Phases of Capitalist Development

Also by Robert Albritton

A JAPANESE APPROACH TO STAGES OF CAPITALIST DEVELOPMENT

DIALECTICS AND DECONSTRUCTION IN POLITICAL ECONOMY

Also by Makoto Itoh

POLITICAL ECONOMY FOR SOCIALISM

POLITICAL ECONOMY OF MONEY AND FINANCE (*with Costas Lapavitsas*)

THE BASIC THEORY OF CAPITALISM

THE JAPANESE ECONOMY RECONSIDERED

THE WORLD ECONOMIC CRISIS AND JAPANESE CAPITALISM

Phases of Capitalist Development

Booms, Crises and Globalizations

Edited by

Robert Albritton
Associate Professor of Political Science
York University
Toronto
Canada

Makoto Itoh
Professor of Economics
Kokugakuin University
Tokyo
Japan

Richard Westra
Lecturer in Political Science
School of Social Science
College of the Bahamas
Nassau
Bahamas

and

Alan Zuege
Department of Political Science
York University
Toronto
Canada

Editorial matter and selection © Robert Albritton, Makoto Itoh,
Richard Westra and Alan Zuege 2001
Chapter 7 © Makoto Itoh 2001
Chapter 8 © Robert Albritton 2001
Chapter 17 © Bob Jessop 2001
Chapter 18 © Richard Westra 2001
Chapters 1–6, 9–16 © Palgrave Publishers Ltd 2001

First published 2001 by
PALGRAVE
Houndmills, Basingstoke, Hampshire RG21 6XS and
175 Fifth Avenue, New York, N. Y. 10010
Companies and representatives throughout the world

PALGRAVE is the new global academic imprint of
St. Martin's Press LLC Scholarly and Reference Division and
Palgrave Publishers Ltd (formerly Macmillan Press Ltd).

ISBN 0–333–75316–X hardback
ISBN 0–333–94838–6 paperback

This book is printed on paper suitable for recycling and
made from fully managed and sustained forest sources.

A catalogue record for this book is available
from the British Library.

Library of Congress Cataloging-in-Publication Data
Phases of capitalist development : booms, crises, and globalizations /
edited by Robert Albritton ... [et al.].
    p. cm.
Includes bibliographical references and index.
ISBN 0–333–75316–X
  1. Capitalism. 2. Economic development. 3. Financial crises.
4. Globalization. I. Albritton, Robert, 1941–

HB501 .P4175 2000
338.9—dc21
                                                                00–053063

10   9   8   7   6   5   4   3   2   1
10 09 08 07 06 05 04 03 02 01

Printed in Great Britain by Antony Rowe Ltd, Chippenham, Wiltshire

Contents

Preface

This volume reflects the intellectual interest of the editors in navigating a sprawling research territory in political economy – the study of phases of capitalist development. The idea for the volume originated with Richard Westra following the publication of his article 'Periodizing Capitalism and the Political Economy of Post-War Japan' in *Journal of Contemporary Asia*. That elicited a response from a small US publishing house that proposed he edit a collection of essays on the topic of periodizing capitalism. From there the idea blossomed into the major collaborative effort that is this volume. Following extensive preparatory discussions among the editors, this effort entailed the selection and forwarding of invitations to world-renowned political economists representing a broad range of perspectives. All were asked to focus upon what the editors believed to be the most important questions facing the research domain of phases of capitalist development. Beyond this rudimentary prompting however the contributors were given complete intellectual freedom and encouragement to expound upon or defend their own position. The editors wish to acknowledge the foresight of Palgrave Publishers for agreeing to publish such an extended collection of essays.

Notes on the Contributors

Robert Albritton is a Professor of Political Science at York University in Toronto, Canada. His recent publications include *A Japanese Approach to Stages of Capitalist Development; Dialectics and Deconstruction in Political Economy*; and 'The Unique Ontology of Capital' in *Marx's Theories Today*.

Sabah Alnasseri is Assistant Lecturer in Political Science at the Johann Wolfgang Goethe University Frankfurt/Main, Germany. Sabah is working on a PhD thesis which deals with the political economy of the social formations in Arabic space, with a primary focus on the crises since the 1970s, and is the author of various articles on this subject.

Giovanni Arrighi is a Professor of Sociology and Director of the Institute for Global Studies in Culture, Power and History at The Johns Hopkins University. His books include *The Geometry of Imperialism; The Dynamics of Global Crisis* (co edited); *The Long Twentieth Century: Money, Power and the Origins of Our Times*; and *Chaos and Governance in the Modern World System* (co-edited with Beverly Silver).

John R. Bell teaches in the School of Liberal Studies at Seneca College in Toronto. He is the author of 'Dialectics and Economic Theory' in Albritton and Sekine, *A Japanese Approach to Political Economy*.

Ulrich Brand is a Research Assistant in Political Science at the Johann Wolfgang Goethe University Frankfurt/Main, Germany. His PhD thesis treated the political role of non-governmental organizations from the perspective of a materialist state theory and regulation theory, with a special emphasis on the ecological crisis and politics of biodiversity. He has recently published the book *Reflexionen einer Rebellion: Chiapas und ein anderes Politikverständnis*.

Alex Callinicos is a Professor of Politics at the University of York, United Kingdom. His books include *Marxism and the New Imperialism* (co-edited); *Making History; Theories and Narratives*; and *Social Theory*. He is currently writing a book on equality.

Guglielmo Carchedi is a Senior Research Officer at the Faculty of Economics and Econometrics of the University of Amsterdam, Holland. He is the author of several books and articles in the fields of sociology, economics and methodology. His last books are *Class Analysis and Social Research; Frontiers of Political Economy*; and *Marx and non-Equilibrium Economics* (co-edited with Alan Freeman). He is now completing a Marxist analysis of European economic integration.

Simon Clarke is a Professor of Sociology, University of Warwick, United Kingdom, and Scientific Director, Institute for Comparative Labour Relations Research (ISITO), Moscow. His publications include *Keynesianism,*

Monetarism and the Crisis of the State; Marx's Theory of Crisis; Management and Industry in Russia (a series of four books); and *The Formation of a Labour Market in Russia.*

Gérard Duménil is a Research Director at the Centre National de la Recherche Scientifique, MODEM, University of Paris X-Nanterre. He is the author of *Le Concept de loi économique dans 'Le Capital'; Marx et Keynes face à la crise*; and (with Dominique Lévy): *The Economics of the Profit Rate: Competition, Crises and Historical Tendencies in Capitalism; La Dynamique du capital: un siècle d'économie américaine* and *Au-delà du Capitalisme.*

Alan Freeman is a Professor of Economics at the University of Greenwich, London. His publications include *Ricardo, Marx, Sraffa* (co-edited with Ernest Mandel) and *Marx and non-Equilibrium Economics* (co-edited with Guglielmo Carchedi). He has also published articles on the economic crisis, uneven development and alternative economic accounting methods.

Makoto Itoh is a Professor of Economics at Kokugakuin University in Tokyo and Emeritus Professor of the University of Tokyo. His books include *The Basic Theory of Capitalism; The World Economic Crisis and Japanese Capitalism; Political Economy for Socialism; Political Economy of Money and Finance* (with Costas Lapavitsas); *The Japanese Economy Reconsidered* (in preparation); and numerous works in Japanese.

Bob Jessop is a Professor of Sociology, Lancaster University, Lancaster, United Kingdom. His publications include *The Capitalist State; Nicos Poulantzas; Thatcherism; State Theory; The Future of Welfare States* (forthcoming); and *Regulation Theory* (forthcoming). He is currently researching the restructuring of welfare regimes in advanced capitalism and the implications of the so-called knowledge revolution for the future dynamic of global capitalism.

Samuel Knafo is at the Department of Political Science at York University, Toronto. His research focuses on Marxist economics and the historical roots of financial globalization.

David M. Kotz is a Professor of Economics at the University of Massachusetts at Amherst and Research Associate at the Political Economy Research Institute at the University of Massachusetts. His recent publications include *Social Structures of Accumulation: The Political Economy of Growth and Crisis* (co-edited); and *Revolution from Above: The Demise of the Soviet System* (with Fred Weir).

Dominique Lévy is a Research Director at the Centre National de la Recherche Scientifique, CEPREMAP, Paris. Recent books include (with Gerard Duménil): *The Economics of the Profit Rate: Competition, Crises and Historical Tendencies in Capitalism; La Dynamique du capital: un siècle d'économie américaine*; and *Au-delà du capitalisme.*

Alain Lipietz is a Member of the European Parliament (Green group), a Member of the Economic Analysis Council of the French Prime Minister, and a Research Director at the Centre National de la Recherche Scientifique, CEPREMAP, Paris. He is the author of several books including: *Mirages and*

Miracles: The Crises of Global Fordism; Towards a New Economic Order: Post-fordism, Ecology and Democracy; Green Hopes: The Future of Political Ecology; La société en sablier: le partage du travail contre la dechirure sociale; and *The Wealth of Regions* (forthcoming).

Jason W. Moore is at the Department of Sociology at The Johns Hopkins University. He has published reviews and articles on world capitalism, environmental history, and labour geography in *Antipode; Critical Sociology;* and *Review: A Journal of the Fernand Braudel Center.*

Stephen Resnick is a Professor of Economics at University of Massachusetts at Amherst. His publications include (with Richard Wolff) *Knowledge and Class: A Marxian Critique of Political Economy* and *Economics: Marxian versus Neoclassical;* several entries in *The Encyclopedia of Political Economy;* (forthcoming) *Class and Its Others* (co-edited with J.K. Gibson-Graham and Richard Wolff) and *The Rise and Fall of the USSR: A Class Analysis* (with Richard Wolff).

David L. Rigby is an Associate Professor of Geography at the University of California, Los Angeles. He is author of *The Golden Age Illusion: Rethinking Postwar Capitalism* (with Michael Webber). His other publications and research interests span evolutionary models of technical change, regional growth theory, and uneven development.

Thomas Sablowski is a Research Assistant in Political Science at the Johann Wolfgang Goethe University Frankfurt/Main, Germany. Recent publications include 'Italien nach dem Fordismus: Regulation und organische Krise einer kapitalistischen Gesellschaftsformation'; 'Shareholder Value gegen Belegschaftsinteressen; and Der Weg der Hoechst AG zum 'Life-Sciences'-Konzern' (together with Wolfgang Menz and Steffen Becker).

Thomas T. Sekine was a Professor of Economics and Social and Political Thought at York University, Toronto from 1968 to 1994. He is currently teaching at the School of Commerce, Aichi-Gakuin University, Japan. His recent publications include *A Japanese Approach to Political Economy: Unoist Variations* (co-edited with Robert Albritton) and *An Outline of the Dialectic of Capital,* 2 volumes.

Kees van der Pijl is a Professor of International Relations at the School of European Studies, University of Sussex, United Kingdom. His publications include *The Making of an Atlantic Ruling Class; Wereldorde en machtspolitiek; Vordenker der weltpolitik; De greep nar de macht; De flat;* and *Transnational Classes and International Relations.*

Michael J. Webber is a Professor of Geography and Environmental Studies at the University of Melbourne. His publications include *The Golden Age Illusion: Rethinking Postwar Capitalism* (with David L. Rigby); *Putting the People Last* (co-edited with Mary Crooks); and *Global Restructuring: the Australian Experience* (with Robert Fagan). His other publications and research interests span the areas of location theory, urban planning, industrial development and regional growth.

John Weeks is Professor of Development Economics and Director, Centre for Development Policy and Research at the School of Oriental and African Studies, London. Publications include: *Capital and Exploitation; A Critique of Neoclassical Macroeconomics*; and, most recently, 'The Essence and Appearance of Globalization: The Rise of Finance Capital' in *Globalization and The Dilemmas of the State in the South* and 'Latin America and the High Performing Asian Economies: Growth and Debt' in *Journal of International Development* (forthcoming).

Richard Westra is a Lecturer in the School of Social Science at The College of the Bahamas. His most recent publication is 'A Japanese Contribution to the Critique of Rational Choice Marxism' in *Social Theory and Practice*.

Jens Winter is at the University of Bremen, Germany and Research Assistant on the project 'International Regulation of Labour and National Employment Relations: The Case of the Regional Labour-Regime, North American Agreement on Labour Cooperation (NAALC) between the USA, Mexico and Canada', and has written on the role of space and the state in the post-Fordist debate.

Alan Zuege is at the Department of Political Science at York University in Toronto researching the political economy of internationalisation. He is a contributing editor of the *Socialist Register* and has recently published articles in *Monthly Review* (with Gregory Albo); *Socialist Register 2000*; and in the collection, *Die Strategie der 'Neuen Mitte'*.

Introduction

There exists no more pressing a task at the dawn of the new millennium than to produce in-depth knowledge of the political economy of capitalism – knowledge not only of capitalist development at the current conjuncture, but of capitalism's past and its possible trajectory in the future. It is precisely to this endeavour, then, that this volume seeks to contribute.

The periodization of capitalism together with the study of its phases of development are a research territory that has figured prominently within the political economy tradition over the last century, and its modalities of analysis have become increasingly sophisticated and wide-ranging. Yet the various schools of thought in this literature have evolved in relative isolation from each other and enjoyed few outlets for the creative cross-fertilization of ideas. What this volume accomplishes therefore is something highly unique: for never before has new and original work of such a distinguished roster of scholars, representing the most important schools of political economy, been assembled under one cover. The contributors are based in nine different countries – Australia, The Bahamas, Canada, England, France, Germany, Holland, Japan and the United States – and represent a variety of academic disciplines – economics, geography, history, international relations, political science and sociology – making this volume a genuinely international and interdisciplinary effort. And all have previously made path-breaking interventions in the political economic study of phases of capitalist development. It is the editors' sincere hope as such, that this collection of essays representing divergent perspectives will spark an expanded interest in scholarly engagements over what are certainly the most important questions of political-economic research today.

The theoretical point of departure for this volume is the view that capitalism since its inception has been far from uniform. Key to improving our understanding of capitalism is the attainment of greater clarity regarding the specific forms capitalism has assumed in the successive phases of its existence. That which is of paramount concern, and the point around which the most intense debate swirls, is the characterization of the period following the Second World War. The stakes here are certainly the highest. For as we enter the new millennium, the interpretation of the political economy of this most recent past will impact profoundly upon our political and economic strategizing for the future. Some of the vital questions the contributors address with respect to the foregoing are: How should the post-war period be characterized, and was it marked by just a single form of capitalist development? How have economic stagnation, the internationalization of capital and financial instability contributed to defining the present stage of capitalist development? Does the current conjuncture represent a new phase of capitalism, a transition between capitalist phases, a transition away from capitalism, or a post-capitalist phase? What variables are most felicitous for constructing a theory of capitalist phases: the capital–labour relation, hegemonic blocs, national systems of innovation, characteristic commodities, leading technologies, or economic sectors, and so on? Should the study of phases of capitalist development commence with particular national models of capitalism or at the global dimension of capital, or possibly some combination of the two? And, how can knowledge of capital's logic or 'capital in general', the question with which it is widely accepted that Karl Marx grappled in his historic *Capital*, now contribute to the theorizing of phases of capitalist development?

While the study of phases of capitalist development has been an explicit concern of left political economy, its research agenda squarely faces the issues that mainstream economics is now increasingly forced to confront. For much of the twentieth century, the application of formal mathematical modelling techniques to depict the economic affairs of the advanced Western societies captivated scholars and provided a foundation for private and public decision-making. Simply understood, the belief was that, though extremely abstract, these models captured the operation of that purported *constant* of Western advancement – the capitalist market – and hence could be consistently marshalled for predictive purposes. The potency of mainstream economic modelling appeared to be confirmed by capitalism's longevity and purported triumph in the face of rival social systems. In the closing decades of the twentieth century, however, the smug complacency of orthodox economics has been eroded by rapid and unforeseen transformations, mounting global instabilities and the propensity for recurrent crises. Indeed, even in the mainstream business press it is no longer uncommon to find the dangers of present trends compared to those that culminated in the period of depressions and world wars that began the century. In this environment economists have been prodded to leave the terrain of technical scholasticism in order to make sense of the world outside of abstract theory – a task of course involving precisely those questions about the variegated forms assumed by capitalism that are at the core of this volume.

To sum up, we hope that although the immediate purpose of this volume is to spur academic discussion, it contains insights useful to social movements, left parties and progressive policy actors. What knowledge could be more crucial as we enter the twenty-first century than knowledge that clarifies the main structural trends of capitalism's past, present and future?

1
International Relations and Capitalist Discipline

Kees van der Pijl

My aim in this chapter is to look at the interconnections between phases of the imposition of the discipline of capital; phases in the international circulation, or world market movement, of various forms of capital; and phases in the geopolitical spread of a 'heartland' of capital, originally centred on England and the lands of English settlement. My argument is that as the new millennium begins, a combination of the discipline of capital with the interests of the most powerful states not only is undermining global production but is actually jeopardizing humanity's existence on the planet.

Let me first outline what I mean by the phrase 'discipline of capital' and how we can understand it – in light of the theme of this collection – as a 'phased' phenomenon, before discussing how it is imbricated with world politics.

Capital and the state system

Capitalist development itself represents a historical stage in the progressive evolution of humanity's metabolism with nature. It applies when mobile wealth has become a quasi-independent social force which reproduces itself through the workings of a competitive system of exploiting wage labour, enlarged by coercive appropriation. In a crucial passage in the *Grundrisse*, Marx states that capital 'is not, as the economists believe, the *absolute* form for the development of the forces of production ... it is a discipline over them, which becomes superfluous and burdensome at a certain level of their development' (Marx 1973: 415).

The miraculous multiplication of productive forces and parallel opportunities for enrichment, the praise of which has been sung from the *Communist Manifesto* to last week's issue of *Business Week*, sets apart capitalist development from all prior patterns of organizing the social labour process. Marx and Engels hence interpreted capitalist development as a momentous force towards removing, in principle, the need for the exploitation of

1

humans by humans – a point not likewise emphasized in the financial press of course.

All historical modes of organizing the social labour process, its distributive order, and the material and ideological power relations by which they are upheld, have been characterized by exploitation. However, because the progress in developing the productive forces is necessarily a result of intensified social cooperation at the same time, capitalist society develops under two contradictory aspects: social inequality, related in particular to advancing processes of commodification; and planned interdependence, or socialization of labour (*Vergesellschaftung*). Classes develop along the lines of cleavages drawn by exploitation, by patterns of unequal distribution and power, as well as (under capitalist development) by the inner tension between the moments of marketization and privatization on the one hand, and the moment of *Vergesellschaftung* on the other.

Socialism in this perspective develops within capitalist society rather than violently breaking into it. Hence phases of capitalist development are also moments of growth of a potential alternative order, even if its realization remains necessarily mediated by class struggles. As Gramsci notes, socialism is 'a historical process, a development from one social stage to another that is richer in collective values' (Gramsci 1977: 53). The real configuration and drift of the class structure registers this development in the sense that the socialization of labour in advanced capitalist society produces a new class, the managerial cadre. Normally, this cadre operates as the executive arm and governing class of the ruling bourgeoisie. But as the 1970s have demonstrated, mass movements for democracy and workers' power can push these cadres towards privileging the moment of socialization over that of commodification. Neo-liberal globalization for one thing denotes the counterattack to this trend by renewing the subordination of these cadres as part of a pervasive reimposition of the discipline of capital over society (van der Pijl 1998: chapter 5).

There are three phases of imposing the discipline of capital. In each of them, it reaches deeper into the society–nature metabolism, provoking its own forms of resistance. First, there is the process of *original accumulation*, the stamping of the commodity form on social relations including relations of production. The second is the capitalist *production* process, the exploitation of living labour-power, in which the technical labour process, with all that it implies in terms of human autonomy and creativity, has to be subordinated to the process of expanding value, the 'valorization' of capital invested. The third is the process of social *reproduction* in its entirety, which likewise has been made subject to the requirements of capital accumulation. This includes the biosphere as well as what we may conveniently call, to distinguish it from work, 'daily life'. 'Phases' here overlap and complement each other, as the discipline of capital works its way to the actual productive –reproductive core of social life. Yet the advance is real, comprising original accumulation first, then production flanked by original accumulation, and finally, the productive–reproductive system as a whole but still driving forward certain forms of original accumulation.

The internationalization of capital constitutes a second 'phased' aspect of capitalist development. It is closely related to the phases of capitalist discipline, but it is also more concrete as it takes into account the dimension of space. Capital has historically internationalized as: (1) the internationalization of the circuit of capital in commodity form (trade linked to capitalist productive processes); (2) the internationalization of the circuit of money capital (foreign investment in capitalist production, both portfolio flows and foreign direct investment); and (3) the internationalization of productive capital itself, by the transnational socialization of labour within firms (Palloix 1975: 78). The more developed form again presumes and includes the results of the earlier one(s).

With each advance, class struggles elicited by the imposition of capitalist discipline become more complex, as more aspects of life are involved in dealing with the disciplinary pressures represented by capital. The conflicts that result from these pressures, and the mediations by which they are relayed through the social structure, become more varied as well. The idea of classes as vast standing armies, ready to jump on each other, loses credence accordingly, and some authors have duly concluded that class is a thing of the past (Pakulski and Waters 1996). But as long as the conditions of exploitation have to be imposed, they will be collectively resisted as well.

Let us now see how this may relate to international politics. One key aspect of capitalist society is the moment of alienation. Alienation is the form taken (under the conditions of an exploitative society) by the tendency towards *objectification* proper to historical humanity. Objectified social practices, structures and beliefs in such societies assume the status of quasi-independent social forces, no longer the *result* of the social labour process, but prior to and above it. Thus capital, and the commodity form of social relations it dictates, appear to people as life-giving, supernatural powers which must be obeyed as if society (or nature) has no independent existence, needs, or limits. Critical theory begins when these alienated social forms are recognized as such and analyzed as epiphenomena of the social labour process. As Mark Rupert writes, '[T]he process of objectification and the continual reconstruction of the nature/society relation are ontologically primary and account for the nature of human social beings in any given historical epoch' (Rupert 1993: 69).

States, too, grow out of certain development processes in society before they impose themselves as a quasi-external force on their own social foundations. And even if this 'alien' quality may gradually descend from the heights of divinely sanctioned absolutism to a much nearer 'relative autonomy', the modern state retains its distinction from society and cannot be identical to it as long as the exploitation of society and nature is mediated and sustained by alienation.

Relations *between* societies are necessarily structured by these patterns of objectification/alienation as well. The common sense understanding of world politics looks at states as self-sufficient entities confronting each other in an ahistorical universe. The diplomat's paradigm assumes the autonomy and potential antagonism of each sovereign state. Its doctrinal codification as 'realism', however, belongs to the modes of thought which, like economics, remain encapsulated within alienated consciousness. Just as in economic theory, commodities in the market appear to encounter each other only on account of their own quality and price rather than as mediated, objectified forms of social relations, so relations between states are understood by realists not in terms of a 'deep, internal relation prior to and constitutive of social actors but as an external joining of states-as-actors' (Ashley 1986: 287).

The 'deep, internal relation' of capitalist development obviously is capital, private enterprise united in the competitive exploitation of wage labour. It emerged in England first, and from the confrontation with France onwards, international relations, too, evolved into a vector along which the discipline of capital is imposed and resisted.

Growth of a Lockean heartland in the global political economy

The reasons why capitalist development obtained its historic centre in north-western Europe reside in the relative scarcity of labour (stimulating productivity-raising innovation), and in the huge proceeds from overseas trade once American silver allowed Europeans to break into Asian trade networks (Frank 1998). Why capitalist development more specifically took off in England has two further reasons.

One is the type of state–society relation established by the Glorious Revolution of 1688 and outlined by Locke in the *Two Treatises of Government* – a state 'serving' a self-regulating civil society and allowing the expansion of private enterprise under a flexible system of common law. Certainly England developed an activist state first, which during a short phase in the seventeenth century imposed its authority on society and unified the feudal mosaic of local autonomies into a single whole. However, a long tradition of social self-regulation and resistance to the encroaching monarchy dating back to the Norman invasion was synthesized with a new confidence of the mercantile interests to conduct their own affairs without more than the state guarantee of property under the law, and this soon displaced the tentacular, 'Hobbesian' state again (Rosenstock-Huessy 1961: 293).

The second reason resides in colonial settlement. Emigration from the British Isles to North America and Australia also transplanted a common language and culture, including the Lockean political culture favouring free enterprise. In the colonial struggles with France in North America and India which were part of the Spanish War of Succession (1701–14), the Austrian War of Succession (1740s) and the Seven Years' War (1756–63), the presence of British settlers proved a decisive advantage in achieving victory – as it had been in prior rivalry with Holland (Arrighi 1978: 57–8).

These two processes in combination demarcated a transnational space which in the words of the historian of the British Commonwealth enabled the 'system of interlinked groups, organizations and societies within the greater community... to avoid in a very large measure the growth of rigidities and compartmentalization in its political, economic and social structure' (Hall 1971: 106). The concept of a *Lockean heartland*, which I use to denote this integrated core of the global political economy, borrows from Sir Halford Mackinder's geopolitical nomenclature (see Evans and Newnham 1992: 123). Mackinder in 1904 used 'heartland' for the Tsarist Russian Empire, and argued the centrality of the Eurasian land mass in world politics on account of British-imperial setbacks and the new strategic importance of railways. In fact, Britain declined only if one sticks to a strictly national, 'little-England' concept of its place in world history. As Henk Overbeek has noted:

> Capitalism is not a social formation located within the confines of a particular portion of the available global space (be it a nation-state or, as in Britain, a 'multinational state'), but it is a global social formation, with the historical evolution of social forces tendentially also becoming global in character.
>
> (Overbeek 1990: 3)

The development of capital to global dimensions has been mediated by the growth and consolidation, in successive contests including war, of this Lockean heartland. France became the model for all later contenders. Thus, while in Britain original accumulation occurred in a world market and transnational context, in France it was pursued from above, by the state – consolidating tributary forms of exploitation to the breaking point (Lefebvre 1976, II: 35–6). This was not a matter of strategic 'choices' being made on either side of the channel, but the differential evolution of sets of social forces emerging from a common, feudal-Christian civilization. The outcome of social and international struggles, partly of course preordained by geography and climate, led to a balance of forces which in France turned out to be less favourable to the roving, commercial element to carve out a sphere of self-regulation against the dynastic centralizing power. While the Glorious Revolution gave Parliament control of public finances, which lowered interest rates on public debt and made private investment easier (Cameron 1991: 195), in France, on the other hand, public works and Colbertism generally (later rationalized under Napoleon) reinforced the confiscation of the social sphere by the state. In Britain, the backlash produced by the French revolution in turn reinforced the idea – expressed notably by Ure and

Bentham – that the strictest discipline over the workers was an essential requirement for capital's proper functioning (Thompson 1968: 888; Meeus 1989: 126).

The common characteristic of the imposition of the discipline of capital in the phase of original accumulation resides in the breaking of the traditional mould of agrarian existence by commodification. Through a range of inter-mediate forms, wage labour replaced personal subservience, usually by social dislocations caused by famine, migration or war. Urbanization is a key variable here – not because industry is necessarily located in the city (it often is not), but rather because the commodification of social relations in the countryside pushes people living off the land directly, into the confines of the city where they are linked to food production and to their own employment by means of markets (Schwartz 1994: chapter 5). But in what-ever form original accumulation takes place, there occurs what sociologists call *anomie* among those put under the new discipline – the loss of norm-ative coherence which creates a susceptibility to new forms of collective consciousness. This becomes more acute if the transformation proceeds in a shock-like fashion. It is this normative vacuum striking large masses of people driven into the unknown which creates the opportunity for mass mobilization. Original accumulation as a result creates the preconditions for a type of social revolution characteristically accompanying the definition of a new world role for a given state (in practice, after the establishment of the English lead, a contender posture) – if not triggering national unification to begin with (Rosenstock-Huessy 1961). In our own age, anomic masses streaming into a new urban environment in Iran heaped up the explosive material for what became the 1979 Iranian Revolution, which has been compared to what happened in Russia prior to 1917 (Hough 1990: 48).

Britain remained virtually unchallenged as an industrial power until late in the nineteenth century. With 2 per cent of the world's population, it still in 1860 accounted for 40 to 45 per cent of world industrial production. As Senghaas (1982: 29) observes, the rest of the world accordingly was threa-tened with peripheralization and the strongest states adopted the state-led catch-up pattern pioneered by France to maintain their independence.

Now the efforts of contender states to resist peripheralization by the expanding heartland, can be viewed under two aspects. One is the build-up of a rival production system allowing the late-comer country to hold its own in the confrontation. This highlights the aspect of competition, and supports the realist view of world politics. The protective demarcation of a separate sovereignty also in the economic sphere precludes integration. But the con-stitution of a modern state, as well as the forced marches of industrialization necessarily taking its clues from the more advanced rival, also move the contender state forward in time to the very threshold of the Lockean state–society configuration itself. SS ideologues during the Second World War studied the structure of the British Commonwealth to copy its features in the expanded European space occupied by the Nazis including Russia (van der Pijl 1996: 168) – but that prospect, too, went under in the defeat.

The second aspect is the simultaneous widening of the sphere of circulation for capital by adding new centres of production, which circuits of commodity, money and productive capital can be latched onto. Around these circuits, transnational socialization of labour and class formation may then develop to the point where the inter-state confrontation is undermined, especially on the side of the contender state. In this light one may interpret, for instance, the German opposition against Hitler led by Goerdeler, and the role of comparable 'comprador liberals' in other contender states (van der Pijl 1984: 128–30 and *passim*).

One can imagine the advantage enjoyed by the English-speaking world ever since the Monroe Doctrine (that is, from 1823 on) as the moment of real challenge including war and the threat of war, has been absent from it. Even allowing for trade rivalries and other economic friction, the heartland could always utilize fairly directly the opportunities for deepening the socialization of labour and redistribute relative economic power peacefully. Hence, the material and ideological regressions which the contender states have experienced in the wake of lost wars or otherwise failed catch-up episodes, and which have contributed to producing the often extreme doctrines under which the contender effort was resumed, have generally not affected the 'eternal liberalism' of the heartland.

The widening of the sphere of circulation of commodity capital linking different national industrial economies can be gauged from the distribution of productive capacity in textiles, the dominant sector of first-generation industrialization. In Table 1.1, cotton spindlage capacity in the heartland is set at 100, so that the widening of circulation within the heartland, and the growth of the contender economies relative to the heartland, can both be read from the table. From this table we may also see how *war* works out negatively in the contender posture, most clearly in case of the defeated party. The *Pax Britannica* was a prosperous peace for the English-speaking world first, because the rival industrial capacity of the three main contenders, which stood at a third in 1834, declined to a quarter by 1867. Of course, by then, new contenders were coming to the fore, in new sectors.

Britain also dominated world trade, more particularly the circuit of capital in commodity form (trade linking centres of capitalist production) which was the dominant form of internationalization at this stage. In 1860, French export of manufactures stood at 38.5 per cent and Germany's at around 20 per cent of Britain's manufacturing exports (Senghaas 1982: 32, table 3). France, only by the coincidence of the US Civil War, recovered briefly from the setback of the Cobden–Chevalier free trade treaty concluded with Britain in the same year – before disappearing behind the US and even behind Germany after Prussia had defeated Austria first and then itself unified the north in the moment of victory over France.

Table 1.1   Heartland–contender development in cotton spindlage and major wars

Total for heartland = 100	1834	1852	1861		1867		1913
Great Britain	87.7	76.6	72.9		81.0		64.5
				CIVIL WAR			
United States	12.2	23.4	27.1		19.0		35.5
Contenders						FRANCO-PRUSSIAN WAR	
France	21.9	19.1	12.9		16.9		8.6
				AUSTRO-PRUSSIAN WAR			
Germany	5.5*	3.8	5.3	WAR	4.8		12.6
Austria-Hungary	7.0	5.9	4.2		3.6		5.6

*1836.
Source: Calculated from Landes (1969: 215, table 5).

Already in the nineteenth century, the circuit of money capital, too, was projected to the international level. It notably combined Britain and the United States into an Atlantic 'swing mechanism', in which periods of real accumulation absorbing capital, alternated after 1840. From 1870 on, Canada, Australia and Argentina also became part of it, with the City of London serving as the pivot (Williamson 1968: 82). Accumulated French foreign investments in the early 1850s amounted to half the British figure; by 1914, when the British had amassed a stock of 20 billion pounds sterling, France's stood at slightly more than a tenth, and Germany's at around half that (Kenwood and Lougheed 1971: 43, table 3; 45, table 4; and 47). Nearly 50 percent of British investments were made in the US and the settler colonies, and amid much 'English-speaking' propaganda by Cecil Rhodes and his associates, the steel magnate Andrew Carnegie and others, the UK and the US in 1911 concluded an Arbitration Treaty outlawing war between them. In the same year the foundations of the British Commonwealth were laid at the Imperial Conference (Hall 1971: 67).

In this age of new heavy industries (of which the steel–railway complex was the most important and politically sensitive), the major powers moved to assist capital in imposing discipline on a vastly expanded industrial proletariat. As British industrial and trade pre-eminence eroded, the Hobbesian confiscation of the social sphere by the state, which characterized the new contenders, namely Germany and to a lesser extent, Austria-Hungary and Russia, proved well suited to deal with the challenges facing their ruling classes. They also found a ready formula for mobilizing their nations behind the catch-up effort in nationalism, protectionism and welfare, which effectively redirected the masses' aspirations from socialism to 'a place under the sun' (Cox 1987: 157). While the state-monopolistic drive also permeated the English-speaking countries on account of parallel structural trends (productive restructuring as well as the increasing imperialist struggle over contested spheres-of-influence), the heartland yet reasserted its unity. Aided by Russia and the USSR, it could defeat the German–Austrian challenge even when Italy and Japan threw in their weight with the contenders in the Second World War.

In Table 1.2, the widening of the sphere of circulation of capital is documented for the steel industry. The world wars also led to redistribution within the heartland (into which France had become integrated without shedding its 'Hobbesian' antecedents). But the three main contenders, which in 1938 drew roughly level with heartland production, still stood at two-thirds as late as 1957, of course in a completely changed geopolitical configuration. Yet the presentation underlines the effect of war on the comprehensive heartland–contender equation.

Henceforth, the challenge to capitalism becomes largely external to it, a contest of 'systems'. In the 1930s, the rise of the automotive complex in the United States and the recasting of social relations and economic policy towards a welfare state format and Keynesian demand management already reached beyond the state-monopolistic phase into what I call, by reference to the synthesis with renewed internationalization of capital, corporate liberalism. The Marshall Plan after 1945 extrapolated the New Deal synthesis

Table 1.2 Heartland–contender development in steel production and the world wars

Total for heartland = 100	1880	1900		1910		1925	1938		1950[+]	1957[+]
				FIRST WORLD WAR			SECOND WORLD WAR			
United States	42.8	61.3		72.8		75.5	62.7		78.3	74.5
Great Britain	44.2	29.5		17.8		12.3	23.5		14.4	15.6
[France]	13.0	9.3		9.4		12.2	13.7		7.3	9.9
Contenders										
Germany/FRG	23.6	38.2		36.0		12.0	51.8		10.5	18.2
			RUSSO-JAPANESE WAR							
Russia/USSR	9.9	13.0		9.7		3.1	39.6		23.8	34.7
Japan	–	–		–		2.2	14.3*		4.3	9.4

*1939. [+] Steel plus finished iron.
Sources: Calculated from Hexner (1943: 324–5, appendix VI); Economic Commission for Europe (1959: 22, tables 16, 17).

to Western Europe and served to uphold military expenditure in the context of the cold war. Foreign direct investment was again overwhelmingly sourced from the main heartland economies, the US and the UK (see Stopford and Strange 1991: 17, table 1.1). If we take the car industry as an indicator of this phase, the USSR and its bloc never even had a chance to catch up, and its efforts in this sector never matched the challenge it could still pose in heavy industry (Stopford and Strange 1991: 17, table 1.b).

As Table 1.3 documents, auto production could shift emphasis within the heartland as Western Europe caught up with US living standards. Japan, in the wake of its defeat in 1945, avoided the cost of political confrontation by adopting a peaceful contender role, as what Castells calls a 'vassal state' of the West (Castells 1998: 277). The USSR, however, victorious but devastated in the Second World War, had to bear the brunt of a sustained arms race. In the critical post-war transition years, 1953–65, the USSR defence expenditure was three times the West European average and ten times that of Japan (Maddison 1971: 137).

When the microelectronics revolution made its impact on capitalist development, the Soviet bloc was completely outcompeted by the next round of contenders, both vassal states such as Taiwan and South Korea and the biggest Latin American producers. Its 22.7 per cent share of non-OECD machinery and transport equipment exports to the OECD, in 1973, had dwindled to 4.6 per cent in 1987 (van Zon 1994: 38). But the contender posture of the USSR by then had already been reduced almost completely to the military-diplomatic dimension until it gave up and collapsed in 1991.

However, even if successive contender states historically have not been able to follow the heartland in terms of leading industries, their industrialization has proceeded in the older sectors. Thus in textiles, the heartland states until the 1990s entrenched themselves in a cartel, the Multi-Fibre

Table 1.3 Heartland–contender development in passenger car production, 1960 and 1982

Total for heartland = 100	1960	1982
USA	54.4	31.3
Canada	2.6	5.1
EEC (incl. UK)	42.0	61.3
Australia	1.0	2.3
Contenders		
Japan	1.3	43.3
USSR	1.1	8.3
Brazil	0.3	3.0

Source: Calculated from Dicken (1986: 283, table 9.1).

Agreement, before control of the industry was effectively taken over by big corporations operating in a liberalized world market (Underhill 1998: 200). In this, only very recent, new setting, Asian vassal states will compete with heartland corporations in capital-intensive textile production, while the clothing industries of 'emerging giants like China and India will do well, especially if their domestic markets expand at the same time as export prospects improve as [MFA] quotas are removed' (Underhill 1998: 253). In other words, capitalist textile production is on its way to becoming global two hundred years after the industrial revolution in England, but only after big capital from the heartland states was able to take over world market control from the prior cartel.

The second-generation basic industries, too, have continued to grow on a world scale even if the contender states have not been able to follow heartland industrial development in newer sectors. If we take the example of steel, China in 1997 became the biggest producer in the world with 107.6 million tonnes of annual production, just ahead of Japan. Presented as in Table 1.2, this would amount to 52.1 per cent of the heartland's production (the US plus the four main EU producers). Russia still stands at 22.4 per cent, Ukraine at 11.9, India at slightly less. Of course, the Asian vassal producers, Japan (as China, around 50 per cent), South Korea (20.6 per cent), and so on, form a class of their own.[1] Thus one could still argue that in the very long run, the productive discipline of capital will transform all the world's states into components of a global industrial system. However, here we must remind ourselves that the discipline of capital, along with the shift to intensive consumption generated by the automotive type of industrialization, moves into the reproductive sphere as well, compounding all prior processes of capitalist development.

The spectre of a crisis of exhaustion

The third phase in the imposition of the discipline of capital, as indicated, concerns the sphere of reproduction of social life in its entirety. There is a synchronizing quality to this form of capitalist discipline because it affects, among other things, the planetary biosphere irrespective of the particular phase of imposition of capitalist discipline prevailing locally.

Now the world's resources and human capacities should not be envisaged as a fixed stock of things, as the famous 'Limits to Growth' report still did (see Houweling 1999), but as a substratum to be mobilized as productive forces for capitalist exploitation. It is capital which defines the productive forces in their dialectical unity with particular relations of production (Palloix 1995: 27). With the deepening of capitalist discipline to include the natural foundations of humanity's existence and the most intimate aspects of social life (indeed the reproductive ones), the capacity of the biosphere and daily life to renew themselves according to their own requirements and rhythms is prejudiced. This was the limit to market economy highlighted by Polanyi (Polanyi 1957).

'Exhaustion' of the capacity of society and nature to support capitalist discipline in this perspective becomes the unifying meaning of 'crisis' – comprising all sorts of internal economic imbalances and disproportions in addition to the destruction of the social fabric and the biosphere. Hence it intersects with, and undermines, the linear process of industrialization under the *productive* discipline of capital. As Rainer Funke has argued in an article published posthumously in 1978, the capitalist mode of production is still developing in terms of commodification, but the moment of crisis is becoming manifest in what he calls 'the mounting incapacity of capitalism to "grow into" an existing infrastructural basis' (Funke 1978: 227–8).

My thesis is that a crisis of exhaustion is threatening a global society held together by capitalist discipline. That is the 'Y2K' problem the world really faces. This crisis can be specified as follows. First, a crisis of exhaustion of the biosphere will most directly compound the ongoing processes of original accumulation–urbanization in the poorest parts of the world. Second, a crisis will occur of the internationalization of capital, characterized by a regression from international socialization of labour to disjointed circuits of money capital with a strongly speculative bent, undermining the world's productive capacity. Finally, there will come a crisis of the geopolitical expansion of the Lockean heartland – entailing a withering of transnational civil society and a regression to bellicose imperialism.

In those parts of the world where original accumulation is still in progress, and where it constitutes the locally most salient form of the imposition of the discipline of capital, the crisis of exhaustion as a result of capital's penetration into the sphere of reproduction in its entirety raises the spectre of 'super-disasters'. The International Federation of Red Cross and Red Crescent Societies in its latest report warns of the prospect of what it calls 'chain reactions of devastation'. Of the 50 fastest-growing cities in the world, 40 are in earthquake zones, while half of the world's population lives in coastal regions often exposed to rising sea levels and cyclones. Most of them are in zones of original accumulation.[2]

Clearly, no heartland status can exempt any part of the globe from this crisis of exhaustion, although some countries of course have assets bolstering their relative survival capacity. The World Bank in 1995 made an attempt to recalculate the world's wealth by country, not by looking at the traditional economic assets only, but also by reference to its 'social capital' and related human assets; and to the quantity and quality of its natural resources. From Table 1.4, we may get an indication of the capacity to survive of today's world. It is one sign of the vast resources marshalled by the Lockean heartland that even in this calculation, in which reproductive potential is added to productive, two of the original English settler states head the list.

Table 1.4 World Bank's 10 richest countries by latest measure ($ per capita)

		Sources of wealth (% of total)		
	Est. wealth	Human resources	Produced assets	Natural capital
1 Australia	835 000	21	7	71
2 Canada	704 000	22	9	69
3 Luxembourg	658 000	83	12	4
4 Switzerland	647 000	78	19	3
5 Japan	585 000	81	18	2
6 Sweden	496 000	56	16	29
7 Iceland	486 000	23	16	61
8 Qatar	473 000	51	11	39
9 UAE	471 000	65	14	21
10 Denmark	463 000	76	17	7

Source: World Bank, as in *Financial Times*, 18 September 1995.

In the dimension of the successive stages of internationalization, or world market movement, of capital, the crisis manifests itself in a regression from the emerging productive world economy to financial speculation. In the 1970s, processes of runaway internationalization of production from the heartland meshed with national industrialization strategies of a range of new contender states, antagonists and vassals alike. Calling this the 'new international division of labour' is a rather lapidary way of analyzing a contradictory and highly dynamic situation which soon became engulfed by the neo-liberal economic strategies of the Atlantic ruling class and the new round of confrontation with which it met the challenge. The concept applied, at best, to a belated internationalization of production from the big continental-European countries and has little applicability elsewhere (Ruigrok and van Tulder 1995: 129). Yet the Third World strategy for a New International Economic Order (NIEO) (while likewise failing to appreciate the dynamic nature and drift of the processes involved) was an attempt to transform the fleeting division of labour into a real, conscious *Vergesellschaftung*, that is, to impose a normative unification and a degree of planning on it, relayed through the United Nations system. Not unexpectedly, this NIEO project was favourably received among the cadre element in the heartland (van der Pijl 1998: 156–8). Materially, it would have facilitated a global productive economy in which the globalizing trends in textile and steel production, referred to above, would be embedded in a political regime of some equitability instead of in a liberalized context under the World Trade Organization (into which, incidentally, China has still to obtain entry).

The US-initiated policy to slam the brakes on credit-financed Third-World and Soviet bloc industrialization imposed radical fiscal discipline on the contenders by suddenly and radically reducing dollar inflation, while simultaneously contracting hoped-for export markets in the heartland. This strategy has proven successful (certainly in the longer run) in throttling contender state industrialization. It also has imposed a regime of micro-economic rationality on politics, subordinating democratic, internally generated policies to what Gill calls the *new constitutionalism* of international capital and its institutions (Gill 1995).

The high real interest rates which were the result of the monetarist intervention entailed a massive redistribution of profits and wealth from productive enterprise to financial institutions, fuelling a huge international circuit of money capital. Already in 1990, US securities transactions with foreigners, which still amounted to 9 per cent of gross domestic product (GDP) in 1980, had risen to 93 per cent; Japan's equivalent figure rose from 7 to 119 per cent. In the same decade, the stock of international bank lending rose from a value of 4 to 44 per cent of the combined GDP of the OECD countries. The markets for financial derivatives continued to grow in the 1990s. Futures and options on interest rates, currency and stock market indexes in combination tripled from 1992 to 12.2 trillion US dollars outstanding in 1997; interest rate swaps and options and currency swaps in combination grew from 5.3 to 28.7 trillion US dollars in the same period.[3] As I have documented elsewhere, profit distribution in the main capitalist economies became heavily skewed towards money capital (van der Pijl 1998: 60, table 2.5).

The drainage on society's wealth exerted by these non-productive profit strategies has resulted in enrichment of the richest and relative immiseration of the vast majority of the world's population. Table 1.5 gives the shares of the five quintiles of world income for four years. As transpires from this table, polarization really became marked in 1980 and after, entailing among others the halving of the share of the second 20 per cent in 1990 compared with 1965.

Marx interpreted the growth of financial forms of enrichment as a crucial 'moment of transformation' in capital's real historical development (Marx, *Capital*, vol. iii). The explosion of unregulated finance would, in his view, at

Table 1.5   Shares of world income 1965–1990 (per cent of total world income)

	1965	1970	1980	1990
Richest 20%	69.5	70.0	75.5	83.4
Second 20%	21.2	21.3	18.3	11.3
Third 20%	4.2	3.9	3.5	2.1
Fourth 20%	2.9	2.8	2.2	1.8
Poorest 20%	2.3	2.2	1.7	1.4

Source: Adapted from Sweezy (1998: 12).

some point provoke state regulation in order to safeguard the material reproduction of society. This would become critical if accompanied by a second transformative process, the crystallization of the 'collective worker' and its capacity to organize production without capitalist interference. In this latter moment, he saw the constructive aspect of a transformation towards an 'associated mode of production' (Marx 1965: 454–6). Here one may see how the inner tension in capitalist development between commodification and socialization or *Vergesellschaftung*, ultimately reaches a stage where the two can no longer be reconciled.

The collective worker should be imagined as the unity, forged in a democratic process of mass mobilization and debate, of cadres and workers. Fundamental social change depends on the capacity of the most advanced elements of these social categories to transcend short-term considerations of a pecuniary or status nature and unite in an effort to save the integrity of social life and planetary existence, and to that end roll back the discipline of capital.

This leads me to the third aspect of the imminent crisis of exhaustion caused by capital's comprehensive discipline on society and nature – the destruction of the capacity of the Lockean heartland to really grow to global proportions. Locke envisaged the state as serving an essentially self-regulating civil society by upholding the structures for private association under the law. Private enterprise did flourish under this particular state–society configuration, but has meanwhile evolved into an unsustainable discipline over the planet which *also undermines civil society itself*. Indeed the destruction of the life-supporting capacity of the biosphere by pollution, climate change and straight exhaustion (of fresh water supplies, fish stocks, minerals, and so on) is coupled increasingly to exhaustive demands placed on society in the productive sphere. Management techniques and ideologies such as quality circles and benchmarking tend to intensify work to unsustainable levels, while accumulation strategies directed at leisure and recovery time extend pressures deep into daily life (van der Pijl 1998: 45).

The combination of the neo-liberal delegitimization of the state and its actual abandoning of tasks in the sphere of social protection, with the exhaustion of the civil sphere, produces particular forms of degeneration of public life. In a recent article, Robert Cox has indicated that the retreat of the state and the underdevelopment of civil society (understood as a realm of private association and terrain for the development of democracy) attracts forces of decay, which he discusses under two headings: exclusionary populism and the covert world. Exclusionary populism mobilizes the resentment against certain aspects of neo-liberal globalization behind xenophobic, racist, or religious-fundamentalist programmes. The covert world 'comprises intelligence services, organized crime, terrorist groups, the arms trade, money-laundering banks, and secret societies' (Cox 1999: 14). These two worlds overlap of course, but so do the supposed illegal and undemocratic forces within states – including the developed heartland states.

In this light I would also interpret NATO's punitive expedition against rump-Yugoslavia in the spring of 1999. This war was launched as key zones of the envisaged 'one world under capital' – Russia, the vassal states of East Asia, Brazil, Venezuela – have descended into crisis. Expansion of the heartland now has slid back to a ruthless imperialism. While the Central European expansion of NATO has proceeded in response to the aspirations of the local ruling elites – a standard phenomenon of the heartland's expansion so far (Holman 1998), the violent forward push into the Balkans as a result of Yugoslavia's collapse clearly lacks such a transnational class component. Rather, this push seems motivated by the need to intimidate Russia (where criminal privatization and the collapse of the state are destroying the foundations of organized social life, though that country still commands huge resources for a renewed challenge to the heartland) as well as China (the ascendant contender). US and British appetites for the raw material resources of the Caspian area also are hardly concealed.[4]

The spectre of super-disasters in the zones of original accumulation; the regression of the internationalization of capital to speculative movements of funds across the globe prejudicing production and pushing entire continents over the brink economically; and the slide into punitive war – these together are darkening the horizon of capitalist development profoundly. Of course, the final hour of capitalism has been declared so often that few would risk their reputation on trying again. Yet if one looks at the phases of capitalist development in the longer historical perspective, the need to theorize its transcendence is probably more urgent than ever.

Notes

1   OECD iron and steel statistics reported in *Financial Times*, 23 October 1998.
2   *Financial Times*, 25 June 1999. See Schneider (1989: chapter 6) on the impact of the greenhouse effect.
3   *Financial Times* 17 July 1998. See *The Economist*, World Economy Survey, 19 September 1992.
4   At the Washington NATO summit of April 1999, with war raging in rump-Yugoslavia, the US, UK and Turkey sponsored the formation of GUUAM, a political-economic alliance of Georgia, Ukraine, Uzbekistan, Azerbaijan and Moldova. See Reuters dispatch, www.russia.today.com, 4 May 1999; and Amineh (1999).

2
The Fortunes and Misfortunes of Post-Fordism

Alain Lipietz

In times of crisis there is a tendency to idealize the declining social order as a lost paradise. This is now the case with 'Fordism', the model of development which characterized the post-war Golden Age in the West, and was partially imitated in models of 'import-substitution' in the Third World. The logic of Fordism secured rising standards of living and provided a feeling of security to workers. The crisis of Fordism in the 1970s gave rise to a period of experimentation with new models. Among them, one model in particular seems increasingly dominant on a world scale, but still faces serious contenders. Consolidated around the North Atlantic rim, it is especially well represented, and thus well studied, in the United States. While appealing to capital, it is not at all appealing to workers. But nowhere in the genes of capital is it inscribed that what is good for capital is also good for workers, and even less for nature!

The new model of development which has triumphed on both sides of the Atlantic, and which we call the 'neo-Taylorist', 'flexible' or 'liberal productivist' model, is much less stable than its predecessor. It is cyclical like capitalism in the nineteenth century, but its transnationalization renders these cycles particularly dangerous. However, it is not the only possible form to succeed Fordism, even within a capitalist framework. Other models have emerged that are less 'liberal' (in continental Europe and in Japan). They remain highly competitive and better preserve the interests of workers, even if they also suffer from instabilities linked to transnationalization.

I have described the development of Fordism in earlier works: its crisis; the dangers of the responses to the crisis by the United States, Britain and France; as well as the multiplicity of models that have appeared across the globe (Lipietz 1987; 1992b; 1997b). I will thus be brief in resketching these analyses, which I will present in the simplest form through a focus on the *social question* (drawing especially on the French context) in the period of 'after-Fordism', which raises issues of exclusion, precariousness and increasing inequalities of income and position. From the perspective offered by this lens, which highlights important features of the current transition, the

Fordist social order will be called: the *'hot-air balloon society'* and the Atlantic (flexible) after-Fordist order: the *'hourglass society'*.

In the first section, I will present the causes of the crisis of Fordism and the two paths chosen to move beyond it. In the second section, I will concentrate on the characteristics of the flexible model: its social consequences and macroeconomic regime. Finally, I will offer an evaluation of the relative situation of the different models in the world at the end of the twentieth century.

From the hot-air balloon society to the hourglass society

The history of capitalism is not linear. It may be viewed as a succession of models of development with points of bifurcation and regression. Thus the decline of Fordism has brought a new model of development in its wake, one described by two American radicals as 'The Great U-Turn' (Bluestone and Harrison 1988).

The hot-air balloon society

The model of development we call Fordism rested on three pillars:

1. A particular organization of labour (a 'technological paradigm') – Taylorism – which allowed rapid and continuous gains in productivity from the beginning of the century onwards. It rested on the opposition in the workplace between those who conceive (engineers, administrators and technicians) and those who execute (manual and less-skilled workers).
2. A macroeconomic logic (a 'regime of accumulation'), based in this case on the systematic redistribution of productivity gains to every social class, particularly to all workers, in the form of regular increases in purchasing power. This effective demand sustained accumulation during the post-war Golden Age by creating a growing market for mass production. This is why we have come to speak of this model as Fordism – in homage to Henry Ford, who mass-produced automobiles and encouraged employers to raise wages so that those vehicles would be bought. The model is also called 'Keynesianism' – in homage to John Maynard Keynes, who demonstrated the role of insufficient effective demand during the crisis of the 1930s.
3. A 'mode of regulation', or, a package of governing rules which, in the context of Fordism, entailed a centralized and rigid system of redistributing productivity gains, stabilized by a network of collective bargaining, social legislation and the welfare state (the system of social security). It is for this reason that we sometimes refer to the most organized forms of Fordism as 'the social-democratic model'.

The pattern of income distribution under Fordism takes the form of a pot-bellied hot-air balloon – few wealthy, few poor and many in the middle

– which rises continuously and as a whole. The hierarchy of wages is rigidly fixed by collective agreements. Wealthy classes, middle classes and working classes all successively gain access to the same structure of consumption, which increases according to similar trajectories that differ in time. The lifestyle of engineers precedes the lifestyle of technicians by a few years which, in turn, represents the future lifestyle of skilled labour who are themselves opening the path for semi-skilled labour. For a different analogy, we can imagine a society on an escalator where social distances remain the same, but where everyone rises together. Newcomers, such as rural-to-urban migrants and immigrants, stand on the last stair.

The image of the hot-air balloon is, above all, a descriptive one. To represent the distribution of income in a more practical manner, we can present incomes on a vertical axis and add, to each segment of this axis, a horizontal axis representing the portion of population enjoying an income within this segment. In this way, we obtain a kind of spinning top, a 'strobiloïde' of incomes (taken from *strobilos* or spinning top in Greek). Figure 2.1 represents such spinning tops of different countries at different dates. Since the aim is to represent the inequalities and not the general income level of those countries at a given time, all these spinning tops have the same surface representing the totality of households of the country. The level of the median income[1] is indexed at 100, the 'half-median' level at 50, and so forth. A strobiloïde in a developed and Fordist country must not touch the ground: almost no one has an income of zero. As we move up the scale, we find some poor households near the bottom, but as we proceed, we reach a 'belly' at the levels where the largest portion of households are found. Moving higher still, we find the upper middle classes who constitute a smaller group. The spinning top gets thinner, and tapers progressively as it reaches even higher incomes where we find fewer and fewer people.

Let us examine a few of these spinning tops. In Figure 2.1, the left part represents the end of the 1970s. We can see that the population in Sweden is concentrated around the median, while the Netherlands falls just a bit under it. These are the countries that typify 'social democracy' in the post-war period. Already, Great Britain and the United States can be distinguished from these models: we find far fewer people in the middle, more rich and poor, and already (in the United States) many that are extremely poor. These countries, which initially invented Fordism and the welfare state, are less 'egalitarian' than the continental European countries that subsequently developed them. We can also imagine what the form of a strobiloïde would take in Brazil or India – a big drop of paint with its bottom flat on the ground – with 70 per cent of the population having little or no income, 25 per cent middle class, and some very rich. This pattern is much more inegalitarian than the richer countries.

In Fordist – or social democratic – countries, strobiloïdes of income have the form of a spinning top. Why then use the image of a hot air balloon?

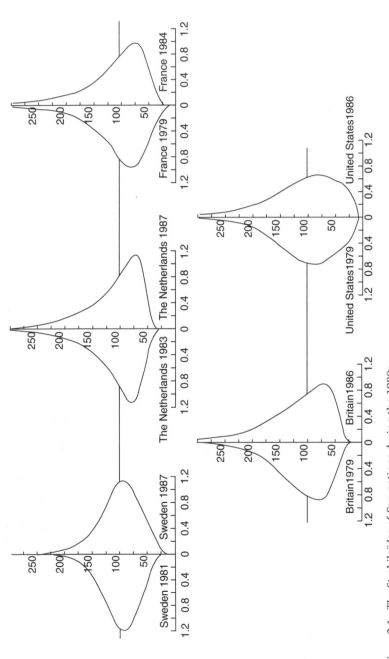

Figure 2.1 The Strobiloïdes of five nations during the 1980s.

Source: Louis Chauvel, 'Inégalités singulières et plurielles: les évolutions de la courbe des revenues disponibles', *Revue de l'OFCE*, no. 55, octobre, 1995.

First, because a real spinning top rests on the ground, which is not an accurate representation of the distribution of income. More importantly, the image of a hot-air balloon evokes a *'physiology'* – an internal macro-economic logic – characteristic of Fordism. It is in fact the mass of income of wage-earners, largely situated around the median income, that enables the whole of the economy to rise, like the mass of hot air caught within the belly of the hot-air balloon, between the tight chimneys of the top and the bottom, that elevates the aircraft.

This is, indeed, the logic of mass consumption. Kalecki, the great Polish economist who, from his London refuge during the inter-war period, iden-tified the missing link between Marx and Keynes, wrote: 'Wage earners spend what they earn, capitalists earn what they spend.' We will revisit the second part of this sentence later. The meaning of the first is evident. Most wage-earners – workers, employees and lower managers – spend almost everything they earn, or save in order to consume later. The part of income distributed in wages is immediately returned for goods produced, which are practically sold in advance. This was the driving force of the Golden Age of Fordism (1945–75): a stable and sustained growth of production made pos-sible because purchasing 'power' and the 'willingness' to purchase were nearly equal. With collective agreements, contracts of indefinite duration, mechanisms to increase progressively the minimum wage, we can be certain that 'effective demand' will increase commensurate with gains in productiv-ity. We can thus invest continuously to increase production. In the case of pregnant women, the sick, retired and unemployed people, the welfare state exists to guarantee a permanent wage. The consumption of Fordist workers is both stable and growing. This is completely different for capitalists and high wage-earners, since they shift from consumption to savings in a cyc-lical pattern. We will return to this later on.

The crisis of Fordism

The Fordist wage relation was characterized, most of all, by the combination of Taylorist principles of labour organization and rigid forms of wage con-tractualization which ensured regular growth in the purchasing power of workers (social legislation, collective agreements, the welfare state). This capital–labour compromise came into crisis from both sides at the beginning of the 1970s. On the one hand, what we call 'globalization' – the extensive internationalization of markets and productive networks without a corre-sponding international harmonization of wage compromises – brought competitive constraints to centre stage. On the other hand, the Taylorist organization of labour exhausted its capacity for the rationalization of labour. Hence, from both sides (competitiveness and profitability) the rigid-ity of wage contracts came to appear as a barrier.

The first cause of the crisis, globalization, is the best-known. It represents the official explanation for the crisis and serves as a justification for the 'only way out': reduce wages. This explanation is in fact also accepted by the majority of union militants, of alternative environmentalists, and can be considered true. But it does not tell the whole story. It does not explain the crisis of those sectors not subject to international competition (the majority of economic activity); it does not explain why countries such as Germany and Japan are, despite their higher wages, more competitive than France; and it does not explain how the 'Four Tigers' of Asia have, despite rising wages, managed to surpass Britain where wages are now lower than in Singapore and even South Korea.

The second cause is more subtle. One of its associated propositions must be examined with care: the notion that technological change will make production so efficient as to lead to the *end of work*. Jeremy Rifkin (1995) brilliantly defends this thesis. According to him, if firms used the best techniques available there would hardly be need for labour at all. Against Rifkin's position, however, one might recall that the old refrain, 'Machines kill jobs', has been around for centuries now; that productivity increases were higher under Fordism than they are today (twice as high in France: 5.2 per cent per year from 1949 to 1974 and 2.6 per cent since 1974); and that, in any case, the central issue remains of how better to redistribute the gains of productivity, in the form of either increases in purchasing power (as in the Fordist era) or reductions in the working day. To this, defenders of the Rifkin thesis might respond: 'Yes, but these are now ruled out by international competition', which brings us back to the previous objection, the globalization thesis.

The crisis of the Fordist organization of labour is actually a bit more complex. If all firms do not use the best techniques available, it is because they must buy them (invest) and, in order to do this, they must increase their profits. The prevention of the Y2K bug has revealed the amortization of computer hardware and software in even the most prestigious firms – this at a time when the productivity gains furnished by Fordist techniques, which come from machines that are more and more costly and automated, and designed by legions of engineers and technicians, are less and less able to cover the necessary investments which have made them possible. In other words, the efficiency of capital (the value of the product over the value of equipment) is decreasing continuously: by 43 per cent in France since 1965 (Figure 2.2). In order to buy new equipment, the first and oldest strategy for investors is of course to increase their share of profits (the marginal rate) and thereby lower the portion for labour, either by making people work more, or by paying them less, or both, but in each case by repudiating the Fordist compromise of the post-war era.

The two paths from the crisis

In both explanations (globalization and the crisis of Taylorism), the path forward always implies, at first, the same solution: a decrease in wages. This

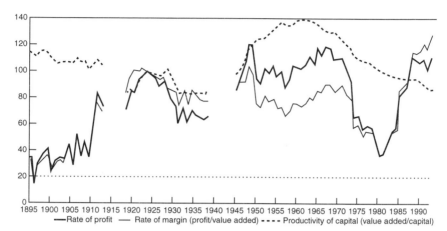

Figure 2.2   The rate of profit and its components: France – base 100 in 1924.

is what British, American and French employers did from 1978 onwards. Since the low point of 1982, French employers have restored their profit rate, which tripled in the following 10 years (Figure 2.2). The rate of profit (profit over invested capital) is nothing other than the rate of margin (profit over value-added), multiplied by the efficiency of capital (value added over capital invested). Even if the second has a 'tendency to fall' (as Marx would say), the rate of profit can be re-established by a more rapid reduction in the portion allocated to wages.

Today in France, as in the United States, the crisis is over for capital. The rate of profit has been restored to the level enjoyed from the 1950s to 1970s. Who has paid for this? In large part the workers. They continue to produce more each year. Productivity in France, despite a slower pace, has increased by 30 per cent in 12 years. But there has been no decrease in the annual hours of work, nor any increase in real wages, from 1982 levels. The portion of the national product allocated to wage earners has dropped dramatically and this has more than compensated for the reduction in the efficiency of capital.

In the United States, the situation for workers is even worse. In every economic branch, at all levels of qualification for women, as well as for men, the length of annual work has increased by a month since the 1970s. Americans worked 320 hours more than Germans each year, and for a lower wage (at least until the mid-1990s). The average wage has decreased by 10 per cent in real terms since 1973. Simply to maintain the living standards of 1973, an American worker today must work 245 hours more each year (Schor 1991). In Britain, the breakdown of norms regarding the length of working hours is such that those norms have practically lost all meaning.

In the Anglo-Saxon countries, even more than in France, the threat of unemployment and the elimination of legislation regulating the conditions of work have been central to bringing this mounting pressure to bear on workers. Thus, the first way out of the crisis of Fordism has entailed the destruction of rigid social compromises: the notorious path of '*flexibiliza-tion*'. This route was chosen by Anglo-Saxon countries, Southern Europe and France: a 'Brazilianization' resulting in 'neo-Taylorism', upholding Taylorist principles of labour organization, reinforced by computer technologies, but without the advantages Fordism previously offered to workers. Fortunately, this is not the only path left.

Other national capitalisms have explored a new compromise based on the 'mobilization of human resources', or the mobilization of workers in the competitive battle for productivity and quality. This path involves actively promoting growth in the productivity of labour, without necessarily relying on increasingly sophisticated and costly machinery. New compromises based on this strategy can be negotiated at the level of the firm (as in Japan), of a branch (as in Germany, in Northern Italy, and in general in the Alpine Arc), or of an entire society (Scandinavia). These compromises always imply the maintenance of a certain rigidity of social benefits, in exchange for the negotiated involvement of workers (Lipietz 1997b).

The lesson of the 1980s, from the point of view of capitalists (the point of view of competitiveness), is the victory of the second model over the first. As in Atlantic capitalism, rates of profit have been restored to levels similar to those before the crisis, but by completely different means. In countries still using Fordist methods, and which rely heavily on technology to improve the efficiency of labour, the efficiency of capital (the value added divided by the costs of the capital invested) has decreased continuously since the end of the Second World War (Figure 2.2). In models based on the negotiated involvement of workers, the decrease in the efficiency of capital is erased, while the product of labour, increasingly qualified compared with other countries, is sold at higher and higher prices on the world market. The result: Germany and Japan, despite having the highest wages in the world, have consistently garnered a trade surplus with the United States since the 1980s, whereas the United States has continuously posted a deficit of 7 to 20 billion dollars per month in the same period.

The first model can still survive in neo-Taylorist regions of high flexibility, either by specializing in low-skill industries or by realizing breakthroughs in branches employing mainly engineers (this is the case mostly in the United States, but not in Britain). Hence, we are witnessing a new international division of labour between a highly skilled centre, with higher and more rigid wage contracts, and an increasingly flexible periphery. This new inter-national division of labour is being organized in Europe following a North-East–South-West axis running from Scandinavia (where high-tech champions like Nokia are prospering) to Ireland and Portugal. France lies somewhere in the middle, suffering in the face of competition from countries that work 'better than her' (Germany) and others which are less costly (Spain).

The hourglass society

From the range of possible solutions to the crisis, it is clear that France chose, as early as the 1970s, and especially since the second half of the 1980s, the path of 'flexibilization'. The political, ideological and institutional strategies initiated from 1978 onwards in the Anglo-Saxon countries, in Southern Europe and in France under Prime Minister Raymond Barre – in the name of the struggle against inflation, for competitiveness, and for the restoration of firms' profitability – marked the end of Fordism. In the process, a new model has taken its place since the 1980s: the 'liberal productivist' model based on 'neo-Taylorism', which has fundamentally reshaped society in the form of an hourglass.

Flexibilization and social disruption

The flexibilization of the wage relation, with a notable shift away from rigid ties to the firm, and the progressive reduction in the range of guarantees of unemployment insurance, have globally weakened workers and the lower middle class. The result has been an increase in profits, especially profits distributed in the form of financial gains, as well as higher wages for senior managers and directors. This in turn has resulted in the concentration of income in the classes who save (leaders of industry and commerce and the upper tier of wage earners). The social elevator is going down again as the hot air balloon deflates and becomes an hourglass.

The image of the hourglass is also both descriptive and 'physiological' (Lipietz 1996). First, the pattern of income distribution shifts from the image of the hot air balloon to one of an hourglass (Figure 2.3). It deflates at the centre where we find the middle classes, to take the form of what we call the 'two-thirds' society, with a shrinking median third. Indeed, the first to deflate Fordism in this manner were the British and Americans led by Margaret Thatcher and Ronald Reagan. The problem is not only the coexistence of rich people, shrinking middle classes and a marginalized third. Rather it is also the process that tears apart this society, deflating the middle and emptying most of its contents below, while a small segment is pulled to the top: the Anglo-Saxon yuppies and all who, in the second half of the 1980s, were the beneficiary of '*la France qui gagne*' ('The France which wins' in the words of Laurent Fabius, the prime minister at the time).

We should now look at the bottom of this hourglass society. The strobiloïde of the United States speaks for itself. With increasing economic instability and uncertainty, it is the lower-middle and popular classes which are pushed towards the bottom, into conditions of precariousness, extreme poverty and sometimes outright exclusion. The precarious worker is at the same time poor and precarious, two distinct conditions. In terms of purchasing power, poor workers today are wealthier than many workers in

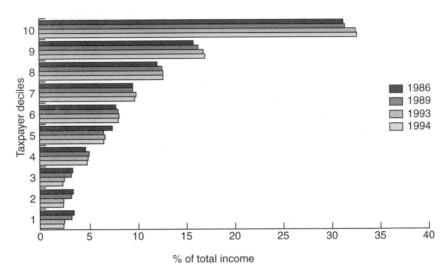

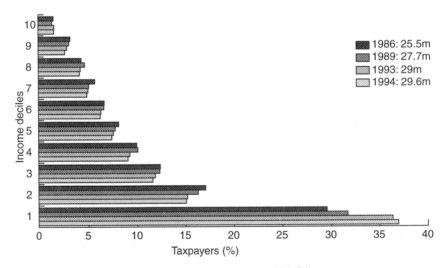

Figure 2.3   The evolution of the hourglass society (1986–94).

1960. But they have no job security; it is nowadays much more difficult to plan for the future and to raise children with the expectation they will be upwardly mobile socially. People at the bottom are perceived as enemies to people in the middle, not because they really threaten them in the labour market, but because this bottom provides an image of what the future may hold for those in the middle. It is the suffering of the declining white middle class that fuels the fire of racism today.

The fragmentation of the wage-earning class

The English journalist Will Hutton (1996) speaks of the '30–30–40 society': 30 per cent excluded, 30 per cent precarious, 40 per cent stable, with each segment further differentiated internally by income. In France, we may not be there yet, but we are nevertheless witnessing a division of incomes into four groups.

1. A highly qualified segment benefiting from the growth in social productivity through high wages: this is the modern bourgeoisie and petty bourgeoisie, engineers and managers. In periods of growth (as the one experienced by the United States in the second part of the 1980s and the 1990s), they see their income rise considerably, raising the issue of how this income is used, which will be examined later.
2. A segment of permanent and relatively skilled workers. These are the survivors of the old Fordist wage relation. This relation only applies now to middle managers, technicians and middle-range civil servants (the 'intermediary' professions).
3. A segment of workers in low wage and precarious employment. Although their formal contracts may not be precarious (interim, short-term, part-time), there is a widespread apprehension that their employers could reduce them all to such a position. However, in periods of growth, these workers are hired *en masse*, almost giving the impression of full employment. Their income, much like the income of those in the second category, may therefore increase, but much less so than the income of those in the first category. This wage stability prevents economic 'booms' from becoming inflationary.
4. A final segment of people permanently excluded from employment.

The emergence of a *permanently* 'unemployable' sector (the word is atrocious!), the excluded, is a novelty in the core capitalist societies. This group is no longer a 'reserve army', but a population that capitalism does not need any more, not even to discipline stable workers with the threat of dismissal. This permanent exclusion results from two features of hourglass societies.

The machine of exclusion

First, capital no longer tends to hire all the 'proletariat', but only those it needs, according to the machines it owns and the markets it perceives. However, mechanization reduces the demand for labour in an economy where growth is insufficient and working time is not reduced. This situation, where a mass of workers is no longer in reserve, but is permanently useless to capital, is classic in the underdeveloped countries (we call it a 'Lewisian situation'[2]). But in 'neo-Taylorist' countries which are more developed, there is simply no need for under-skilled labour. Pressured on two fronts in international competition, by countries seeking to 'mobilize their human resources' (for example, Germany, Japan) and by the new industrialized economies where unskilled labour costs much less, 'neo-Taylorist' countries (United States, Great Britain, France) can hope only to preserve qualified tasks in the Taylorist organization of labour, and relocate others to the Third World – or themselves become Third World countries. This Brazilianization is a tendency already at work, but we are still far from its full realization![3]

Attempting to bring wages into alignment with Irish, Spanish then Brazilian competition, means, for a country like France, resigning itself to the drift towards Third World status. In the United States the situation is already so 'Lewisian' that excluded people are shamelessly deprived of their citizenship status and even basic human rights. President Bill Clinton has even recently supported a Republican law depriving young single women (mostly Afro-Americans) of family allowances if they abandon their studies. In Roman antiquity, the 'proletariat' constituted the lowest class, useful to the city only for its lineage (*proles*): that is, for producing children. Clinton and the Republican Congress seem to be excluding Afro-Americans to such an extent that the United States does not even need their children. The best that this '*underclass*' can do is disappear with its useless lineage. In this case, we cannot simply talk of exclusion, but of expulsion. An 'underclass' is expelled from humankind, deprived of individual rights. Let us remember that the care of children and the right to establish a household (be it single-parent or otherwise) are not rights tied to citizenship, but to the 'human being' as defined by the Universal Charter of the United Nations. These are not granted to residents of a country because they belong to a nation, but owed to them by society because they are humans. This process of expulsion, an extreme feature of the hourglass society, is thus always more or less linked to racism, taking root in ethic differences, and constituting the poor as a race apart.

In France, these excluded persons are, for the most part, immigrants and youth of foreign origin. In the last century they were very numerous in France, a country that lost vast numbers of men in the world wars and was in need of children up until 1945. The dazzling economic success of Fordism pushed France to look for labouring hands across Europe and Africa, despite a rural exodus towards cities and the repatriation of the French from Algeria. In 1965, immigration reached the previous peak of 1930, and immigrants comprised 7.4 per cent of the population by 1975. But with the crisis of Fordism, the flow of immigration was interrupted, except in cases of family reunion; and the process of exclusion began. If people of colour are the first to be targeted as 'supernumerary', the threat in fact looms for all poor people: street youth, the homeless, all of whose physical appearance offends the 'included'. Thus the image of the hourglass is still imperfect, because the grains of sand at the bottom of the hourglass remain within it. The machine of exclusion more closely resembles a centrifuge, whose velocity expels those no longer useful to post-industrial society.

The macroeconomy of the hourglass society

We can now turn to the internal logic – the physiology, the regime of accumulation – of the hourglass society. Let us revisit Kalecki's words: 'Wage earners spend what they earn, capitalists earn what they spend.' In Fordism, the largest share of national income is distributed to wage earners 'around the median income', who spend everything they earn. This is not the case with the 'capitalists', that is, entrepreneurs and beneficiaries of the distribution of interests and dividends. They have sufficient money to secure savings which are lent to firms in order to invest, if they wish to do so. Hence the amount saved from national income is actually spent only if firms invest it. If they do not, sales slow down, stocks accumulate, and production decreases. Finally, the income saved that has not been spent is no longer available: it is cut off from what firms can hope to gain. Hence the notion that 'capitalists earn what they spend'. 'What they spend' must here be understood in two senses: either they spend directly (big cars, yachts, caviar) or they save it as households but spend it (invest it) as entrepreneurs.

The return of cycles

This reasoning is of course highly simplified. Besides direct consumption and investment, there are two other important outlets for production: exports and government spending. Exports in excess of imports (like in Japan or Germany) or public spending in excess of taxes can thus stimulate production, but evidently not in all countries at the same time or in a permanent fashion.

In the hot-air balloon society, since the amount of wages represents some 70 per cent of the total product, firms have no worries about effective demand: they will never lack consumers. In an hourglass society, this percentage drops dangerously close to 50 per cent (56 per cent in France in 1994). Will the other half of the national income be spent or not? This depends on the mood of the wealthy (their 'animal spirits' as the great economist, Joan Robinson following Keynes would have said). Either capitalists and high-income households, encouraged by the rise of profits, spend freely: they buy luxury goods and they invest – business is going well enough to justify their investments. Or they start worrying about signs of weak demand from households – entrepreneurs slow down their investments, and the wealthy increase their savings; in the end, the absence of a 'willingness to buy' provokes the fall in production they had anticipated.

The economic dynamic of hourglass societies is thus profoundly cyclical: at some points the wealthy save too much and production declines, at other points they spend too much and production gets carried away. The theory of cycles was, from Marx's time to the 1950s, the grand issue of political economy. It has been a bit neglected during the Fordist era, but with the emergence of the hourglass society it has become fashionable once again. Today, however, two features contribute to the acceleration of these cycles and distinguish them from their pre-war manifestation.

Globalization and financialization

Globalization refers to a growing interdependence among national markets leading towards a unified world market. We are still far from this, but the integration of all national, or at least continental, markets is proceeding apace. Before, when demand would slow down in a country, we could hope to compensate by expanding markets in other countries. Today, a whole continent or even all three great regional blocs (Europe, the Americas and Asia) can find themselves in a slump.

Financialization is at the same time a result and an accelerator of the hourglass society. An increasing portion of the national income that is not automatically consumed is accumulated as financial assets. These assets in turn yield dividends and interest, increasing the income of the wealthiest classes, which is, of course, saved right away. This growing mass of money struggles over shares (shares of ownership of corporations) and obligations (the recognition of a debt by states and firms). Prices of these titles thus increase, and with them the value of the shareholders' wealth. This financial surplus value again raises the income of shareholders, but only virtually: surplus value is appropriated only if titles are sold and this requires the right timing. However, the increase in the price of assets can have a real effect: prompted by the revaluation of their assets, wealthy households may consume even more (the 'Pigou effect') or buy new titles. In the latter case we witness a true 'inflation of assets'.

In search of large dividends, the mass of this speculative money is instantly directed towards the 'juiciest' firms: those pursuing short-term strategies to maximize the value distributed to shareholders, those most effective in squeezing their workers, trimming their 'excess fat', and distributing the greatest share of profit instead of reinvesting it. All of this aggravates the social disruption and economic instability which characterize hourglass societies.

The globalization of financial markets intensifies financialization, because financial capital, in search of a productive base to milk, can play firms (or governments if they prefer bonds) off against one another on a global scale. This is what we call the *world casino society*. Within this mass of capital seeking the most profitable country, capitalized pension funds represent the most significant players. Collecting workers' contributions and investing them to finance workers' retirement, these funds are institutionally obliged to look in the most cynical and opportunistic way for the highest yields to serve the interests of their members. Only certain regions like Northern Italy or Southern Germany escape this short-term horizon, since, for cultural reasons, banking capital remains (for the moment!) intimately tied to industrial capital. It is no coincidence that these local societies are *also* the ones favouring the 'negotiated mobilization of human resources' to move out of the crisis of Fordism (Leborgne and Lipietz 1991).

The trickle-down economy

Naturally, the attraction of significant yields on savings from the casino economy, further enhanced by fiscal measures taken by governments (in the name of 'defending their currency') to attract floating capital to their national territory, further diverts even the wealthier classes away from consumption. A paradox: the more wealth gets concentrated, the more difficult it becomes to convince the rich to consume. But to the single-minded liberal thinker, relying solely on the second half of Kalecki's observation, only the expenditures of the wealthy classes are available to relaunch production. In this way, governments arrive at the conclusion that rich people should be made even richer in order to consume a bit more: to buy a third car, hire a housemaid and gardeners, go to fancy restaurants. Kalecki's formula is thus reduced to the idea that 'wage earners live from the expenses of the wealthy', as in eighteenth-century Europe, or as has always been the case in Brazil. This is the *trickle-down* economy, resembling a fountain whose waters trickle from one basin to the next below (Bowles, Gintis and Weisskopf 1983).

In a trickle-down economy, one should not be surprised to hear governments calling for wage reductions, making sinister cuts in often worthwhile social budgets (housing, culture) in the name of public deficit reductions, while at the same time, begging their citizens to spend more! They are only addressing the highest portion of the hourglass, ready as they are to finance the hiring of servants, the purchase of new cars, and the reduction of fiscal charges on financial profits as long as the balance is directed towards consumption, not savings.

What remains of Keynesianism?

There are still two other ways to finance growth: fiscal policy and monetary policy. Public spending is also an 'effective demand'. When a state levies taxes and spends them, it stimulates demand which is directed at firms, especially when these taxes are levied upon the segments which tend to save more. If production slows down too much, the state can temporarily spend a little more than it receives, even if that means paying back the debts so accumulated when business improves again. Generally, on average, there is no need for states to go into debt. A sufficiently large community must finance annual collective investments from the income of that year. A public deficit is a good thing in periods of low production, but it is important quickly to re-establish balance when the economy is going better: this is called 'anti-cyclical policy'. Unfortunately, in hourglass societies, economic activity tends to languish because wage earners are too poor to ensure a sufficient demand. This is why governments in such societies tend to sink into deficits: they dare not tax the rich (for fear of capital flight) and cannot tax the poor.

The other tool of economic policy is, or rather was, monetary policy. A central bank has the capacity to expand short-term credit. This encourages firms to invest and households to buy lodging. This policy, as we will see, has worked well in the United States in the second half of the 1990s. But what is possible in a country like the United States, which issues the international currency (the dollar), cannot work in countries obliged to equilibrate their balance of payments. This is the case for France. In order to 'keep the franc strong', it becomes necessary to attract mobile capital from across the globe by offering them high interest rates. In the second half of the 1980s, French governments in this way encouraged a 'monetarist' policy favouring quasi-usurious interest rates. Moreover since 1993, with the Maastricht Treaty, the central banks of Europe have become 'independent'. In other words, they now fall under the influence of a group of individuals who cannot be held accountable. They managed to maintain the same policy, despite its ir-rationality, until 1995. Monetary policy escaped from politics. In fact, this stance of the (independent) councils of central banks only reflected the wishes of the financial community – favouring greater yields for those with the means to save money. Hence, the 'money wall' of the 1920s was reconstituted. However, such a monetary policy is not really necessary in hourglass societies: the United States and even Great Britain avoided it by practising 'semi-Keynesianism'.

A four-class society?

The dynamic equilibrium of Fordism can be compared to a game with two adversaries: capital and labour. It was in capital's best interest to limit its pressure on labour or it would have lost its customers. Workers, on the other hand, could not demand wage increases at a pace faster than the growth of productivity or the ensuing 'profit squeeze' would have reduced the pace of investment and job creation.

This logic is no longer valid in the hourglass society. First, as we have seen, the excluded no longer have the potential to be hired. What is earned and spent by 'included workers' does not benefit them: an increase in wages is no longer sufficient to produce new demand and significantly increase produc-tion and employment; rather, it risks getting lost in imports. Moreover, financialization introduces a gap between financial profits and the capacity of firms to invest. Even if wages go down, the capacity to finance enterprises does not necessarily increase. The difference can be captured by finance. The share of income and jobs seems to structure the interest of four different groups: the excluded, included workers (with their own subdivision that we examined earlier), 'active' capitalists (entrepreneurs) and 'passive' capitalists ('rentiers').

However, it is very important to emphasize that these groups, or rather their economic status, do not constitute classes. Rather, they represent statuses or functions. Included workers are potentially excluded; they often belong to the same family. The rentiers are themselves often high wage earners. Entrepreneurs earn a large portion of their income as rentiers (they place their profit instead of investing it themselves) and often remunerate themselves as wage earners in their own firms. Finally, the new middle class (managers, especially senior managers) are also owners of a patrimony that yields interests and dividends.

Only the unity of the excluded and included can successfully pressure the social layers at the top, which occupy the functions of 'capitalists', to compel them to become more 'active' and less 'passive'. However, this unity still needs to be worked out. It must take into account diverging interests which run across it. It must also think strategically about the divergence of interests which it can play upon to divide the three faces of capital: upper management, productive firms and financial capital.

The state of after-Fordism: the end of the 1990s

According to the preceding arguments, there seems to be an intrinsic superiority of the German and Japanese model over the American one. Yet this diagnosis seems to be contradicted by the evidence at the end of the 1990s. I still persist in defending it. The German and Japanese models, based on the involvement and the qualifications of relatively stable workers, are not only more socially equitable (everything is relative) but also more competitive than the American model based on flexibility and the inequality of income. At no time since the 1980s has the trade surplus of Germany and Japan been higher, and this does not only stem from a time lag in the economic conjuncture (that is, the weak imports of both countries). Of course, the abundance of capital seeking opportunities to invest and the high quality of American engineers (the top layer of the neo-Taylorist division of labour) enable the United States to triumph in activities linked to the computer sector. Moreover, the penetration of Japanese capital and, in smaller proportions, European capital is starting to transform American labour techniques. But American competitiveness is not catching up: the United States is accumulating boundless deficits, thanks in part to the particular status of the dollar.

So why then has the United States reached this new century in full expansion, when Europe is stagnating and Asia, after 15 years of growth, is experiencing a terrible crisis? The response is to be found not on the side of technological paradigms but on the side of forms of continental regulation. I have already exposed several times the reason for Europe's paralysis during the 1990s (Lipietz 1997b). First, extremely restrictive budgetary and monetary policy were dictated by the Single European Act (1988) and the Maastricht Treaty (1992), which structured the monetary unification of the continent. Second, there was a collapse of a traditional trade outlet: the former socialist Europe. At the end of this century, with monetary unification achieved, Europe is risking a timid recovery based on low interest rates and a 'benign neglect' regarding the relative strength of the Euro. Meanwhile, the United States, under the brilliant direction of the Federal Reserve, has continued since the late 1980s to practice a semi-Keynesian policy sustaining economic expansion!

In the case of Asia, even more so than in Europe, there is a hierarchy which extends across a wide range of models of development, from the Japanese model to the 'primitive Taylorist' model of Thailand (Lipietz 1997b). Continental regulation has been spontaneously ensured by pegging currencies at the bottom of the hierarchy to the dollar, which was losing value in relation to the yen. No mechanism regulated the growth of demand; this growth was facilitated by rapid industrialization in the region (particularly China) and exports to the rest of the world. Thus, Asia passed through a period resembling the Taylorist model of the inter-war period, experiencing its own 'Roaring Twenties' from 1985 to 1997. As the rest of the world lamented its own deindustrialization and financialization, Asia was becoming an immense economic machine attracting financial capital and driving investment from around the world. Thailand and Malaysia were covered with high rises, and no Korean chaebol was too small to refuse the opportunity to transform itself into an international trust encompassing a wide range of productive branches.

At the time, I emphasized the role of the continuous devaluation of the dollar in relation to the yen, a trend which was precisely reversed in 1997. And I stressed that, in the absence of Fordist regulation of Asian demand, this boom would lead to a crisis of overproduction. As we know, there is always a point at which financial capital realizes that the overaccumulation of productive capital no longer corresponds to any real demand: after the Roaring Twenties came the crash of 1929 and the ten years of the Depression. This is exactly what happened in 1997.

The United States functions even more obviously according to the general macroeconomy of pre-war capitalism. After the deep recession at the beginning of the 1980s, the 'second Reagan' expansion, and the recession under George Bush, Americans are still in 1999 in the midst of a new boom that seems endless, thanks to the intelligent monetary policy of Allan Greenspan. As in all booms that preceded World War II, unemployment has reached a minimum, wages are increasing, share prices are reaching levels that bear no relation to the earnings they yield, and this will continue until the cycle turns around. Moreover, the neo-Taylorist United States is witnessing, at the same time, the proliferation of the 'working poor' (workers living in miserable conditions while still employed), and overqualified and overpaid engineers profiting fully from the multimedia boom. But that too will reach its limits.

We should be surprised that the crisis has not yet arrived. The major difference from the 1930s is precisely that, since Keynes's time, people have learned his monetary lessons even if they have forgotten about the role of effective demand. At the end of 1997, the IMF spent tens of billions of dollars to save Asia: no one played this role towards the United States in the 1930s, nor in fact towards South America in the 1980s. This made it possible to cushion the effect of the Asian crisis on Europe and North America. Today, the three poles of the world economy are desynchronized: Europe is awakening, Asia is faintly recovering, while America is triumphing. Until now, these poles have been able to compensate one another in order to avoid a global economic catastrophe.

But it must be stressed that it is mostly the 'incredible' American expansion, with its massive trade deficit, that is sustaining growth in the world economy and that has helped some Asian countries (especially those with the best internal regulations, like Taiwan) to pull themselves out of their crises. China itself has played an important role in avoiding a crisis comparable to the 1930s, assuming the responsibility of not devaluing its own currency.

For how long can Greenspan's policy keep the world from plunging into the abyss? This accommodating monetary policy sustains a continuous expansion of final demand by the 'Pigou effect' presented earlier: as the price of their assets are climbing, middle-class households can spend on credit, even if they are not saving any more. But precisely there lies the danger: in a capitalist model without redistribution of a Fordist type but with a very 'flexible' labour market, the excess of money creates no inflation in the price of labour or of commodities, but does create it in the price of financial assets. Hence, a crash can occur at any moment in the United States, as in 1930, or even more like Japan at the beginning of the 1990s. Indeed, Japan also experienced impressive growth during the 1980s based on its technological superiority, but this growth was dependent on exports (unlike the United States today) and consumption by the wealthy which rested (this time like the United States) on the inflation of stocks and real estate.

Greenspan's whole policy aims at avoiding such a crash at the end of this century. It will still happen, provoking a cyclical recession in the United States, which will affect the whole world if Europe does not pick up the slack. The new crisis will come from a shortage of demand as it did in 1930. But this time it will be a global shortage. On paper, it could be resolved by a 'worldwide New Deal', erasing Third-World debts, restructuring the American debt, and massively redistributing income to the poorest of this 'hourglass world society', principally in the form of the reduction of labour time. Even then, it would be necessary that this New Deal respects the constraint of environmentally sustainable development, which was not the case with Fordism after the war.

A huge challenge![4]

Translated by Samuel Knafo

Notes

1 The 'median' here refers to the level of income at which half of households gain less.
2 From the studies of Arthur Lewis on Third-World countries.
3 There exists, moreover, a tendency for models of development to cross-breed. In the American 'Kanban Alley' (Ohio, etc.), automobile plants 'import', in part, Japanese methods of labour organization, but without attaining a level of competitiveness which would allow them to export their product.
4 On this challenge, see Lipietz (1992b; 1999).

3
The Disintegration of Capitalism: A Phase of Ex-Capitalist Transition

John Bell and Thomas T. Sekine

Introduction

In this chapter we advance a rather unconventional and perhaps even heretical thesis that capitalism, far from being resurgent as many believe, has already disintegrated so that we are no longer living in a capitalist society, properly speaking. Because the careless and imprecise usage of the term causes many fruitless and aggravating imbroglios, all the more do we need to begin by determining the precise sense in which we employ the term *capitalism* in this chapter.

Generally speaking, the word *capitalism* has two distinct meanings. In one sense, it means 'being a capitalist' or 'acting like the capitalist'. Indeed, a capitalist uses a certain amount of money as 'capital', that is as investment (or advance) in an enterprise of one sort or another, for the purpose of profiting from it. When the word is employed in this sense of 'capitalist activity or behaviour' we refer to it as *capitalism-I*. But the same word often means something more and other than this. It may mean 'a social system to which the spread of such capitalist activities has given rise', or 'a capitalist society'. When the word is used in the latter sense to denote 'a social system organized or integrated capitalistically', we refer to it as *capitalism-II*. The point here is that the presence of *capitalism-I* does not necessarily or automatically lead to (or develop into) *capitalism-II*, though it is often fallaciously believed to do so. Even though the two meanings are not the same, one tends to gloss over the distinction because the conventional wisdom is firmly established to the effect that, if *capitalism-I* is practised sufficiently extensively, then *capitalism-II* will automatically follow. Here the meaning of 'sufficiently extensively' is never unambiguously explained. Since we do not subscribe to this conventional wisdom, we are entitled to claim that *capitalism-II* can wither away, even as *capitalism-I* is reactivated.

The next thing we wish to assert is that *capitalism-II* exists only when, and in so far as, its 'use-value space' is adequately subsumed under the logic (or dialectic) of capital. By a 'use-value space' we mean the concrete-specific

37

historical context within which the real (or substantive) economic life of society evolves. The real economic life of a society is predicated on its production and consumption of use-values: on its metabolic interchange with surrounding nature, whereby a society transforms part of nature into useful products and returns to it the remains of each product's use and consumption. An enormous variety of use-value spaces have existed throughout our history, and it is evident that not all of them can be organized or integrated by the logic of capital. Only those spaces in which many key use-values are capitalistically producible as commodities can be subsumed under the logic of capital, and hence are amenable to capital's control. This claim brings out the distinctive feature of the Marxian approach to economics.[1] For the bourgeois approach presumes that *any* use-value space should be operable capitalistically and therefore be capable of underlying or backing up a capitalist society, whereas the Marxian approach insists on the historical transience of *capitalism-II*.

To drive home this message, let us imagine a rectangular coordinate system in which all points represent a conceivable use-value space (see Figure 3.1). Let the origin refer to that which underlies and supports 'pure capitalism': an ideal use-value space which is perfectly 'commodifiable' (in the sense of being capitalistically manageable) and is, hence, fully amenable to capital's control such that economic life becomes completely subsumable under the logic of capital.[2] Let any point other than the origin represent a

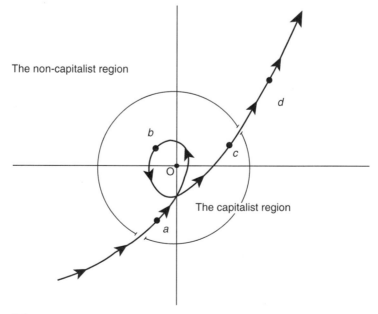

Figure 3.1

historical space which is not perfectly subsumable and which, therefore, leaves externalities outside capital's control. Let us arrange them in such a way that the spaces more readily 'commodifiable', and so more easily amenable to capital's control, are placed nearer the origin. Then, draw a circle around the origin to indicate that the points which fall outside the circle, because they are too far from the origin, cannot internalize externalities to form a capitalist society; whereas those falling inside it, being close to the origin, can do so because the use-value space can support or be integrated into capitalism-II. It is this division of the coordinates into the two categories – those belonging to the *capitalist region* and those not – that indicates the specifically Marxian nature of this investigation. At this point, let us interpret the evolution of human societies by an arrow-marked path which, at one point in history, enters the *capitalist region*, approaching but never reaching the origin, and then departing from this region at another point in history.

It is the task of the bourgeois state to internalize, by means of its economic policies, these misfit elements or externalities and make them broadly subject to the capitalist rules of the market. Historically, the leading bourgeois states took recourse to mercantilist, liberal and imperialist policies which may be viewed as typifying the three major ways of internalizing the externalities that arose in each of the three developmental periods of capitalism.[3] This was the inspiration for Kozo Uno's stages theory of capitalism (Albritton 1991). Different stages of the world-historic development of capitalism are distinguished by the types of use-values, such as wool, cotton and steel which are *dominant* in the economic life at each of the stages, in the sense of shaping the predominant industrial technology of the stage. Technological parameters in turn shape the mode of accumulation of capital which is peculiar to a stage. Thus, the modes of accumulation of merchant capital, industrial capital and finance capital characterize, respectively, the stages of mercantilism, liberalism and imperialism. But each of those modes of accumulation presupposes stage-specific economic policies on the part of the bourgeois state.

In Figure 3.1, a point such as *a*, which is close to the entry gate into the circle, represents a capitalist society at the stage of mercantilism; a point such as *b*, which is in the neighbourhood of the origin, represents one at the stage of liberalism; and a point such as *c*, which is located near the exit gate from the circle, represents one at the stage of imperialism. If none of the three types of economic policies can successfully internalize the externalities, we must admit that we are outside the capitalist region of the diagram, whether at some point prior to the entry gate or at another beyond the exit, and that we are no longer contemplating capitalism-II.

With the concepts and definitions explained above, we shall now proceed to describe the process of the disintegration of capitalism, or the phase of what we call 'ex-capitalist transition'. The thesis amounts to saying, in terms of Figure 3.1, that we find ourselves today at a point such as d which is located, on part of the path of the evolution of human societies, outside the capitalist region.[4]

The age of the great transformation

We turn our attention now to the age of the great transformation, when the imperialist bourgeois state went into decline and ultimately met its demise. We have already shown that, if the bourgeois state dies, capitalism cannot survive. It is our contention that this occurred during the inter-war period. When the First World War ended, and when the peace treaty of Versailles was signed among the belligerent powers, the world economy found itself in a chaotic condition. Not a single country could stabilize its economy by means of traditional economic policies – economic policies of the bourgeois nation-state aimed at controlling *externalities* so as to ensure the integrity of the capitalist market. For the war put an end to the capitalist order which had prevailed before, and the externalities which then arose far exceeded the efficacy of the policies then available to, or conceivable by, the bourgeois state. In order to interpret the nature of the inter-war period, it seems to us instructive to focus on the stark contrast between the 'conservative 1920s' and the 'revolutionary 1930s' as Karl Polanyi (1957) did in his celebrated book *The Great Transformation*.

Indeed, a return to normalcy was piously sought by all the major powers during the decade of the 1920s. In the first half of that decade the devastation caused by the war (together with the attendant confusion) was gradually overcome, until, in the second half of the decade, a 'relative stability' was eventually restored. The ephemeral stability of the world economy in the second half of the 1920s was literally 'relative', in that it entirely depended on a smooth flow of American funds. The United States lent by preference to Germany, which then paid reparations to France and Britain. After irrigating European business and industry together with the spheres directly dependent on them, functionally as well as geographically, the money returned to the United States. As long as this circuit was somehow maintained, the world economy could count on a fragile stability, to the relief of the capitalists and their liberal spokesmen, who naively thought that the pre-war system of self-regulating markets had finally been restored.

During the war, productive facilities outside Europe, especially in Japan and the United States, had been vastly expanded because of the extraordinary outburst of demand. But when European industry recovered from the war-inflicted damage, the world economy was saddled with extreme over-capacity, whether in agriculture, light or heavy industry, or transportation. Since new productive facilities had been built by means of liberal credit, the abrupt cooling-off of the wartime and reconstruction boom resulted in a serious debt and overproduction crisis, making the restoration of the pre-war economic order a practical impossibility. Normally, under such circumstances the bourgeois state, because of its need to stick to the gold standard, would enforce a set of radically deflationary measures, hoping to find a new point of departure, even though that would entail widespread bankruptcies and unemployment. But the social and political climate of the time was hardly attuned to the necessary economic discipline that the restored gold standard would have imposed on society, given that the recent founding of the Soviet Union had inspired the working classes to self-confident and militant action. When the speculative boom in the United States reversed the international flow of money and left the rest of the world starved for funds, it was only a matter of time before a crisis manifested itself. The trigger was pulled by the spectacular crash of share prices on Wall Street in the fall of 1929, which ushered in the decade of the Great Depression.

In retrospect, it is easy to say that the long depression was caused by policy errors. For the authorities, in panic, did push many of the wrong buttons which only aggravated the crisis, deflating the economy when it should have been inflated. But that is just another way of admitting that the right remedy for the occasion exceeded the ordinary run of policy measures available in the arsenal of a bourgeois state. The time was not yet ripe for the novel economic policies which only a welfare state could conceive, sanction and implement.

In the meantime, the sudden rise of fascist regimes, including German Nazism and Japanese militarism, on the one hand, and the sinister entrenchment of Stalinism on the other, began to pose serious threats to the bourgeois state which had proven to be ineffectual in the face of growing crises. Soon it was openly challenged and besieged by the collectivisms of both the right (fascism) and the left (Bolshevism), and its fate was sealed. The bourgeois state now had to choose between death, pure and simple, or a partial survival by radically transforming itself into a welfare state. It is our interpretation that President Roosevelt's New Deal policies and reforms marked the first step towards the reshaping of the American bourgeois state which had sustained capitalism-II into the welfare state which would embrace and nurture social democracy.

Roosevelt won for the government the right to directly involve itself in, and to exert regulatory authority over production, employment, sales, pricing, finance and such other areas as had previously been considered the exclusive province of the private sector. In other words, he succeeded in placing the 'planning principle of the state' alongside 'the market principle of capital' in the management of the national economy, thus substantially broadening the role of the state in economic affairs. The economic policies of the state were no longer restricted to simply preparing the ground for the self-regulation of the capitalist market, by *internalizing externalities*. The state was now deemed responsible for the macro management of the national economy, in which it had to cooperate with capital and labour.

Although the New Deal had this revolutionary aspect, and the size of the federal budget substantially increased during the New Deal period, its pump-priming effect remained minor, and by the time the nation was visited by another crisis in 1937, conservatives had ganged up to prevent Roosevelt from pursuing this type of policy further. It was only the stepping up of arms production, which began in the following year, that finally rescued America from the mire of the Great Depression. It was much the same elsewhere. The fascist states, which had resorted early on to the militarization of their economies, recovered first from the economic doldrums, followed by those countries which abandoned the gold standard to give precedence to domestic over external equilibrium. The others, which held on to gold, fared least well, until they, too, soon had to abandon it in favour of a managed currency system. Thus, on the eve of the Second World War, all countries other than the fascist and the communist ones could be said to have opted for social democracy within the framework of a nascent welfare state.

The Second World War was quite unlike the First in that it was not fought between two coalitions of imperialist bourgeois states, but between an alliance of social-democratic and Bolshevik powers on the one hand, and the axis of the fascist states on the other. Only because the Western powers had previously embraced social democracy within the framework of the welfare state and declared a truce with regard to the internal class war and external rivalry with the Bolsheviks, could they muster sufficient strength to overpower the mortal enemy. In other words, the Western democracies were able to preserve themselves because they had recanted capitalism-II, in deed if not in words, by transforming the bourgeois state into the welfare state.

Even so, immediately after the fall of fascism, the cold war began. The East–West ideological and territorial divisions were interpreted as a struggle between capitalism and socialism. Indeed, strong anti-socialist sentiments survived in the West, especially in the United States, which saw itself as forming a bastion against communism and a sanctuary for traditional bourgeois values. But the fact of the matter was that social democracy and the welfare state had to be consolidated, rather than dismantled, in the West, so as to obviate communist influence. To have restored a bourgeois state at that point would have been little short of suicidal. Even the arch-reactionaries knew that much viscerally. Thus, as the cold war intensified, no major Western power made any reckless move backwards to the regime in which capital lorded over labour, and the oppressed and impoverished masses in turn counted the days to a great socialist uprising.

Unlike communism, the welfare state did not aim to suppress *capitalism-I*; it was rather an opportunistic regime which abandoned *capitalism-II* in order to revitalize *capitalism-I* within a protected safety zone, as it were. Even if that 'noble' goal was desirable, however, the welfare state could not have become an enduring reality unless a new mode of production, often referred to as 'Fordism', evolved simultaneously, a mode of production embodying a new industrial technology, the application of which yielded a large enough value-added to be amicably shared between capital and labour.

Fordism-consumerism and the age of petroleum

When the war ended, the United States was the only major industrial power which managed to preserve its productive facilities intact, and these had to be mobilized urgently to provide for the needs of the devastated and starving world. But that meant that US factories, which were then largely geared to arms production, had to be converted to the production of civilian goods. This conversion occurred relatively smoothly for several obvious reasons. First, there was a strong demand for US products both at home and abroad. In the United States, during the war, the production of civilian goods had to be curtailed in order to step up arms production. Indeed, the demand for consumer goods was restrained by virtually 'forced' savings, such as the subscription to war bonds. A substantial pent-up demand for such goods had, therefore, been created before it was released at the end of the war, as demobilized soldiers returned home seeking new ways of life. Abroad, reconstruction required consumer and producer goods in such massive quantities that they could not be locally procured, so, naturally, American supplies were crucially important. The problem of the 'dollar shortage' was solved, in the first instance, by the Marshall Plan and, later, by the Korean War. Fortunately, there were quite enough idle funds convertible into capital. As war bonds were redeemed, the private sector was suffused with money which could be used to buy consumer goods or invested in order to expand productive facilities. Finally, the rapid expansion of production generated enough employment opportunities, so that household savings remained vigorous, providing more investible funds at low rates of interest. All these factors worked favourably to inaugurate America's post-war industrial regime, which was heavily centred on the production of consumer durables.

Behind this relatively unproblematic conversion from war to peace of the American economy was the fear, quite widely held by government and business leaders, of a returning depression once the post-war flurry would have passed. This led to the Employment Act of 1946, which formally proclaimed the welfare state's commitment to pursue Keynesian macro policies, as well as to involve itself in economic activities with a view to ensuring industrial peace and national prosperity. This established what American economists Hansen and Samuelson called the 'mixed economy'. On the other hand, the United States also asserted its unchallenged leadership as the main architect and guarantor of the IMF-GATT system, which made *Pax Americana* an appropriate reference for the international economic order that was to rule for several subsequent decades. The post-war American economy which emerged against this backdrop was based on the mass production and consumption of consumer durables – on Fordism and consumerism (or the affluent society). These are the two faces of the new age of oil or petroleum,[5] as distinct from the age of coal, which previously supported *capitalism-II*.

Fordism has its origin in F.W. Taylor's 'scientific management', which, with time-and-motion studies, accelerated the mechanical processes of task completion. Taylorism, however, 'culminated in and was transcended by' (Brenner and Glick 1991: 74) Fordism when the conveyor-belt assembly line was introduced. Fordism is best applied to the mass production of consumer durables, typically automobiles. Thus, we shall refer here to the mode of mass-producing consumer durables with an automatic assembly line as Fordism. By consumerism we mean the mass consumption of consumer goods which became typical in the affluent society, that highly urbanized mass society in which a large proportion of the revenue was earmarked for the purchase and maintenance of consumer durables and in which wastefulness in consumption was institutionalized.

Both Fordism and consumerism presuppose the age of petroleum. Coal and oil (petroleum) are both fossil fuels; thus, one may get the impression that they are similar in economic effects as well. Nothing is further from the truth. While coal mining entails the hardship of physical labour and is frequently associated with the macho image of the sturdy collier, oil is pumped out of the ground almost automatically once the well is bored. Unlike coal, oil can not only run internal combustion engines, but it can also replace many natural raw materials with synthetic ones (fibres, resins, detergents, and so on). Thus, it causes power revolutions in both production and transportation, while also pushing the 'disembedding' of industry from agriculture to its limit.[6] With oil, it can even be claimed that, in principle, human beings are finally liberated from the pain and toil of productive labour (labour which produces material objects), such that its mobilization and deployment no longer determine the basic structure of human society.

Unfortunately, petro-technology was not only radically labour-saving, but also environmentally destructive. In the first phase of the petroleum age, which established itself after the Second World War, it was the second of these properties that predominated. This was due to the simple fact that the people who had lived through the privation and shortages of the 1930s and 1940s craved for material amenities. Anything newly produced was valuable and welcome to them. Since the vastly productive petro-technology became suddenly available to them, they blindly let themselves loose in the production and consumption of things both necessary and not-so-necessary. That enabled production to expand more rapidly than the labour–output ratio fell, which resulted in the unprecedented economic growth of the 1950s and 1960s. With the outpouring of mass-produced goods from the Fordist factories, the living standard of the population improved markedly in the highly urbanized, mass consumption society, dubbed 'affluent' or 'consumerist'. Thus, the material foundation of the welfare state, which sought the placation of class struggles, was laid. But the obverse of this benefit was an extensive devastation of the natural environment, which imposed limits and constraints on the affluent society, and which, by the 1970s, was all too apparent. To this question we will return later.

For the reasons already given, petro-technology accomplished a vast expansion of society's productive powers, undreamed of in the previous age of coal and natural raw materials. The sectors which employed such technology grew much more rapidly than other more labour-intensive sectors, such as traditional farming, artisanal production and personal services. Also the high-productivity sectors which yielded more value-added grew at a greater pace than the low-productivity sectors. The former, being more profitable, could afford to pay higher wages than the latter. As the proportion of the former consequently increased at the expense of the latter in the national economy, its overall growth rate rose and yielded (for the same amount of capital consumption) a greater value-added, which could then be amicably shared between labour and capital. This is the reason why the average growth rate (of about 5 per cent) after the Second World War proved to be dramatically higher than the secular average of growth rates (of about 2 per cent) long considered normal previously. Thus, the living standard of the working classes improved very substantially, though unevenly, and the welfare state and its social security programmes expanded satisfactorily, at least until the dreams of President Johnson's 'Great Society' were frustrated by the escalating costs of the Vietnam War.

Social democracy appeared to have achieved a lot within a very short while and relatively painlessly. But the unprecedented growth depended on the crucial assumption that the demand for consumer durables kept expanding. Suppose that it came to a halt and stopped growing, so that industry could at most count only on a replacement demand for consumer durables. Then the high-productivity sectors with a high growth potential would become unprofitable and would have to shrink relative to the low-productivity sectors with a low growth potential (typically in personal and public services[7]), with the result that the growth rate of the economy as a whole would decline. This would mean that the current production of value added by the whole economy would no longer grow rapidly enough, so that its distribution between labour and capital would necessarily become stressful, thus undermining the foundation of the welfare state. The oil crises were a sudden reminder that society had to pay for the squandering of resources and environmental devastation that its productive activities had wreaked. When industry was forced to bear part of this burden, it declared itself paralyzed, especially when the other more threatening trend of the decline in the demand for material amenities was making itself felt. Such a trend seems to have set in during the 1970s when the world economy was severely shaken by the two oil crises.

During the heyday of Fordism, the economies of industrially advanced nations produced a large value added $(v + s)$ for a relatively small capital consumption (c). This fact undergirded industrial peace and the welfare state. Thus, for instance, if society produced 100 (in whatever units), of which it allowed only 20 for stock consumption, 80 could be amicably divided up between labour and capital, with the blessing of Keynes, Galbraith, Rawls and all the other 'liberal' (or social-democratic) thinkers. But if one were suddenly told that from now on the capital-consumption allowance in a GNP of not much more than that of yesteryear should at least be doubled, with only 60 (or less) remaining for distribution between labour and capital, then, regardless of how those 60 were divided, at least one of the two parties would be bound to feel cheated and unhappy. Thus, the shrinkage of the pie means that the former magnanimity must now give way to animosity and invidiousness. Stagflation, the fall from grace of Keynesian economics, industrial decay, declining competitiveness, the upsurge of neo-conservatism and all the rest of the depressing symptoms which then followed close on the heels of the oil crises are all indicative of the fact that the age of social democracy (the decades of the 1950s and 60s) based on Fordism-consumerism had come to an end.

After the curtain fell on this first phase of the petroleum civilization, we passed through the transitional decade of the 1970s before entering the era of post-Fordism and casino capital, which constitutes the second phase of the petroleum civilization.[7]

Uncertainties in the age of post-Fordism and casino capital

There were two main events which supervened in the world economy at the beginning of the 1970s. The first was the oil crises, which led to the establishment of the 'post-Fordist' mode of production superseding Fordism. The second was the fall of the IMF regime, the international currency system based on fixed exchange rates and a gold–dollar standard, which not only incapacitated Keynesian policies, but also let loose the international money games that have wreaked so much havoc in our time.

The effects of the oil crises on industrial restructuring are relatively easier to trace. As soon as the price of crude oil was trebled or quadrupled by the oil cartel, the energy-intensive Fordist production system found itself in a blind alley. Generally speaking, the production of goods that were 'big-heavy-long-and-thick' (*jukochodai*), and hence relatively energy-intensive, had to be de-emphasized in favour of the production of those that were 'small-light-short-and-thin' (*keihakutansho*), and hence relatively energy-saving. This accelerated the adoption by industry of the high technologies which were by then being made ready for commercial applications – notably in microelectronics, new carbon materials and genetics – as firms struggled hard to 'downsize' or to become 'lean', by reducing energy, labour and financial costs. To the extent that the firms succeeded in this conversion, traditional Fordist labour became largely redundant. For the labour that the leading firms increasingly sought at this point was knowledge-intensive. Since the labour market could not adapt to such a change overnight, high rates of unemployment began to threaten all the advanced economies. These varied from country to country according to the speed of the industrial transformation and the institutional and socio-cultural 'rigidities' specific to each.

In the meantime, the shift of the international currency system from fixed to flexible exchange rates stimulated offshore banking, which had been developing as a vehicle whereby those dealing with, and banking in, particular currencies sought to avoid various country-specific regulations. Flexible exchange rates vastly expanded their scope, by accelerating the mobility of capital across borders, while the flood of oil dollars into euro-currency markets fuelled a growing debt crisis. Before these problems were addressed, the deregulation of financial industries, which began in the United States, and the application of new computer technologies, which made possible not only the speedy transmission of messages but of vast sums of funds as well, dramatically altered the parameters of international finance. As a result, business firms operating internationally were exposed and became vulnerable to much greater risks and uncertainty. Thus, the ground was laid for the age of financial innovation and the frenzied money games of casino capital.[8]

Underneath all this was the general trend towards a declining demand for funds (money convertible into capital) on the part of larger corporations. As the economy remained sluggish under stagflation, corporations had little incentive to expand the scale of their operation, which, together with their compelling need for downsizing, meant that their demand for outside funds remained weak. Not only did they borrow less from banks and raise less money from capital markets, but they also supplied their own idle funds for investment in securities. Thus, capital markets and banks were flooded with idle money. When the debt crisis proved that lending to the Third World was a hazardous affair, the mature industrial economies had to seek another way to make use of the excess money which refused to be integrated into real economic activities in production and allied fields. It was not that small producers were adequately provided with necessary funds, but rather, that large concentrations of idle money which could not afford to meddle with costly petty finance sought gigantic projects with huge stakes, or else were 'parked safely' by means of speculation in marketable securities. Often they preferred the second option, so the path was open for them to initiate money games by introducing financial innovations.

It is the two tendencies discussed above which define the age of post-Fordism and casino capital. They should each be understood as one aspect of a necessary whole rather than as separate phenomena concurring for some contingent reasons, for together they confirm the signs of an approaching demise of even *capitalism-I.*

The age of petroleum, in both its Fordist and post-Fordist phase, fundamentally characterizes the process of the disintegration of capitalism. Petro-technology, as mentioned before, is both labour-saving and environmentally destructive. If in the Fordist phase only the second aspect was apparent, the first aspect too makes itself felt unambiguously in the post-Fordist phase. When consumers became increasingly satiated with ordinary goods in the 1970s, manufacturers could not simply mass-produce ordinary goods and expect the market to absorb them without demur. They had to sell novelties and accept the rapid obsolescence of their plants and equipment, which weighed heavily on their R&D and capital costs. The pressure on firms today to supply innovative goods for narrow and fleeting markets has become intense. Thus they inevitably owe much to gadget inventors, while making little net profit for themselves. That is why they remain poor employers, even when they do relatively well, so that 'jobless growth' becomes the rule. In the meantime, the high-consumption society continues to spew out many noxious substances into the environment far more rapidly and massively than the self-cleansing capacity of the earth can handle, inexorably suffocating the matrix of our existence. The second aspect of petro-civilization thus continues unabated.

Obviously, mature industrial economies tend to depend much less on productive labour than previously (productive labour being that which society applies to nature in order to transform part of it into useful objects or use-values). For the kind of labour that advanced industrial societies demand has become more intellectual than manual, and thus should be viewed as unproductive service labour, even when it is employed in the so-called productive (non-tertiary) sectors. It is true that 15 to 16 per cent of manufacturing jobs still require manual labour (Drucker 1986), but these tend to be increasingly shifted to the *maquiladora*-type districts of newly industrializing economies. As the leading industries restructure themselves in developed countries, presumably at the expense of the Third World, they recover the value-added productivity they had previously lost under the impact of high energy costs. However, a typical example can be cited to show that this in no way solves the distributional problem, thus foreclosing any chance of social democracy's revival.

According to Miyazaki (1990), the unit price of a typical integrated circuit can be decomposed into the following: the direct materials cost of 3 per cent, the direct labour cost of 12 per cent, the indirect cost of 80 per cent, and the profit of 5 per cent. Most of the indirect cost is believed to be made up of 'knowledge costs', which include the cost of research and development. Thus, if we allow, say, 5 per cent of the price for traditional items of the indirect cost such as depreciation, we may roughly claim that the constant-capital component (*c*) of the output price accounts for 8 per cent, the variable-capital component (*v*) for 12 per cent and the surplus-value component (*s*) for 80 per cent. Of this surplus value, however, 75 per cent is, from the outset, earmarked for payment to the knowledge-intensive services of unproductive workers in developing the new commodity, leaving only 5 per cent at the disposal of the firm.

Needless to say, this cost analysis applies only to a particular commodity, and not to the whole productive activity of the economy. But the problem seems no less striking at the macro level, where the general trend is that a much greater proportion of workers than before tends to be employed in the rapidly expanding service (tertiary) sectors. For example, in 1990, 72 per cent of those at work in the United States were employed in the tertiary industries, and the rest in the primary and secondary industries (in passing, the situation was roughly the reverse in 1890, when the non-tertiary industries were then employing 70.2 per cent (Labergott 1966: 118)). The tertiary sector includes industries which are adjunct to productive activities (business-administrative services) and those which are not directly related to them (personal and public-administrative services). As just mentioned, there are undoubtedly many who are employed in the primary and secondary sectors but are not engaged in productive labour strictly speaking. It is, therefore, probably fair to estimate that, in most advanced countries, the proportion of strictly 'productive' workers in the labour force is not much more than 20 per cent. Since the size of the labour force in many advanced countries is typically about half of the population in those countries, we may speculate that the surplus value produced by roughly 10 per cent of the population is supporting the rest. The rate of surplus value must, therefore, be enormous, which suggests that, for any advanced economy, the consequential factor in its proper management lies in the distribution, rather than production, of surplus value.[9]

The productivity of material things remained relatively low up to and including the age of coal, so that the mobilization and deployment of productive labour constituted the primary concern of society. This fact justified not only the first principle of historical materialism, according to which the organization of the production of material things (the economic base or substructure) determined the ideological superstructure of society, but also the primacy of 'economics' as the art of optimally allocating society's resources in order to most efficiently provide for its material needs. Capitalism (in the sense of *capitalism-II*), because it essentially belonged to the age of coal, was the last human society in which the superstructure depended on the particular manner in which productive labour was mobilized and deployed. It was also the society which gave economics the privileged place in the social sciences because of its promise to 'economize' on the use of society's productive resources. But the advent of petroleum changed all this by finally liberating human society from the burden of productive labour.

The popular conception of a 'post-industrial society' in which informa-tion takes precedence over material objects, or software over hardware, does indeed capture, if at a rather superficial level, the fact that our society is no longer obsessed with the production of material wealth. It seems to us that too much of surplus value is being siphoned off to international 'casino' speculators, high-tech gadget inventors, fashion designers of eccentric tastes and many other apparently not-so-useful 'unproductive' workers, leaving only a trifle to genuinely deserving businesses as profit. Does this situation not remind us of the nightmare of the stationary state which once torment-ed Ricardo? The dialectic of capital also speaks to this possibility. The abso-lute rent that landed property carves out of surplus value, prior to its distribution as profits to different branches of industry, has an upper limit such that, if it is exceeded, the working of the law of value becomes adulter-ated and capitalism ceases to exist (Sekine 1997, II: 122).

No matter how large the surplus value may be that society produces, if too much of it accrues to rent, interest and the incomes of society's non-pro-ductive service providers, thereby leaving little profit accruing to capitalist producers, the accumulation of capital will languish. There are two ways in which this sort of situation could come about. The first could occur if the use-value space is such as to satisfy all material conditions in favour of capitalist production, but not enough profit accrues to the capitalists to prod them to accumulate because of an institutional impediment, such as landlordism. This kind of situation, which sometimes arises *before* capitalist production has had a chance to develop, can be relatively easily remedied by reforms or policies aimed at removing such an impediment. Secondly, how-ever, there are also cases in which the existing use-value space lacks the material conditions which would make capitalist production a viable pro-position. Under these conditions, capitalist production cannot earn high enough profits, even though no specific institutional impediment exists inhibiting capital accumulation. Such a deep-rooted, systemic malady, in a capitalist economy, could not be cured by conventional reforms. It seems that we are today faced with this second sort of situation. Only in this light can we properly evaluate the present hyperactivity of casino capital.

A mature industrial economy, in which the living standard of the masses and middle classes improves, generates more savings than can be invested in real capital formation, leaving a great quantity of funds 'idle' in the sense of not finding credible borrowers – ones who will convert them into real capital. Such idle funds have no other place to go than markets where existing assets, real and financial, are traded. Thus, it has become a wide practice for individuals and firms to 'park' funds temporarily in marketable securities for the purpose either of earning incomes or of realizing specula-tive (capital) gains. This practice has been called 'fund management'. As long as production continues to grow, the funds saved will be converted into real capital in due course, so that one resorts to fund management only in the interim. But with the coming of the post-Fordist age, as production loses its former vigour, fund management begins to assume a usurpatory role in the economy, upsetting the latter's so-called 'fundamentals'. Flexible exchange rates, the deregulation of financial services, the application of computer technology, the invention of a variety of new financial commodities, especially derivatives – together with the kind of sophisticated financial engineering which thrives in the profitable use of said derivatives – all combine to transform sound fund management into high-stakes money games which attract and mesmerize what has come to be called casino capital.

Yet derivatives together with the other new financial instruments are necessary products of today's business environment which is suffused with risks. A judicious use of options, swaps, and futures enables ordinary business firms to hedge against unforeseeable market risks (due in particular to the volatility of commodity prices, exchange rates, interest rates, or equity prices), and works much like an insurance policy, so that no right-minded businessman can sensibly afford to do without them. The sad thing, however, is that from this perfectly legitimate act of self-protection by real businesses, we cannot separate speculative gambles. Their very effort to circumvent market instabilities has an inherent tendency to magnify them. If a firm hedges against a risk, the risk hedged against does not disappear. It is simply handed over to the counter-party. It is sometimes said that the use of derivatives enables the transfer of a given amount of risk from those who can least afford to bear it to those who can most afford to do so. But the redistribution of risks does not occur in such an idyllic fashion. Large institutions supposed to be equipped with greater capacity to deal with derivatives tend to concentrate many stakes, and magnify them with high leverages, before playing a sort of Russian roulette. These firms too can err, and if they crumble, they destabilize the market far more severely and irrevocably than when small failures occur spread out thinly over the market. These complications arise because hedging against market risks is an altogether different thing from insuring against certain genuinely 'insurable' uncertainties.

In the meantime, large institutional investors (such as pension funds, mutual funds, investment trusts, insurance companies, hedge funds and so on) to whom individual and corporate savers entrust their funds play a dominant role in securities markets. They hire professional fund managers to valorize their holdings for the benefit of clients. Large institutional investors tend to be conservative because their investments are subject to various regulations, as indeed they ought to be. But such regulations are often frustrating to 'talented' fund managers, who, to demonstrate their acumen, move to hedge funds. Some of them, especially those of the global-macro type, have triggered upheavals in international financial markets (witness the 1992 British pound crisis, the 1994 Mexican peso crisis, the 1997 Thai baht crisis, the 1998 Russian rouble crisis), and thereby caused much need-less suffering. With their highly leveraged 'off the balance sheet' gambles in colossal amounts, hedge funds too have at times gotten themselves into trouble (as witnessed in the LTCM crisis in September 1998), forcing the United States and other leading monetary authorities to bail them out so as to avoid putting the world economy itself in peril, the scale of their opera-tions posing a far more serious threat than smaller crises dispersed in time and space. Thus, in our era, the effort to circumvent market instabilities tends rather to magnify them.

It is, therefore, our intuition that hedging against market risks is an altogether different thing from insuring against certain genuinely 'insur-able' uncertainties. Yet it does not seem to us that today's trade in derivatives is an anomaly that can be easily controlled by regulatory measures. For it reflects, in our view, the systemic malaise, *die Krankheit zum Tode* (Sickness unto death), of the post-Fordist economy in which idle funds routinely fail to be converted into real capital. It was in order to turn these *unloanable* funds into an instrument of genuine chrematistics or profit-seeking that a pair of Nobel-prize talents (Robert Merton and Myron Scholls) had to be enlisted to pull off a 'financial innovation', involving a widespread use of derivatives. But has their meritorious achievement reduced or increased economic instabilities? Perhaps the collapse of one or more of the rapacious hedge funds with which they consult will one day soon trigger the stampede of casino capital which will finish *capitalism-I*, just as the crash of 1929 and the ensuing depression ended *capitalism-II*.

Conclusion

Today, the popular conception still lingers that there has been no discernible break between our present society and a traditional and more genuine capitalism, although various ambivalent appellatives have been invented to describe the change: 'revised or modified capitalism', 'state-monopoly capitalism', 'present-day or contemporary capitalism', and so forth. But these, in our view, are evasive and empty names, which do not come to terms with what has happened in the past seventy-five years.

In this chapter we have tried to show that, during the Great Depression of the 1930s, *capitalism-II* ended its life and was followed by social democracy. The latter, as a regime of political expediency rather than an historical society, sought industrial peace and a truce in the class struggles in a largely middle-class, mass society. It did achieve these goals, though by chance, because of the timely evolution of petroleum technology, the spectacular productivity of which enabled an amicable division of value added between capital and labour, securing the basis for social democracy and industrial peace in the context of Fordism-consumerism. But when the demand for material wealth slowed down it immediately got into trouble. The coming of the oil crises, which coincided with the satiation of the affluent society,[10] required a radical reorganization of industry in the course of which post-Fordism superseded Fordism. At this point, the application of high technologies, still broadly within the confines of the petro-civilization, pushed production (the provision of material wealth) to its limit.

Our society is no longer production-centred as was capitalism-II. We have come a long way from *capitalism-II*, to which we shall never return. For social democracy, which followed it, further enforced our production-centred way of life, until it, having passed through Fordism, has now reached an impasse.[11] This means that, as we face the present economic slump which is characteristic of the age of post-Fordism and the retreat of social democracy, we must learn at least one crucial lesson. That is, that the present slump cannot be overcome by once again restructuring the economy in such a way as to make it more productive, profitable and competitive, that is by further counting on the efficacy of the market principle of capital. We no longer have the context in which it works. Organizing the production of material amenities by the capitalist principle of chrematistics makes sense only for a particular period of human history and for a given range of technologies in use-value production. It is not a viable proposition today, for to try to organize education, medical care, social services and public goods by the same principle will only frustrate us and lead us astray. It is therefore time to look for a society in which we can live, and are entitled to do so, without being directly or indirectly involved with the capitalist exercise of making profits. The phase of ex-capitalist transition points to such a society.

We have yet to ascertain the clear contours of the historical society that looms on the horizon. But in parallel with Polanyi's exchange, redistribution and reciprocity, we too can think of the three modes of integrating the economy: the capitalist principle of the market, the planning principle of the state and the cooperative (or mutual aid) principle of the community. Capitalism tended to rely exclusively on the first of these, while social democracy tried to support the first with the second. In both cases, it was the production-centred economy that was sought. If, at present, we seek a non-production-oriented, happy and fulfilling society, we may have to learn how to make use of the long-neglected third principle.

Notes

1 We distinguish between being ideologically Marxist and being in the Marxian intellectual tradition. See Sekine (1997: I, 20).

2 Note that the 'zero' on this plane represents an ideal 'use-value space' which does not exist in fact. It is only at this point of origin that economic theory, which is nothing other than a logical definition of capitalism by capital itself, is in full operation. Such economic theory is systematically expounded in Sekine (1997).

All historically (really) existent use-value spaces are to be positioned at some distance from the origin, such that the farther away they are from the origin the less they embody the logic of capital. Only the origin belongs to capital, whereas all other points on the plane belong to us, humans. If theory belongs to capital, history is ours.

3   While pure economic theory operates as an autonomous (self-dependent and closed) system, only by presupposing an ideal (imaginary rather than really existent) use-value space, real capitalism in history must always live with a real use-value space, which is bound to breed some externalities. For this reason, it cannot dispense with the bourgeois nation state, which prepares the ground, a theatre stage, for capitalism's performance.

4   To empiricists it appears that economic life today is far more extensively 'commodified' than before. Indeed, many things which could not be produced and sold in the market are now available as commodities, and the world market for commodities has grown in breadth and depth. But all this is due to the fact, that the bourgeois states transformed themselves successfully into welfare states, preserving capitalism-I in return for the abolition of capitalism-II.

5   We use expressions such as the age of petroleum, petro-civilization, and so on, to highlight the main feature of the use-value space, which, we believe, can no longer belong to the *capitalist region* of Figure 3.1. If bourgeois analysts universalize the working of the (self-regulating) market to all use-value spaces, and overlook the significance of the advent of petroleum, that is only expected. But their critics, who proclaim themselves to be historical materialists, are often just as heedless of this important fact. They appear to believe that the logic of capital is so versatile as to be able to adapt to any use-value space. But it was Marx who taught that human relations in society are crucially dependent on material conditions involving use-values.

6   It was Karl Polanyi who first spoke of 'the disembedding of economy from society' in modern times, a concept which parallels the contention of historical materialism that the economic base determines the ideological superstructure of society. But the most fundamental 'disembedding' occurs, in our view, when manufacturing ceases to be part of agriculture – what we call 'the disembedding of industry from agriculture'. From that follows a whole series of other disembeddings: of technology from ecology, of science from wisdom, of man from nature, of the rational space-time from the life-world, of economy from society, of *gesellschaft* from *gemeinschaft*, and so on. Particularly relevant in this connection is Colin A.M. Duncan's perceptive book (1996).

7   It is an egregious error to claim that the age of petroleum is already past because of our increasing reliance on nuclear power. Imagine that coal suddenly disappeared. Despite some discomfort, our civilization would survive. But, if the supply of oil were to be cut off, our economic life would grind to a halt. Our economic life is still fully dependent on this remarkable fuel.

8   The expression 'casino capital' is inspired by the felicitous title of Susan Strange's (1997) celebrated book, *Casino Capitalism*, though she does not herself talk of 'casino capital' as such. The dialectic of capital justifies two unproductive forms of capital, namely loan-capital and commercial capital (which includes bank-capital as a special case), as specialized forms of capital which take over specific functions of industrial capital. This is due to the fact that, by socializing idle funds which the motion of industrial capital routinely generates (loan-capital) and by selling its commodities more professionally and expertly (commercial capital), their

operations enable industrial capital to produce more surplus value than it could otherwise. But, in the pure theory (or definition) of capitalism, there is surely no room for such a thing as 'casino capital', a chrematistic operation in money games which makes no contribution towards rendering the production of surplus value more efficient, but, if anything, hinders and disrupts it. The increasing prominence of the operation of casino capital, which does not belong to the definition of *capitalism-II*, is another testimony to its disintegration. Just as merchant capital and money-lending capital were the forms of capital theoretically and historically prior to industrial capital, 'casino capital' may be thought to be a dominant form of capital after the enfeeblement of industrial capital. It shares with money-lending capital the property of Hegelian 'measurelessness' (Sekine 1997, I: 103; 1986, I: 209), meaning that it can undermine sound capitalist activities.

9   The term 'surplus value' is used in a somewhat metaphoric way to indicate the money value of surplus products, since the law of value does not apply, strictly speaking, to today's economy, which corresponds to the use-value space represented by a point like d outside the 'capitalist region' in Figure 3.1.

10 Our thesis that we are by now satiated with material wealth may be challenged on the ground that only a small proportion of the world population is privileged to live in an affluent society, and moreover the indigent in affluent societies still retain an appetite for material amenities. True enough, but irrelevant. For there is no core (affluence) without periphery (poverty) in the 'capitalist' world system, as Wallerstein would claim quite judiciously. But we cannot claim that we shall forever remain immune from satiation with material wealth because poverty will always exist in the periphery. See the following note.

11 'The desire of food is limited in every man by the narrow capacity of the human stomach; but the desire of the conveniences and ornaments of building, dress, equipage, and household furniture, seems to have no limit or certain boundary.' This famous quotation from Adam Smith (1979, I: 181) has constituted the most fundamental premise of economics for the past two hundred years. It is this premise that is being challenged today.

4
Capitalist Development in World Historical Perspective

Giovanni Arrighi and Jason W. Moore

The particular way in which we periodize capitalist history largely depends on the temporal and spatial horizons of our observations and on the conceptual frameworks that underlie those observations. Most periodizations have been based on observations and conceptual frameworks that refer implicitly or explicitly to national dynamics of capitalist development. This is a perfectly legitimate and useful way of analyzing and periodizing capitalist development, provided that we do not conflate the dynamic of capitalist development as it unfolds in specific national (or sub-national) locales with the dynamic of capitalist development as it unfolds in a 'world' consisting of a large number and variety of such locales. Although these two dynamics influence one another, each has a logic of its own and must be treated as an object of analysis in its own right.

Our argument in this chapter is that the world dynamic of capitalist development is something more and different that the 'sum' of national dynamics. It is something that can be perceived only if we take, as the unit of analysis, not individual states but the *system* of states in which world capitalism has been embedded. More specifically, we shall argue that from this holistic perspective the initial formation and subsequent expansion of the world capitalist system to its present all-encompassing global dimensions can be broken down into four, partly overlapping 'systemic cycles of accumulation'. Each of these cycles consists of two distinct *phases* of capital accumulation, a phase of material expansion and a phase of financial expansion. In spite of this similar composition, systemic cycles of accumulation are not mere cycles, because each has been associated with a widening or deepening of world-scale processes of capital accumulation. As such, they constitute distinct *stages* of the transformation of the world capitalist system from being *a* 'world' among many 'worlds' to becoming the historical social system of *the* entire world.

Financial capital and systemic cycles of accumulation

Our conceptualization of systemic cycles of accumulation as stages of capitalist development originates in two observations. One is the widely held perception of a close parallel between the beginning and the end of the twentieth century (see, among others, Gordon 1988; Arrighi 1994; Harvey 1995; Hirst and Thompson 1996). Crucial in this respect is the centrality of 'finance capital' in the two periods. At the beginning of the twentieth century, this centrality gave rise to liberal and Marxist theories of 'finance capital' and 'imperialism' as jointly inaugurating a new phase of capitalist development (Hobson [1902] 1938; Hilferding [1910] 1981; Bukharin [1915] 1972; Lenin [1916] 1952). At the end of the century, this same centrality has given rise to the idea that 'globalization' and associated 'financialization of capital' inaugurate an equally new phase of capitalist development. The language and concepts have changed but the idea that finance capital constitutes a new, latest, highest phase or stage in the development of capitalism is at least as widely held today as it was a century ago. Is it possible that this discursive recurrence of finance capital as a new, latest, highest stage of capitalist development conceals its factual recurrence within a cycle too long to be detected within the time horizon ordinarily deployed in the analysis of capitalist development?

The second observation, derived from Fernand Braudel (1982; 1984), suggests an affirmative answer to this question by pointing to the short-sightedness of early twentieth-century characterizations of finance capital as a new phase of capitalist development.

> Hilferding ... sees the world of capital as a range of possibilities, within which the financial variety – a very recent arrival as he sees it – has tended to win out over the others, penetrating them from within. It is a view with which I am willing to concur, with the proviso that I see the plurality of capitalism as going back a long way. Finance capitalism was no newborn child of the 1900s; I would even argue that in the past – in say Genoa or Amsterdam – *following a wave of growth in commercial capitalism and the accumulation of capital on a scale beyond the normal channels for investment*, finance capitalism was already in a position to take over and dominate, for a *while at least*, all the activities of the business world.
> (Braudel 1984: 604; emphasis added)

The idea that long before the early twentieth century the accumulation of capital through the purchase and sale of commodities 'on a scale beyond the normal channels for investment' enabled finance capitalism 'to take over and dominate, for a while at least, all the activities of the business world', is a recurrent theme of the second and third volumes of Braudel's trilogy *Civilization and Capitalism*. It underlies Braudel's contention that the essential feature of historical capitalism over its *longue durée*, that is, over its entire lifetime, has been the 'flexibility' and 'eclecticism' of capital rather than the concrete forms it assumed at different places and at different times.

Let me emphasize the quality that seems to me to be an essential feature of the general history of capitalism: its unlimited flexibility, its capacity for change and *adaptation*. If there is, as I believe, a certain unity in capitalism, from thirteenth-century Italy to the present-day West, it is here above all that such unity must be located and observed.

(Braudel 1982: 433)

In certain periods, even long periods, capitalism did seem to 'specialize', as in the nineteenth century, when '[it] moved so spectacularly into the new world of industry'. This specialization led many 'to regard industry as the final flowering which gave capitalism its "true" identity'. But this is a short-term view.

[After] the initial boom of mechanization, the most advanced kind of capitalism reverted to eclecticism, to an indivisibility of interests so to speak, as if the characteristic advantage of standing at the commanding heights of the economy, today just as much as in the days of Jacques Coeur (the fourteenth-century tycoon) consisted precisely of *not* having to confine oneself to a single choice, of being eminently adaptable, hence non-specialized.

(Braudel 1982: 381; translation amended as indicated in Wallerstein 1991: 213)

These passages can be read as a restatement of Karl Marx's general formula of capital, $M–C–M'$. Money capital (M) means liquidity, flexibility, freedom of choice. Commodity capital (C) means capital invested in a particular input–output combination in view of a profit. Hence, it means concreteness, rigidity, and a narrowing down or closing of options. M' means *expanded* liquidity, flexibility and freedom of choice. Thus understood, Marx's formula tells us that capitalist agencies invest money in particular input–output combinations, with all the loss of flexibility and of freedom of choice that goes with it, not as an end in itself. Rather, they do so as a *means* towards the end of securing an even greater flexibility and freedom of choice at some future point in time. Marx's formula also tells us that, if there is no expectation on the part of capitalist agencies that their freedom of choice will increase, or if this expectation goes unfulfilled systematically, capital *tends* to revert to more flexible forms of investment, first and foremost to its money form. In other words, the 'preference' of capitalist agencies for liquidity increases and an unusually large share of their cash flows tends to remain in liquid form.

This second reading is implicit in Braudel's characterization of 'financial expansion' as a symptom of maturity of a particular phase of capitalist development. In discussing the withdrawal of the Dutch from commerce around 1740 to become 'the bankers of Europe', Braudel suggests that this withdrawal is a recurrent world-systemic tendency. The same tendency had already been in evidence in fifteenth-century Italy, and again around 1560, when the leading groups of the Genoese business diaspora gradually withdrew from commerce to exercise for about seventy years a rule over European finances comparable to that exercised in the twentieth century by the Bank of International Settlement at Basle – 'a rule that was so discreet and sophisticated that historians for a long time failed to notice it'. After the Dutch, the tendency was replicated by the English during and after the Great Depression of 1873–96, when the end of 'the fantastic venture of the industrial revolution' created an overabundance of money capital (Braudel 1984: 157, 164, 242–3, 246).

After the equally fantastic venture of so-called Fordism-Keynesianism, US capital since the 1970s has followed a similar trajectory. Braudel does not discuss the financial expansion of our days, which gained momentum in the 1980s, that is, after he had completed his trilogy on *Civilization and Capitalism*. Nevertheless, we can easily recognize in this latest 'rebirth' of finance capital yet another instance of that recurrent reversal to 'eclecticism' which in the past has been associated with the maturity of a major capitalist development. '[Every] capitalist development of this order seems, by reaching the stage of financial expansion, to have in some sense announced its maturity: it [is] *a sign of autumn*' (Braudel 1984: 246; emphasis added).

In light of these observations, we may interpret Marx's general formula of capital (M–C–M') as depicting not just the logic of individual capitalist investments, but also a recurrent pattern of historical capitalism as world system. The central aspect of this pattern is the alternation of epochs of material expansion (that is, M–C phases of capital accumulation) with phases of financial rebirth and expansion (that is, C–M' phases). In phases of material expansion, money capital 'sets in motion' an increasing mass of commodities (commoditized labour-power and gifts of nature included); and in phases of financial expansion an increasing mass of money capital 'sets itself free' from its commodity form and accumulation proceeds through financial deals (as in Marx's abridged formula M–M'). Taken together, the two epochs or phases constitute a full *systemic cycle of accumulation* (M–C–M').

Starting from these premises (and relying on Braudel's dating of the recurrent switches of the leading agencies of world-scale processes of capital accumulation from trade and production to high finance) we can identify four systemic cycles of accumulation: a Genoese-Iberian cycle, stretching from the fifteenth century through the early seventeenth; a Dutch cycle, stretching from the late sixteenth century through the late eighteenth; a British cycle, stretching from the mid-eighteenth century through the early twentieth; and a US cycle, stretching from the late nineteenth century through the current phase of financial expansion. Each cycle is named after (and defined by) the particular complex of governmental and business agencies that led the world capitalist *system*, first towards the material and then towards the financial expansions that jointly constitute the cycle. The strategies and structures through which these leading agencies have promoted, organized and regulated the expansion or the restructuring of the capitalist world-economy is what we shall understand by regime of accumulation on a world scale. The main purpose of the concept of systemic cycles is to describe and elucidate the formation, consolidation and disintegration of the successive regimes through which the world capitalist system has expanded from its late-medieval regional embryo to its present global dimension.

As the above periodization implies, consecutive systemic cycles of accumulation overlap with one another at their beginnings and ends. This is because, historically, phases of financial expansion have not just been (to paraphrase Braudel) the 'autumn' of a major development of world capitalism. They have also been periods of transition from one leadership and regime to another in world-scale processes of capital accumulation. They have been the time when the organizing centres of the subsequent cycle emerged interstitially within the structures of the cycle that was drawing to a close, and gradually acquired the capacity to lead world capitalism through a new phase of material expansion.

The historical underpinnings of this conceptualization and periodization of world capitalism have been laid out in detail in two studies, one focused on the cycles themselves (Arrighi 1994) and one on transitions from cycle to cycle (Arrighi and Silver *et al.* 1999). Here we shall limit ourselves to elucidate the logic and mechanisms that underlie the dynamics of the cycles and the transitions. We shall focus first on financial expansions as *recurrent phases* of world capitalism from its earliest beginnings right up to the present. We shall then deal more specifically with systemic cycles of accumulation as *stages* of capitalist development.

The logic and mechanisms of financial expansions

Let us begin by emphasizing that phases of material and financial expansion are both processes of the world capitalist system – a system which has increased in scale and scope over the centuries but has encompassed from its earliest beginnings a large number and variety of governmental and business agencies. Material expansions occur because of the emergence of a particular bloc of governmental and business agencies capable of leading the system towards wider or deeper divisions of labour that create conditions of increasing returns to capital invested in trade and production. Under these conditions profits tend to be ploughed back into the further expansion of trade and production more or less routinely; and, knowingly or unknowingly, the system's main centres cooperate in sustaining one another's expansion. Over time, however, the investment of an ever-growing mass of profits in the further expansion of trade and production inevitably leads to the accumulation of capital 'on a scale beyond the normal channels for investment', as Braudel put it, or, as we would say, over and above what can be reinvested in the purchase and sale of commodities without drastically reducing profit margins. Decreasing returns set in; competitive pressures on the system's governmental and business agencies intensify; and the stage is set for the change of phase from material to financial expansion.

In this progression from increasing to decreasing returns, from cooperation to competition, the relevant organizational structures are not those of the units of the system but those of the system itself. Thus, with specific reference to the latest US cycle, the relevant organizational structures are not merely those of the vertically integrated, bureaucratically managed corporations, which were only one component of the bloc of governmental and business agencies that led world capitalism through the material expansion of the 1950s and 1960s. Rather, they are the organizational structures of the cold war world order in which the expansion was embedded. As the expansion unfolded, it generated three closely related tendencies that progressively undermined the capacity of those structures to sustain the expansion: the tendency of competitive pressures on US corporations to intensify; the tendency of subordinate groups to claim a larger share of the pie; and the tendency of US corporations to hoard the profits of the material expansion in extraterritorial financial markets. Already in evidence in the late 1960s and early 1970s, these were the tendencies that triggered the change of phase from material to financial expansion (Arrighi 1994: chapter 4; Silver and Slater 1999: 211–16).

As Robert Pollin has pointed out, the idea of recurrent and protracted phases of financial expansion poses a basic question: 'Where do the profits come from if not from the production and exchange of commodities?' As he suggests, this question has three possible answers, each pointing to a different source of profits. First, some capitalists are making money at the expense of other capitalists, so that there is a redistribution of profits within the capitalist class but no expansion of profits for the capitalist class as a whole. Second, profits for the capitalist class as a whole expand because financial deals enable capitalists to force a redistribution of wealth and income in their favour, either by breaking previous commitments to workers and communities or by inducing governments to squeeze their populations to make payments to their capitalist creditors. Finally, 'financial deals can be profitable on a sustained basis . . . if [they enable] capitalists to move their funds out of less profitable and into more profitable areas of production and exchange' (1996: 115–16).

In our conceptualization of financial expansions, each of these three sources of profitability plays a distinct role. The first source provides the link between the crises of overaccumulation that signal the end of material expansions and the beginning of the financial expansions that follow. Thus, at the onset of each financial expansion,

> an overaccumulation of capital leads capitalist organizations to invade one another's spheres of operation; the division of labor that previously defined the terms of their mutual cooperation breaks down; and, increasingly, the losses of one organization are the condition of the profits of another. In short, competition turns from a positive-sum into a zero-sum (or even a negative-sum) game. It becomes cut-throat competition.
>
> (Arrighi 1994: 227)

In and by itself, this source of profits does not provide a plausible explanation of the long periods of financial expansion – longer, as a rule, than half a century – that have intervened between the end of every phase of material expansion and the beginnings of the next. Nevertheless, cut-throat competition among capitalist agencies consolidates what we may call the 'supply' conditions of sustained financial expansions. That is to say, by accentuating the overall tendency of profit margins in trade and production to fall, it strengthens the disposition of capitalist agencies to keep in liquid form a growing proportion of their incoming cash flows.

Sustained financial expansions materialize only when the enhanced liquidity preference of capitalist agencies is matched by adequate 'demand' conditions. Historically, the crucial factor in creating the demand conditions of all financial expansions has been an intensification of interstate competition for mobile capital. Braudel says nothing about such a competition, in spite of Max Weber's observation that it constitutes 'the world-historical distinctiveness of [the modern] era' (1978: 354). Whereas in pre-modern times the formation of world empires swept away freedoms and powers of the cities that constituted the main loci of capitalist expansion, in the modern era these loci came under the sway of 'competing national states in a condition of perpetual struggle for power in peace or war... The separate states had to compete for mobile capital, which dictated to them the conditions under which it would assist them to power.' This competitive struggle has created the largest opportunities for modern capitalism, 'and as long as the national state does not give place to a world empire capitalism also will endure' (Weber 1961: 249).

The occurrence of financial expansions in periods of particularly intense interstate competition for mobile capital is no mere historical accident. Rather, it is the outcome of a double tendency engendered by particularly rapid, extensive and profitable expansions of trade and production. On the one hand, capitalist organizations and individuals respond to the accumulation of capital over and above what can be reinvested profitably in established channels of trade and production by holding in liquid form a growing proportion of their incoming cash flows. This tendency creates an overabundant mass of liquidity that can be mobilized directly or through intermediaries in speculation, borrowing and lending. On the other hand, territorial organizations respond to the tighter budget constraints that ensue from the slowdown in the expansion of trade and production by competing intensely with one another for the capital that accumulates in financial markets. This tendency brings about massive, system-wide redistributions of income and wealth from all kinds of communities to the agencies that control mobile capital, thereby inflating and sustaining the profitability of financial deals largely divorced from commodity trade and production (Pollin's second source of financial profits). All the *belles époques* of finance capitalism – from Renaissance Florence to the Reagan and Clinton eras, through the Age of the Genoese, the periwig period of Dutch history and Britain's Edwardian era – have been the outcome of the combined if uneven development of these two complementary tendencies (Arrighi 1994: 11–13, 16, 105, 172–4, 231, 314–17, 330; Arrighi and Silver *et al.* 1999: especially chapter 3).

Finally, Pollin's third source of financial profit – the reallocation of funds from less to more profitable areas of material production and exchange – comes into the picture, not as a critical factor that makes financial deals profitable on a sustained basis, but as a factor in the *supersession* of financial expansions by a new phase of material expansion. Particularly illuminating in this connection is Marx's observation that the credit system has been a key instrument, both nationally and internationally, of the transfer of surplus capital from declining to rising centres of capitalist trade and production. Like Weber, Marx attributed great importance to the role played by the system of national debts pioneered by Genoa and Venice in the late middle ages in propelling the initial expansion of modern capitalism.

> National debt, i.e., the alienation of the state – whether despotic, constitutional or republican – marked with its stamp the capitalistic era. . . . As with the stroke of an enchanter's wand, [the public debt] endows barren money with the power of breeding and thus turns it into capital, without the necessity of its exposing itself to the troubles and risks inseparable from its employment in industry or even in usury. The state-creditors actually give nothing away, for the sum lent is transformed into public bonds, easily negotiable, which can go on functioning in their hands just as so much hard cash would.
>
> (Marx 1959: 754–5)

Since Marx's core argument in *Capital* abstracts from the role of states in processes of capital accumulation, national debts and the alienation of the assets and future revenues of states are dealt with under the rubric of 'primitive accumulation' – Adam Smith's 'previous accumulation', 'an accumulation not the result of the capitalist mode of production, but its starting point' (Marx 1959: 713). This conceptualization prevented Marx from appreciating the continuing historical significance of national debts in a world capitalist system embedded in states continually competing with one another for mobile capital. Nevertheless, Marx did acknowledge the continuing significance of national debts, not as an expression of interstate competition, but as means of an 'invisible' inter-capitalist co-operation that 'started' capital accumulation over and over again across the space-time of the world capitalist system from its inception through his own days:

> With the national debt arose an international credit system, which often conceals one of the sources of primitive accumulation in this or that people. Thus the villainies of the Venetian thieving system formed one of the secret bases of the capital-wealth of Holland to whom Venice in her decadence lent large sums of money. So was it with Holland and England. By the beginning of the 18th century.... Holland had ceased to be the nation preponderant in commerce and industry. One of its main lines of business, therefore, [became] the lending out of enormous amounts of capital, especially to its great rival England. [And the] same thing is going on to-day between England and the United States.
>
> (Marx 1959: 755–6)

Marx never developed the theoretical implications of this historical observation. In spite of the considerable space dedicated to 'money-dealing capital' in volume III of *Capital*, he never rescued national debts and the alienation of the state from their confinement to the mechanisms of an accumulation that is 'not the result of the capitalist mode of production but its starting point'. And yet, in his own historical observation, what appears as a 'starting point' in one centre (Holland, England, the United States) is at the same time the 'result' of long periods of capital accumulation in previously established centres (Venice, Holland, England). To use Braudel's imagery, each and every financial expansion is simultaneously the 'autumn' of a capitalist development of world-historical significance that has reached its limits in one place and the 'spring' of a development of equal or even greater significance that is about to begin in another place.

This conceptualization of systemic cycles of accumulation generates the periodization of capitalist history summed up in the diagrammatic representation of Figure 4.1. As the figure shows, Joseph Schumpeter (1954: 163) was perfectly justified in suggesting that, in matters of capitalist development, a century is a 'short run'. As it turns out, in matters of development of the world capitalist system, a century does not constitute even

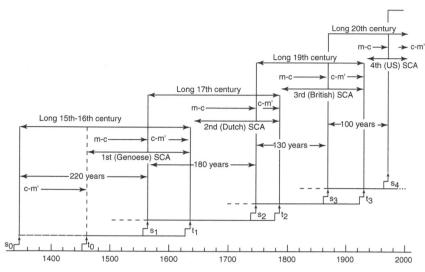

Figure 4.1 Long centuries and systemic cycles of accumulation (SCAs).

a 'short run'. Thus, Immanuel Wallerstein (1974) borrowed Braudel's notion of a 'long sixteenth century' (1450–1640) as the proper unit of analysis of what in his scheme of things is the first (formative) stage of the capitalist world-economy. Eric Hobsbawm (1987: 8–9) similarly speaks of a 'long nineteenth century' (1776–1914) as the appropriate time frame for the analysis of what he envisages as the bourgeois-liberal (British) stage of historical capitalism. In our representation we have not two but four 'long centuries' as the appropriate time frame for the analysis of the rise, full expansion and eventual supersession of the agencies, strategies and structures that define distinct systemic cycles of accumulation. The long centuries that encompass the cycles overlap because, as a rule, the agencies, strategies and structures of each cycle (in short, their regimes) formed and rose to preeminence during the phase of financial expansion of the preceding cycle.

All long centuries thus consist of three distinct segments or periods: (1) a first period of financial expansion (stretching from S_{n-1} to T_{n-1}) in the course of which the new regime of accumulation develops within the old – its development being an integral aspect of the full expansion and contradictions of the latter; (2) a period of consolidation and further development of the new regime of accumulation (stretching from T_{n-1} to S_n) in the course of which its leading agencies promote, monitor and profit from the material expansion of the world capitalist system as a whole; (3) a second period of financial expansion (from S_n to T_n) in the course of which the contradictions of the fully developed regime of accumulation create the space for, and are deepened by, the emergence of competing and alternative regimes, one of which will eventually (that is, at time T_n) become the new dominant regime.

Borrowing an expression from Gerhard Mensch (1979: 75), we designate the beginning of every financial expansion (and therefore of every long century) as the *'signal* crisis' (S_1, S_2, S_3, and S_4 in Figure 4.1) of the dominant regime of accumulation. It is at this time that the leading agency of systemic processes of accumulation begins to switch ever more massively its capital from trade and production to financial intermediation and speculation. The switch is the expression of a 'crisis' in the sense that it marks a 'turning point', a 'crucial time of decision' when the leading agency of systemic processes of capital accumulation reveals, through the switch, both a positive and a negative judgement. The negative judgement concerns the possibility to go on profiting from the reinvestment of incoming cash flows in the trade and production of commodities, that is, in the existing M–C–M' circuit. And the positive judgement concerns the possibility of prolonging in time and space its leadership and dominance through a greater specialization in high finance, that is, in an M–M' circuit.

This crisis is the 'signal' of a deeper underlying systemic crisis, which the switch to high finance nonetheless forestalls for the time being. Indeed, the switch can do more than that. It may turn the end of material expansion into a 'wonderful moment' (a *belle époque*) of renewed wealth and power for its promoters and organizers. To a different extent and in different ways it has done so in all four systemic cycles of accumulation. However wonderful this moment might be for those who benefit most from the end of the material expansion, in past cycles it has never been the expression of a lasting resolution of the underlying systemic crisis. On the contrary, it has always been the preamble to a deepening of the crisis and to the eventual supersession of the still dominant regime of accumulation by a new one. We call the event, or series of events, that lead to this final supersession the *'terminal* crisis' (T_1, T_2, T_3 in Figure 4.1) of the dominant regime of accumulation, and we take it to mark the end of the long century that encompasses the rise, full expansion and demise of that regime.

As shown in the figure, our assessment is that the present US regime has already experienced its signal crisis – a crisis which we situate around 1970 – but not yet its terminal crisis. Two closely related questions then arise: (1) Is the US cycle bound to end like all previous cycles in a terminal crisis? (2) And if it is, what new paths of world capitalist development, if any, can be expected to emerge out of the terminal crisis? These questions cannot be answered by treating systemic cycles of accumulation as mere cycles, as we have done so far. Rather, even the most tentative of answers requires that we deal with them as *stages* in an evolutionary process of expansion and transformation of world capitalism.

Systemic cycles of accumulation as stages of capitalist development

Let us begin by noticing that all the long centuries depicted in Figure 4.1 consist of three analogous segments and are all longer than a century, but over time they have grown shorter. That is to say, as we move from the earlier to the later stages of capitalist development, it has taken less and less time for systemic regimes of accumulation to rise, develop fully, and be superseded. This speed-up can be gauged with some precision by comparing the periods of time that separate successive signal crises. These periods measure the time that it has taken successive regimes, first, to become dominant after the signal crisis of the preceding regime and, second, to attain the limits of their own capabilities to go on profiting from the material expansion of the world-economy. As shown in Figure 4.1, this time has decreased steadily, from about 220 years in the case of the Genoese regime, to about 180 years in the case of the Dutch regime, to about 130 years in the case of the British regime and to about 100 years in the case of the US regime.

While the time taken by successive regimes of accumulation to rise to dominance and attain their maturity has been decreasing, the size and organizational complexity of the leading agencies of these successive regimes has been increasing. The latter tendency is most clearly perceived by focusing on the 'containers of power' (that is, on the states) that have housed the 'headquarters' of the leading capitalist agencies of the successive regimes: the Republic of Genoa, the United Provinces, the United Kingdom and the United States.

At the time of the rise and full expansion of the Genoese regime, the Republic of Genoa was a city-state small in size and simple in organization which contained very little power indeed. Deeply divided socially, and rather defenceless militarily, it was by most criteria a weak state in comparison with and in relation to all the great powers of the time, among which its old rival Venice still ranked fairly high. Yet, thanks to its far-flung commercial and financial networks the Genoese capitalist class, organized in a cosmopolitan diaspora, could deal on a par with the most powerful territorialist rulers of Europe, and turn the relentless competition for mobile capital among these rulers into a powerful engine for the self-expansion of its own capital (Arrighi 1994: 109–32, 145–51).

At the time of the rise and full expansion of the Dutch regime of accumulation, the United Provinces was a hybrid kind of organization that combined some of the features of the disappearing city-states with some of the features of the rising nation-states. A larger and far more complex organization than the Republic of Genoa, the United Provinces 'contained' sufficient power to win independence from imperial Spain, to carve out of the latter's seaborne and territorial empire a highly profitable empire of commercial outposts, and to keep at bay the military challenges of England by sea and France by land. This greater power of the Dutch state relative to the Genoese enabled the Dutch capitalist class to do what the Genoese had already been doing – turn interstate competition for mobile capital into an engine for the self-expansion of its own capital – but without having to 'buy' protection from territorialist states, as the Genoese had done through a relationship of political exchange with Iberian rulers. The Dutch regime, in other words, 'internalized' the protection costs that the Genoese had 'externalized' (Arrighi 1994: 36–47, 127–51).

At the time of the rise and full expansion of the British regime of accumulation, the United Kingdom was not only a fully developed nation-state and, as such, a larger and more complex organization than the United Provinces had ever been. In addition, it was in the process of conquering a world-encompassing commercial and territorial empire that gave its ruling groups and its capitalist class a command over the world's human and natural resources without parallel or precedent. This command enabled the British capitalist class to do what the Dutch had already been able to do – turn to its own advantage interstate competition for mobile capital and 'produce' all the protection required by the self-expansion of its capital – but without having to rely on foreign and often hostile territorialist organizations for most of the agro-industrial production on which the profitability of its commercial activities rested. If the Dutch regime relative to the Genoese had internalized protection costs, the British regime relative to the Dutch internalized production costs as well (Arrighi 1994: 43–58, 174–238).

Finally, at the time of the rise and full expansion of the US regime of accumulation, the US was already something more than a fully developed nation-state. It was a continental military-industrial complex with sufficient power to provide a wide range of subordinate and allied governments with effective protection and to make credible threats of economic strangulation or military annihilation towards unfriendly governments anywhere in the world. Combined with the size, insularity and natural wealth of its domestic territory, this power enabled the US capitalist class to 'internalize' not just protection and production costs – as the British capitalist class had already done – but transaction costs as well, that is to say, the markets on which the self-expansion of its capital depended (Arrighi 1994: 58–74 and chapter 4).

This steady increase in the size, complexity and power of the leading agencies of world capitalist development is somewhat obscured by another feature of the temporal sequence sketched in Figure 4.1. This feature is the double movement – forward and backward at the same time – that has characterized the sequential development of systemic cycles of accumulation. For each step forward in the process of internalization of costs by a new regime of accumulation has involved a revival of governmental and business strategies and structures that had been superseded by the preceding regime.

Thus, the internalization of protection costs by the Dutch regime in comparison with, and in relation to, the Genoese regime occurred through a revival of the strategies and structures of Venetian state monopoly capitalism which the Genoese regime had superseded. Similarly, the internalization of production costs by the British regime in comparison with, and in relation to, the Dutch regime occurred through a revival in new, enlarged and more complex forms of the strategies and structures of Genoese cosmopolitan capitalism and Iberian global territorialism, the combination of which had been superseded by the Dutch regime. And the same pattern recurred once again with the rise and full expansion of the US regime, which internalized transaction costs by reviving in new, enlarged and more complex forms the strategies and structures of Dutch corporate capitalism which had been superseded by the British regime (Arrighi 1994: 57–8, 70–2, 243ff.).

This recurrent revival of previously superseded strategies and structures of accumulation generates a pendulum-like movement back and forth between 'cosmopolitan-imperial' and 'corporate-national' organizational structures, the first being typical of 'extensive' regimes – as the Genoese and the British were – and the second of 'intensive' regimes – as the Dutch and the US were. The Genoese and British 'cosmopolitan-imperial' regimes were extensive in the sense that they have been responsible for most of the geographical expansion of the world capitalist system. Under the Genoese regime, the world was 'discovered', and under the British it was 'conquered'.

The Dutch and the US 'corporate-national' regimes, in contrast, were intensive in the sense that they have been responsible for the geographical consolidation rather than expansion of the world capitalist system. Under the Dutch regime, the 'discovery' of the world realized primarily by the Iberian partners of the Genoese was consolidated into an Amsterdam-centred system of commercial entrepots and joint-stock chartered companies. And under the US regime, the 'conquest' of the world realized primarily by the British themselves was consolidated into a US-centred system of national markets and transnational corporations.

This alternation of extensive and intensive regimes naturally blurs our perception of the underlying, truly long-term, tendency of the leading agencies of systemic processes of capital accumulation to increase in size, complexity and power. When the pendulum swings in the direction of extensive regimes – as in the transition from the Dutch to the British – the underlying trend is magnified. And when it swings in the direction of intensive regimes – as in the transitions from the Genoese to the Dutch and from the British to the US regimes – the underlying trend appears to have been less significant than it really was.

Nevertheless, once we control for these swings in the pendulum by comparing the two intensive and the two extensive regimes with one another – the Genoese with the British, and the Dutch with the US – the underlying trend becomes unmistakable. The development of historical capitalism as a world system has been based on the formation of ever more powerful cosmopolitan-imperial (or corporate-national) blocs of governmental and business organizations endowed with the capability of widening (or deepening) the functional and spatial scope of the world capitalist system. And yet, the more powerful these blocs have become, the shorter have been the life-cycles of the regimes of accumulation they have brought into being – the shorter, that is, has been the time it has taken for these regimes to emerge out of the crisis of the preceding dominant regime, to become themselves dominant, and to attain their limits as signalled by the beginning of a new financial expansion. In the case of the British regime, this time was 130 years, or about 40 per cent less than it had been for the Genoese regime; and in the case of the US regime it was 100 years, or about 45 per cent less than for the Dutch regime.

This pattern of capitalist development, whereby an increase in the power of regimes of accumulation is associated with a decrease in their duration, is reminiscent of Marx's contention that '*the real barrier* of capitalist production is *capital itself* ' and that capitalist production continually overcomes its immanent barriers 'only by means which again place these barriers in its way on a more formidable scale' (Marx 1962: 245).

> The contradiction, to put it in a very general way, consists in that the capitalist mode of production involves a tendency towards absolute development of the productive forces... regardless of the social conditions under which capitalist production takes place; while, on the other hand, its aim is to preserve the value of existing capital and promote its self-expansion (i.e. to promote an ever more rapid growth of this value)... It is that capital and its self-expansion appear as the starting and closing point, the motive and purpose of production; that production is only production for capital and not vice versa... The means – unconditional development of the productive forces of society – comes continually into conflict with the limited purpose, the self-expansion of capital. [If the] capitalist mode of production is, for this reason, a historical means of developing the material forces of production and creating an appropriate world-market, [it] is, at the same time, a continual conflict between this... historical task and its own corresponding relations of social production.
>
> (Marx 1962: 244–5)

This contradiction between the self-expansion of capital on the one side, and the development of the material forces of production and of an appropriate world market on the other, can in fact be reformulated in even more general terms than Marx did. For historical capitalism as world system of accumulation became a 'mode of production' – that is, it internalized production costs – only in its third (British) stage of development. And yet, the principle that the real barrier of capitalist development is capital itself, that the self-expansion of existing capital is in constant tension, and recurrently enters in open contradiction, with the expansion of world trade and production and the creation of an appropriate world market – all this was clearly at work already in the first two stages of development, notwithstanding the continuing externalization of agro-industrial production by the leading agencies of capital accumulation on a world scale.

In both stages the starting and closing point of the expansion of world trade and production was the pursuit of profit as an end in itself on the part of a particular capitalist agency. In the first stage, the 'Great Discoveries', the organization of long-distance trade within and across the boundaries of the far-flung Iberian empire(s), and the creation of an embryonic 'world market' in Antwerp, Lyons and Seville were to Genoese capital mere means of its own self-expansion. And when around 1560 these means no longer served this purpose, Genoese capital promptly pulled out of trade to specialize in high finance. Likewise, the undertaking of carrying trade among separate and often distant political jurisdictions, the centralization of entrepot trade in Amsterdam and of high-value-added industries in Holland, the creation of a worldwide network of commercial outposts and exchanges, and the 'production' of whatever protection was required by all these activities, were to Dutch capital mere means of its own self-expansion. And again, when around 1740 these means no longer served this purpose, Dutch capital – like Genoese capital 180 years earlier – abandoned them in favour of a more thorough specialization in high finance.

From this angle of vision, in the nineteenth century British capital simply repeated a pattern that had been established long before historical capitalism as mode of accumulation had become also a mode of production. The only difference was that, in addition to carrying, entrepot and other kinds of long-distance and short-distance trade and related protection and production activities, in the British cycle extractive and manufacturing activities – that is, what we may call production in a narrow sense – had become critical means of the self-expansion of capital. But around 1870, when production and related trade activities no longer served this purpose, British capital moved fast towards specialization in financial speculation and intermediation, just like Dutch capital had done 130 years earlier and Genoese capital 310 years earlier.

The same pattern was repeated 100 years later by US capital. This latest switch from trade and production to financial speculation and intermediation – like the three analogous switches of earlier centuries – can be interpreted as reflecting the same underlying contradiction between the self-expansion of capital and the expansion of world trade and production, which in our scheme corresponds to Marx's 'development of the productive forces of [world] society'. The contradiction is that the expansion of world trade and production was in all instances mere means in endeavours aimed primarily at increasing the value of capital and yet, over time, it tended to drive down the rate of profit and thereby curtail the value of capital. Thanks to their continuing centrality in networks of high finance, the established organizing centres are best positioned to turn the intensifying competition for mobile capital to their advantage, and thereby reflate their profits and power at the expense of the rest of the system. From this point of view, the present reflation of US profits and power follows a pattern that has been typical of world capitalism from its earliest beginnings. The question that remains open, and to which we shall now turn by way of conclusion, is whether this long-established pattern can be expected to result in the future as it did in the past in the replacement of the still dominant regime by another regime.

Possible futures

Systemic cycles of accumulation describe both patterns of recurrence and patterns of evolution. Figure 4.1 only shows the pattern of recurrence that consists of alternating phases of material and financial expansion and the pattern of evolution that consists of a speed-up of world-scale processes of accumulation from cycle to cycle. It does not show the pattern of recurrence that consists of alternating extensive ('cosmopolitan-imperial') and intensive ('corporate-national') stages of world capitalist development. Nor does it show the increasing scale and scope of successive cycles. As we have seen, this increasing scale and scope can be gauged both by the greater size and power of the cycles' organizing centres relative to their predecessors and by the progressive internalization of costs within the structures of successive regimes. Figure 4.2 complements and supplements Figure 4.1 by focusing specifically on these patterns.

Were the future of world capitalism fully inscribed in its past patterns of recurrence and evolution – which is even less likely to be the case in the present than it was in past transitions, as we shall presently see – the task of forecasting what to expect over the next half century or so would be straightforward. Our expectations would be the following. First, within 10 or at most 20 years that US regime would experience its terminal crisis. Second, over time (let us say, in another 20 years or so) the crisis would be superseded by the formation of a new regime capable of sustaining a new material expansion of world capitalism. Third, the leading governmental organization of this new regime would approximate the features of a 'world-state' more closely than the United States already has. Fourth, unlike the US regime, the new regime would be of the extensive ('cosmopolitan-imperial') rather than of the intensive ('corporate-national') variety. Finally, and most important, the new regime would internalize reproduction costs, that is, the kind of costs that the US regime has tended to externalize ever more massively.

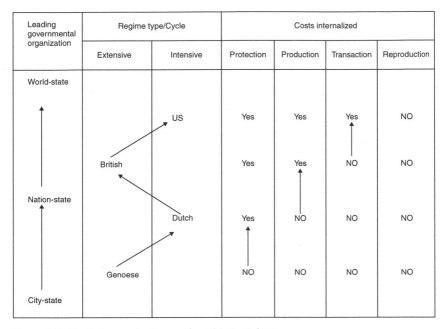

Leading governmental organization	Regime type/Cycle		Costs internalized			
	Extensive	Intensive	Protection	Production	Transaction	Reproduction
World-state						
		US	Yes	Yes	Yes	NO
	British		Yes	Yes	NO	NO
Nation-state						
		Dutch	Yes	NO	NO	NO
	Genoese		NO	NO	NO	NO
City-state						

Figure 4.2 Evolutionary patterns of world capitalism.

It is certainly within the realm of historical possibilities that these expectations will actually be fulfilled. But their fulfilment is neither the only nor, indeed, the most likely of possible futures, because transitions from one regime to another are not fully inscribed in previously established patterns. Established patterns of recurrence and evolution show that the *succession* of emergent developmental paths that over the centuries has propelled the expansion of the world capitalist system to its present, all-encompassing global dimensions, has not been a purely random process. But the emergence of a newly successful developmental path in the course of each and every transition has been contingent upon, and thoroughly shaped by, a range of historical and geographical factors that were themselves transformed and recombined by the competition and struggles that underlie financial expansions.

The patterns we observe *ex post*, in other words, are as much the outcome of geographical and historical contingencies as they are of historical necessity. In speculating *ex ante* about future outcomes of the present transition, therefore, we must pay equal attention to occurrences that fit into past patterns of recurrence and evolution and to occurrences that do not, that is, to significant anomalies that can be expected to make future outcomes deviate from past patterns. An in-depth analysis of the dynamic of the present transition in comparison with past transitions (Arrighi and Silver *et al.* 1999) has identified a number of such anomalies, three of which deserve particular attention as a warning against any mechanical projection of past patterns into the future.

First, in past transitions financial expansions were characterized by the interstitial emergence of governmental-business complexes that were (or could be plausibly expected to become) more powerful both militarily and financially than the still dominant governmental-business complex – as the US complex was relative to the British in the early twentieth century, the British complex relative to the Dutch in the early eighteenth century, and the Dutch relative to the Genoese in the late sixteenth century. In the present transition, in contrast, no such emergence can be detected. What we observe instead is a bifurcation of global military and financial resources that has no precedent in earlier transitions. As in past transitions, the declining but still dominant (US) complex has been transformed from the world's leading creditor into the world's leading debtor nation. As in no past transitions, however, military resources have become more than ever concentrated in the hands of the still dominant complex, while the emerging creditor nations can at most aspire to become military powers of no more than regional significance (Arrighi and Silver *et al.* 1999: 88–96, 275–8).

Second, and closely related to the above, the world's emerging creditor nations (most notably Japan and the overseas Chinese diaspora operating out of Taiwan, Hong Kong and Singapore) all belong to a non-Western civilization (the China-centred regional world system) and are organized politically in city-states (one sovereign, Singapore, and one semi-sovereign, Hong Kong), a semi-sovereign province (Taiwan) and a military protectorate of the United States (Japan). This constitutes a double anomaly, because in past transitions the change of guard at the commanding heights of world capitalism always involved a shift of financial power from the non-Western to the Western world, and within the Western world, from city-states and semi-sovereign political formations to empire-building nation-states of increasing scale and complexity. The anomalous bifurcation of military and financial power is thus accompanied by an equally anomalous reversal of the tendency towards an increasing concentration of financial power in the hands of *Western* states of growing size and complexity (Arrighi and Silver *et al.* 1999: 141–50, 263–70, 286–9).

Third, and probably most important, past transitions were all shaped by escalating social conflict. But escalating social conflict was far more a consequence than a cause of the inter-capitalist competition and struggles that underlay financial expansions. In the present transition, in contrast, social conflict has precipitated and shaped the financial expansion from the very start. Indeed, in a very real sense the present financial expansion has been primarily an instrument – to paraphrase Immanuel Wallerstein (1995: 25) – of the containment of the combined demands of the peoples of the non-Western world (for relatively little per person but for a lot of people) and of the Western working classes (for relatively few people but for quite a lot per person). The financial expansion and associated restructuring of the global political economy have undoubtedly succeeded in disorganizing the social forces that were the bearers of these demands in the upheavals of the late 1960s and 1970s. At the same time, however, the underlying contradiction of a world capitalist system that promotes the formation of a world proletariat but cannot accommodate a generalized living wage (that is, the most basic of reproduction costs), far from being solved, has become more acute than ever (Arrighi and Silver *et al.* 1999: 211–6, 282–6).

The combination of these anomalies points to the pitfalls involved in any simple extrapolation into the future of the long-term tendencies depicted in Figure 4.2. Social pressures for the internalization of reproduction costs within the structures of world capitalism have not been eliminated. And yet, the bifurcation of military and financial power and the decentralization of financial power in otherwise politically weak states do not augur well for an easy or imminent accommodation of those pressures. This does not mean that there are no solutions to the crisis of overaccumulation that underlies the ongoing financial expansion. Rather, it means that the crisis has more than one possible solution – some involving a continuation of past patterns, others their reversal, and still others the emergence of new patterns. Which particular solution will eventually materialize depends on an ongoing process of struggle that for the most part still lies in front of us.

5
Class Struggle and the Global Overaccumulation of Capital

Simon Clarke

This chapter addresses a central theme which recurs through many analyses, particularly on the left, of the current crisis of world capitalism, which see this crisis in terms of the erosion of national forms of economic regulation by the internationalization of capital, and the corresponding failure to develop new trans- or inter-national forms of regulation. I want to argue, from within a Marxist perspective, that the contradiction between the global character of capital accumulation and the national form of the state is not a new phenomenon, but has been a characteristic of capitalism since the earliest stages of commercial capitalism, underlying the historical development of capitalist states within the international state system. In periods of sustained accumulation on a world scale this contradiction is suspended, as the internationalization of capital opens up opportunities for capital and for the state. In periods of crisis, the contradiction re-emerges. From this point of view, the present crisis is not a manifestation of a transition from one stage of capitalism to another, but is rather an expression of the contradictory form of the capitalist mode of production, which manifests itself most dramatically in periodic crises.

After a brief theoretical and historical discussion I will concentrate on the post-war cycle, which I will explore from a global perspective which focuses on the world system not as an aggregation of discrete national economies and nation-states, but as a global economy and a system of nation-states. Although this gives the chapter a high level of generality, I think that such a level has some validity in describing tendencies common to all the nation states and 'national economies' comprising the international capitalist system.[1]

Capitalist crisis or regulation crisis?

The instability in the world economy since 1974 has cast serious doubt on our understanding of the post-war boom and, more broadly, of the contemporary stage of capitalist development. From the late 1950s to the early

1970s the overwhelmingly dominant view was that the post-war boom marked a qualitatively different phase of accumulation, characterized variously by the emergence of the Keynesian welfare–warfare state, of state monopoly capitalism or, more recently, of the Fordist 'regime', or 'social structure', of accumulation. This phase was marked by the dominance of the technology of mass production, a growing degree of monopoly, a collaborationist system of industrial relations, and the stabilization of accumulation by the nation-state.

Although the re-emergence of the immanent crisis tendencies of capital accumulation since 1974 has made it clear that the stability of the post-war boom was considerably overemphasized, it has not led to a serious re-examination of the belief that the war marked a fundamental break in the history of capitalism. Instead the crisis has been widely interpreted as a crisis of the post-war phase of capitalism, and a period of transition to a new stage, whose contours are not yet clear, but which is marked by new production technologies, increased competition on a global scale, flexible industrial relations systems, and a marked reduction in the ability of the nation state to regulate accumulation.

For many on the left, neo-liberalism is the capitalist politics appropriate to the transition phase, the outcome of the breakdown of the forms of regulation typical of the post-war boom in the face of the rapid internationalization of capital. The current phase of the crisis indicates the limits of neo-liberalism, its resolution demanding new forms of regulation and more extensive political intervention at the national and international level, which provides the opportunity for the left to develop a new politics appropriate to the new phase of accumulation.

It is my belief that this kind of analysis focuses on relatively superficial and transitory features of capitalism, which are one-sidedly elevated to defining features of a distinctive stage of capitalist development. The crisis is then seen only as a crisis of particular 'modes of regulation' of capital accumulation, which can be resolved by developing new forms of regulation, rather than being seen as a crisis which expresses the contradictory form of accumulation itself. Theoretically this distracts attention from more fundamental and enduring features of capitalism. Politically it cuts us off from the lessons of history, and tends to validate an opportunistic and divisive politics. A central feature of this analysis, and one of its most fundamental weaknesses, lies in its understanding of the relationship between capital and the state, and particularly of the relationship between the internationalization of capital and the national form of the state.

Global capitalism and nation states

Capitalism has been a global phenomenon since its origins in the commercial capitalism of the middle ages, which grew up on the basis of trading networks that extended from China and India to the Atlantic seaboard of Europe, unconstrained by national boundaries or local sovereignties. From the thirteenth to the fifteenth centuries all the crowned heads of Europe were, at one time or another, in hock to the Italian bankers, whose financial power and international connections enabled them to dictate their terms to the haughtiest of monarchs. By the early modern period domestic prosperity depended on commercial success in international markets, the solvency of the state depended on its reserves of world money.

The penetration of capital into production rooted capital more firmly within the territorial jurisdiction of particular monarchs, but such capitalist development still depended on the penetration of world markets. It was the commercial expansion of the seventeenth and eighteenth centuries which paved the way for Britain's industrial revolution, whose momentum depended on British capital's access to world markets as sources of supply and as outlets for its expanding product, and so on the liberalization of international trade and payments, through which the dynamic of capital accumulation was extended on a world scale.

Adam Smith had already noted the extent to which the cosmopolitanism of capital enabled it to evade the jurisdiction of the nation state. In considering the sources of public revenue Smith noted that interest, as a pure net product, should in principle bear the highest burden of taxation. However he immediately noted the impracticality of such a proposal: 'the proprietor of stock is properly a citizen of the world, and is not necessarily attached to any particular country. He would be apt to abandon the country in which he was exposed to a vexatious inquisition, in order to be assessed to a burdensome tax, and would remove his stock to some other country where he could either carry on his business, or enjoy his fortune more at his ease' (Smith 1910, 5, 2, art. 2).

The subordination of the nation state to global capital did not come about without considerable resistance. A central focus of popular agitation throughout the nineteenth century was the issue of the currency, as production was sacrificed on the altar of gold in periodic crises. Although such agitation personalized this constraint, identifying it with the greed, corruption and privileges of the bankers, the bankers' power was only the expression of the dominion of world money, through which the powers of the nation state were subordinated to capital accumulation on a world scale. The gold standard, which for the populists was the symbol of the bankers' power, embedded the subordination of the nation state to the imperatives of global accumulation within the constitution. Thus the formal adoption of the gold standard was an essential component of the formation of the modern nation state, the subordination of the state to global capital being the essential complement to the domestic jurisdiction of the nation state. In Britain this subordination was enshrined in the constitution with the resumption of gold convertibility after the Napoleonic Wars.

The capitalism of the mid-nineteenth century was marked by a cosmopolitanism which envisaged the effective dissolution of the nation state as a political body as it was reduced to its essential tasks of the protection of property and the administration of justice, enforcing laws whose universality was guaranteed by their eminent rationality. The rise of an organized working class in the second half of the nineteenth century revealed the political naivety of such a utopian dream, but the dream still contained an element of reality.

Economic liberalization from the 1840s to the 1860s, which was the condition for the full participation of particular nations in the dynamics of capital accumulation, and the rapid dissolution of pre-capitalist forms of production, destroyed the economic, social and political foundations of the nation states which emerged from the middle ages. However, the crisis of 1873, which was the first global capitalist crisis, shattered the cosmopolitan dream, as the pressure of overproduction unleashed competitive and class struggles which, combined with the fiscal, monetary and financial impact of the crisis on public finances, precipitated a crisis of the state. The response to this crisis was the political and economic reconstruction of the state, which involved, among other things, the rapid reconstitution of the emerging liberal state on an unequivocally national basis. However, such a reconstitution could only take place within the context of a global capitalist system. Thus it did not involve the independent formation of discrete and independent political units, but rather the demarcation of national jurisdictions within a new imperialist system of nation states. Thus the rise of the modern national democratic state was closely associated with the development of an international political system, beyond the reach of any democratic processes, and the subordination of nation-states to global capital in the constitutional form of the gold standard, whose generalization dates from the last quarter of the nineteenth century, a process which was only completed when the adherence of the US to the gold standard was finally confirmed with the Republican victory in 1896.

Although the modern nation-state is constituted politically on a national basis, its class character is not defined in national terms. The class character of the capitalist state is most fundamentally determined by the separation of the state from civil society, and the corresponding subordination of state and civil society to the rule of money and the law. However, the capitalist law of property and contract transcends national legal systems, and world money transcends national currencies. Thus the subordination of the state to the rule of money and the law, which is the foundation of the constitutional form of the capitalist state, confines the state within limits imposed by the contradictory form of the accumulation of capital on a world scale. Consequently the national form of the capitalist state can be defined only as a condensation, or nodal point, of an international state system. In this sense the formation of a truly international, transnational or world state would mark not a rational adaptation of the capitalist state to the global character of capital accumulation, but a fundamental transformation of the state form, which could only be based on an inversion of the relationship between capital and the state, between politics and economics, an inversion which would hardly be consistent with the continued existence of the capitalist mode of production.[2]

Although the class character of the state is defined globally, at the same time the political stability of the state has to be achieved on a national basis, which presupposes, in general, that the state is able to secure the expanded reproduction of domestic productive capital which is the principal source of the incomes of the population and the revenues of the state. On the one hand, this is the only basis on which the relative surplus population can be absorbed, and so the social reproduction of the working class reconciled with its subordination to capital. On the other hand, it is the only basis on which the state can secure its revenues, and so meet increasing demands on its resources.

The national form of the capitalist state determines the form in which the inherent contradictions of capital accumulation confront the state. The contradiction inherent in capitalist accumulation, between the tendency to develop the productive forces without limit, and the need to confine the development of the productive forces within the limits of profitability, unfolds on a world scale, as capital seeks to overcome local barriers by developing the world market as a source of raw materials and an outlet for surplus capital and commodities. So long as capital is able to overcome the barriers to accumulation by global expansion its inherent contradiction is suspended. However, once this expansion approaches its limits the barriers to accumulation reassert themselves and the contradiction comes to the surface.

This contradiction appears to the state in the form of the barriers to the sustained accumulation of domestic productive capital presented by the overaccumulation of capital on a world scale. Although the state cannot resolve the contradictions inherent in capital accumulation, it can contain the political impact of those contradictions to the extent that it is able to secure the integration of the accumulation of domestic productive capital into the accumulation of capital on a world scale. The limits on the ability of the state to achieve this are partly set by the particular conditions of domestic accumulation and by the national form of the state, but are more fundamentally defined by the form of the international state system and the dynamics of global accumulation of which it is a part.

During periods of sustained accumulation on a world scale, the liberalization of international trade and payments and the corresponding internationalization of capital define a horizon of opportunity through which to secure domestic prosperity and social and political harmony. However, as the overaccumulation and uneven development of capital present growing barriers to accumulation on a world scale, international competition intensifies, debts begin to mount, sources of credit dry up, and the accumulation of domestic productive capital falters. The internationalization of capital now appears not as an opportunity but as a barrier, in the form of the pressure of international competition and the burden of international debt. As the pressures increase, the first response of the nation state might be to throw up barriers to the international movement of commodities and capital, in the vain attempt to sustain the accumulation of domestic productive capital. However, the crisis has not arisen as a result of the internationalization of capital but, on the contrary, because the attempt of capital to overcome the barriers to accumulation by penetrating world markets has reached its limits as overaccumulation appears on a global scale. The change from one phase of the cycle to the other is not in the *fact* of the global character of capital accumulation but in its *form*.

The internationalization of capital is not a cumulative process, but a cyclical one, as political and administrative barriers to the mobility of capital are thrown up in the wake of the crisis. Although the internationalization of capital might reach new heights, and might appear in very different institutional forms, in each successive cycle, there is not a fundamental qualitative difference involved. From the vantage point of the 1930s the post-war internationalization of capital appears dramatic, but it is not clear that it is fundamentally different from the internationalization that marked the mid-Victorian boom a century before. However, rather than pursue this comparative perspective further, it is time to turn to the implications of this analysis for an understanding of the present crisis.

The internationalization of capital and the limits of the nation-state

Fundamental to the conventional interpretations of the post-war boom is the belief that the increased penetration of the state into civil society from the 1930s transformed the laws of motion of the capitalist mode of production by establishing modes of regulation which could contain the tendency to overaccumulation and crisis. According to this view, the limits of these modes of regulation were determined by the fact that they were established on a national basis, and so have been progressively undermined by the internationalization of capital.

It is certainly true that the freedom of the nation-state to pursue an independent economic policy has been severely reduced since the 1970s by the growing pressure of international competition and by speculative movements of international money. However, the internationalization of capital was not the source of the recurrent crises of the last quarter of the century. The growing pressure of international competition expressed not so much the internationalization of capital, as the growing overaccumulation of capital on a world scale. Indeed the internationalization of capital has continued to be the means by which capital has sought to overcome the barriers to accumulation as the more dynamic capitals, with the growing encouragement of the state, seek to conquer world markets. 'Internationalization' is a threat to backward capitals, but it is also an opportunity for the more advanced. Similarly the speculative movements of international money expressed not the breakdown of earlier 'national' modes of regulation, but the uneven development of capital which underlay the growing imbalances in international payments which international capital was called on to finance. The internationalization of money capital made it possible to sustain accumulation, despite such imbalances, by the massive expansion of international credit. Thus the crisis is not the result of the internationalization of capital, but rather expresses the fact that such internationalization has approached its limits.

The belief that the post-war boom was based on the institutionalization of modes of regulation of accumulation through which the accumulation of capital was subject to the direction of the nation state is equally false. While the state certainly intervened more actively in regulating accumulation, this did not involve an inversion of the relationship between capital and the state. State intervention has been circumscribed throughout the post-war period by the contradictory form of accumulation on a world scale. The tendencies towards the internationalization of capital and the liberalization of capitalist regulation are by no means new, but have been the dominant tendencies ever since the Second World War, central features of the boom as much as of the crisis.

The state and the market in the post-war boom

The wartime need to subordinate the accumulation of capital to the rapid expansion and restructuring of the productive forces had led the state to develop a dense network of institutions of planning, regulation and control. The immediate post-war priority was the reconversion of military production to peacetime needs. However this task was a relatively simple one, and was achieved remarkably quickly. The much more difficult task was that of the reconstruction of the social relations of production.

For the left, the wartime interventionist apparatus provided a basis on which to develop new forms of democratic planning to bring social production under social control. For the bourgeoisie, on the other hand, the priority was not to develop but to dismantle this interventionist apparatus, to bring social production back within the limits of capital. However, this latter task could not be achieved immediately, for the legacy of war was an enormously uneven development of the forces of production, not only sectorally but also geographically, marked primarily by the overwhelming dominance of US productive capital which underlay the post-war 'dollar shortage'. In similar circumstances rapid liberalization after the First World War had provoked an acute crisis, with intense class struggles, financial instability, the destruction of productive capacity and the devaluation of capital, culminating in the crash of 1929 and ensuing depression. The priority of the bourgeoisie was to avoid repeating this experience by using the interventionist apparatuses of the state to restructure the productive forces, on the one hand, and to develop appropriate financial institutions, on the other, which could ensure a smooth restoration of the liberal order. Although the details of this strategy differed from one country to another, the task was a global one, coordinated by US capital and the US state.

The issue of post-war reconstruction was a fundamental class issue. The social and political strength of the working class made immediate liberalization inconceivable, even in the US. However the widespread retention and development of the apparatus of wartime intervention in the reconstruction period, involving nationalization, the development of instruments of bureaucratic and fiscal intervention, and a pervasive network of economic and financial controls, did not necessarily represent a victory for the working class. Behind the rhetoric of 'national reconstruction' lay a struggle over the form of that reconstruction. However, this struggle did not appear transparently as a class struggle.

The idea of national reconstruction was a myth not only because it glossed over the class issue, but also because the uneven development of the forces of production made reconstruction on the basis of national self-sufficiency inconceivable. The priority of national reconstruction was to expand exports, which would provide outlets for the surplus products of the more highly developed branches of production and provide the means of international payment with which to purchase urgently needed means of production and subsistence. Thus national reconstruction could take place only within the framework of international reconstruction. Accordingly the class struggle over the form of national reconstruction was severely circumscribed by the struggle over international reconstruction, which soon set the Soviet bloc against the Atlantic alliance. The class character of the national reconstruction effort was determined not by the greater or lesser degree of state intervention, but by the global context within which such intervention took place. In the emerging Soviet bloc, reconstruction took place within a framework of planned trade dominated by barter relationships on the basis of political control from the centre. In the emerging capitalist bloc, reconstruction took place within the framework of international trade and financial liberalization, in which payments imbalances were accommodated by enormous flows of international aid, military expenditure and financial investment.

The foundations of the post-war boom were undoubtedly laid by the activity of the state in the reconstruction period. However, the crucial feature of this activity was not so much the ability of nation-states to sponsor the restructuring of the productive forces, nor even to contain the aspirations of the working class in order to force up the rate of profit, but the success of the US-dominated effort to rebuild a system of international trade and payments through which international flows of money capital could accommodate the uneven development of the forces of production on a world scale. The removal of state controls on the international movements of commodities and capital was both a precondition and a result of this reconstruction strategy. The liberalization of the international financial system then made possible the rapid internationalization of capital, through which the most advanced capitals were able to suspend the barriers to accumulation presented by the limited extent of the domestic market, and so sustain accumulation in the face of the tendency to overaccumulation and crisis. It was the sustained accumulation of the post-war boom, based on the rapid internationalization of capital and liberalization of the international movements of commodity, money and productive capital, which made possible the national policies of Keynesian interventionism and economic planning, whose success enabled politicians then to claim that they had tamed capitalism.

Internationalization of capital and the crisis of overaccumulation

The crisis tendencies of post-war accumulation appeared from the mid-1960s as the overaccumulation and uneven development of capital, accommodated by the expansion of credit and reinforced by rising government expenditure, generated growing inflationary pressure and imbalances of international payments. The enormous post-war growth of the credit system made it possible to overcome periodic crises and to sustain accumulation, at the cost of rising inflation. However this was not a feature of new modes of regulation. What was new was the willingness of governments systematically to pursue inflationary credit policies in the attempt to stave off crises, a policy which capitalists had vigorously, and largely successfully, opposed in the past.[3] Thus inflationism did not express a change in the form of the state, but a shift in the balance of class forces, expressed through the political pressure of the working class, institutionalized in the welfare state and in the system of industrial relations which was a legacy of the post-war settlement.

By the early 1970s the boom was entering its speculative phase on a global scale, leading to the inflationary crisis of 1974. Attempts by the more vulnerable powers to resolve this crisis on a national basis, whether by inflationary Keynesianism or by direct intervention to sustain domestic production in the face of intensified international competition, were largely unsuccessful, such policies raising further barriers to accumulation and so reinforcing inflationary pressures by sustaining backward capitals at the expense of the more dynamic capitals. The ability of national governments to pursue such policies was limited by the growing pressure of international competition and by speculative movements of international money. However, this pressure was but a symptom of the increasing overaccumulation and uneven development of capital on a world scale. Indeed the crisis arose not because of the extent of internationalization, but because such internationalization had come up against its limits, as the further expansion of the world market intensified international competition and as the growth of international credit was unable to accommodate growing payments imbalances.

The growing overaccumulation and uneven development of capital through the 1970s led not only to an economic crisis but also to a deepening political one. The 'post-war settlement' had secured the social and political integration of the working class in the metropolitan capitalist countries through the systems of industrial relations and the welfare system. In the boom these 'modes of regulation' of the working class could even prove functional to sustained accumulation, reconciling the working class to the intensification of labour and a high degree of mobility in exchange for guaranteed employment, rising wages and welfare benefits as capital sought to develop the productive forces without limit. However, the growing overaccumulation and uneven development of capital from the late 1960s increasingly brought the tendency to develop the productive forces without limit into contradiction with the need to confine the development of the productive forces within the limits of capitalist social relations of production. The growing pressure of competition in the face of the overaccumulation of capital eroded profits and public revenues, leading to an intensification of the class struggle. The attempt of the state to confine these struggles within the institutional forms of industrial relations and the welfare state by inflationary means only served to exacerbate the crisis by further eroding the international competitiveness of domestic productive capital and by increasing monetary and financial instability, so that the crisis increasingly unleashed a class struggle over the institutional forms of industrial relations and the welfare state.

The crisis of Keynesianism did not express the barrier to domestic capital accumulation presented by international capital, but rather expressed the barrier presented to the realization of the material aspirations of the working class by the need for capital to subordinate the development of the productive forces to the social form of capitalist production. The barrier to the aspirations of the domestic working class was not competition from foreigners; it was the social form of capitalist production. The rise of neo-liberalism did not express the thwarting of the ambitions of the nation state by international capital, but the success of the right in exploiting and intensifying the divisions in the working class opened up by the crisis in the attempt to secure a resolution of the crisis on the basis of capital.

The crisis of 1974 was a classic overaccumulation crisis. Although the immediate response of several states was to pursue deflationary policies, in order to force accumulation back within the limits of profitability, such policies soon provoked industrial and political conflict, so that the US in particular reversed its stance. The stagflation of the 1970s was essentially an expression of the global balance of class forces, as working-class pressure continued to force nation-states to pursue inflationary domestic policies, within limits dictated by capital through the financial markets. However, such inflationary policies served only to intensify the crisis of domestic productive capital and led to a growing polarization which counterposed neo-liberal 'monetarist' strategies of the right, based on subordination to the dynamics of the global accumulation of capital, to 'corporatist' strategies, based on the protection and regulation of the accumulation of domestic productive capital by the nation state, that were generally espoused by the left. The crisis of 1979 marked a decisive shift in the balance of class forces, with Britain and the US joining Germany and Switzerland in the conservative camp, imposing a global depression that saw the massive devaluation of surplus capital and destruction of surplus productive capacity, escalating unemployment and an intense offensive against the working class on the part of both capital and the state which sought not so much to force down wages as to restructure the institutional forms of industrial relations and the welfare state through which workers had sought to realize their material aspirations, in order to subordinate the reproduction of the working class to the reproduction of capital.

However deep was the recession of 1979–81, and however great were its social costs, it was not sufficient fully to restore the conditions for sustained accumulation, nor did it remove the tendency to overaccumulation and crisis. As in the 1970s, restrictive fiscal policies were soon reversed, and global accumulation renewed on the basis of Reagan's military Keynesianism. However the massive defeat suffered by the working class in the early 1980s enabled capital and the state to confine working class aspirations within the limits of profitability, so that accumulation was sustained in the metropolitan centres without the emergence of significant inflationary pressures. Meanwhile surplus capital found new outlets for productive investment, particularly in East Asia, where 'modernizing states' played a key role in providing the institutional infrastructure for accumulation and in preparing an educated, motivated and disciplined working class. Nevertheless, the intensification of labour and rapid technical change provided opportunities for surplus profit which stimulated the overaccumulation and uneven development of capital to a historically unprecedented degree, which was sustained by an explosion of domestic and international debt, financed not so much by credit expansion as by the diversion of surplus capital into unproductive and increasingly speculative channels.

The crisis and the crash

The stock market crash of 1987 raised the spectre of 1929 and 1873, throwing into fundamental doubt the belief that modern capitalism was a qualitatively different phenomenon from its earlier forms of existence. Although the crash of 1987 revealed only too clearly the fragile basis of the boom of the 1980s, it was not in itself an event of fundamental significance, being confined to a devaluation of fictitious capital. The immediate impact of the crash was effectively neutralized by easing credit, by bailing out banks and by precarious international cooperation to regulate currency markets. However, the crash was only an expression of the deeper crisis, of the global overaccumulation and uneven development of capital, which international financial Band-Aid does nothing to resolve. Nevertheless, such measures were able to restore confidence because beneath the froth of speculation there still appeared to be opportunities for soundly based productive investment to drive accumulation forward, in the first instance in the economies of the Asian Tigers, but more fundamentally in the breaking down of the last major political barriers to the globalization of capital. The collapse of the Soviet bloc at the end of the 1980s served to distract attention from the crisis of global capitalism, despite the fact that the 'crisis of socialism' was, as much as anything, itself a result of the overaccumulation and uneven development of capital on a world scale, which impacted on the Soviet bloc in the form of the increasing pressure of world competition, the growing cost of escalating military expenditure, and the enormous burden of hard-currency debt (Clarke *et al.* 1993).

The post-war reconstruction boom had been based on the reintegration of the global capitalist economy on the basis of the dismantling of the barriers to the free movement of commodities that had been erected in the inter-war period as national governments had sought to protect their domestic economies from the ravages of depression. The integration of any particular national economy into the global accumulation of capital through the liberalization of trade implied an expansion of opportunity for capitals oriented to the world market as a source of raw materials and means of production or as an outlet for their products, but a threat to those backward capitals which could not compete against foreign imports. While the sustained accumulation of capital depends on breaking down all local barriers to its expanded reproduction, the short-term costs are not borne by those who might enjoy the more uncertain long-term gains. The issue of liberalization versus protectionism was an issue that divided both capitalists and the workers who depended on them for a living within each particular country and was an issue that could only be resolved politically, the outcome being determined primarily by the extent to which the material and social conditions of production within the national borders were conducive to participation in the global processes of accumulation.

Colonialism and imperialism had already laid the foundations for a postwar boom based in the first instance on a global division of labour between advanced manufacturing in the metropolitan centres of accumulation and the extraction and export of primary produce from the peripheral regions. Those peripheral national economies in which a significant manufacturing industrial base had been developed within the protectionist framework of the depression and war years were much less well placed to participate in the boom, since full liberalization implied opening their markets to imported manufactures from the metropolitan centres and the consequent destruction of the established manufacturing base. Most of the more developed countries of southern Europe and Latin America, as well as South Africa and India, retained the corporatist and protectionist structures which sought to preserve domestic manufacturing production and employment while relying on expanded exports of primary products to sustain domestic accumulation, a strategy which was equally the basis for the construction of the Soviet bloc, which presented itself to the Third World as the model for such a national-patriotic mode of development.

Through the 1970s and 1980s a gap in productivity, and correspondingly in both wages and profits, progressively opened up between those capitals which were integrated into the processes of global accumulation and those which had sought protection behind national frontiers. However, the wider the gap, the more difficult it was to leap across. The backward capitals had neither the financial nor the technical resources to reconstruct domestic production which had lost its place on the world market. The only possibility for a restructuring of domestic productive capital was on the basis of direct investment by more advanced foreign capitals, whose prospects depended in turn not only on the liberalization of trade but also on the liberalization of capital flows and a congenial and stable political environment. 'Globalization' through the last quarter of the century was, therefore, by no means an automatic process, but rather the result of an extended period of economic and political crisis at the national level, that gave rise to intense class and political struggles, which progressively shifted the balance of class forces on a global scale.

By the end of the 1980s it appeared that 'liberalization' and 'stabilization' were the key to economic success, as the dynamism of those economies which had followed that path contrasted with the stagnation of those which had resisted. The ideology and policies of 'structural adjustment' were the basis of an increasingly aggressive offensive on the part of the international financial institutions, for whom it had become the unproblematic key to success. Since the strategy was associated with breaking down the regulatory role of the nation state it could even be associated with a crusade for democracy and human rights and freedoms, all interpreted in the negative sense of freedom from coercive regulation. However, while interventionist and protectionist policies of the nation state might be barriers to the integration of the national economy into global accumulation, their destruction was by no means a guarantee of such integration. Those countries which had adopted such policies as the outcome of domestic class and political struggles through the 1970s and 1980s were not distinguished by the greater wisdom or rationality of their political leaders, but by the fact that they were the countries in which the objective conditions for the success of such policies were the most well developed. By the end of the decade, those economies which retained substantial barriers to global integration were those in which such integration threatened massive economic destruction with only the most nebulous prospects of renewed accumulation: Brazil, Argentina, South Africa, India and the Soviet Union were all economies which had highly developed but globally uncompetitive manufacturing (and to a growing extent even primary producing) sectors and a mature and organized industrial working class. While protectionism could not prevent continuing decline, liberalization promised accelerated destruction of the established productive base and intensified class and political conflicts which could only undermine the prospects of renewal on the basis of foreign direct investment. Nevertheless, the longer these countries postponed their integration into the global economy, the deeper into crisis they fell and the worse their prospects became. Thus, while globalization was by no means automatic, it was nevertheless the inevitable expression of the dynamic of capital accumulation which was given a renewed stimulus in the aftermath of the stock market crash of 1987.

With the collapse of the Soviet bloc and economic reform in China new horizons opened up before global capital in the 1990s, to supplement the more limited opportunities presented by the Asian Tigers and the opening of Latin America. For the first time since 1914 capital was free to roam the whole world in search of profitable outlets for investment. However, the amount of capital seeking such outlets was growing at a massive rate as the flow of capitalized surplus value was augmented and even dwarfed by voluntary savings attracted by the prospects of speculative gains and the forced savings of workers, who were increasingly compelled to provide for their own subsistence in periods of ill-health and old age by investing in insurance-based systems of provision which were rapidly displacing socialized provision. Thus, the renewed global boom in the accumulation of productive capital was overlain by an even greater boom in speculative investment channelled through the world's financial institutions.

It is of the essence of speculative investment that it promises fabulous returns at the risk of catastrophic losses, but while fabulous returns drive the speculative boom forwards, catastrophic losses risk bringing down the whole system. The international movements of capital drove accumulation forwards through the 1990s, but these movements were increasingly dominated by speculative investments in property and fictitious capital on a scale far beyond anything that could be justified by the production and appropriation of surplus value. As the speculative inflation of stock and real estate prices led yields to fall far below the prevailing rates of interest, the speculative dimension of the boom became ever more predominant, driven by the institutional interests of financial intermediaries in sustaining the boom with other people's money. Like all such speculative booms, it could be sustained only by the constant influx of new investments and discovery of new outlets for the expanded capital, both of which were provided by privatization. On the one hand, the privatization of health, welfare, pensions and social insurance put vast sums of money into the hands of the financial institutions to fuel the speculative boom. On the other hand, the privatization of public assets provided new outlets for surplus capital.

The fact that capitalist accumulation always and everywhere takes the form of the overaccumulation and uneven development of capital implies that capitalist accumulation will always be interrupted by crises marked by the devaluation of capital and the destruction of productive capital. However, while every local crisis has wider repercussions, and risks setting off a chain reaction which can lead to a general crisis, such a generalization of the crisis is by no means necessary, provided that the losses can be redistributed rather than being cumulative. The financial crises of 1987 and of 1997–8 raised the spectre of a global crash, but in each case their impact was localized and confidence was restored in the belief that the crash was merely a superficial local disturbance which had been the result of exceptional circumstances. A brief period of soul-searching, with calls for the development of new modes of financial regulation, particularly at the international level, was soon forgotten as the locus of speculation moved on, leaving devastation of the real economy in its wake.

It is important neither to overemphasize nor to underestimate the significance of the periodic financial crises which mark the course of capitalist accumulation. Financial crises are the most dramatic but also the most superficial expressions of the fundamental contradiction underlying capitalist accumulation that derives from the subordination of the production of things to the production and appropriation of surplus value and that gives rise to the overaccumulation and uneven development of capital on a world scale. The devaluation of capital and destruction of productive capacity is not just the Armageddon that hovers over the horizon, but the threat that faces every capitalist every day. Overaccumulation and uneven development appears not only in the dramatic form of financial crises, but also in the everyday reality of capitalist competition which impels capitalists constantly to seek to intensify labour, extend the working day, force down wages and transform the forces of production in order to survive. Capitalist competition compels every capitalist to intensify the exploitation of his own workers as his contribution to the struggle to intensify the exploitation of the working class as a whole. It is this everyday struggle over the production and appropriation of surplus value in every individual workplace and every local community that is the basis of the class struggle on a global scale.

The inevitability of the crisis tendencies of capital and the permanence of class struggle does not determine either the form or the outcome of such crises and class struggles. If left unfettered, the tendencies of global accumulation will certainly lead to a further growth in global imbalances, in international competition, in inter-imperialist rivalries, and in financial and political instability. It is equally certain that if the crisis tendencies of global capitalist accumulation are not contained, they will provoke a political crisis of neo-liberalism, both nationally and internationally, the outcome of which we cannot predict. However, we know, from bitter historical experience, how powerful are the forces of nationalism once opportunistic politicians have unleashed them. We know how rapidly old alliances can crumble, and we know how rapidly new blocs, often extremely unlikely ones, can form. We know how fast, once such bloc formation is under way, conflict can escalate, and economic differences become political confrontations, which in turn lead to military engagements. We know how rapidly an epoch of global prosperity, underpinning prospects of world peace and international harmony, can become an epoch of global confrontation, culminating in war. If such a prospect seems unlikely now, it seemed equally unlikely a century ago.

However such developments are not inevitable. While the contradictory mode of capitalist accumulation and development may be unchanged and unchanging, the economic, social and political forms through which the underlying contradictions are expressed, the struggles in which they are embedded and the outcomes to which those struggles give rise are not imposed by any economic logic. The political outcomes are determined by the political responses to emerging economic difficulties, the biggest dangers of which lie in the renunciation of internationalism in the name of a resurgent nationalism. In the current political conjuncture there are grounds for optimism, but certainly no room for complacency. The East Asian crisis has provoked a renewal of the democratic and working-class movements in the countries most affected, while the direction that China will follow remains uncertain. The collapse of the Soviet bloc has certainly stoked the fires of inter-imperialist rivalry in the scramble to carve out spheres of economic and political influence, and it has resurrected some of the ugliest forms of nationalism in both East and West. But it has also fuelled the spirit of internationalism which has already proved an inspiration, especially to the young, in the peace movement, the world development movement, the ecological movement, and in the more traditional movements of international trades union and political solidarity. The collapse of the Soviet bloc makes the task of contracting a new international order, which the global environmental crisis has already placed firmly on the agenda, an even more pressing political priority, but at the same time it has swept away many of the political barriers to the formation of an organized movement for liberation which can bring together the whole range of trade union, labour and other non-governmental organizations on a global scale.

Notes

1 This analysis is developed theoretically and historically, from rather different angles, in Clarke (1988a) and Clarke (1990c).
2 On the theory of the capitalist form of the state, see the papers collected in Holloway and Picciotto (1978) and Clarke (1990c).
3 The main exceptions being the German social-democratic government after the First World War, and populist US administrations since the nineteenth century.

6
The State, Globalization and Phases of Capitalist Development

David M. Kotz

The quarter century following the end of the Second World War is often called the Golden Age of capitalism, in light of the relatively rapid and stable economic growth in the major industrialized capitalist countries in that period. However, that was by no means the only long period of relative prosperity in world capitalist history. Two others that have been identified ran from the mid-1840s to the mid-1870s and the mid-1890s to 1913 (Mandel 1975: 122; Gordon *et al.* 1982: 9). The intervals between these vigorous long-term expansions have seen poorer economic performance by a variety of measures. This alternation between long periods of rapid growth and long periods of slow or no growth has led some analysts to refer to 'long swings' in capitalist economies.[1]

The social structure of accumulation theory offers an explanation for such long swings based on the creation and then collapse of successive sets of institutions that are favorable for capital accumulation.[2] Such a set of growth-promoting institutions, which includes political and cultural as well as economic institutions, is referred to as a social structure of accumulation (SSA). According to this theory, the construction of a new SSA leads to a long (20 to 30 years) period of rapid accumulation, while the eventual demise of that SSA, due to contradictions and stresses that build up during the period of rapid accumulation, ushers in a period of relative stagnation, which in turn ends only when a new SSA is built. Since each SSA is a historically new configuration of institutions that differs from its predecessors, each successive long period of rapid accumulation can be regarded as a new phase of capitalist development. SSAs have both national and international dimensions – a distinct SSA develops in each country, while a set of common international institutions regulates the international aspects of capitalist accumulation.

For example, Bowles *et al.* (1990) describe the domestic aspect of the post-Second-World-War SSA in the US as consisting of a 'capital-labour accord' (a set of institutions promoting peaceful capital-labour relations), a 'capitalist–citizen accord' (a set of institutions regulating relations between the citizenry and the capitalists) and the 'containment of intercapitalist rivalry' (a set of institutions regulating competitive relations among large enterprises). They call the international dimension of the post-war SSA *'Pax Americana'*, which refers to such institutions as the Bretton Woods monetary system and the US readiness to intervene politically and militarily around the world to protect capitalist interests.[3]

According to the SSA theory, the post-Second-World War SSA broke down during 1966–73, bringing the Golden Age to an end by the latter year. Since 1973 economic performance in the industrialized capitalist economies has been significantly inferior to that of the Golden Age. Table 6.1 illustrates this, showing the growth rate of gross domestic product (GDP) for several major capitalist economies in 1950–73 and 1973–97.

While Japan and the major Western European economies have been relatively depressed in the 1990s, the US is often portrayed as rebounding to great prosperity over the past decade. Table 6.2 shows two indicators of economic performance, GDP and labour productivity growth rates, for the US economy for various sub-periods during 1948–98.[4] This table shows that the Golden Age began to lose its lustre in the US after 1966, when several institutions of the post-war SSA began to break down (Bowles *et al.* 1990: chapter 4). It also suggests that the reports of prosperous conditions in the US economy in the 1990s do not reflect any turnaround of long-term growth trends.

Column 1 of Table 6.2 shows that the GDP growth rate slowed down somewhat in 1966–73. However, the GDP growth slowdown in 1973–9 was much sharper. The 1980s expansion was more tepid than that of the much condemned 1973–9 period, and the 1990s expansion barely improved on the 1980s.[5] Column 2 of Table 6.2 shows that the high rate of labour productivity growth recorded in 1948–66 gave way to markedly reduced increases in 1966–73. In 1973–9 productivity growth practically disappeared. After 1979 it recovered somewhat but has remained well below the 1948–73

Table 6.1 Growth rate of real gross domestic product for six major capitalist countries (percentage increase per year)

Country	1950–73	1973–97
USA	3.8	2.5
UK	3.0	1.8
Germany	6.0	2.1
France	5.0	2.1
Italy	5.6	2.4
Japan	9.2	3.3

Sources: For US: *Economic Report of the President* (1985: 243; 1992: 300; 1999: 328). For other countries: Maddison (1995: 83); *Economic Report of the President* (1999: 454).

Table 6.2 Growth rate of real gross domestic product and labor productivity for the US economy (percentage increase per year)

Period	(1) *Growth rate of real GDP*	(2) *Growth rate of Labour productivity*[a]
1948–66	3.95	2.44
1966–73	3.45	1.57
1973–79	2.69	0.50
1979–89	2.45	1.24
1989–98	2.47	1.15[b]

[a] Annual rate of increase in real gross domestic product per hour worked in the nonfarm business sector. The figure for total hours worked in 1997 was estimated.
[b] Through 1997, not 1998.
Sources: Column 1: *Economic Report of the President* (1985: 243; 1992: 300; 1999: 328); US Department of Commerce (1999). Column 2: Lum and Yuskavage (1997); US Department of Commerce (1986; 1998; and 1999).

level (which averaged 2.20 per cent per year). Productivity performance in the 1990s has been worse than that of the 1980s.[6]

As of this writing, some twenty-five years have passed since the end of the last long-swing expansion, and there is no evidence in the economic data for the major capitalist countries that a new SSA, and with it a new phase of capitalist development, has yet emerged. This chapter argues that the construction of a new SSA has been blocked by world developments which are hindering the reconfiguration of the capitalist state as part of a new SSA. These world developments are the increased globalization of capitalism and the demise of state socialism.

The state and social structures of accumulation

The development of each successive SSA in history has involved the reconfiguration of key institutions that affect capital accumulation, including the form of capitalist enterprises, relations among enterprises, the labour process, relations among classes, the role of the state, and the dominant ideology. The reconfiguration of the state has been particularly important in the construction of each SSA. The state has a major effect on the conditions of capital accumulation, not only directly but also indirectly through its effects on all other institutions that affect accumulation – for example, on the form of the capitalist enterprise, on inter-enterprise relations, and on class relations. The direction of reconfiguration of the state in the past has been toward a more interventionist role in relation to the economy in each successive SSA.

In the US, the state played an important but limited role in the mid-nineteenth-century SSA, including financing and building transportation improvements, encouraging immigration, and providing cheap land at the frontier. The state played a more interventionist role in the early-twentieth-century SSA, including the first steps toward actively regulating business. In the post-Second-World-War SSA in the US, the state played a very active role, including supervision of capital–labour relations, regulation of the macroeconomy via fiscal and monetary policy, oversight of the financial sector, promotion of growth through public investment in economic infra-structure and education, and provision of income security to individuals. The state played a highly interventionist role, with variations in the specifics, in all the major capitalist countries in that period. The heavily state-managed capitalism of that era produced the Golden Age performance noted above.

Since the end of the Golden Age, successive governments in the US and Europe have sought to promote more vigorous capital accumulation but so far without success. The dominant direction of attempted reconfiguration of the state has been the reverse of the previous historical trend, moving back toward the relatively less interventionist state of capitalism's past.

In the US, state intervention in the economy has been reduced by the administrations of both Republican and Democratic presidents, starting midway through the term of President Jimmy Carter in 1978. There has been deregulation of sectors of business that had been regulated since early in this century, such as transportation, power and communication. Regulation of the financial sector, which dated to the 1930s, has been substantially loosened. The state has also withdrawn from Keynesian-type macroregulation. While the central bank does seek to actively forestall inflation, the former government commitment to stabilizing real output and stimulating aggregate demand growth was renounced in the early 1980s and has not been reintroduced.

State regulation of labour–management relations to encourage peaceful collective bargaining was an important part of the previous SSA in the US. This has been replaced by a state policy varying from outright hostility to labour unions and collective bargaining to a neutral stance that leaves large corporations free to continue their heightened resistance to serious collective bargaining. The welfare state has been sharply reduced since the late 1970s, when President Carter first called for cutbacks in social spending. All state income maintenance programs have been pared back, including the overwhelmingly popular social security retirement pension program. The longstanding federal commitment to support those without a means of income was rescinded in 1996. Investment in public infrastructure, one of the most obviously essential state supports for capital accumulation, declined by nearly one-third as a percentage of GDP from 1966 to 1997.[7]

The judicial and legislative branches of the US government have been leading the effort to pare back economic activism in the 1990s. A remarkable series of US Supreme Court decisions in June 1999 resurrected the long-dead doctrine of states' rights, harking back to the pre-monopoly capital era when business interests had successfully used that doctrine to block the rise of an interventionist federal government.[8] In June 1998, Congress came close to destroying the fiscal basis of modern government in the US. The dominant Republican Party leadership led a drive to weaken the Internal Revenue Service (IRS). Congressional hearings presented the IRS as a kind of Gestapo that was terrorizing citizens. One area in which the US has long been a world leader is in the collection of taxes, and the US has historically collected a relatively high proportion of taxes owed by law. Had the bill introduced by the Republicans passed unaltered, payment of taxes would have become more voluntary than mandatory. Even the amended bill that passed (the IRS Restructuring and Reform Act of 1998) significantly weakened the ability of the IRS to collect the taxes necessary for a functioning state. By May of 1999 IRS seizures of property from tax delinquents had declined by 98 per cent from two years earlier.[9]

Since the Thatcher era in the UK, the state has followed a similar course to that of the US. The UK's 'New Labour' government under Prime Minister Tony Blair has been continuing many of the economic policies of Thatcherism, particularly regarding state intervention in the economy. In continental Western Europe there has been great pressure to move in this direction as well. However, enormous popular resistance has so far limited such 'reforms' there.[10]

Some have suggested that the neo-liberal agenda of removing the state from the economy, to let the market rule, has created a new SSA. However, if an SSA is understood to mean not just any set of institutions that affect capital accumulation but a set of institutions that effectively promotes rapid and stable accumulation, then the continuing absence of rapid long-run growth in the industrialized capitalist countries is inconsistent with the claim that we now have a new neo-liberal SSA. The historical evidence suggests that the neo-liberal policy direction runs counter to the requirements for reconfiguring the state as part of a new SSA. A new SSA requires a state that can intervene in the economy in new ways so as to manage capitalism more effectively.

World capitalism seems to be suffering from an inability to reconfigure the state as part of a new SSA. Recently capitalism has produced rapid technological innovation and has avoided severe capital-labour conflict. It may be that the failure to find the right state role is the main obstacle to the creation of a new SSA and with it a new phase of capitalist development entailing rapid long-term capital accumulation.

Globalization

As Marx and Engels noted 150 years ago in the *Communist Manifesto*, the capital accumulation process has a powerful tendency to break down barriers that stand in its way. The boundaries of the nation-state are a good example. The geographic space of the nation-state was important to the initial development of capitalism. It provided a large region with a single currency and the absence of barriers to commerce, thus creating the large market necessary for capitalist development. However, capitalist accumulation from the start tended to push beyond the boundaries of the nation-state. In early capitalism the drive to accumulate benefited from the existence of precapitalist empires and also fostered the building of new multi-national empires. In the fifty years prior to the First World War, capitalist exchange became increasingly internationalized as international trade and foreign investment both grew rapidly. However, a large part of that trade and investment took place within the European colonial empires and hence was not really exchange between different political sovereignties.

The internationalization of capitalist exchange was interrupted during 1914–45, by two world wars, socialist revolution, depression, and fascism. The colonial system collapsed after the Second World War, and a new capitalist world economic order was built, often referred to as the Bretton Woods system. Under that system trade and investment became free to cross former empire boundaries. Certain features of the Bretton Woods system were favourable for the expansion of both international trade and investment, such as the fixed currency exchange rates. However, the Bretton Woods system permitted moderately high tariffs and controls on capital flows. The system was a compromise between the primarily national, state-guided capitalism favoured by some of the system's designers and the more fully open world economy that had been sought by others.[11]

The Bretton Woods system collapsed during 1967–73, as part of the collapse in that period of the SSA that had supported the Golden Age. The ensuing decades have witnessed a process of increasing globalization of capitalist exchange. Most observers believe that capitalism has become more globalized than in any previous era, although there is no universal agreement about this among analysts. While we cannot do full justice to the many issues surrounding globalization here, a review of some evidence suggests that globalization has been increasing in ways that are tending to undermine the ability of the capitalist state to effectively support capital accumulation.

Indicators of globalization

Globalization is usually defined as an increase in the volume of cross-border economic interactions and resource flows, producing a qualitative shift in the relations between national economies and between nation-states (Baker *et al.* 1998: 5; Kozul-Wright and Rowthorn 1998: 1). Three kinds of economic interactions have increased substantially in past decades: merchandise trade flows, direct foreign investment and cross-border portfolio investments. We will briefly examine each.

Table 6.3 shows the ratio of merchandise exports to gross domestic product for selected years from 1820 to 1992, for the world and also for Western Europe, the US and Japan. Capitalism brought a five-fold rise in world exports relative to output between 1820 and 1870, followed by another increase of nearly three-fourths by 1913. After declining in the inter-war period, world exports reached a new peak of 11.2 per cent of world output at the end of the Golden Age in 1973, rising further to 13.5 per cent in 1992. The 1992 figure was over 50 per cent higher than the pre-First-World War peak.

Merchandise exports include physical goods only, while GDP includes services, many of which are not tradable, as well as goods. In the twentieth century the proportion of services in GDP has risen significantly. Table 6.4

Table 6.3 Merchandise exports as a percentage of GDP

Year	World[a]	Western Europe	US	Japan
1820	1.0	n.a.	2.0	n.a.
1870	5.0	10.0	2.5	0.2
1913	8.7	16.3	3.7	2.4
1950	7.0	9.4	3.0	2.3
1973	11.2	20.9	5.0	7.9
1992	13.5	29.7	8.2	12.4

[a] The 'world' data cover 56 countries, which accounted for 93 per cent of world output and 87 per cent of world population and exports in 1992.
Source: Maddison (1995: 38).

Table 6.4 World merchandise exports as a percentage of world non-service GDP

Year	World merchandise exports as a percentage of world non-service GDP
1820	1.2
1870	6.2
1913	12.2
1950	11.0
1992	31.3

Source: Menshikov (1997).

shows an estimate of the ratio of world merchandise exports to the good-only portion of world GDP. This ratio nearly tripled between 1950 and 1992, with merchandise exports rising to nearly one-third of total goods output in the latter year. The 1992 figure was 2.6 times as high as that of 1913.

Western Europe, the US and Japan all experienced significant increases in exports relative to GDP between 1950 and 1992, as Table 6.3 shows. All of them achieved ratios of exports to GDP far in excess of the 1913 level. While exports were only 8.2 per cent of the total GDP of the US in 1992, exports amounted to 22 per cent of the non-service portion of GDP that year (*Economic Report of the President* 1999: 338, 444).

Many analysts view foreign direct investment as the most important form of cross-border economic interchange. It is associated with the movement of technology and organizational methods, not just goods. Table 6.5 shows two measures of foreign direct investment. Column 1 gives the outstanding stock of foreign direct investment in the world as a percentage of world output. While this measure has more than doubled since 1975, it is not much greater today than it was in 1913. Column 2 shows the annual inflow of direct foreign investment as a percentage of gross fixed capital formation. While this measure increased rapidly between 1975 and 1995, it is still quite low in absolute terms, with foreign direct investment accounting for only 5.2 per cent of gross fixed capital formation in 1992.

Not all, or even most, international capital flows take the form of direct investment. Portfolio flows (such as cross-border purchases of securities and deposits in foreign bank accounts) are normally larger. One measure that takes account of portfolio as well as direct investment is the total net movement of capital into or out of a country. That measure indicates the extent to which capital from one country finances development in other countries. Table 6.6 shows the absolute value of current account surpluses or deficits as a percentage of GDP for 12 major capitalist countries. Since net capital inflow or outflow is approximately equal to the current account deficit or surplus (differing only due to errors and omissions), this indicates the size of

Table 6.5   Foreign direct investment

Year	(1) World stock of foreign direct investment (% of world output)	(2) World foreign direct investment inflows (% of world gross fixed capital formation)
1913	9.0	n.a.
1960	4.4	1.1
1975	4.5	1.4
1995	10.1	5.2

Source: Baker *et al.* (1998: 9).

Table 6.6   Current account surplus or deficit as a
percentage of GDP (weighted average for 12 countries)

1910–14	3.8
1950–54	1.8
1970–74	1.4
1990–96	2.7

Note: The absolute values of surpluses and deficits are averaged. The
twelve countries are major participants in international investment
from Western Europe, North America, the Far East, and Latin
America.
Source: Baker et al. (1998: 11).

net cross-border capital flows. While the ratio nearly doubled between 1970–
74 and 1990–96, it remained well below the figure for 1910–14.

While cross-border net movements of capital have not been impressive,
the same cannot be said of cross-border gross capital movements.[12] In recent
times a very large and rapidly growing volume of capital has moved back
and forth across national boundaries. Much of this capital flow is speculative
in nature, reflecting growing amounts of short-term capital that are moved
around the world in search of the best temporary return. No data on such
flows are available for the early part of this century, but the data for recent
decades are impressive. During 1980–95, cross-border transactions in bonds
and equities as a percentage of GDP rose from 9 per cent to 136 per cent for
the US, from 8 per cent to 168 per cent for Germany, and from 8 per cent to
66 per cent for Japan (Baker et al. 1998: 10). The total volume of foreign
exchange transactions in the world rose from about $15 billion per day in
1973 to $80 billion per day in 1980 and $1260 billion per day in 1995. Trade
in goods and services accounted for 15 per cent of foreign exchange transactions in 1973 but for less than 2 per cent of foreign exchange transactions in
1995 (Bhaduri 1998: 152).

While the cross-border flows of goods and capital are usually considered to
be the best indicators of possible globalization of capitalism, changes that
have occurred over time within capitalist enterprises are also relevant. That
is, the much-discussed rise of the transnational corporation (TNC) plays a
role here, where a TNC is a corporation which has a substantial proportion
of its sales, assets and employees outside its home country.[13] TNCs existed in
the era before the First World War, primarily in the extractive sector (such as
petroleum and mining). In the period since the Second World War many
large manufacturing corporations in the US, Western Europe and Japan
became TNCs.

The largest TNCs are very international measured by the location of their
activities. One study found that the 100 largest TNCs in the world (ranked
by assets) had 40.4 per cent of their assets abroad, 50.0 per cent of output

abroad, and 47.9 per cent of employment abroad in 1996 (Sutcliffe and Glyn 1999: 125). While this shows that the largest TNCs are significantly international in their activities, all but a handful have retained a single national base for top officials and major stockholders.[14] The top 200 TNCs ranked by output were estimated to produce only about 10 per cent of world GDP in 1995 (Sutcliffe and Glyn 1999: 122).

Some portion of world trade in goods takes place between the subsidiaries of a TNC. Reliable data on such intra-firm trade are scarce. One sees figures of 30 per cent to 40 per cent cited, as guesses at the percentage of intra-firm trade in world trade, but there is no way to determine their reliability. An unknown part of intra-firm trade merely represents sales to marketing subsidiaries abroad.

Consequences of globalization

At the close of the twentieth century, capitalism has become significantly more globalized than ever before. The most important features of globalization today are greatly increased international trade, greatly increased short-term speculative capital flows, and a major role for large TNCs in manufacturing, extractive activities, and finance, operating worldwide yet retaining in nearly all cases a clear base in a single nation-state. The earlier wave of globalization before World War I took place within a world carved up into great colonial empires, which meant that much of the so-called 'cross-border' trade and investment of that earlier era actually occurred within a space controlled by a single state.

The rapid rise in merchandise exports began during the Bretton Woods period, as Table 6.3 has shown. So too did the growing role for TNCs. These two aspects of the current globalization had their roots in the post-war era of state-managed capitalism. This suggests that, to some extent, globalization reflects a long-run tendency in the capital accumulation process rather than just being a result of the breakdown of the Bretton Woods system and/or the rising influence of neo-liberal policies. On the other hand, the extremely rapid increase in cross-border short-term capital flows does appear to reflect the breakdown of the previous system and perhaps the influence of neo-liberal policies in the past two decades.

The enormous growth in short-term speculative capital flows has introduced a new element of instability into the international capitalist system. The Asian financial crisis which began in the summer of 1997 made this clear, when a sudden and massive reversal from inflow to outflow of short-term capital sank one Asian economy after another. However, the great increase in speculative capital flows could be reversed relatively easily, by means of various reforms that have been proposed since the Asian financial crisis (such as transactions taxes). In any event, it is the increase in trade, not the speculative capital flows, that presents a major problem for the construction of a new SSA.

An important consequence of globalization in this period has been to make capitalism significantly more competitive, particularly for large corporations. The Golden Age was characterized by significant monopoly and oligopoly power within the major capitalist economies, as many perceptive analysts have noted (Baran and Sweezy 1966; Galbraith 1967). The rapid growth of trade has changed the situation faced by large corporations. For example, in the US the rate of import penetration of domestic manufacturing markets was 2 per cent in 1950; it rose to 8 per cent in 1971 and 16 per cent by 1993, an eight-fold increase since 1950 (Sutcliffe and Glyn 1999: 116).

The high level of world trade reached before the First World War occurred within a system based much more on specialization and division of labour. That is, manufactured goods were exported by the advanced capitalist countries in exchange for primary products, unlike today when most trade is in manufactured goods. In 1913 62.5 per cent of world trade was in primary products (Bairoch and Kozul-Wright 1998: 45). By contrast, in 1970 60.9 per cent of world exports were manufactured goods, rising to 74.7 per cent in 1994 (Baker *et al.* 1998: 7).

The valid observation that globalization has weakened labour because of capital's increased mobility has led some to draw the seemingly reasonable conclusion that globalization has thereby strengthened capital. However, such a conclusion is oversimplified. While offering advantages to capital in its relation to labour, globalization has created problems for capital-capital relations and for the ability of capital to use the state for its own ends. The current form of globalization has been undermining the possibility of reconfiguring the state to usher in a new period of rapid capital accumulation. It does so in two ways, one structural and the other based on class relations.

The structural aspect is the well-known tendency of increased global interdependence to limit the ability of individual states to regulate capital. Any state regulation that might increase costs of production in the home country creates problems in a globalized marketplace, if competitor countries do not have similar regulations. Even regulations undertaken, partly or entirely, to benefit capital in the long-run would encounter this obstacle, since the short-run costs of such regulations might threaten the survival of domestic industries. A version of capitalism based on a big, interventionist national state might face viability problems in the short run even if it were superior over the long run, if the taxation required to support it undermined the competitive position of domestic industry.

However, the structural aspect of this problem should not be exaggerated. If the political will is present, it can be overcome. For example, a nation-state willing to violate international free trade and investment rules can protect its regulatory programs against international pressures. If states retain political sovereignty within the world system – which large capitalist states still do – then the structural limits on state regulation of capital coming from globalization are, it must be concluded, limited.

There is another, more significant effect of globalization on the state. That is a class relations effect. Specifically, globalization undermines the class coalition which has in the past served as the political basis for the various versions of the regulationist state that have emerged in the twentieth century. In mature capitalism a regulationist state has rested upon support from two main groups, big capital and the working class.[15]

For example, in the US large corporations emerged and grew powerful in the last three decades of the nineteenth century, producing a division between big and small business. A significant part of the new big business leaders came to support government regulation of various aspects of the economy in the pre-First-World-War years (Weinstein 1968). By 1945 support for an interventionist state by big business became much more solid. By contrast, small business remained adamantly opposed to the big, interventionist state. This division was reflected in the sharp political differences in the decades immediately following the Second World War between the Business Roundtable, a big-business organization which often supported interventionist programs, and the US Chambers of Commerce, the premier small-business organization, which hewed to an anti-government stance.

When large corporations achieve significant market power and become freed from fear concerning their immediate survival, they tend to develop a long time horizon and pay attention to the requirements for assuring growing profits over time. They come to see the state as a potential ally. By contrast, the typical small business faces a daily battle for survival, which prevents attention to long-run considerations and which places a premium on avoiding the short-run costs of taxation and state regulation. This explains why pro-interventionist big business, in alliance with organized labour, provided the main political base for establishing an interventionist state in the US during 1933–48, while small business interests remained in opposition.

Globalization has transformed big business from a supporter to an opponent of the interventionist state.[16] It has done so partly by producing TNCs whose ties to the domestic markets for goods and labour is limited. More importantly, globalization tends to turn big business into small business. The process of globalization has sharply increased the degree of competitive pressure faced by large corporations and banks, as competition has become a worldwide relationship.[17] Even if those who run large corporations and financial institutions recognize the need for a strong nation-state in their home base, the new competitive pressure they face shortens their time horizon. It pushes them towards support for any means to reduce their tax burden and lift their regulatory constraints, to free them to compete more effectively with their global rivals. While a regulationist state may seem to be in the interests of big business, in that it can more effectively promote capital accumulation in the long run, in a highly competitive environment big business becomes unable to support such institutions.

The second political support for the interventionist state has been the working class, which historically has been able to gain significant material benefits from the regulationist state. Globalization has been weakening the working-class and trade union movement in the mature capitalist countries, as capitalists play off the working class of one country against that of other countries with the ever-present threat of capital flight and/or import competition.

The relative political weight of the working class and big capital in constructing the post-war regulationist state varied from one country to another. Sweden represents one extreme of the working class playing the leading role, with big capital accepting the transformed system, while the US represents the opposite pole, with far-seeing representatives of big capital playing the leading role with the organized working class in a secondary, supportive position. But with labour weakened and big capital hostile, no effective political base remains for the regulationist state.

The demise of state socialism

After 1945 world capitalism faced a serious rival social system – the state socialism of the USSR and its bloc in Eastern Europe, soon supplemented by China. During 1989–91, the USSR and Eastern Europe suddenly abandoned state socialism and began the effort to install capitalism in its place.[18] Through a more gradual process China had, by that time, shifted onto a similar trajectory of replacing state socialism by capitalism.

One can view the demise of state socialism as an aspect of the globalization of capitalism, in a certain sense. Its disappearance made capitalism a fully global system geographically for the first time ever.[19] Yet the more significant meaning of 'globalization' of capitalism refers not to the percentage of the world that it covers but to the extent to which capitalist systems in the world are economically integrated with one another. Hence, the demise of state socialism deserves to be treated as a distinct factor that has been affecting the role of the capitalist state.

The sudden demise of the rival system of state socialism has contributed to the difficulty of reconfiguring a new regulationist state in capitalism in several ways. First, it weakened the working-class in capitalist countries. Since the late nineteenth century the vision of a socialist alternative to capitalism had played an important role in the development of the working-class movement in advanced capitalist countries. While the socialist movement split after the Russian Revolution into communist and social democratic wings, both wings were hit hard by the sudden demise of state socialism, which was widely interpreted as demonstrating that socialism is an unworkable system and that there is no alternative to capitalism. As socialism of any sort lost legitimacy, the working-class movement as a whole was significantly weakened politically, which reduced its ability to press for a regulationist state.

Second, the demise of state socialism was widely interpreted as proving that any form of state regulation of the economy was doomed to failure. This gave strength to the ideological foes of state regulation and made it more difficult to make the case for a new regulationist state.

Third, fear of the rival system had been an important reason why big capital had previously been so supportive of a regulationist state. Concern that the workers might 'turn to communism' had encouraged acceptance of welfare state measures, and fear of being outperformed economically by the rapidly growing state-socialist economies had fostered support for state interventions aimed at accelerating capital accumulation.

Fourth, the existence of the rival bloc had fostered a degree of unity among the major capitalist states unseen in earlier eras of capitalism. The sharp rivalry among major capitalist states, which had dominated capitalist history until 1945, became muted as they sought to maintain a united front, under US leadership, against the Communist enemy. This greatly facilitated the construction and smooth operation of the international institutions of state-regulated capitalism during the Golden Age.

Given its many impacts, one can make a case that the existence of a relatively strong rival social system was a critical factor in the maturation of state-regulated capitalism after the Second World War. The capitalist celebration at the sudden and unexpected disappearance of that rival system may have been premature. Its disappearance has contributed significantly to the difficulty in reconfiguring a new state-regulated capitalism, without which there may be no new period of rapid and stable capital accumulation.

Conclusions

The globalization of capitalism in this era, both in the sense of growing economic integration within the capitalist world and in that of the full geographic spread of world capitalism, has presented an obstacle to the development of a new regulationist state. Without such a regulationist state, it is difficult to see how a new SSA can arise, and with it a new phase of rapid capitalist development. Without a new SSA, we are likely to see, both internationally and within individual countries, a trend of growing conflict, instability and uneven development. With economies growing slowly or not at all, the conflicts between capital and labour, and between rival capitalists, will have a zero-sum character and hence are likely to intensify. The absence of an effective regulationist state will leave the economy prone to sharp swings and severe crises. The divergence in the fortunes of different regions, industries and occupations, which has been widening since the end of the Golden Age, is likely to widen still further. The stresses on the social order will increase over time.

The obvious resolution to this problem in the development of globalized capitalism would be the emergence of a global capitalist state. If the world-scale concentration of capital developed sufficiently through cross-border mergers, one could imagine a world capitalism in which many world markets came to be dominated by a few gigantic firms operating within the regulation of an international capitalist state. The global monopoly capitalists would form the political base for such a global regulationist state.

However, while such an eventuality cannot be ruled out for the distant future, it seems to be an impossibility in the near future. The cultural and political reality of humankind, anchored in a much smaller geographic scale, would seem to rule out the emergence of a world state in the foreseeable future.[20] If monopolization does arise on a world scale in the absence of any genuine global state able to regulate it, the problems of global capitalism would only be accentuated.

A more feasible resolution would be the development of a bloc system in the world. Three major political–economic blocs might develop, one in North America dominated by the US, one in Western Europe dominated by Germany, and one in East Asia dominated by Japan. In each bloc there might develop, not necessarily a full regional state, but sufficiently developed multilateral institutions within each bloc to permit the construction of new SSAs in the major countries of each bloc. While such a bloc system might permit a new period of more rapid and stable capital accumulation, history suggests that bloc systems tend to produce serious international conflicts.[21]

Economic or political events might intervene to change the possibilities regarding the emergence of a new regulationist state. A major economic crisis could erupt – for example, following the bursting of the stock market bubble in the US. A serious world depression might create favourable conditions for the emergence of a new activist state. A fascist regime could arise in a major peripheral country, Russia being the most likely. Alternatively, a socialist regime could emerge in a major peripheral country, such as Brazil or Russia. Such a shift, rightward or leftward, in one or more major peripheral countries, could change the world's political dynamics in ways that might foster regulationist states elsewhere.

There is also the possibility of a revival of the working-class movement in the industrialized capitalist countries, possibly in response to the conditions described above, of intensifying conflict, instability and uneven development. This might prod big capital back towards support for a regulationist state, and it might also open the possibility of finally superseding capitalism in its heartland.

Notes

Research assistance for this paper was provided by Li Minqi and Elizabeth Ramey. Helpful comments on an earlier draft were given by Samuel Bowles, Dan Clawson, James Crotty, Gerald Epstein, Robert Pollin, and Mohan Rao, although they bear no responsibility for the final outcome. Research funding was provided by the Political Economy Research Institute at the University of Massachusetts at Amherst.

1 Gordon *et al.* (1982) offer empirical evidence for the existence of such long swings.
2 See Kotz *et al.* (1994) for a full explanation of the social structure of accumulation theory.
3 The regulation theory explains long-run changes in capital accumulation in a manner that has some similarities to the SSA theory. See Kotz *et al.* (1994: chapter 5) for a discussion of the similarities and differences between the regulation and SSA theories.
4 Table 6.2 measures economic growth using business cycle peak years for the US economy as beginning and end points, to show long-run performance. The only exceptions are 1966, which was three years before the next peak but marked a turning-point in several important economic series, and 1998, which is the latest year for which data are available as of this writing.
5 The expansion of the 1990s did finally bring the unemployment rate below 5 per cent, as slow growth in labour productivity led to the creation of a large number of low-wage, low-productivity jobs. The low inflation of the late 1990s in the US has been due to a combination of factors, including a labour movement lacking the power to raise wages much even when labour markets tightened and dropping world prices for raw materials due to depressed conditions in much of the world.
6 The increase in output per hour worked is the basis for long-run growth of profits. Capitalists can increase profits for a time by reducing workers' living standards and/or increasing the intensity of labour (as occurred in the US in the 1990s), but those processes have natural limits.
7 *Economic Report of the President* (1999: 326, 350). Investment in public infrastructure here includes gross investment in non-military structures and equipment by all levels of government.
8 In three related decisions, the court ruled that state governments were immune from lawsuits charging them with violation of federal laws (*New York Times*, 24 June 1999, A1, A22). The US Supreme Court has even flirted with overturning the longstanding interpretation of the interstate commerce clause of the US Constitution that has formed the basis of all federal regulation of business over the past century.
9 *New York Times*, 18 May 1999: C11. An anonymous IRS tax collector was quoted as saying, 'With this new law, if somebody says "I'm not paying," then we just say "thank you" and leave.'
10 It appears that pressure on Japan to pare back its interventionist state has come largely from abroad, and this pressure has for the most part been successfully resisted so far.
11 The British economist John Maynard Keynes and US Treasury official Harry Dexter White fought for a system of national capitalisms, while the international bankers and corporations favoured an open world economy. For an account of this struggle, see Block (1977: chapters 3–5).

12 A country that experienced large inflows and outflows of capital of equal magnitude during a year would register zero net capital flow.

13 Some definitions require significant dispersion of activities over some minimum number of different countries.

14 Sutcliffe and Glyn assert that 'we are not convinced that there [is] yet any' TNC that is 'so international in ownership, production, and management that it no longer has a basic nation state' (Sutcliffe and Glyn 1999: 126).

15 A somewhat different class alliance gave rise to the developmental state in late-developing capitalist countries, such as Japan, Turkey or South Korea.

16 In recent decades large US corporations and banks that formerly supported foundations that advocate an active government role in the economy, such as the Brookings Institution, have become big donors to neo-liberal foundations such as the American Enterprise Institute and the Heritage Foundation. As a result, such right-wing foundations, which previously had to rely mainly on contributions from small business, have become very wealthy and influential.

17 Jeffrey Garten, the dean of the Yale School of Management, remarked that American corporate CEOs today 'feel they are in a brutally competitive world, and they think they are in a race for their lives' (*New York Times*, 18 July 1999, sec. 4: 4). No serious analyst would have described the mindset of US big business in such terms in the 1950s or 1960s, when large corporations made large profits almost every year, avoided price competition, and rarely suffered an annual loss.

18 See Kotz with Weir (1997) for an analysis of the reasons for the demise of state socialism.

19 Before 1917, capitalism had not yet fully spread to all parts of what came to be called the Third World.

20 In an earlier era of capitalism, with new technologies of transportation and communication, brought the world the modern large-scale nation-state and its associated national consciousness. One could point to current communication and transportation technologies which are tending to produce a world culture and consciousness. However, there is no reason to predict that more local loyalties and identities will be superseded any time soon.

21 See Kotz *et al.* (1994: 307–15) for a discussion of a possible future bloc system.

7

Spiral Reversal of Capitalist Development: What Does It Imply for the Twenty-First Century?

Makoto Itoh

The attempt to reinterpret history in terms of its phases of development closely reflects our efforts to understand the contemporary age and to gain perspective on the future. It should be our common concern to characterize the current period of crisis and restructuring since 1973 from the point of view of phases of capitalist development. For this purpose, the preceding phase of high economic growth lasting about a quarter century particularly needs to be re-examined. As the issues surrounding the phases of capitalist development are most suitably approached from Marxist political economy, it is helpful first to start with a brief review of the classic concerns in the literature on periodizing capitalism, beginning with Marx himself.

Marx, Lenin and Uno

Marx

In Marx's *Capital* as well as in his other works, different phases of capitalist development were not yet a major concern. Marx's preoccupation was the basic theory of the capitalist economy in general. Unlike classical political economy and neo-classical economics, Marx's theory identified the historically specific and transitory nature of capitalism. In the narrowly limited view of classical political economy (and later of neo-classical economics), the capitalist market economy was regarded as a natural and harmonious social order. Marx's theoretical system in *Capital* presented a thorough critique of such a naturalist view of the capitalist economy, by showing the historical character of both the market economy and the capitalist economy.

According to Marx, the forms of a market economy existed from the ancient world, mainly as intersocial economic relations. For the first time in capitalism, however, labour-power is socially transformed into a commodity, and an extensive commodity economy is formed, as capital organizes the social production of commodities by means of commodities. The labour process, existing 'independently of any specific social formation' (Marx 1976: 283), and as the basic process of social life mediating and regulating the metabolism between human beings and nature, then becomes totally embraced by the forms of the market economy as the basis of the valorization of capital.

Lenin

Lenin's *Imperialism* (1917) practically opened a new area of research. Its major concern was not the capitalist economy in general but 'the highest stage of capitalism', as its subtitle suggests. It presented 'a composite picture of the world capitalist system' (Lenin 1965: 3) with concrete data and facts since the late nineteenth century. Lenin used Hilferding's concept of 'finance capital', based upon the joint-stock company, and supplemented it with an analysis of monopoly. However, while Hilferding deduced the notion of finance capital from Marx's theory of money and credit almost at the same abstract level of research as in *Capital*, Lenin's study began with more concrete historical processes in the major heavy industries and financial institutions of the main capitalist countries.

Based on Marx's theory of the capitalist economy in general, Lenin developed a historically concrete analysis of the different phases of capitalist development based on changes in the leading industry, the dominant form of capital, and the forms of rivalry among economic powers in the world market. Often, however, the methodological significance of Lenin's *Imperialism* has been misinterpreted. For example, some regard it as a new model of monopolistic capitalism replacing the old model of competitive capitalism in *Capital* at the same level of basic theory. This type of interpretation seems to provide authority for the views of many contemporary political economists that their models of recent capitalism serve as a replacement for the older models, including the basic theory in *Capital*.

Uno

Against such inclinations, Kozo Uno's methodological argument that Marxist political economy should be systematically broken into three different levels of research is effective. The first level would comprise the basic theory of the capitalist economy in general, which was presented in *Capital*. Uno attempted to purify and complete such a theoretical system based on *Capital* in one of his main works (Uno 1980). We see in that work that the historical facts referred to in *Capital* are mostly of an illustrative nature and omissible from the main body of theoretical analysis of the capitalist economy in general.

The second level of research would develop a stages theory of world capitalist development on the foundation of the basic principles at the first level. This level would involve the concrete examination of the historical development of the dominant forms of capital, their main industrial bases, and the characteristic economic policies of the leading states at each stage. Uno proposed three stages of capitalist development: mercantilism, liberalism and imperialism. In the first stage, mercantilism, the dominant capital was British merchant capital, based upon the growth of the woollen industry. The second stage, liberalism, was dominated by British industrial capital with its centre in the cotton industry. In the third stage, imperialism, the different types of finance capital which appeared in Germany, Britain and the USA with the development of heavy industries assumed dominance.[1] Lenin's *Imperialism* should be located at this level of research, where concrete historical facts and analysis of national economies cannot be omitted. The tasks and contents of such a stages theory of capitalist development should not be confused with those of the basic principles of capitalism.

The third level of research would deal with the historical development and contemporary context of an individual capitalist economy. The world economy after the First World War must also be analysed at this level as a more concrete empirical study. According to Uno, this is because after the First World War capitalism entered into a transitional period towards socialism, and governments felt a need to counter the external and internal threat of socialism, and therefore given such a high degree of government intervention in the economy, that there could no longer be a stage of capitalism with its own logic of development. The first and the second levels of research should be used as frames of reference to guide this third level of concrete empirical analysis. Socialist parties and socialist movements in each country and in each period are particularly able to plan concrete tactics upon the ground of political economic research at this level, not just on the basis of research at the first and the second level.

Using the basic principles of the capitalist economy as a fundamental frame of reference, the concrete studies of institutional and political factors at the second and third levels of research are organically focused on the process of capital accumulation. In this regard, Uno's approach and other Marxist approaches to phases of capitalist development differ methodologically from studies by the historical school, institutional school, or recent evolutionary economics. However, since there are interests which overlap with the studies of these latter approaches, especially the role of cultural, historical and institutional differences among societies in economic development, mutual cooperation with them or utilization of mutual achievements is fully possible.

The period of high economic growth

I learned a lot from Uno's original attempts to restructure Marxist political economy, and follow his lead on the distinction between levels of research. I therefore assume that capitalist development since the First World War must be subject to the third level of concrete empirical analysis. However, this period is not homogeneous, and needs to be broken into at least three phases. The first phase is the stormy inter-war period, in which the 1930s period of great crisis must be further distinguished as a sub-phase from the period of world capitalist restructuring in the 1920s. The second phase is the period of high economic growth after the Second World War until 1973, and the third is the period of continuous crisis and restructuring through the last quarter of the twentieth century.

Among these three, the second phase formed the most stable pattern of capitalist development. More than a few names have been proposed to characterize this stable pattern, for example monopoly capitalism, state monopoly capitalism, state capitalism, welfare state capitalism, Fordism, *Pax Americana*, and consumerism. The difficulty in deciding upon a uniform label reflects the complexity of this phase. One advantage of placing the analysis of this phase at the level of the concrete empirical analysis of capitalism is avoiding the problem of choosing a single label which consists of a more or less one-sided simplification. Instead we can try to draw upon the contents of these various characterizations to provide a proper synthetic perspective.

In treating stages of capitalist development at the intermediate range of theory, we should indeed be able to avoid over-generalizing certain aspects of capitalist development in each period. On the other hand, however, we must not miss the trends of capitalist development which stretch across several phases. The specific features of each phase should therefore be clarified in combination with these longer trends studied at that third level of concrete historical analysis.

Trends away from competitive free market capitalism

From this perspective we can see that, for about a century since the late nineteenth century, the capitalist world system reversed the direction it took during the stage of liberalism in a spiral way, tending to restrict free market competition in the following four ways.

1. With the development of heavy industries, giant joint-stock companies grew. They tended to form monopolistic organizations in order to avoid cut-throat competition and to earn monopolistic profits by controlling the prices of their products.
2. In heavy industries, experienced and muscled male workers were needed in mass numbers and were employed together in large workplaces. As a result, trade unions grew among them as well as among the increasing numbers of workers in the public sector. Unions attempted to restrict free competition in the labour market, in order to defend workers' class interests. On the basis of this growth of labour movements, socialist movements and socialist consciousness could also develop.

3. In accord with these trends, the economic role of nation states was reinforced. Imperialist colonial and tariff policies were strengthened to suit the economic needs of monopolistic firms. With these spiral evolutionary characteristics, the stage of imperialism has been also called neo-mercantilism. Social policies to cope with labour and agricultural problems were adopted to obtain national support for imperialism and also to defend the capitalist order against socialism. Two imperialist world wars further extended large-scale state intervention into the market economy to mobilize national economic power. The military-industrial complex was later maintained to a large extent in the context of the cold war. The great crisis of the inter-war period generated the New Deal and Keynesian employment policies. Social-democratic welfare state policies became positively promoted by European countries as a counter-vailing power against socialism. The resulting growth of public sectors (providing stable employment) also favoured trade union movements.

4. As the Soviet type of socialism developed and multiplied, especially after the Second World War, to cover about 30 per cent of the area and 35 per cent of the population of the globe, the capitalist world market system appeared to face a serious challenge from this growth, which limited its own territorial expansion. Socialist movements of various kinds also tended to gain strength within both the central and peripheral capitalist countries. The need to counter these socialist advances was clearly a factor which led to the increasing role of the state through the cold war period.

Thus the basic historical trend for the capitalist world system to expand its competitive market order throughout the world was in fact restricted and reversed for almost a century. The basic vitality of the capitalist world system with its free competitive market seemed to have been diminished. Just as the capitalist world system was born in the mercantilist stage through the midwife of political-military state intervention, its vitality seemed to wan as it opted increasingly for reintensified political-military state intervention.

So long as the economic roles of massive firms and hypertrophic states grew, the socio-economic significance of communal human relations was weakened in people's consciousness and often undermined in practice. Socialist movements including social democracy in the advanced industrial countries were influenced by these developments, tending to focus on issues of state power and state policy with a social base grounded in the trade unions of big businesses. Besides the economic demands of workers' movements, pacifist anti-war movements mobilized opposition to state policies. While the state was the focus of many issues, cooperative movements, feminism, and ecologism were not yet incorporated into the main evolutionary thrust of capitalism or socialism.

Along with the trends restricting the competitive free market, however, the advanced industrial countries in the period after the Second World War achieved an exceptionally high rate of real economic growth without serious economic crisis or depression, unlike in previous phases. Thus this period was called the 'Golden Age' of capitalism (Marglin and Schor 1990).

Keynesianism or Fordism

Statism in the capitalist world during this period took the particular form of Keynesianism. After the instability of the monetary and financial system and the excessive accumulation of monopolistic industrial capital played such an important role in the devastating Great Crisis beginning in 1929, a managed currency system was introduced, which enabled states to operate flexible Keynesian macro-demand policies. The Bretton Woods system integrated the managed currencies internationally with fixed exchange rates, and served as a stable frame for the capitalist world system under Keynesianism. As Keynesian economics enhanced its prestige by furnishing the theoretical basis for economic policies which seemed remarkably successful in maintaining economic growth, more than a few Marxists put forth models of contemporary capitalism that similarly assumed the effectiveness of monetary and fiscal state policies. This tendency was especially evident in the models of state monopoly capitalism and state capitalism.

Although the expansion of effective demand was an important basis for continuous economic growth in this period, it is dubious whether this was achieved just by state monetary and fiscal policies operating 'from above', except in the earlier years of reconstruction after the Second World War. Amid rapid economic growth, the annual increase in tax revenue more and more enabled states to build necessary infrastructures. The Keynesian type of fiscal policy with budget deficits became unnecessary and was not pursued in many capitalist countries, though a consistent monetary policy to keep real rates of interest low remained effective for capital accumulation. Under the cold war framework, as the theories of military capitalism underlined, military expenditure was kept at a high level, especially in the US, and worked as a sort of military Keynesianism. The economic effect of this policy, however, steadily decreased and became negative for the US economy by the time of the Vietnam War. Still, in so far as Keynesianism was presented as an abstract general theory which asserted the effectiveness of monetary and fiscal policies for maintaining full employment, it was extremely difficult for many to understand why it suddenly became ineffective in the 1970s.

The apparent success of Keynesianism in the period of high economic growth needs another type of explanation, an explanation 'from below', within the dynamism of capital accumulation. To this end, the French Regulation School presented the model of the Fordist regime of accumulation, which emphasized the rise in real wages in line with the increase in productivity by means of an explicit or implicit capital–labour accord.[2] This was an effective critique of Keynesianism and an important contribution to the clarification of the basic logic of capitalist development in this period. This model of Fordism accords with social democracy in highlighting the effective role of trade unions and the supplemental role of welfare state policies for economic growth.

Nevertheless, the model of Fordism was presented as if it were an abstract theoretical model of contemporary capitalism which replaced Keynesian theory. It was regarded as a new model of capitalism substituting for the older model of imperialism or the even older model of competitive capitalism in *Capital*. At such an abstract level, it was not combined with more concrete historical analysis of the conditions favourable for capital accumulation and suitable for the development of Fordism. As a result its weakness was in the difficulty to explain, within its own theoretical framework, why the successful process of continuous economic growth had to end, not unlike the weakness of Keynesian theory.

Concrete conditions for high economic growth

Four historical conditions can be identified as forming an essential framework for high economic growth in this period.

The first was the strong international competitive power of the US economy. This condition was necessary to maintain the convertibility of dollars into gold as a stable foundation of the Bretton Woods international monetary system along with US overseas public expenditures and private investment on a large scale.

The second was the availability of a series of technological frontiers for producing more and more sophisticated consumer durables by massive industrial investment in fixed capital. The expansion of effective demand by working people on the model of Fordism was essential for marketing sophisticated consumer durables such as the various electric home appliances and cars produced by means of increasing the scale of mass production. The relevancy of the model of Fordism must be understood in this historical context.

The third condition was the continuous increase of relatively cheap primary products in the world market, largely from Third-World countries. Among others a cheap and plentiful supply of oil from Middle Eastern countries at a price of less than two dollars per barrel was an essential precondition for the constructing high-energy-consuming type of social structure of mass consumption.

The fourth condition was the availability of a sufficient number of docile workers with a suitable level of education to be adaptable to the changing technologies in the advanced countries, as capital accumulation continuously expanded employment. The primary sources capital could draw upon to absorb the wage workers it needed for its expanded accumulation included workers released from the war mobilization, the latent industrial reserve army in agriculture, the increasing participation of women in labour markets, immigrant foreign workers and the growth of population.

As I have argued elsewhere in greater detail (Itoh 1990), the period of high economic growth was facilitated by these concrete historical conditions. The apparent success of Keynesianism and the virtuous circle of the Fordist model could not exist without them. When these conditions were undermined, Keynesian policies could not prevent the end of the 'Golden Age', and instead promoted inflationary crisis and stagflation after 1973, and subsequently had to be abandoned.

The spiral reversal of historical development

The Bretton Woods international monetary system actually collapsed when the US lost its economic hegemony in international trade and was no longer able to maintain the convertibility of dollars into gold. The transition to a system of floating exchange rates ignited highly unstable developments in money and finance. In the advanced capitalist countries, this was combined with the overaccumulation of capital in relation to the inflexible supply of labour-power and primary products as a result of a continuous process of high economic growth, causing speculative and vicious inflation – the destructive inflationary crisis and stagflation of the 1970s. Then in the 1980s, the counter-inflationary monetarist policies with the crowding-out effect of the huge budget deficit in the Reagan administration raised the US rate of interest. The international disparity in rates of interest was greatly widened, and this triggered massive international speculative trading of currencies, securities and derivatives. Huge bubbles swelled successively in Japan and the surrounding Asian countries, among others since the late 1980s with a lowered rate of interest and their burst has created enormous economic difficulties. Although the US economy enjoyed a strong recovery in the 1990s, along with a prosperous stock market, the US bubble boom may also collapse. Especially the lowered real income of the majority of workers would then eventually limit the expansion of the US market in the long run.

In this period of recurrent economic crises and instability, the survival efforts of capitalist firms have led to the introduction of ever more sophisticated information technologies. Along with the wide-ranging impact of the information revolution, the current phase of capitalist development has spirally reversed its tendency over the past century to restrict competitive free markets in five ways. Consequently the competitive market order has been revitalized all over the world.

1. In the restructuring process, capitalist firms have introduced microelectronic (ME) automation systems into both factories and offices. They could thus raise labour productivity elastically by relatively smaller units of investment. Multiple models of cars, electric appliances and clothes can be flexibly produced by the same automated production lines to sell in individualistic consumer markets. As product lines

become more diversified and rapidly changing, monopolistic price control among industrial firms becomes difficult to form and maintain, and competitive rivalry is greatly intensified both domestically and internationally.

By means of ME information technologies, capitalist firms have also increased flexibility by relocating manufacturing and business sites, thereby reinforcing global competition across borders. Regional economic development has become more uneven as most rapidly growing tertiary sectors such as finance, trading and other services tend to concentrate their activities in big business centres.

The financial market has also become widely globalized and has intensified competition across different financial areas and sectors.

2. As ME automation spread in factories, offices and shops, capitalist firms could dispense with a large part of their skilled and experienced workers, while they increased flexible forms of irregular employment such as housewife part-timers, seasonal workers and temporary workers often sent from other companies. The employment of cheap foreign workers, in many cases without work permits, has also increased. The international mobility of the labour force has thus continuously increased as an aspect of the globalization of the market economy.

As a result of these trends, traditional trade unions have suffered a decline in their rate of organization and a weakening of their social position. Workers are segmented into different types of employment and have to compete with various kinds of cheaper workers in the labour market. Hence, the labour market too has been restructured into a more competitive market. Capitalist firms are able flexibly to choose different types of workers in combination to economize operational costs. Unlike in the 1960s period of rapid economic growth under the 'Fordist regime of accumulation', trade unions have consistently failed to raise real wages despite increased labour productivity. Even a decline of real wages has become a reality for many workers. The unevenness of wage rates and income distribution has therefore increased conspicuously even within the advanced capitalist countries.[3]

3. In the meantime the economic role of the state has been much reduced as a result of the failure of Keynesianism to solve prolonged stagflation and the cumulative fiscal crisis of the state. Since the beginning of the 1980s, neo-liberalism with its ideological commitment to the competitive free market has replaced Keynesianism as the dominant policy stance in the capitalist world. Public enterprises have been privatized and deregulation has promoted freer market competition everywhere. State expenditures in welfare, education and medical services have been reduced, and the number of public servants has been cut back. These neo-liberal policies are not merely a reaction to the failure of Keynesianism, but have deeper roots in the real trend to revitalize the competitive capitalist market

throughout the world. At the same time, neo-liberalism clearly stands against trade unionism, social democracy and, above all, socialism.

4. Accompanying these changes, the globalization of the market economy has regained momentum. Capitalism seems to be restoring its vitality through an historic crisis by returning to its original mother sea of the world market. The contemporary characteristics of economic globalization, however, include the widespread use of microelectronic information technologies, the multinationalization of capitalist firms in many business areas including manufacturing, and the increased speculative flow of money and finance throughout the world. National states have become less effective as regulators or controllers of national capitals as capital has intensified its multinational activities. The economic intervention of the state has been weakened with the intensified globalization of multinational capitalist firms.

The strong trend towards globalization is also used as an ideology to support neo-liberal policies such as deregulation, tax reduction for the wealthy and capitalist corporations, and a more open market economy. The Washington–IMF axis tends to represent this ideology and often advises others to follow the American model of business and market order as a *de facto* world-standard for all economies in the age of globalization.

5. While the capitalist economy has spontaneously striven to restructure through continuous economic crises, mainly by introducing ME technologies as well as new policies, the Soviet type of socialism with its hypertrophied inelastic state and party bureaucracy was unable to change either its industrial technologies or its type of socialism in the face of economic stagnation. The difficulty of transforming the economic order through restructuring eventually led to the dissolution of the regime itself in Eastern Europe and the USSR, via the increased demands for a market economy and democracy as well as growing ethnic and nationalist tensions.[4] As a result, the move towards a capitalist market economy in one way or the other has been pursued in Russia and most of the East European countries.

China has maintained the leadership of the Communist Party and is experimenting with a socialist market economy rather successfully measured in terms of economic growth since 1978. Vietnam and Cuba are following this experiment. However, the socialist market economy in these countries no longer seems to be an oppositional economic order, but instead has become a more open market for multinational capital.

All of these systemic changes in the former centrally planned economies have globally re-extended the space for multinational capitalist firms to invest and merchandise. Both the actual and ideological grounds for globalization and neo-liberalism were advanced by these systemic changes.[5]

The strong tide of capitalist globalization with mega-competition and neo-liberalism is not the product of a simple linear historical evolution of capitalism since its origins and development. It signifies a spiral historical reversal backward, after a century of attempts by capital, workers and states to regulate the free competitive market, as well as by socialism to construct planned economies without a free market. In the midst of the current transformations underway, as we have seen, capitalism is restoring the competitive vitality of the market economy in the depths of its historical crisis. Correspondingly, individualism and competitive freedom in the market order, not concerns for substantial economic equality or fraternity, have become the dominant ideology in the world.

Implications for the new century

The second historical spiral twist

Capitalism is full of paradoxes both in its basic workings and in its historical development. The periodization of capitalism into phases therefore does not necessarily imply a linear progress towards socialism along a single trajectory. Schumpeter's creative destruction occurs not just in regular business cycles, through phases of periodic crisis and recession, but also on a larger scale in the unexpected turns taken through great depressions like the late nineteenth century, the 1930s, and the current period.

Unexpectedly, capitalist development in our age entered a process of spiral historical reversal back towards competitive free market capitalism with a strong tendency towards globalization. It is the second large-scale spiral reversal in the history of capitalist development. The first reversal turned capitalist development from competitive free trade with a tendency to globalization, to a reintensification of state power, nationalism and market regulation. The development and spread of Soviet socialism accentuated the tendency for regulatory statism as a reaction among capitalist countries.

The second historical reversal of capitalist development toward deregulated competitive market capitalism is then also accentuated by the unexpected dissolution of Soviet socialism. Uno's understanding of world history after the First World War as a transitional period toward socialism is in trouble. The progress towards socialism in world history may contain spiral twists to and fro on a large scale, just as does the world history of capitalism.

These reflections suggest that the neo-liberal belief in the victory of free market capitalism on a global scale and the so-called failure of socialism in the last phase of the twentieth century is not a final conclusion to history. Broader options for the mass of people must surely be reopened among different types of capitalism and socialism in the twenty-first century.

Disillusions of neo-liberalism and fundamental problems of capitalism

Despite its belief in the economic efficiency and rationality of a competitive free market order, neo-liberalism has already revealed its inability to deliver on its promises. Under neo-liberal economic policies of deregulation, the instability of monetary and financial systems has greatly increased throughout the world, and caused the devastating swelling and bursting of speculative bubbles in Japan and other Asian countries, among others. Neo-liberalism arrogantly asserts that these destructive developments are due to imperfections in the transparent competitive market. This neglects the historical reality that capitalist market economies cannot be the purely individualistic social orders found in orthodox textbooks, but rather are always based upon various non-market political and communal human relations, such as nation states, political parties, families, local communities, trade unions, and cooperatives. The ideologies of neo-liberalism and globalization shift the burden of the economic and fiscal crisis onto the mass of working people, to the benefit of transnational corporations and the wealthy. Emergency economic policies place priority on public spending to rescue big businesses and banks, neglecting the needs of the vast majority. Neo-liberalism is unmistakably reintensifying the class-divided nature of contemporary society, with results that are especially obvious in the widening gap in income distribution.

As neo-liberalism is based upon the spiral historical reversal of capitalist development, reviving its fundamental vitality in the competitive market, its limitations are deeply rooted in the basic historical contradictions of the capitalist economy itself. Indeed the capitalist economy is increasingly demonstrating its intrinsic limitations in this period of recurrent crises. Capital accumulation has revealed the difficulty of maintaining the balance between the demand and supply of human labour-power as a commodity in the labour market. The managed currency system with floating exchange rates has heightened financial instability. And capitalist societies have become increasingly polarized between a small group of wealthy asset owners and a repressed mass of workers suffering under conditions of worsening economic inequality. The capitalist economies are clearly exploiting and devastating both human beings and nature with renewed intensity, and deepening social and ecological crises around the world.

Thus, the phase of capitalist development in the current economic downturn after the period of high economic growth signifies not just a new mode of contemporary capitalism, but also a revival of its fundamental workings and contradictions. The basic principles of the capitalist economy as theorized in *Capital* have in fact become *more* directly relevant to understanding the current phase of capitalism than in preceding phases. This suggests as well that socialism, as a fundamental critique and alternative to the capitalist economic order, could conceivably regain its relevancy in the new century if the failures of the Soviet type of socialism can be theoretically and practically overcome. Indeed it is dubious whether alternatives confined within the framework of capitalism, such as a return to Keynesianism, can solve all the serious problems in contemporary capitalism.

Diversification in globalization

To open up the full range of possible paths for the restructuring of political and economic orders in the twenty-first century, it is noteworthy that the process of globalization in our age is not necessarily homogenizing the economic systems of the world. Despite economic globalization and 'the great civilizing influence of capital' (Marx 1973: 409), which homogenizes the style of production and consumption everywhere in the world, there is a paradoxical counter-tendency generating a diversification of politico-economic systems.

In the preceding phase of high economic growth, the US economic system represented the leading model for the rest of the capitalist world. In the analysis of the French Regulation School, it was assumed that the same Fordist regime of accumulation spread from the US to the other advanced capitalist countries in that period. By contrast, the same Regulation School today underlines the diversification of trajectories among advanced capitalist countries in the period of after-Fordism. Three distinct models of restructuring are identified as the most important. The US model of neo-Fordism raises the productivity and intensity of labour without redistributing the fruits to its workers. The Swedish model of Volvoism strengthens the basis of social democracy, especially by offering workers greater participation in decision-making. While the Japanese model of Toyotism flexibly rotates multi-skilled workers within firms by maintaining their loyalty and cooperation. In the Asian countries surrounding Japan, there is even further diversity of political-economic orders.

Why has the diversification of economic systems become so conspicuous in the recent process of restructuring and globalization? An important factor to consider when answering this is the flexible adaptability of information technologies (Pgano 1999). In contrast to the dominant industrial technologies which shaped the Fordist regime of accumulation by constructing huge plants for the mass production of more or less uniform models of consumer durables, information technologies have reopened opportunities for different sizes of plants and business firms and types of business. At the same time, information technologies have enabled capital to use various types and levels of workers, flexibly and in combination, both domestically and internationally.

In addition, multinational firms in the form of joint-stock companies can organize their internal operations in many different ways. For example, firms now have greater flexibility in how they divide internal departments, branches and factories, and what degree of independence these operations are given. There are different ways to organize vertical and horizontal relations within firms and on the shop floor. The capitalist market economy cannot dissolve societies completely into atomic individuals. It must leave intact both communal and authoritative non-market human relations, such as those within firms, and within families. In such non-market human relations, historical, cultural and habitual traditions tend to be resilient and to diversify across different societies, even though they are also subject to constant change.

Multinational firms make the most of both the qualitative and quantitative diversity of societies by means of information technologies. If all societies became truly homogenous, firms would no longer need to invest abroad. For multinationals, one of the most important motivations to invest abroad is to make use of and combine different social conditions. In this way, multinationals take advantage of the diversity of social orders in the distribution and rationalization of their activities, at the same time as they promote the globalization of economies.

The tendencies of diversification interact with processes of regional economic integration as well. It is often argued that the regional integration of Europe through the formation of the European Union (EU) enhances the mobility of capital and labour-power across borders, and thereby offers a suitable environment for contemporary multinational corporations. EU integration is assumed to be a desirable path for economic recovery and growth. What will the future reveal? EU integration will further increase the pressures towards homogeneity in Europe. Can Europe solve its high rate of unemployment and economic stagnation and become a growing centre of the world economy? Or can Asia with its characteristic heterogeneity maintain its dynamism and achieve higher economic growth as a region? Such a comparison of the dynamism of these two regions is another interesting issue from the perspective of diversification and globalization tendencies as we move into the twenty-first century.

Tendencies towards diversification are not limited to the paths of capitalist development either. China, with its high economic growth, is showing viability as a socialist market economy despite the various problems that remain to be solved in the future. Vietnam and Cuba are following this model of socialism. The Russian Communist Party is regaining support among the Russian people for its programme to restore a socialist planned economy on the basis of public ownership of the primary means of production combined with political democracy. The feasibility of various models of market socialism is also being re-examined at the level of theory (see for instance Bardhan and Roemer 1993).

Just as with the different phases of capitalist development in world history, we see a synchronic diversity of politico-economic orders in the current world, despite a strong trend towards the globalization of capitalism.

This suggests that people in different countries and regions have a range of alternatives available to them beyond the narrow limits of neo-liberalism and the US model in forging their own social path of progress in the new century.

Notes

1   The contents of Uno's stages theory of capitalist development were presented in Uno (1971), while his methodology of Marxist political economy as a whole was presented in Uno (1962). See Itoh (1980: chapter 1) for a more detailed account of Uno's original contributions to political economy. An important attempt to apply and extend Uno's stages theory of capitalist development is Albritton (1991). Albritton added a fourth stage of consumerism, which was typically formed in 1950s–1970s. I am still hesitant to break with Uno's methodology, which completed the stages theory of capitalist development with the classic stage of imperialism, and treated the periods after that at the level of concrete empirical analysis. Albritton's inclusion of neo-liberalism together with Keynesianism as representative ideologies of this fourth stage seems also difficult to follow and rather confusing, as it obscures an important historical turn of capitalist development in our age, on which this chapter concentrates.
2   The French Regulation School was given a basis for further development by Michel Aglietta (1979), followed up and extended to the more recent phase of capitalist development by Boyer (1986) and Yamada (1991) among others.
3   Even in the Japanese economy, for example, the inequality of income distribution has conspicuously increased. Although the Japanese economy formed a relatively egalitarian society through the period of high economic growth, it has largely lost this characteristic since then. Tachibanaki (1998: 5–6) revealed that the degree of unevenness of Japanese income distribution increased rapidly in the recent decade. The Gini coefficient of Japanese income distribution before tax rose remarkably by almost 0.1 in 1980–92. This has resulted in the striking fact that the unevenness of income distribution in Japan is now greater than that in the US.
4   For further detail, see Itoh (1995).
5   Thus, just after the collapse of the USSR, Fukuyama (1992) presented the view that world history had come to an end with the final victory of the capitalist free market economy and liberal democracy over Marx's socialism.

8
Capitalism in the Future Perfect Tense

Robert Albritton

Every day capitalists speculate on all kinds of 'futures', often referred to as 'derivatives', suggesting the possibility of gambling on almost any kind of future as long as through an operation of derivation an underlying asset can be given a commodity form and a price.[1] As Barings Bank discovered, these new financial products can sometimes be costly. Which only goes to show that predicting the value of a particular currency on a particular future date is difficult given the huge number of variables involved. Thirty years ago, no one could have predicted the incredible proliferation of derivatives in recent years.[2] And yet, however much the derivative form expands, capitalism itself has not yet been packaged as a derivative. Capitalists do not want to consider that one could gamble over the future of capitalism as a whole. For them capitalism is forever.

While capitalists speculate about the future all the time, in the social sciences these days such speculation is discouraged. Like capitalists I want to speculate about the future, but unlike them I shall speculate about the future as a transition away from capitalism. Also, contrary to their multivariable quantitative speculation, my speculation will be about structural constraints that place limits on capitalism's future. It is my argument that if we place ourselves imaginatively in the year 2100, we will look back on the twenty-first century as the century of transition away from capitalism. Given the past predictions of capitalism's imminent demise, it is natural to approach this topic with caution. Also, to argue that capitalism is faced with insuperable structural constraints does not say anything about the creation of socialism. What follows capitalism could be even more barbaric, unless we seize the opportunities that will be presented in this century to move towards democratic socialism. Thus I certainly do not want to be understood as presenting any sort of mechanical or automatic transition from capitalism to socialism. Instead I want to think carefully and systematically about the limits of capitalism and its possible end.

Further, it is beyond the scope of this chapter to discuss all of the contradictions and structural constraints that may in the future weaken or undermine capitalism. Rather, I shall use the levels of analysis approach developed by Japanese political economists Uno and Sekine to focus my analysis.[3] Central to this approach is first of all an emphasis on clarifying what capitalism is by theorizing its inner logic. In order to discuss the end of something, it helps to be clear about precisely what it is that is coming to an end. Second, this inner logic never operates without interventions and resistances at the level of history, resulting in a vast plurality of capitalist forms. And this move from the theory of capital's inner logic to the complexities of historical development is mediated through the use of levels of analysis. Following Uno and Sekine, I shall call these levels: the level of the theory of pure capitalism, the level of stage theory (no teleology intended),[4] and the level of historical analysis. In what follows I shall consider what each level might contribute to thinking about the possibility that capitalism will have come to an end by the end of the next century.

The theory of pure capitalism

In order to theorize capital's inner logic, we must imagine a society in which all production is production of commodities by commodified labour-power organized by capitalists to maximize profits. In such a society capital is 'self-expanding value', and this implies that economic social relations are reduced totally to value that operates commodity-economically without outside support to expand itself. In short, we must imagine an economy totally governed by markets, and we must imagine that markets are totally self-regulating. It follows that there is no organized human intervention into the economy in the form of extra-economic force, whether by the state, by organized capitalists, or by organized workers. And all individuals are either capitalists, workers, or landlords. Capital only becomes self-expanding when the use of money to make more money subsumes the labour and production process. If capital is simply buying cheap and selling dear as in M–C–M', then capital can redistribute wealth, but it cannot create new wealth. It is the commodification of labour-power that is crucial to converting capital from a circulation form into a production relation that becomes the economically dominant principle for a whole historical epoch of capitalist expansion and penetration.

In his *An Outline of the Dialectic of Capital*, Sekine demonstrates that even in this purely capitalist society where capital is assumed to always get its own way, in the long run, the rate of profit must fall 'when the technological base of the aggregate-social capital advances'.[5] It is beyond the scope of this chapter to present his mathematical proof, but the argument is essentially as follows. The higher the level of capitalist productivity, the more and faster must productivity increase to maintain the same rate of profit. While capital never contemplates its own end in a purely capitalist society, we can do so in history. For productivity means essentially that fewer and fewer workers produce more and more, and this would reach a limit with total automation. This must imply total unemployment, total lack of profit, and total inability for anyone to buy the product – in other words, the end of capitalism. Of course, in history capitalism would come to an end long before the rate of profit fell to zero.

This feature of capitalism that Postone has called the 'treadmill effect' proves that capitalism must be mortal, but it is not a 'teleology' in the usual sense of the word.[6] A teleology in this context would imply the realization of a particular end to history as, for example, socialism, but I am only arguing that capitalism must be followed by something else, where 'the something else' could be various possibilities including a vast array of barbarisms or socialisms.

At this level of analysis we are also limited in what we can say conclusively about exactly when or how capitalism might actually come to an end. In a purely capitalist society the falling rate of profit can only be counteracted by raising the rate of exploitation, which in turn can only be raised by increasing productivity (because of competition capitalists cannot by themselves and in the short run increase the length of the working day or increase intensification by very much). In history and with the help of the state, capitalists have discovered various ways to maintain profit rates other than increasing productivity. These include lowering wages, intensifying labour, lengthening the working day, finding cheaper sources of constant capital, redistributing wealth, socializing costs, and subsidizing profits. All of these, however, are rather short-term and limited as compared to increasing productivity. For example, lowering wages too much either could lead to an underconsumption problem or could threaten the very reproduction of the working class. Lengthening the working day or intensifying labour have clear physical limitations. Finding new deposits of higher quality or more accessible raw materials is less and less likely given the extensiveness and intensiveness of the search heretofore. In fact, the cost of many constant capital inputs are likely to rise in the future as supplies of various resources run low. Redistributing wealth through regressive taxation, debt slavery and other measures is also severely limited by underconsumption or by the likelihood of resistance by those being ripped off. Resistance is also likely to place limitations on the use of public funds to socialize costs and subsidize profits. For some time, profit rates have been maintained more by these latter methods than by increased productivity. This is a clear sign that we are in a phase of transition away from the most recent stage of capitalism that I refer to as 'the stage of consumerism'.[7] Since some of these methods may depend increasingly on force or their failure on our ability to resist, the length of the transition and the forms its takes cannot be predicted, though it is difficult to see capitalism persisting for another hundred years.

If pure capitalism is the management of economic life by a commodity-economic logic, then there are two basic, extreme types of alternatives to capitalism: one is a top-down command economy and the other is a bottom-up democratic-socialist economy. Something approximating either of these could follow capitalism and while the democratic economy option is clearly preferable, it is also the more difficult to realize.

Stage theory

A careful study of Sekine's dialectical theory of capital reveals that labour-power, land and money are the three commodities that capital has the most trouble managing commodity-economically, even in a purely capitalist society. All three are implicated in periodic crises, and at the level of stage theory we are particularly interested in the degree to which each of these economic variables is commodified and how the typical forms and degrees of commodification are supported ideologically, legally and politically in different stage-specific modes of capital accumulation. Finally, when capitalism will have come to an end, we would expect significant decommodification of each of these commodities – above all labour-power.

Elsewhere I have argued that capitalism should be periodized according to four basic stages: mercantilism, liberalism, imperialism and consumerism.[8] At each stage I attempt to theorize the modes of capital accumulation that are most decisive and typical for the stage. This is aided by the fact that for each stage there is a kind of 'golden age' when capital was accumulating most successfully. For the stage of mercantilism the golden age of capital accumulation is most apparent in England between 1700 and 1750, for liberalism it is in England between 1840 and 1870, for imperialism it is in Germany and the US between 1890 and 1914, and for consumerism it is in the US between 1950 and 1970. Each stage is named for the dominant type of state policy and ideology that supports capital accumulation. Thus the stage of mercantilism is so named because the accumulation of capital through a putting-out system is supported by mercantilist ideologies and state policies, and similarly consumerism implies that the production of consumer durables by transnational corporations is supported by consumer-ist ideologies and state policies.

In each stage, capital accumulation always centrally involves a particular organization of capital, a particular capital–labour relation, and particular sectors that are the dynamic centre of capitalist expansion. Thus the stage of mercantilism centrally involves a putting-out system organized by merchant capital most typically and expansively in the putting-out production of woollens. The stage of liberalism is centred around competitive light indus-try organized by entrepreneurial capital most typically in cotton manufac-turing. The stage of imperialism is centred around monopolistic heavy industry organized by finance capital most typically in the steel industry. The stage of consumerism is centred around consumer durable industries organized by transnational capital most typically in the auto industry.[9]

Except for the first stage when capitalism was still embryonic, all subsequent stages had golden ages that lasted 20 to 30 years. The periods between these golden ages are transitional and are marked by the turbulence of economic crises, revolution and war. The length of the transitional phases vary greatly depending in part on how radical the change is from one stage to the next. For example, the change from putting-out production to factory production is arguably more radical than that from the centrality of light industry characteristic of liberalism to the dominance of heavy industry characteristic of imperialism. It is not surprising then that the transition from the golden age of mercantilism to the golden age of liberalism was some 90 years and was marked by the American and French revolutions, whereas the transition from liberalism to imperialism marked by the great depression of 1873 lasted only about 20 years.

I agree with Arrighi's argument that progressive phases (golden ages) of capital accumulation are marked by the expansion of material production, whereas transitional phases are marked by the predominance of financial capital that redistributes wealth more than it creates new wealth.[10] Thus the golden age of consumerism in the US between 1950 and 1970 was marked by rapid material expansion, whereas all the indices of material growth have fallen since the early 1970s as we move increasingly into a global economy marked by financial wheeling and dealing that Susan Strange has labelled 'casino capitalism'.

According to my analysis, we are now in a phase of transition away from consumerism, which may of course have interesting sub-phases. The big question is whether this transition will lead to yet a new golden age (or stage) or away from capitalism.

The decommodification of labour-power

At least some degree of the commodification of labour-power is perhaps the most necessary condition for the existence of capitalism. In a purely capitalist society the commodity form is fully established and this implies that labour-power is totally commodified. In such a situation the following conditions would ensue: (1) workers would be totally separated from the means of production, (2) there would be no organized human intervention into the labour market (trade unions, state policy, and so on), (3) workers would be mobile, (4) on average they would receive the value of their necessary labour, and (5) capital would be totally indifferent to labour-power except as a value-expanding commodity input into the production process. Of course in history none of these five conditions of total commodification is ever met completely on a global scale. Yet these criteria are useful benchmarks for measuring the degree of commodification.

These conditions are not of equal importance since it is the separation of workers from the means of production and the existence of a competitive labour market that are crucial. Thus any move that increases worker control over the means of production or lessens the competitiveness of labour markets is a move towards the decommodification of labour-power. Inroads on capital's absolute property rights over the means of production achieved through collective bargaining, legislatively, or through popular opinion may in some cases be important steps towards decommodification. Similarly protections against the extreme insecurity generated by a purely competitive labour market may also be seen as moves towards decommodification. At some point, which cannot be precisely specified, worker control over the means of production and protection of workers against the market whip of economic insecurity would produce a decommodification of labour-power inconsistent with the successful continuation of capitalism. Such a point would imply that capital could no longer successfully reverse the process of decommodification through recommodification.

As the only commodity input that can add more value than its cost to the product, labour-power is ultimately the source of all profit. In history capitalism has always benefited to some extent from forced labour, but at its core it has always featured reliance upon labour markets and formally 'free' wage slaves. Indeed, it is this formal freedom that capitalists like to point to as they sing the praises of capitalism as opposed to those terrible systems of forced labour, which they condemn even as they utilize them as sources of cheap labour to increase their profits.[11]

Each golden age features a core sector of production that with its forward and backward linkages serves as the main engine of growth. In the stage of liberalism it is cotton manufacturing that is particularly expansive. Cotton manufacturing not only provided the most new industrial jobs in Britain, but it stimulated the growth of transportation systems (ships and railways), of coal mining, of iron production, of machine production, of clothing production, and clothing retail.

The capitalist production relations in the stage of liberalism are most developed in England, but even there the class of wage labours was not a majority of the population. The number of factory workers was third after domestic servants and agricultural workers, and while some agricultural workers were wage workers, many were also petty commodity producers.[12] Labour-power may have been the most commodified that it ever is in history in Britain in this stage. Trade unions as a principal form of worker self-organization were weak and legislation favoured competitive labour markets. While the labour-power that was commodified was very commodified, large segments of the population remained outside the labour market even as Britain became the 'workshop of the world'. Of course, outside Britain the percentage of the population participating in the labour market was smaller yet. Thus while British labour markets where competitive in this stage and the labour-power that was commodified was quite commodified, a great deal of the total labour, though possibly influenced by wage labour, could not really be considered commodified. Furthermore, while this stage featured weak unions and a 'New Poor Law' that removed poor relief from able-bodied men unless they submitted to the discipline of workhouses, there were many rules both formal and informal about skill and about who could do what kind of labour.[13] Also there were many forms of worker organization from informal shop-floor organization to embryonic craft unions. Furthermore, status consciousness was very strong and capitalists often attempted to gain worker cooperation through various forms of paternalism. Thus even in this stage in cotton manufacturing in Britain, labour-power was far from being totally commodified.

The stage theory of consumerism, derived from the golden age of capital accumulation in the US from 1950 to 1970, presents a picture in which a greater proportion of labour-power is commodified, but on average it is commodified less than in the stage of liberalism. The harsh effects of labour market competition are softened by extensive 'safety nets', and strong trade unions make some inroads into management rights. For example, in the American auto industry management can no longer fire workers at will, workers can grieve mistreatment, the speed of the line has limits, there are limits on forced overtime, and management must take some responsibility for health and safety. These moves towards the decommodification of labour-power reflect the power of workers and the need to placate them in order to preserve the labour market and capitalist control over the means of production. Also, the possibility of this rather costly degree of decommodification depended on the continuing prosperity and high growth rates of the US economy.

While this is significant, proof that the degree of decommodification of labour-power associated with the golden age remained within the confines of the continuation of capitalism is the subsequent recommodification that has occurred since 1970 in the phase of transition away from the golden age. The trend in this phase of transition is towards the increasing dominance of financial capital as high rates of material expansion of wealth are increasingly replaced by financial wheeling and dealing that tends to redistribute wealth more than it creates new wealth.

It is my argument in this chapter that the phase of transition away from consumerism is also a phase of transition away from capitalism. Thus it is my claim that the current apparent recommodification of labour-power is not the harbinger of a new golden age of capitalism, but is the product of a hypertrophic financial capitalism that through globalization has managed to inject radically increased degrees of competition into labour markets. This is in line with my claim that financial capital tends to redistribute wealth more than create new wealth. On a global scale this means that wealth is redistributed from working people to capitalists, from poorer countries to richer countries, from debtors to creditors, from consumers to capitalists, from smaller capitalists to larger, from taxpayers to capitalists, and finally from all non-financial capital to financial capital.[14] This redistribution can have only a limited life span because the growing inequality and insecurity that results will lead to resistance and to mounting underconsumption problems that will generate crises.

Besides the growing inequality, there are other reasons to believe that the recommodification of labour-power will have a limited life span. Principal of these is growing global unemployment and underemployment. According to ILO statistics, approximately one-third of the global workforce is unemployed or underemployed. In the US, according to official statistics, unemployment averaged 4.8 per cent in the 1960s, 6.2 per cent in the 1970s, and 7.3 per cent in the 1980s.[15] While the statistics for the 1990s will probably be better than those for the 1980s this will be due to the bubble economy that has largely improved employment in the US at the expense of the rest of the world.[16] Furthermore, most of the new jobs in the US are low wage.[17]

Even if the short-term growth rate of global capitalism should pick up for a while and population growth should decline, the advance of labour-saving technologies will radically reduce the demand for workers. As productivity advances and fewer and fewer produce more and more, radical changes will be required including a 30-hour work week, a guaranteed annual income and improved safety nets, an increase in paid community service work, and improved access to education and training. All of these changes will tend to support the decommodification of labour-power. For example, as people work less hours they will have more time for self-organization and participatory democracy. A guaranteed annual income above the poverty line will mean that people will not have to accept low-paying sweatshop jobs and will become free from the whip of economic insecurity that drives competitive labour markets.

The decommodification of land

Throughout much of the world and much of the history of capitalism a great deal of land has been held by landlords whose aim has been to preserve and expand their land holdings across generations. Also land has been controlled by states. As a result, while formally commodified, the wholesale buying and selling of land in competitive markets has been constrained. It is primarily in the US that land has been open to unbridled capitalist exploitation from early on. The result has been terrible environmental destruction and the development of an industrially based agribusiness that is tied in with the chemical and biotech industries. This combination has proved to be effective in radically improving short-term agricultural productivity at the long-run cost of degrading the land, polluting the water, exhausting water supplies, and damaging human health.

Unsustainable agriculture is only one byproduct flowing from the com-modification of the land. Rapid depletion of non-renewable resources, the destruction of rain forests and other old growth forests, the building of dams, and urbanization have also been facilitated by a commodification of the land that has taken its toll. The commodification of land is really the same thing as the commodification of nature, and the effect is to subord-inate nature to the imperative of short-term profit.

The neo-liberal policies promoted by financial capital have largely thwarted the efforts of environmental movements to improve our relation with nature. Environmental protection legislation has been eroded and has often not been enforced. Even the gutless Kyoto agreement to limit green-house gas emissions already seems to be a dead letter, as such emissions increase every year. In their search for environmental policies consistent with the market, some neo-liberals have proposed ecological taxes, but so far no one has taken up this proposal with much enthusiasm since it would increase the cost of commodities for the poor and reduce the profits of the rich. Indeed, a truly radical system of 'ecological taxes' would internal-ize all environmental costs and benefits into the price system resulting in a system of ecological prices, or in other words of planned prices in opposition to market prices. But the alternative price structure would only be accept-able after a redistribution of wealth that would not penalize the poor. All of this implies a radical move away from capitalism towards democratic socialism.

Our relation to the earth is in a state of deep crisis, which short-term profit orientations can only worsen. There is simply no alternative to long-range planning when it comes to preserving the environment. This must among other things result in the decommodification of land, a decommodification that is followed by a very different kind of relation to the land. The land needs to be viewed as something like a sacred trust that each generation does its best to preserve and even improve for future generations.

The decommodification of money

In a purely capitalist society the role of the state in connection with money is simply to passively make the currency official. Unlike labour-power and land, money is a capitalistically produced commodity, and yet unlike all other such commodities it is the universal equivalent. In order for money to be commodity-economically managed it must be gold and convertible cur-rency. Both monetary and non-monetary gold are produced by the gold industry, and a certain percentage of circulating gold can be replaced by gold symbols. If the total commodity value that needs to be circulated exceeds the total of circulating money, then some portion of idle money will become active, non-monetary gold will become monetary gold, and a greater portion of material and human resources will be devoted to gold production (Sekine 1997, I: 65). In other words, the supply of money is regulated by value, as is the supply of all other commodities.

At the level of stage theory, money is never totally regulated by the motion of value, though the closest it comes is in the stage of liberalism. In the history of capitalism the gold supply depended first on pillage and second on new discoveries of gold deposits – its supply never had the flexibility assumed in pure capitalism. At the level of stage theory, we can no longer assume a single unified monetary system: rather there is an international, national and sometimes regional or local monetary system with varying degrees of autonomy or interpenetration. Also, both credit money or fiat money can be easily overissued, causing inflation. Balance of payments shortfalls may cause too much gold to leave the country thus undermining the domestic monetary system. Finally, given the importance of having a relatively fine-tuned money supply for a healthy economy, the state or the central bank has always stepped in to some extent to regulate the money supply.

In the stage of liberalism, a number of fortuitous circumstances conspired to make a gold-based monetary system work quite well. The Bank of England had by then become a strong central bank committed to maintain stable gold prices, and Britain so dominated the global economy that the international monetary system was to a large extent a projection of Britain's domestic monetary system. Debt expansion was constrained by small state expenditures, balanced budgets, and self-financing industry. Enough gold flowed into the monetary system due to significant gold discoveries throughout the world. Thus while the Bank of England did manipulate the money supply to some extent and costs of adjustment could generally be passed on to weaker countries because of British hegemony, yet even at the more concrete level of stage theory, it is accurate to theorize a high degree of commodity-economic management of money in the stage of liberalism.

In comparison, when we theorize the management of money in the stage of consumerism, it is definitely less commodified, though the quasi-political management of money characteristic of this stage is meant to at least partially imitate the stability of the gold standard, while giving nation-states enough autonomy to effectively utilize counter-cyclical Keynesian policies. Other currencies were to be pegged to the US dollar, which was to be pegged to gold at 35 dollars per ounce. All countries were to be committed to stable exchange rates, and governments were expected to buy or sell their currency in foreign exchange markets to maintain stable exchange rates. A country facing chronic balance of payments deficits could alter their exchange rate, but changes of over 10 per cent would require the approval of the International Monetary Fund.

This system worked to some extent because of the hegemony of the US and because of the cold war that spawned international liquidity by continually sending US dollars abroad. Eventually, however, this spawning contributed to severe balance of payments deficits, debt expansion, and inflation in the US economy. And these tendencies ultimately forced the US to break with the gold standard in favour of freely fluctuating currencies in the early 1970s. It is these changes that signal the end of the 'golden age' of consumerism and mark the beginning of the phase of transition away from consumerism. This is the beginning of the slowdown in the rate of growth of the global economy, of growing unemployment, of huge debt expansion including ecological debt, and the growing separation of money and finance from the real economy.[18] The golden age has been followed by a 'leaden age'.[19]

Does this ending of the gold standard mean that money has become completely decommodified in the sense that it has no connection with value whatsoever? I think not. And that is because we now have human institutions that attempt to do the same thing as the gold standard, that is, to maintain the market regulation of money as much as possible, interfering only when deflation or inflation indicate the need. In today's global economy it is international currency markets, the flow of international finance and the International Monetary Fund that play the disciplinary function that the gold standard played in the nineteenth and early twentieth centuries. Thus the partial decommodification of money could be seen as a strategy to maintain and advance the commodification of other dimensions of capitalism and hence to promote its continuation. It is necessary to distinguish between forms of partial decommodification that can be viewed as compromises forced upon capitalism in one area to strengthen its hold in other areas as opposed to decommodification that undermines capitalism altogether. Or in other words, we need to distinguish between decommodification that buys time for capitalism and decommodification that diminishes its life span.

Current trends towards the deregulation and globalization of money and financial markets combined with unprecedented debt expansion tend to generate an international bubble economy in which the monetary economy continually threatens the real economy by its instability and hypertrophy.[20] Since the Second World War a deep global crisis that could have served the function of bringing the monetary economy back in line with the real economy has not been allowed to occur. Indeed, such a depression would likely be considerably worse and more protracted than the 1929 depression, jeopardizing the future of capitalism. In order to avoid global depression significant economic actors, whether political units or corporations, are no longer allowed to go bankrupt. Instead debt expansion has been allowed to mushroom to enormous proportions and along with it a global financial system, run by creditors determined not to be paid back in inflated currencies even if it means advocating the most inhumane austerity policies that increase inequality and unemployment.

Governments are being forced to dance to the tune of financial capital as the big creditors increasingly run the world.[21] Speculative runs on national currencies can overnight spin economies into disaster, high debt levels transfer wealth from poor countries to rich countries and result in a new form of debt slavery, and the IMF with its 'structural adjustment policies' waits in the wings to impose austerity policies which are about as successful in helping countries get out of debt as old-fashioned debtor prisons.

It is in the interest of creditors to expand debt as much as possible consistent with some possibility of being paid back. The problem is that debt can become a vicious circle with indebtedness breeding yet deeper indebtedness, since all savings that might go to investment must instead go to pay off debt. Casino capitalism can and does reduce entire nations to beggary, as we have seen in Russia and elsewhere.

The partial commodification of money that has in the past served to keep the monetary economy at least periodically in line with the real economy has been replaced by a monetary economy driven by financial speculators to the point where the casino economy now subsumes and radically destabilizes the real economy, wreaking havoc throughout the world. Nearly all the money in the world today is credit money and we know that credit money, which has always had a political dimension, has now become more political than ever before. But this politics is hidden behind ever more deregulated and globalized money and financial markets which appear to be free and impersonal. It is precisely in these kinds of markets that the powerful creditors of the world can continue to transfer the worlds' wealth into their hands. This transfer of wealth from debtors to creditors has become so dominant in the world that actual production has come to play second fiddle. In the current phase of transition away from consumerism, 'rentier' capitalism, referred to in the past by thinkers such as Hobson, Lenin, Hilferding and Bukharin, has reached heights that they could not even have imagined.

What we are witnessing is an apparent recommodification of money by the freeing-up of money and financial markets. Thus it seems on the one hand that money and finance are regulated by perfectly competitive global markets more than ever before. On the other hand, money has become disconnected from gold, and despite human efforts to imitate the gold standard through institutions like the IMF, the money economy is in continual danger of spinning out of control in its disconnection from the real economy. Indeed, the case has been made that at no time in capitalist history has the money economy been at the same time so large and so cut off from the real economy.[22] This is another indication that we are currently not simply in a phase of transition to a new stage of capitalism, but away from capitalism altogether.

Given how fundamentally important money and credit are to human welfare, it is crucial that we find democratic and egalitarian ways of managing them. And this would require a decommodification that is not designed to imitate the gold standard, but instead is designed to meet human needs through democratic controls. To the extent that the current decommodification involves politically hidden hands manipulating markets for the benefit of the few, the cost is radically increased inequality on a global scale and the massive human suffering that results from the drastic depreciation of national currencies or the bursting of speculative bubbles.

While, in the short run, international regulations such as the Tobin tax or regulations of the banking sector might diminish the destabilizing effects of speculation, in the long run it seems unlikely that the money-economy can be brought in line with the real-economy without a deep global depression.[23] In so far as reforms are effective they will not be reforms that aim to 'recommodify money' by freeing up money and financial markets; rather, they will be reforms that further decommodify money by increasing democratic controls over it.

Labour-power, land and money

Decommodification may always tend to lead away from capitalism, but this leading away may be regressive or progressive. To replace wage labour with forced labour is a regression that is less damaging to capitalism than replacing wage labour with cooperative labour. It is this latter change that would tend to radically undermine capitalism. Similarly, to relate to the land as a permanent trust to be democratically controlled is far more radically undermining of capitalism than totalitarian state control of the land. Finally the current monetary system drains power away from localities into the hands of superpowerful financial institutions, and hence, as a reaction, we find experiments with new forms of grassroots financing.

While the pressures against the further commodity-economic management of labour-power, land and money in the coming century are real and ultimately insuperable, there is no guarantee that the ensuing decommodification will not lapse into some kind of regression that will take the form of totalitarianism or fascism. Decommodification presents an opportunity to radically democratize the economy, but mass movements will have to rise to the occasion. The existence of computer technology increases the possibilities of working out effective ways of replacing market prices that privilege short-term profit with prices that reflect a wide range of human values including ecological values.

I have outlined some of the main pressures constraining labour-power, land and money towards decommodification. These pressures are increased when we consider each element as it resonates with the others. The low wages and insecurities of the labour market and worsening working conditions are exacerbated by the ecological crisis, land speculation bubbles, debt expansion, cutbacks in the safety net and in the social wage, structural adjustment policies, currency depreciations, and unstable monetary and financial systems. The ecological crisis is deepened by the extreme competition and growing inequality that sacrifices all to short-term profit. And monetary instability increases as new debt continues to expand even as there is less and less ability to pay back old debt. Indeed the competition among creditors for sound debtors has become so extreme that often caution is thrown to the winds in courting seemingly sound debtors, as we have seen recently in South Korea and elsewhere.

The positive feedback or resonance between the pressures to decommodify labour-power, land and money also mean that the transition away from capitalism will be marked by increasingly severe crises. Indeed the crisis tendencies are becoming pronounced as capitalism runs up against the limits of the exploitability of both land and labour-power. Capital has flooded into export-oriented Asian economies marked by disciplined, low-wage work forces; minimally enforced environmental restrictions; cheap land, energy and infrastructural inputs; tax breaks; and business-friendly governments. These advantages are relatively short-term, as we have seen even in the case of such a miracle economy as that of Japan. A capitalism whose profits depend primarily on the superexploitation of labour-power and land along with financial wheeling and dealing is a capitalism in decline.

Besides the short-term instabilities created by the sudden entry into and exit out of various markets by financial capital, there is the long-term spectre of stagnation and underconsumption on a global scale. Both previous great depressions were preceded by pronounced increased inequality. With growing inequality, effective demand diminishes and profit rates in industry decline as competition increases and along with it the rate of merging and cartelization. As profit rates in industry decline, more capital shifts to the financial sector, but this simply exacerbates the inequality, and hence the vicious circle becomes more vicious.

Transition away from capitalism

One implication of my argument is that neo-liberal ideology and policy are essentially the expressions of financial capital early in a phase of transition away from capitalism. Because neo-liberalism's policies are already proving to be totally bankrupt in dealing with the major problems that we face, it will be relatively short-lived. Neo-liberalism may well be capitalism's swansong, though it is perhaps a travesty to compare something lacking in grace and beauty to a swan.

One of Marx's mistakes was underestimating the difficulties involved in creating democratic socialism even after the success of a popular insurrection. Capitalism so radically disables our cooperative and democratic capabilities that it must be a long and difficult struggle to achieve a society that breaks with the deep-seated alienation of capitalism. I do not for a moment think that we can achieve anything like democratic socialism without passing through a period of enormous global upheaval. We will need to apply all the intelligence we have to design human institutions that can serve long-term human needs as opposed to short-term profits. As a start we will need to ameliorate the obscene inequality that exists in the world.

However long the transition away from capitalism takes, I suspect that by the end of the twenty-first century, markets, driven by short-term profits, will be viewed as terribly crude ways of coordinating social information precisely because such huge amounts of information are left out as 'externalities'. I do not mean to imply that in a democratic-socialist society there will be no use of markets at all. Rather markets will be designed and utilized only in so far as they can promote democracy, equality, freedom and security.

Democratic socialism is a process that started long ago and will never be complete, just as justice will never be complete. It will always be possible to move towards a more just and more democratic society. The tasks associated with moving towards socialism in the coming century will be difficult, but if we are to have a future that is not a nightmare, it is in this direction we must move.

Notes

1 According to Tickell (1999: 251) the average daily turnover of derivatives is $880 billion.
2 Tickell (1999: 251) claims that '[T]he nominal value of derivative contracts outstanding in 1995 was estimated at $30,602 billion ... a growth of over 2800% in ten years.'
3 Besides the important work of Uno and Sekine, see my *Dialectics and Deconstruction in Political Economy* for an outline and defence of the epistemology of this approach. Also while Itoh's work falls into a different sub-school of Uno theory, it is important as part of the general corpus of work inspired by Uno.
4 'Stages' is not meant to imply a teleology as in 'stages of growth'; rather it simply refers to a level of theory and a way of periodizing capitalism.
5 Sekine (1997, II: 53).
6 For a slightly different version of this see Postone's (1993: 347) discussion of the 'treadmill effect'.
7 I theorize the 'golden age' most fully realized in the US between 1950 and 1970 as 'the stage of consumerism', because it is consumerist policies and ideologies that play the central role in supporting capital accumulation (Albritton 1991).
8 I differ with Sekine, who believes that we have been in a phase of transition away from capitalism since the stage of imperialism (1920s) and that there is no capitalist stage after the Second World War.
9 My position on the centrality of the consumer durable industry is similar to that of regulation theory, but on many other issues I differ from them. See my 'Regulation Theory: A Critique', in Albritton and Sekine (1995).
10 Arrighi (1994) extracts this idea from Braudel and develops it further.

11   During phases of transition capital tends to rely more on force, precisely because maintaining or increasing the rate of profit depends less and less on increases in productivity and more and more on various forms of redistribution of wealth or on superexploitation as in 'free production zones' (see McMurtry 1999).

12   Albritton (1991: 127).

13   This and the points immediately following are discussed in Albritton (1991: 129–31).

14   Interest as a portion of profit was 3.8 per cent in 1950–73 and from 1990 to 1996 it grew to 24 per cent. (Brenner 1998: 209). This indicates the radical shift in predominance from industrial capital to financial capital.

15   Official statistics grossly underestimate the real unemployment because they count as unemployed only those who are currently actively seeking work and because they do not include all those who want full-time work but can only find part-time work.

16   Average unemployment in the OECD countries excluding the US is as high as in the 1929 depression (Brenner 1998: 2).

17   One-third of the workers in the US earn less than $15,000 per year (Brenner 1998: 250).

18   From 1978 to 1995 the top 100 US companies laid off an average of 22 per cent of their work force (Brenner 1998: 200). In the 1990s workers in the US averaged annually 164 extra hours of work as compared with workers in the 1970s (van der Pijl 1998: 44). The average rate of profit for the G-7 countries was 40 per cent lower in the period 1970–90 as compared with the period 1950–70 (Brenner 1998: 7). Real wages in private business in the US are down 12 per cent between 1973 and 1990 (1998: 3). In 1997 personal bankruptcies in the US rose from $30 billion for the previous year to $44 billion (Wade and Veneroso 1998: 17).

19   'Leaden age' comes from Pollin (1996: 109).

20   Singh (1999: 7) and Fine *et al.* (1999: 72–3).

21   In the recent SE Asia meltdown private debt was converted into public debt, ultimately forcing the debtor to pay for mistakes that were at least partially those of the creditors (Singh 1999: 96). Further, international financial institutions came up with a $57 billion bailout for South Korea almost overnight, while the same institutions took years to agree to $10 billion in debt relief for desperately poor countries unlikely to ever pay back their debts anyway (Singh 1999: 101).

22   For example, see McMurtry (1999).

23   In 1970 about 90 per cent of foreign exchange transactions were directly related to the real economy whereas now it is around 5 per cent (Chomsky 1998: 19). Not only has financial speculation become predominate, but the resulting crises nearly always produce bailouts that shift horrible burdens of adjustment onto the backs of working people.

9

Periodizing Capitalism: Technology, Institutions and Relations of Production

Gérard Duménil and Dominique Lévy

Introduction: competing criteria

Few, if any, would contend that nothing has changed within capitalism, or assert that historical change can be assessed on purely quantitative grounds. Rather, the major difficulty in periodizing capitalism is the existence of various *competing* criteria. Many will insist the central factor to consider is the metamorphosis of institutions, firms in particular (their size and the related forms of competition, the division of labour, and so on), but a wide variety of economic and social institutions are also at issue, such as the legal framework, or the state (its involvement in economic affairs or the pattern of international relationships). These viewpoints are clearly reflected in the various labels applied to periods of capitalism: imperialism, state capitalism, monopoly capitalism, state monopoly capitalism, managerial capitalism, Keynesianism, Fordism, neo-liberalism, and so on. Further complexity is added with the broad heterogeneity existing among the various segments of a national economy and among countries.

There is nothing troubling in this diversity of approaches. Capitalism is obviously a complex social system, whose analysis requires the combination of various interrelated components. However, all criteria cannot be placed on the same footing: a hierarchy must be imposed on these aspects of capitalism, and the way they are combined is certainly not neutral.

This chapter is divided into five sections:[1]

First, 'Historical tendencies and structural crises' sets out an initial, simple periodization based on the historical profiles of technology and distribution, in particular the movements of the profit rate which successively diminished in the late nineteenth century, rose from the early twentieth century to the 1950s or 1960s, and then declined again. Three structural crises are distinguished: one in the 1890s, the Great Depression, and one in the 1970s. A new phase, analogous to the first half of the twentieth century with its rising profit rate, may now have been underway since the mid-1980s.

The second section discusses the transformations of 'Institutional frameworks and policies'. The first major set of events was the occurrence of the *corporate* and *managerial* revolutions, and the emergence of modern finance, at the turn of the century. The Great Depression created the conditions for the second set of events: the emergence of the institutions of Keynesianism and the welfare state, in the wake of the New Deal and the Second World War. The crisis of the 1970s provided a foundation for the rise of neo-liberalism, upsetting this institutional framework.

The third section, 'Long waves', compares our analysis with long-wave theory.

The fourth section, 'Relations of production, classes and domination', interprets the above changes in capitalism to the broader Marxist framework of 'historical materialism' – relations of production, class patterns and power relations (class struggles, hegemony and compromise). Both the separation between *ownership* (concentrated in modern financial institutions) and *management* (in large corporations), and the involvement of the state in economic affairs are depicted as actual transformations of relations of production.

The fifth section, 'Can neo-liberalism stop history', questions the ability of neo-liberalism to interrupt the gradual assertion of the managerial feature of our societies. More than ever, managers direct the economy, including financial firms themselves. Rather than halting this evolution, neo-liberalism is described as an attempt to lead the present evolution of capitalism along a specific path, simultaneously favouring private institutions as opposed to public institutions, and redirecting the actions of some of the institutions of Keynesianism (central banks, the IMF, and so on) toward the interests of finance.

Historical tendencies and structural crises

This section is devoted to an initial, straightforward approach to the periodization of US capitalism based on technology, distribution and structural crises.

Three phases in the evolution of the profit rate

The examination of the major variables describing technology and distribution in the US economy, from the Civil War to the mid-1980s, suggests a first periodization in three phases. As shown in Figure 9.1, the secular trend of the profit rate was approximately horizontal, but three distinct periods can be defined (as suggested by the trend line). The first phase stretches from the Civil War to 1900 or the First World War, the second phase corresponds

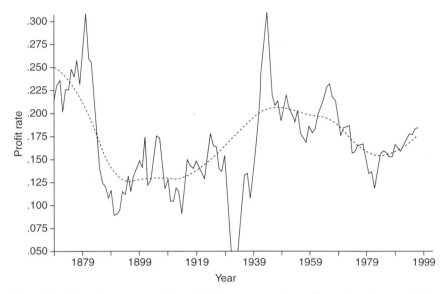

Figure 9.1 The private, non-residential US economy: the profit rate (continuous line) and its trend (dashed line) (1869–1997).
Profit rate = (net product − Labor compensation)/fixed capital. We use BEA data for recent years. The sources for the earlier years are given in Duménil and Lévy (1993).

approximately to the first half of the twentieth century and the third phase stretches from the end of the second period to the mid-1980s.

This periodization is not specific to the profit rate, and a similar profile is observed for the ratio of output to the stock of capital, or the 'productivity' of capital. Other variables, such as labour productivity or the hourly real wage (total compensation), are trended upward, but their growth in the three successive periods was slow, rapid and slow, in comparison with their secular trend. A similar pattern is also observable for the capital–labour ratio, an indicator of the mechanization of production, but the growth rates were, in turn, rapid, slow and rapid. These observations confirm the relevance of this periodization in three phases. (Since the labour cost and labour productivity moved in tandem, the share of profits remained approximately constant.)

Concerning technology and distribution, the trends prevailing during the later decades of the nineteenth century and during the decades following the Second World War up to the mid-1980s are similar in many respects, and appear unfavourable. The growth of labour productivity and of the real wage was slow; the capital–labour ratio rose sharply; the stock of fixed capital increased more rapidly than output (the productivity of capital declined); the profit rate diminished and the growth rate of real wages remained smaller than its secular average. The features of these periods echo Marx's analysis of historical tendencies in volume III of *Capital*, and can be labelled 'periods *à la Marx*'. Conversely, in spite of the Great Depression, the second period appears strikingly favourable: the growth rates of labour productivity and of the real wage rate were comparatively large, and the productivity of capital and the profit rate *increased*.

Two distinct types of structural crisis

Directly associated with this pattern of evolution are two *structural crises* with strong similarities, one in the late nineteenth century and one during the 1970s and 1980s. By 'structural crises', we mean rather long periods, as distinct from the usual recessionary episodes of the business cycle. In addition to the unfavourable trends of technology and distribution, they can be characterized by sluggish accumulation, large business fluctuations, and lasting unemployment (possibly in combination with financial instability). Following Marx, we interpret these structural crises as the typical outcomes of periods of actual decline of the profit rate. Low profit rates are detrimental to accumulation, and contribute to business cycle fluctuations; slow accumulation and recurrent recessions are responsible for large and lasting unemployment rates.

The nature of the Great Depression of the 1930s was thoroughly different from that of the above two crises. Paradoxically, the depression occurred during a period of favourable technical change. The problem was the large *heterogeneity* among firms and a still immature institutional framework for the stabilization of the macroeconomy. The rapid changes underway were concentrated within one segment of the economy, the large corporations backed by finance, whereas the technology and organization of other smaller and still traditional firms were becoming more and more obsolete. The recession in 1929 began a process of devaluation and destruction of the capital invested in this lagging component of the economy. Only extreme demand and credit policies could possibly have avoided the dramatic contraction, vigorously bolstering the activity of the more advanced sector in order to compensate for the disappearance of the older one.

The depression contributed to the acceleration of the transformation of technology and distribution initiated at the beginning of the century, eliminating backward firms, but only provisionally interrupted the movement of the major economic variables during those years. For example, the progress of labour productivity was affected by the depressed levels of activity, but its pattern was resumed after the depression.

A new phase?

An examination of Figure 9.1 suggests that a new phase might be at present in progress, initiated at some point during the 1980s. Were this the case, history would repeat itself as far as the movements of these variables are concerned.

The profit rate fell considerably during the 1970s. In 1982, it was only 57 per cent of its average value during the decade 1956–65. In 1997, it was about at its level of 1970. Thus, the recovery since the mid-1980s is significant, but partial: 65 per cent of the decline between the 1956–65 decade and 1982 has been recovered to date. Interestingly, most of this recovery resulted from the increase of the productivity of capital, while the share of profits only rose slightly. (Recall that profit rate = productivity of capital × share of profits.) This rise of capital productivity since 1982 is reminiscent of the upward trend of this variable during the first half of the twentieth century, our second period, and provides a crucial clue in the identification of a new phase. More and more, recent trends suggest that US capitalism has entered such a new phase and, if this movement is confirmed, *four phases will be apparent since the Civil War.*

Institutional frameworks and policies

This section is devoted to the transformation of institutions and policies: the corporate and managerial revolutions, the emergence of the 'Keynesian compromise', and the reassertion of the power of finance in neo-liberalism.

The new rise of capitalism in the early twentieth century, as managerial capitalism

It is not possible to disconnect the trends of technology and distribution in the twentieth century from the transformations of the institutional framework of modern capitalism. A prominent aspect of this relationship was the evolution of firms and of the forms of ownership. The new technology implemented in the late nineteenth century required larger units of production, and its development was naturally echoed by the emergence of larger enterprises. Small traditional firms, owned by individuals or families, were not adapted to the development of gigantic structures such as railroads. But the increase in *size* actually required new methods of management and large funds to be collected.

The main features of the period can be briefly sketched as follows (Duménil *et al.* 1997). In the late nineteenth century, as the economy was sliding along a trajectory *à la Marx*, the progress of industry and transportation created unprecedented competitive tensions. A network of agreements, pools and trusts was developed by firms attempting to avoid the pressures on their profit rates. This movement was later labelled 'loose consolidation', meaning that previously independent firms organized to share markets or profits, to fix minimum prices, and so on, preserving their existence as separate entities. The antitrust legislation discouraged these organizations, but there was no reversal. Instead, this legislation only favoured new forms of 'tight consolidation', in which independent enterprises were actually *merging* into larger units with common ownership. When the economy recovered from the depression of the 1890s, a sudden wave of incorporation occurred in a few years, right at the turn of the century, known as the 'corporate revolution'. A totally new institutional framework was shaped, whose cornerstone was the large corporation backed by finance. There was, however, a second aspect to this emergence of the institutions of modern capitalism, the *managerial revolution* (Chandler 1977), which is too often described in a reductionist manner as Taylorism or Fordism. The organization of production and all aspects of management in general were now performed in these firms by a broad pyramid of managerial and clerical personnel.

This managerial revolution allowed for new degrees of efficiency. The purpose of management, in the broad sense of the term, is to maximize the profit rate. The problem in the previous forms of technical change was the subordination of the progress of labour productivity to the addition of large masses of fixed capital. This is what mechanization is about in the configuration (manifested in the rising composition of capital) described by Marx in his analysis of the tendency for the profit rate to fall. Conversely, the assembly line, the typical form of mechanization in the first half of the century, did not materialize into a strongly rising capital-labour ratio. The growth rate of this variable was actually *reduced* in comparison to the latter decades of the nineteenth century. But the assembly line is only one example among others. Managing inventories or liquidity has similar effects on the profit rate, as well as improved commercial practices. The extension of this new technology and organization required several decades. Overall, the managerial revolution must be seen as the major counter-tendency to the falling profit rate in the entire twentieth century.

These technological achievements of the first half of the twentieth century finally accounted for the new trends of distribution. The new efficiency manifested in the progress of labour and capital productivity cannot explain the larger rate of growth of real wages and the protection of the welfare state independently of the struggle of workers, *but it created conditions conducive to these improvements*.

The New Deal and the Keynesian compromise

In the nineteenth century, the stability of financial institutions was in the hands of private institutions, more specifically the upper fraction of the monetary and financial system. Large banks, mostly New York banks, were acting as reserve banks, sensitive to the variations of the stock market or to movements within the banking system itself, modifying interest rates and influencing the flows of credit. Special devices were developed during financial crises in order to avoid the suspension of payments by banks. Although these actions impacted on business conditions, they were not directly targeted to stabilizing the macroeconomy. The creation of the Federal

Reserve in 1913 modified this framework, but the earlier reluctance to directly influence economic activity still prevailed during the 1920s.

The monetary and financial institutions proved unable to stem the collapse during the three first years of the Great Depression. Despite the eagerness of finance to preserve its hegemony, the government and the administration were forced into action. The intervention of the state in economic affairs was direct and decisive. The national banking vacation was declared, and the state controlled the reopening of the viable fraction of the system and took care of unsound debts. The economy was organized in 12 groups (the codes) where firms shared markets and fixed minimum prices and minimum wages, under the aegis of the National Industrial Recovery Administration (the most extreme components of this system did not survive the depression) (Duménil and Lévy 1999b).

However, it is only during the war that the ideas of Keynes spread to the US, and that it became relevant to refer to a Keynesian revolution, concerning macro policies, stock market operations and international capital flows. Beyond Keynes's specific recommendations, this social compromise also included several far-reaching elements: (1) a crucial component was the rise of the purchasing power of wage-earners and the social protection of the *welfare state* (echoing the first achievements of the *Progressive Era* in the early twentieth century); (2) unions became important partners in the management of the new social order and new legislation defined the rights of salaried workers; (3) state intervention concerning education and scientific research grew to a considerable extent; (4) as is well known, other countries went even further, involving the state directly within segments of the productive system.

In the late 1960s, economists and, more generally, social scientists forecasted the end of crises and a new affluent society. Not every aspect of the picture was rosy, but these decades appear retrospectively as outstanding. This new age of capitalism actually combined, on the one hand, the *managerial* traits inherited from the revolution in organization initiated in the wake of the crisis of the late nineteenth century with, on the other, the *Keynesian* features ushered in by the Great Depression and the Second World War.

The new trajectory *à la Marx*, neo-liberalism, and a possible fourth phase

The US economy returned to a trajectory *à la Marx* after the war. Efficient management was still necessary because the new organization constantly required the care of managerial and clerical personnel, but the heroic age of revolutions and dramatic improvements belonged to the past. Most of the lagging segment of the economy had been eliminated during the depression and the war, and the profit rate during the 1950s and 1960s remained very high – but the decline was underway.

With the fall of the profit rate, accumulation slowed down, and the tensions on distribution (between salaried workers, firms and finance) were exacerbated. They resulted in a surge of inflation. Keynesian policies of demand management delayed the crisis but were not adequate to cure the structural crisis of the 1970s. Inflation was eroding the income of finance, which had, in addition, never accepted its setback during the Keynesian compromise of the era after the Second World War. During those years, finance had been active in building a new international framework at a distance from domestic regulations. The converging interests of 'eurobanks', of rising multinational corporations, and of the US government created the conditions for *a restoration of the power of finance* (Helleiner 1994). A sharp policy about-face occurred with the election of Margaret Thatcher and Ronald Reagan – the products of an underlying social shift in power.

The new framework is now known as *neo-liberalism*. It is hardly necessary to recall here its main components: quasi-zero inflation, pre-eminence of the stock market, corporate governance, stagnating wages, progressive erosion of the welfare state and regulations, pension funds and private health insurance, free international mobility of capital, and so on. Neo-liberalism was devised in order to restore the interests of capitalists. Zero inflation protects the purchasing power of lenders. It diminishes the inducement to borrow and favours reliance on the stock market. The control of labour costs and deregulation have an obvious positive impact on the profitability of firms.

The new trend upward of the productivity of capital and of the profit rate, apparent since the mid-1980s, is very much like that of the first half of the twentieth century (our second phase), reflecting the new performance of management, technology and organization. The restoration of the productivity of capital probably relates to the information revolution, potentially a new revolution in management (Duménil and Lévy 1999a). Thus, the possible fourth phase in the profile of technology in the twentieth century is clearly associated with a new set of institutions and policies.

A synthesis?

Obviously, the difficulty in the periodization of capitalism is in combining the above elements into a coherent whole. The various categories of events do not necessarily coincide in time.

Consider the first phase, corresponding to the first pattern *à la Marx*. It led to a structural crisis in the late nineteenth century. From these circumstances derived a large institutional transformation, the corporate and managerial revolutions, introducing a new age, *managerial capitalism*. To this point, the picture appears rather unambiguous and we can be content with the image of a single phase from the US Civil War to the turn of the century.

The purely technical and distributional approach of the first section of this chapter runs, into problems, however, with the outbreak of the Great Depression. We interpret the depression as a 'cost' of the diffusion of th e managerial revolution, the inability to control the threat posed bythe underlying heterogeneity of technology within a backward institutional framework. A new element must be introduced into the analysis: the lag in the maturation of the 'management' of the macroeconomy. The acquisition of this new social skill actually *followed* from the depression and the second World War, which created the conditions for its development.

Thus, considering the period stretching from the US Civil War to the Second World War, and abstracting from the crisis years, we are left with two main phases: (1) the period *à la Marx* in the late nineteenth century; (2) the early twentieth century up to the Great Depression, when the new course of technical change and distribution was in progress, but the macroeconomic revolution had not yet occurred (or was only embryonic). The period of the depression and the Second World War represented an important transition marked by the elimination of the older segments of the economy and the establishment of a new social compromise.

Up to the mid-1960s, the effects of the managerial revolution and of the Keynesian framework were still felt, although the first manifestations of the new unfavourable trends became rapidly apparent after the war (when the economy followed a new trajectory *à la Marx*). In its first steps, the consequences of the new unfavourable course of technical change were provisionally offset by the stimulation of the activity and inflation, but this period culminated in the structural crisis of the 1970s. In the wake of the turn to neo-liberalism, new policies and rules were implemented, at first aggravating the crisis, but new, more favourable technological trends seem observable from the mid-1980s onwards (note that we do not mean here that the new technological trends can be imputed to neo-liberalism).

Thus, three phases can be distinguished after the Second World War: (1) up to the 1960s, the large profit rate levels were preserved, despite the early effects of the new trajectory *à la Marx*; (2) the manifestation, in the late 1960s and 1970s, of the new trajectory *à la Marx*, still in the context of the Keynesian compromise, and (3) the new neo-liberal course and the possible emergence of new technological trends. The structural crisis of the 1970s linked the two latter periods.

Obviously, the extension of this analysis beyond the horizon of the US economy adds further complexity. Japan and Europe followed the US with some delay concerning the favourable trends of the second period (the catching-up), the new trajectory *à la Marx*, and the structural crisis. The present international financial instability has now created threats similar to those of the Great Depression, but within a significantly different institutional environment.

Long waves

Obviously, the profile of the profit rate displayed in Figure 9.1 is quite evocative of long waves: apparently the profit rate is taken into oscillations of nearly one century. A first difference with standard long-wave analysis is that we place greater emphasis, in our periodization of US capitalism, on the profile of technology and distribution than on the growth rate of output or prices. Considering the secular trend of output in the US, in constant dollars, since the Civil War, no obvious periodization is apparent as is the case for the profit rate, the labour cost, or the productivities of labour and capital.

A closer examination reveals, however, that growth and accumulation are also part of the same movements as technology and distribution. Figure 9.2 displays a moving average of the growth rate of a constant dollar measure of the net product in the US (dashed line), which abstracts from short-term

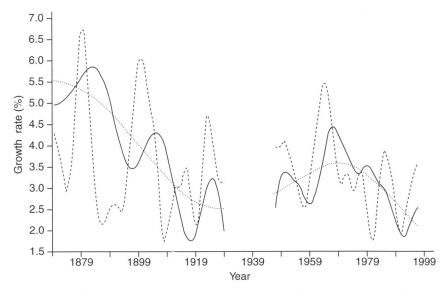

Figure 9.2   US private sector: growth rates of the net product (dashed line) and fixed capital stock (continuous line), both in constant dollars (1869–1997). In order to avoid short-term fluctuations, what is displayed in the figure is a *moving average*. For legibility, the lines have been deleted for the depression years and the Second World War. The figure also displays the trend line (dotted line) of the growth rate of the capital stock.

fluctuations. The figure also depicts a moving average of the growth rate of the stock of fixed capital in constant dollars (continuous line), and the trend line of this growth rate (dotted line). The following observations can be made:

First, the periodization in three phases introduced in the first section is actually evident in this figure, though in a less conspicuous manner than for the previous variables. Both concerning output and capital, the growth rates tended to decline up to the First World War; an upward trend was then apparent, culminating during the 1960s; finally a new downward trend was observed.

Second, large fluctuations of both production and accumulation are manifested during the first phase of decline of the profit rate. It is easy to recognize the crises of the 1870s, 1890s and the turbulence around 1907. The second of these crises, the structural crisis of the late nineteenth century, was the largest, longer and more profound.

Overall it is difficult to identify cycles of 40 or 50 years *à la Kondratieff*. From technology, distribution, accumulation, and growth, we read out longer secular movements. Accumulation and growth before the First World War reflect large 20-year cycles reminiscent of Kuznets's cycles (Kuznets 1952).

Yes, the actual declines of the profit rate – a recurrent tendency within capitalism – led *twice* to structural crises. This mechanism is in line with Marx's description of the consequences of a fall of the profit rate. But these crises created the conditions for a restoration of the profit rate, at least once, maybe twice. But one should be cautious concerning any mechanistic interpretation of these movements. The Great Depression had causes of its own, and it is not clear that these three crises were separated by the succession of an expansionary and a recessionary phase (phases A and B) *à la Kondratieff*.

Even if their causes may differ, recurrent structural crises define important benchmarks in the periodization of capitalism, though not in isolation, and with very specific traits. The common feature of the *three* structural crises is that they provided the conditions for large institutional transformations, and new class configurations (leaderships and compromises).[2]

Relations of production, classes and domination

The present section analyzes the transformations of twentieth-century capitalism, using basic Marxist concepts such as relations of production, modes of production and classes.

Managerial capitalism

Relations of production in the strict sense

History has not confirmed the views of Marx and Engels concerning socialism. Our interpretation is, however, neither that capitalism represents the ultimate stage of the maturation of human society nor that the 'true' proletarian revolution was simply postponed. Not only must the struggle for the elimination of classes remain on our agenda, but history is, indeed, still moving ahead. *A new transition, similar to the one between feudalism and capitalism, is underway. It will lead to a post-capitalist order, with a new managerial ruling class.*

Several aspects of the evolution of production and accumulation since the late nineteenth century must be interpreted as actual transformations of *relations of production and class patterns*:

1. *The separation between ownership and management.* The emergence of large corporations at the turn of the century and the corresponding separation between finance and managerial personnel represented a fundamental shift in the capitalist ownership of the means of production, that is, the metamorphosis of a crucial aspect of relations of production.[3] Private ownership was not destroyed, but a considerable distance was created between the owners and the managers of firms. The functions of the 'active capitalist' were delegated to salaried workers.

2. *The social pattern of ownership.* The ownership of the means of production became more and more concentrated within financial institutions, under the aegis of large capitalists. These institutions controlled the funds of a large population of anonymous holders of securities. The delegation of management to salaried personnel, described above, also occurred within these financial institutions. This broad set of institutions, their specific relationships to large capitalists and small holders, and their upper management define the contours of a social entity labelled *finance.*

3. *The hierarchy of wage-earners.* Correspondingly, several divisions are apparent within salaried wage-earners. (a) One must first distinguish between productive workers, on the one hand, and managerial and clerical personnel, on the other. More than ever, the workers were compelled to produce according to rules defined and controlled by managerial and clerical personnel. The distance created by capitalist production between the workers and the productive means widened considerably. (b) Within the managerial personnel, initiative was concentrated in the hands of the upper fraction of the group, and execution at the bottom.

Parenthetically, Marx clearly anticipated these events. He saw in the separation between ownership and management, and the new forms of ownership, a preliminary step toward the collective ownership of the means of production.

Class patterns

Two class contradictions are at issue which correspond, respectively, to the old capitalist framework and to the new managerial features:

1. The traditional capitalist opposition between *capitalists* and *workers*.
   (a) From this viewpoint, managerial and clerical personnel – from the top to the bottom of the hierarchy – assume the traditional functions of the individual active capitalist as manager of his or her firm. (b) Also from this viewpoint, smaller holders of securities share some aspects of the condition of large capitalists, though in a subordinated fashion.
2. The new opposition between *managerial personnel* and the new dominated class of *'managed' personnel*, by which we mean clerical personnel and production workers.

The complexity of contemporary class patterns is the expression of the dialectical coexistence of these two contradictions (Duménil and Lévy 1994). A single person can belong to the upper and lower fractions of each contradiction. For example, an engineer can be part of the collective worker within the workshop and, simultaneously, belong to *management*. The rank-and-file accountant performs a capitalist task, but is clearly part of *'managed' personnel*. The separation between white- and blue-collar workers still echoes the distinction between clerical personnel and production workers among the new dominated class, but it is gradually loosing its relevance.

Within contemporary capitalism, there is some overlap between the two ruling classes, the old and the new. An 'interface' exists between ownership and management. This is the world of top management and boards of directors, where owners still engaged in some form of management interact with managers who are subsidiarily owners (that is, who hold portfolios of shares). This interface is essential to the preservation of capitalist ownership in a system where ownership and management are basically separated.

Other components of the transformation of relations of production

The managerial revolution primarily affected relations of production within firms, but the new control of monetary and financial mechanisms at the macroeconomic level of the state also affected capitalist relations of production. This control can be interpreted as a second 'managerial revolution' – independently of its actual targets, full employment or price stability – and it always represented a crucial, political issue in the evolution of capitalism.

That the state may interfere with monetary and financial mechanisms was viewed, with some reason, by finance as eroding a crucial aspect of capitalist ownership. Credit and the corresponding issuance of money is directly related to the *accumulation of capital*. The preliminary saving of profits is not a prerequisite to capital accumulation, and the total amount of capital invested within firms can be increased by credit. In a nutshell: credit creates capital. Finance always considered the control of these mechanisms as one of its basic prerogatives.

These new managerial institutions of capitalism also affected the nature of *wage labour*. Within capitalism, labour-power is basically treated as a *commodity*, with its use and exchange values. It is purchased according to the needs of capitalist production, and paid as it is used. Any step toward the recognition of a *right* to work or of a *right to dispose of a certain income*, independently of the demand from capitalists, modifies the 'conditions' of salaried labour. These conditions define another aspect of the relations of production.

A last feature of the evolution of capitalism was the gradual extension of the process of 'socialization', already stressed by Marx, beyond the limits of strictly *economic* mechanisms with respect to education, health, police and other forms of social control. Their concrete analysis lies beyond the limits of the present study, and we will only stress here their double *capitalist* and *managerial* feature: (1) The way these 'social' functions are performed within modern capitalism expresses the necessities of the *reproduction* of the system as capitalist (Bihr 1989). (2) These functions are also part of a broader process of socialization overstepping the limits of capitalism. In both instances, and independently of their more or less 'democratic' or 'elitist' features, they echo the managerial transformation of our societies.

Thus, the use of the expression managerial capitalism in this study is broader than what is (or used to be) meant by it, since it purports to encompass all aspects covered above, with their dual determination. Managerial capitalism is a hybrid social formation combining specifically capitalist traits and a new managerial logic which foreshadows a new mode of production. Two distinct social 'logics' can be detected within contemporary societies: (1) the traditional capitalist rules of the game, with the maximizing of the profit rate as basic principle, and the private (though collective) ownership of the means of production, and (2) new forms of socialization within firms, financial institutions, and outside, which progressively transcend the limits of private ownership, ensuring more and more cooperation and coordination beyond the large antagonistic features of the system.

Ruling classes and class compromise

Power configurations

The reference to relations of production defines a first fundamental level of analysis in the interpretation of the history of capitalism, and there is a straightforward correspondence between these transformations and the evolution of class patterns. There is, however, a second level of analysis, more political and directly related to the state, from which this evolution must be considered. It is that of *power relationships*, either the leadership or domination of a particular class or class fraction, or the existence of given compromises within the various sections of the ruling class or classes. This notion of *class compromise* can be extended further to include other intermediate classes, or even the workers themselves. In this broad sense, it accounts for the configurations in which class power is exercised in general, which combine violence and conciliation. Thus, the transformations described in the first two sections of the chapter are determined to a considerable extent by *class struggle*. Both the confrontation between dominated classes and ruling classes, and the internal contradictions within ruling classes, are at issue.

Within contemporary 'democracies', the regimes do not necessarily change with the succession of leadership and compromises, but mechanisms are at work, similar to those described by Marx in his historical analysis of capitalism. The notion of 'regimes' itself is too narrow, and it would be more appropriate to resort to broader concepts such as large *power configurations* or *junctures*. In the US since the Civil War, and in other major capitalist countries with significant qualification, four such junctures can be identified:

1. The domination of industrial capitalists, and the compromise with small producers (unsettled by the trust movement in the late nineteenth century).
2. The coexistence of the new finance and managers in the wake of the separation between property and management at the beginning of the century, under the hegemony of great financiers (Morgan, Rockefeller and others), and the compromise with traditional capitalists.
3. From the Great Depression to the beginning of the 1970s, the setback of finance (limited in its scope), the increased autonomy of managerial personnel (both in the private and public sectors), and the compromise with the workers.
4. The reassertion of the power of finance within neo-liberalism, the dissolution of the compromise with the workers, and the reduction in the autonomy of managerial personnel, within firms and within the state.

The transformations of the relations of production, which echo the progress of productive forces, define a first set of phenomena where the reference to actual *laws* of evolution and a certain degree of economic determinism is relevant. The relationship between the succession of power configurations and these transformations is rather 'flexible', since struggles are at issue, with various potential outcomes.

Managerial capitalism and the Keynesian compromise

The exact frontiers between the evolution of the relations of production and the succession of power configurations are sometimes difficult to define. It is, in particular, difficult to draw a distinct line between the gradual assertion of the managerial features of twentieth century capitalism, on the one hand, and the specific content of the Keynesian compromise, on the other hand:

1. The various fractions of ruling classes utilised the workers' movement in their own fashion. First, in the late nineteenth century, prior to the First World War, the owners of traditional firms used the hostility of workers toward trusts to obtain conservative legislation (the antitrust legislation), but they simultaneously resisted workers' pressures toward better working conditions, unionization and improved living standards. Then, during the Progressive Era, a significant fraction of the owners and managers of the great corporations began to compromise with the workers in these respects (in combination with the repression of the more radical segment of the labour movement, in particular during the First World War). This compromise played an important role in the rise to dominance of large corporations. Thus, the rise of the managerial corporation simultaneously utilized the labour movement and contributed to the gradual establishment of what was described as the welfare state after the Second World War (Weinstein 1968). Many traits of the so-called 'Keynesian' compromise actually belong to this early managerial period.

2. Although the managerial central control of financial mechanisms and of the macroeconomy can be used by any dominating fraction of the ruling classes according to its own interests, it is clear that the institutions of Keynesianism were originally targeted toward full employment, more than toward price stability. The corresponding specific evolution of *wage labour*, the recognition of a quasi-'right' to work, was not inherent to managerialism, but resulted from the political conditions of the Keynesian compromise, in which the new managerial society was asserted (and this accounts for the precarious character of these social achievements).

Thus, the way the managerial and Keynesian traits of the twentieth century were combined is not coincidental, *since the managerial transformation of capitalism in the twentieth century was made possible by the same social tensions which led to the social compromise.*

The capitalist class in the transition

Our overall interpretation of the posture of the capitalists facing the emergence of managerial relations of production can be summarized by three propositions:

1. *Resistance.* A key element in the interpretation of the evolution of modern capitalism is the recognition of the central role played by the reaction of capitalists to the emergence of a new mode of production more in line with the progress of the productive forces, in which their property would be superseded. The resistance of capitalists to this evolution becomes periodically manifest: (a) in the fight of traditional capitalist owners against the rise of the new large corporations, (b) in the widespread

opposition of all groups of capitalists to the increasing intervention of the state in economic affairs up to the Great Depression, and (c) in the rise of neo-liberalism.

2. *Adaptation.* Fractions of ruling classes are, however, also periodically the promoters of large transformations. Thus, the corporate and managerial revolutions can be interpreted as attempts to make compatible the socialization of productive forces and the private ownership of the means of production. The same was true of the control of the macroeconomy and state intervention, although the transformation of the relations of production underlying this transition was 'biased' toward full employment and welfare during a few decades in the Keynesian compromise. This 'bias' was later corrected in neo-liberalism, but the same tensions and stakes are still at issue.

3. *Inflection.* Neo-liberalism can be interpreted as an attempt by the owners of the means of production to *divert* the alliance between managers and other salaried classes in the Keynesian compromise toward a new alliance between themselves and managers (in particular, the upper fraction of management). Since they could not simply consolidate their rule under its traditional forms, that is, freeze the relations of production, they promoted a transition preserving their privileges as much as possible, and finally allowing them to 'merge' rather painlessly with the new ruling class.

Can neo-liberalism stop history?

This section discusses the implications of neo-liberalism for the history of the last century of US capitalism in this study.

Neo-liberalism against the theories of managerial capitalism

The ups and downs of the theory of managerial capitalism reflect the transformations of capitalism itself. From its earliest stages, the development of capitalism promoted the application of science to production and organization. Thus, pre-managerial and, later, managerial interpretations developed since the eighteenth century, often with a highly utopian content and a socialist leaning. Obviously, the managerial revolution in the early twentieth century considerably strengthened this movement, later stimulated by the Great Depression, the Second World War and the Keynesian compromise. It culminated during the 1960s or 1970s, symbolized by the much-celebrated work of John Kenneth Galbraith.[4]

Did the rise of neo-liberalism destroy the theories of managerialism?

1. Yes, in the sense that they have been superseded, and that theories which had too hastily predicted the emergence of a post-capitalist era appear now obsolete. Too many basic capitalist features have reemerged: the

maximizing of the profit rate in the interest of finance, the rise of interest rates, the control of the rise of wages, the subordination of workers, deregulation, and so forth.

2. Our interpretation is that the resurrection of some of the capitalist features of our societies hides the continuing development of new relations of production. The role of managerial and clerical personnel is more critical than ever. Rather than a setback in the evolution of the relations of production or class patterns toward a pre-managerial stage of capitalism, what is at issue within neo-liberalism is *power*: the new hegemony of finance, that is, within contemporary capitalism, the hegemony of capital in general.

Thus, we must confront the following paradox: our societies continue their movement along a managerial path but under a new, strengthened, leadership of capital. Obviously, this leadership is not neutral. On the contrary, it directs the present evolution along one of several possible paths, away from the earlier gradual enlargement of state intervention and the victories of the labour movement, toward new forms of 'socialization' under the aegis of large corporations and, more generally, 'private' interests.

We believe that: (1) managers are not classless; (2) they have a potential for autonomy as a new ruling class in the future; (3) they are dominated by capitalists; (4) their actual power depends of the succession of *social configurations* in which their class power is expressed. Thus, the reference to managerial capitalism remains relevant in spite of neo-liberalism.

A third managerial revolution? Capital allocation after management and macroeconomics

The managerial transformation of capitalism appears to proceed in a stepwise fashion. In the US, the first revolution affected the organization of production and firms in general during the early twentieth century; the second touched the control of the macroeconomy in the wake of the depression, during and after the Second World War. As already noted, neo-liberalism did not reverse these developments. Instead, the managers of firms were awakened to the quasi-uniqueness of the criterion of their action, the *maximizing of the profit rate*, independently of its social costs, and state policies were targeted toward the stability of prices. A new component of the managerial transformation of capitalism seems, however, presently underway: managers are acting within large collective institutions, upstream traditional financial and non-financial firms. It is probably justified to denote this new step as a third *managerial revolution*, a centralization of capital giving new social content to the relationship between ownership and management.

To make more explicit the exact nature of this new revolution, it is important to recall that there are two basic aspects to the maximizing of the profit rate. Organization and technology within firms define a first component, and *the allocation of capital among industries and firms* defines a second component. In this latter respect, the crucial issue, in addition to the capacity to obtain financing (the issuance of shares and debt), is the determination of relative profitability in the present, as well as the assessment of future prospects. Like macroeconomics, this task goes beyond the limits of individual non-financial corporations.

Obviously, there is nothing radically new within neo-liberalism, and the managerial revolution affected finance long ago. Financiers were surrounded by business staffs from the first stages of the emergence of modern finance at the turn of the century. Within contemporary capitalism new steps have, however, been undertaken. Simultaneously, non-financial corporations developed their financial activity and the finance 'industry' has grown in amazing proportions.

Mutual and pension funds are typical of these new institutions of neo-liberalism. They hold a broad fraction of financial investments.[5] They perform the function of allocating capital among industries and firms; they compare profit rates; and they judge the performances of business staffs. Any negative assessment of a firm results in a movement away from its stocks, and makes it more and more difficult and costly for the firm to obtain new financing. From the viewpoint of relations of production, they are, in our opinion, ambiguous:

1. Imposing profitability norms on enterprises on the behalf of shareholders, they reassert a basic capitalist trait of our societies. Relying on *market mechanisms*, they also strengthen traditional capitalist features.
2. Conversely, they also contribute to the emergence of a new form of capitalism without large capitalists, that is, without large individual shareholders, even if this statement is sometimes grossly exaggerated. Some analysts are so impressed by the impersonal features of this new form of capitalist ownership that they interpret the rise to dominance of mutual and pension funds as a true metamorphosis of capitalism, somehow beyond itself. There is no doubt that these 'institutional investors' represent a new opportunity for managers to express their skills, but it is clear that the barriers between capitalists and wage-earners, in general, are not eroded.

The limitation of this 'socialization' is that it is now subject – as is the control of the macroeconomy – to the fundamentally capitalist criterion of the maximizing of the profit rate in a new context freed from the commitments of the Keynesian compromise. This follows from the present hegemony of finance which determines the path along which the managerial skills of the new class must be expressed. But this restriction does not change the content of this evolution, namely, that managers are acquiring, in present day capitalism, a new capability: *the control of the allocation of capital and of the performance of firm management at an unprecedented level of centralization.*

The maximizing of the profit rate offers certain guarantees concerning the efficient use of resources, but its limitations have been often emphasized: this criterion has been criticized on account of its blindness *vis-à-vis* other phenomena, social, human, ecological, and so on; and, it pushes our societies along a specific historical trajectory that it, itself, generates, which will be hard to reverse (specific consumption patterns, ways of life and culture, and so on). Neo-liberalism does not stop history, but determines its *present*, and biases its *future*.

Neo-liberalism, crisis and the new phase

As stated earlier, considering the historical trends of technology and distribution, a new phase seems at present to be underway with an upward trend of the profit rate since the mid-1980s. The relationship of neo-liberalism to this new phase is a politically crucial issue, one that is difficult to settle. More precisely, the problem is the 'imputation' of the new trends to either (separately or, more likely, in combination): a new technological revolution (the 'information revolution'); new managerial achievements; and the new hegemony of finance.

It is obvious that the dramatic rise of real interest rates during the 1980s delayed the recovery of the profit rate as directly experienced by firms, that is, after the payment of interests (and all taxes) (Duménil and Lévy 1999c). The negative impact of high real interest rates has been often documented and, as is widely acknowledged, the policy shock of 1979 added to the crisis in the 1980s, whereas lenders actually benefited from this movement. Non-financial enterprises had difficulty alleviating the burden of interest (net interests, since firms are simultaneously lending and borrowing), but they eventually performed it, stimulating the dramatic rise of the stock market whose role is now central. The costs of neo-liberalism were very large, and the consequences on investment and employment of the encroachment on profitability levels define only one aspect of these costs.

The fundamental issue is, however, the alleged advantages of neo-liberalism in relation to these costs. The question can be posed, at a broader level of analysis, of the potential 'progressivity' of neo-liberalism. How much of the new trends of technology can be imputed to neo-liberalism? *How much of the new possible phase of capitalism?*

Needless to say, we will not answer these questions adequately. A brief comparison with the unique example of a similar upturn that we know of, that of the early twentieth century, can, however, provide some crucial insights into these complex phenomena. The similarity between the two historical circumstances is very large.

Consider first the role of finance in the transformation of firms, technology and management in the early twentieth century. The corporate and the managerial revolutions required the combined actions of (a) managerial and clerical personnel and (b) finance. The former made possible the acquisition of a new level of efficiency within corporations, and the latter provided the funds for the construction and growth of the new large corporations. A similar twofold process has been underway since the 1980s. Finance supports the present merger wave, and new managerial achievements are performed by managerial and clerical personnel, supported by the so-called information revolution. Thus, the role of finance in the new course of capitalism appears central, supporting underlying transformations. The problem can, however, be framed counterfactually: if policies had been different – think of a 'left' alternative better adapted to the structural crisis than Keynesianism – would the upward turn of capital productivity have occurred? When? Earlier or later? What would have been its amplitude and effects? Could the huge wave of unemployment have been avoided? Would the costs of US hegemony for Europe and the Third World have been reduced? That the framework which allowed Europe and Japan to catch up with the US, with a prominent involvement of the state, was obsolete, remains to be proven.

Consider now income and stability. Another characteristic feature of the early twentieth century was the hegemony of finance concerning the control of the macroeconomy and the preservation of monetary and financial stability. The failure of finance to measure up to this task contributed to the Great Depression and, after the depression, allowed for the rise of the public component of managerialism within Keynesianism. This is where the damaging aspect of finance is even more clearly at issue, both in terms of income and concerning instability. (Recall that Keynes suggested the 'euthanasia of the rentier'.) In present day capitalism, finance again delayed the establishment of the new institutional framework required by the preservation of the monetary and financial stability of the international economy, and, even, promoted dangerous procedures (as had been the case during the 1920s). The recent financial crises clearly document the potential of this threat, and account for the new stimulus to impose some controls. The historical experience of the Great Depression has, however, not been forgotten, and the new institutions built after the Second World War have been only partially destroyed (only part of Bretton Woods was dismantled). Despite neo-liberalism, contemporary capitalism is still a managerial capitalism, and its *public component* can be suddenly or gradually pushed to the fore, if required for the continued stability of the system.

In our opinion, it is very unlikely that the capitalist class will disappear from the scene as a result of its excess rigidity causing a major economic collapse. It will rather 'merge' with the new rulers. This explains why the contemporary forms of the transition, in particular its more or less pronounced private or public features, are so important to this class. This is what neo-liberalism is about: the forms and exact contents of a transition.

Notes

1   This chapter borrows from earlier works: Duménil and Lévy (1993; 1996; 1998).
2   As in Ernest Mandel's analysis, we believe that the movements of the profit rate are crucial in the succession of various phases. We also share the view that 'exogenous', in particular political factors, play a prominent role in the starting of a new ascending phase (Mandel 1975 and 1980; see also Achcar 1999).
3   John McDermott emphasizes this transformation of relations of production putting more emphasis on the corporate form of ownership (McDermott 1991).
4   Berle and Means (1932); Burnham (1945); Chandler (1977); Galbraith (1967); Parsons (1954); Veblen (1983). In the early theories of management, managers were identified with a new form of 'rationality', above classes. This was in particular the case in the US during the first years of the managerial revolution, when Adolf Berle and Gardiner Means described managers as a 'neutral technocracy'. The theories which developed during the Keynesian compromise were not very different in this respect (though more ambiguous). This managerial capitalism had superseded business fluctuations and provided the workers with a larger purchasing power and social protection. The views developed in socialist countries, notably in the USSR during the same years, were actually in line with this assessment. Managers have, however, also been depicted alternatively as a new ruling class or as the disciplined agents of capitalists.
5   In the US, in 1998, the ratio of corporate equities held by mutual funds and pension funds, taken together, to those directly held by households is 1.02.

10
Space, Regulation and the Periodization of Capitalism

Sabah Alnasseri, Ulrich Brand, Thomas Sablowski and Jens Winter

The project of periodizing capitalism will remain an inconsequential academic exercise unless it engages in closer reflection on its underlying theoretical foundations. On the basis of such reflection, it should be possible to differentiate concepts of the various stages, phases and crises of capitalist development (concepts which are often conflated) and, above all, to assess the potential of an action-oriented approach with the aim of overcoming entrenched power, exploitation and repression. We will attempt in the following analysis to use our own underlying theoretical concepts of periodization as a means to understand the present social context and the current developmental tendencies of capitalism. To study the breaks and continuities of capitalist development, we take up the regulation approach, an approach we believe can mediate between the Marxist theory of the capitalist mode of production and the concrete analysis of social formations, and thus produce a theory of the periodization of capitalist development.

The main focus of our chapter is the crucial question of the spatial dimension of capital accumulation – something which is usually considered only *en passant*. Social formations, within the framework of Marxist discussion, have usually been identified with nation-states, and international relations studied within the context of discussions of imperialism and dependency. More recently, in the discourse on globalization and the hollowing-out of the regulatory capacity of the nation-state, the need to foreground those aspects relating to the articulation of local, regional, national and international levels has become increasingly apparent.

The space of regulation

The question of the space of capital can be posed on different levels of abstraction. An adequate understanding of the spatial dimension of capitalist development has often been obscured because the relationship between the capitalist mode of production and the nation-state has frequently been conceived not in terms of a historic coincidence, but of a logical necessity.

Let us begin at the level of the mode of production. At this level, capitalism is necessarily linked to a fractionation of space. Where there exists no socially planned production on a global scale, the private investment decisions of capital holders mediated by the competitive process result in an unequal spatial development of capital accumulation and thereby to an economic fractionation of space. Similarly, the political fractionation of space is a presupposition of capital accumulation. The spatial division of classes enables the formation of alliances between sections of the ruling and subaltern classes (Hirsch 1995a: 31ff.). In this respect the fractionation of regulatory space is an important moment of the dynamics of domination and competition.

Despite this structural connection between the capitalist mode of production and the fractionation of space, it would be wrong to deduce the existence of the national form and nation-states from the capitalist mode of production in a functionalist manner. We must differentiate between the inevitability of the fractionation of space and the forms this takes in history. The national form and nation-states must be understood and studied as historical phenomena in their own right. The fractionation of space has not only taken the historical form of a configuration of nation-states and a system of the international division of labour, but has also resulted in an unequal development and fractionation of space *within* nation-states.

Let us move on to the intermediary level of analysis and an engagement with the Marxist approach of the Regulation School (Aglietta 1979). Regimes of accumulation, modes of regulation and modes of development can only be thought of concretely in spatial terms (Schmid 1996: 239). We suggest, however, that space has not been adequately theorized in the traditional regulation approach. Up until now, the spatial framework within which modes of development have been analyzed has been the nation-state. In the regulationist and other Marxist traditions, the concept of *society's total capital* was attached to the nation-state because the *process of the equalization of rates of profit* within and between branches was thought to operate within a national framework. National currency areas limited free competition and effected a *modification of the law of value on the world market* (Aglietta 1974; Krüger 1986: 46ff.). It thus made sense to study regimes of accumulation primarily within the national framework. This framework was stressed in the analysis of modes of regulation as well, in which the nation-state's role in the regulation of money and the wage relation was central. The state is, according to Lipietz, the 'first form of regulation', which guarantees that social formations do not crumble in the face of endless struggles among the competing factions of society (Lipietz 1988). Finally, the Regulation School's spatial emphasis in its analysis of the Fordist mode of development was on the nation-state.

The methodological focus on individual nation-states was also retained in the study of current restructuring, yielding some interesting results.

Leborgne and Lipietz convincingly demonstrated, for example, that there is not just one way out of the crisis of Fordism, but rather the coexistence of a number of national strategies (Leborgne and Lipietz 1992a; Lipietz 1997a). The question today, however, is to what extent this concentration on the nation-state as the constitutional space of a mode of development can be maintained in light of the far-reaching rearticulation of politics and the economy mediated by globalization. More important yet, the methodological question arises of whether there is, at the *general* level, a spatial multidimensionality of accumulation and regulation. If so, this would have been the case in Fordism as well, but because of the predominantly auto-centred development of national social formations in this phase, this spatial multidimensionality was overlooked.

In contrast to the 'traditional' regulation approach, the geographical and space-theoretical work of Ash Amin, David Harvey, Jamie Peck, Adam Tickell, Eric Swyngedouw and others focuses on the contradictory spatial tendencies of accumulation and regulation. This orientation is based on an understanding of the capitalist totality influenced by Lefebvre's analysis of the social production of space, in particular his principle of the 'interpenetration and superimposition of social space' (Lefebvre 1991: 85ff.). Capitalism (in its entire history) is understood as a global matrix of interpenetrating and interfering spaces on global, national, regional and local scales. Its transformation over time can only be analyzed in concrete historical patterns of capital accumulation, in which the social production of these spaces and their condensation into a 'spatial fix' is a necessary but contradiction-ridden process.

First, the spatial organization of the accumulation processes is not simply determined through the structural tendency of its spatial expansion. Capital *per se* produces no 'spatial fix'. This process requires regulation and is thus politically and socially constituted (Scheuplein 1997: 17; Röttger 1997).[1] The intermediary concept of institutional forms can in this way take on a spatial character.

Second, a fundamentally different perspective on the historical and geographical conditions of a stable mode of development is revealed. Social and economic coherence is not necessarily expressed on the level of the nation-state, rather it 'exhibits a series of regularities at a variety of interpenetrating scales' (Swyngedouw 1997: 146).

In the processes of spatial *rearticulation*, displacement and condensation, the *quantitative* and *qualitative* shape of spaces are fundamentally transformed. These processes do not just happen, rather they express the practices of diverse social actors. Actors shape the architecture of spaces, but they merely co-shape it, because this architecture cannot be explained solely as the result of intentional actions. It is the result of *regulation* in a time of a crisis-induced restructuring and is not *a priori* definable.[2] In this respect, the economic and institutional conditions for a new phase of capitalist development can be articulated in a wholly new way and on an entirely new level. To avoid misunderstanding, neither the end nor the complete erosion of the nation-state is entailed in this thesis. The capitalist state and its apparatuses on the national level will remain, just as ever, central media for the regulation of the contradictions and terrains of social struggles, and thus will participate decisively in the formation of a new mode of development.

Hegemonic modes of development and international regulation

The merit of our reflections on the contradictory relations of economics, politics and space is in allowing us to differentiate more effectively aspects of the current process of transformation, and thereby free the analysis from the methodological bias towards the nation state. This will not reduce the complexity of the problem, of course. Quite the opposite; the already multi-faceted analytical levels of the regulation approach will become still more complex once the multi-scaled, historically variable spatial dimensions of accumulation and regulation are incorporated. Our objective at this point will be to use this added complexity to gain perspective on the under-theorized level of international regulation.

Mistral (1986) in particular was preoccupied with forms of international regulation within the framework of the regulation approach, drawing upon regime theory developed in the study of international relations. According to Mistral, an 'international regime of growth' is led by a hegemonic power which takes a leading role internationally in the major change of structures of production and the basic social conditions of the population. A regime here is understood to be an ensemble of modes of behaviour, norms and institutions which further deepen the international division of labour, structuring the range of acceptable paths of national development and facilitating relatively stable accumulation on an international scale. The historically changing regime of growth creates openings for the integration of certain national paths of development into the world market, while it hinders others. Despite this concern with the international level, Mistral's approach was still based fundamentally on the centrality of nation-states.

In this kind of analysis, it is often assumed that a mode of development will be specified through the 'global' hegemony of a state. Other prominent examples include a few works of the Regulation School and, even more representatively, the neo-Gramscian international political economy approach (Cox 1987; Augelli and Murphy 1988; Gill 1990, 1993; Rupert 1995) and the so-called 'Amsterdam School' (Overbeek 1993; van der Pijl 1998). The neo-Gramscian approach heightens our sensitivity to developments on the international levels of action which, although not autonomous, have an effect on nation states. This approach also effectively identifies various relations of force and transformational processes, which are not reducible to the level of the nation-state. Such insights are rewarding in many respects.

Up until now, the concept of *international regulation* has been used in an undeveloped manner. For some, the coherence of production and consumption on an international level is thematized (for example, Lipietz 1986b: 24). For others, international regulation refers to the existence of international organizations or an international hegemony of nation-states. But the difference between the concept of an international regime and that of an 'international mode of regulation' is unclear. In other studies the concept of governance is used (Jessop 1997b). These applications are a further indication of the absence of a distinctive regulationist approach to the theme of international regulation.

We proceed on the basis that the stabilization of capital accumulation on an international level is dependent upon the condensation of social relations in institutional forms of regulation. If these relations are not present, essential economic preconditions would be endangered: the predictability, planning and, especially, security of investment decisions. It is thus crucial to identify both economic and political contradictions on the international plane.

A more precise theoretical concept of international regulation must, against this background, address a few central facts. First, 'international' and 'national' accumulation processes should be understood as a contradictory unity (Hirsch 1993). The conceptualization of the various spatial levels as a contradictory relation of articulation carries with it the implication that the developments of individual peripheral or metropolitan social formations are not simply a function of international relations. Internal relations play a decisive role. This leads us, second, to the question of whether and how independent contradictions in need of regulation develop on the international level. International political and economic developments are always an expression of cooperation and competition in the social alignment process of capital accumulation (Brand and Görg 1998: 48ff.). Third, nation states play a central role in the process of international regulation, that is, they are crucial to the attainment of international compromises. The question as to whether forms of regulation can develop which are relatively autonomous from direct intervention by dominant states requires further research.

The international political system – despite the absence of an international political form comparable to the nation-state – develops its own political institutions which are neither the direct expression of dominant states nor the instruments of ruling classes, nor simply functional for capital accumulation. This significantly extends regime theory. International political institutions (formal organizations, networks, arrangements or regimes) are constitutive of international politics (Zürn 1998: 171ff.). However, the regime-theoretical understanding of international political institutions remains too formal. We understand these institutions as the condensation of the international balance of forces. Their processual character, their interaction with state relations and their involvement in social struggles all need to be taken into account. International institutions attain a certain materiality and can assume a 'relative autonomy', which also means that the power held by dominant states and classes is never complete and must continually be reproduced in international institutions. International politics is not limited to international political institutions, as regime theory often assumes, but encompasses a much wider set of power relationships in which economic, national political and other actors such as non-governmental organizations are important (Cox 1987; Demirovic 1997).

We agree with regulationist and neo-Gramscian studies that claim a stable mode of development, even on the international level, requires hegemonic conditions. It may be helpful, though, to set aside this issue for the moment, so that the *relationship between the mode of development and hegemony* (in the Gramscian sense) can be adequately conceptualized. We consider it useful to conceptualize international hegemony, not in terms of a nation state but in terms of a mode of development. Admittedly, it is true that capitalist modes of development have, until now, developed in individual nation states and from there internationalized. The hegemonic modes of development were equally the basis of the hegemony of a national capital or a national bourgeoisie *and* of the relevant nation state (England in the nineteenth century, the United States in the twentieth). However, there are two reasons for opposing the concept of an international hegemony bound *a priori* to the nation-state. First, it is possible that world economic stability could be sustained by the cooperation of a group of key actors instead of a hegemonic nation-state (Hübner 1990). Second, it is questionable whether we, in view of the present internationalization of capital, can still rely on the notion of a coherent national bourgeoisie. Nation-state hegemony has in the past always meant the hegemony of a national bourgeoisie. But the congruence of class and territory is more questionable than ever.

A mode of development is internationally hegemonic to the extent that relevant classes and class factions in different social formations orient themselves around it. Of course it does not become hegemonic automatically. It is shaped by the struggles between social groups, classes and class factions in the production process as well as in political and civil society. In the hegemonic mode of development a comprehensive class compromise materializes – a condensation of the economic, political and ideological-cultural balance of forces. These relations are, within capitalist societies, structured asymmetrically: the hegemonic mode of development always signifies the hegemony of a class or class faction and their organic intellectuals who organize the consent of the subaltern classes. It does not however necessarily signify the hegemony of a nation-state. Such a concept of hegemonic modes of development emphasizes the significance of the strategic decisions of ruling classes or class factions in the diverse social formations (even peripheral social formations), because every social formation has at its disposal possibilities within the structural selectivity conditioned by the global configuration.

In the following we will attempt to provide a concrete sketch of our periodization of capitalist development with reference to the conceptualization above, focusing on the historical forms of macroeconomic coherence and the spatial configuration of accumulation and regulation. We differentiate three phases in the history of industrial capitalism. First, the phase of the mode of development based predominantly on extensive accumulation, which developed in nineteenth-century England, spread from there, and then reached its limits at the time of the First World War. Second, the phase of the Fordist mode of development based predominantly on intensive accumulation, the roots of which reach back to the beginning of this century, but which could develop fully only after the Second World War, which started in the USA, and which came into crisis by the end of the 1960s. Third, the phase beginning in the 1970s which is characterized principally by the crisis of Fordism and search for a new mode of development. No attempt will be made to establish the empirical basis for this periodization as a whole within the confines of this chapter. Instead, we will focus on the significance of space for the periodization of the mode of development of Fordism and its crisis.

Fordism

If our theoretical premises are correct, a social production of space with a specific articulation of spatial levels was a defining feature in the development of Fordism. During this phase, essential social relations condensed in institutional forms – above all on the level of the nation-state. Special attention here is due to the forms of the wage relation, the national forms of the regulation of money and, more generally, the institutional system of the nation-state with its paramount significance in comparison with political institutions on other spatial levels. An essential characteristic of the Fordist period was, moreover, the decolonization and subsequent development of nation-states at the periphery of capitalism. It would be wrong, however, to make the national level the only unit of analysis. In particular, advanced productive capital was either very internationalized or internationalizing throughout the Fordist phase.

Fordism was founded upon a predominantly intensive regime of accumulation. Although the technical and organizational fundaments for mass production had already been in place since the beginning of the twentieth century, it was only after the Second World War that intensive accumulation in the capitalist metropolises could develop fully. It did so on the basis of a class compromise which allowed the formation of the Fordist norm of consumption. Central to this class compromise, brokered through the institutionalization of trade unions and collective bargaining, was workers' acceptance of their subordination to the capitalist relations of production and the Taylorist organization of work in return for rising real wages. The combined transformation of the labour process and wage-earners' living conditions, the coupling of norms of production and consumption, of productivity and real wage increases, made possible the virtuous circle of prosperity of intensive accumulation. An important component of Fordism was the Keynesian welfare state, which gave antagonistic social forces terrain for compromise. It played a decisive role in the regulation of the wage relation and money and provided welfare benefits, not only securing the political-ideological basis of the Fordist compromise but also driving forward intensive accumulation.

The extent of auto-centred development of home markets, often seen as a defining characteristic of the Fordist mode of development, in fact varied greatly among economies during this period, according to factors of size, population and historical patterns of development. In this context, the smaller countries found niches within the international division of labour, through the export of goods or services not produced by Taylorist-Fordist methods of standardized mass production (machines, luxury articles, agricultural products, raw materials, financial services), earning the currency needed to fuel imports of typical Fordist mass products and to develop mass consumption. Conversely, Fordist-Taylorist production methods were implemented in places where, depending on the prevailing balance of social forces, no compatible Fordist norm of consumption could be established for the working class: in this case, a low-wage export strategy corresponded to a backward home market development.

Fordism could only really unfold as a hegemonic mode of development in a small number of countries – primarily in the Atlantic area. Its effectiveness was however not limited to this space, rather it set in motion worldwide copycat effects (Lipietz 1992a: 193f; Hirsch 1995a: 70). American multinational corporations and the US state played a central role in the internationalization of the Fordist model, which was grounded not only on the attraction of the 'American way of life' but also on the application of coercion (Rupert 1995). Fordism can therefore be identified as a 'worldwide configuration' of different national regimes of accumulation with varying degrees and modes of world market integration, articulating a set of national and international institutional forms which lent these modes of development temporary stability.

Because of the relatively stable economic and political hegemonic relations in the capitalist as well as state socialist regions, international regulation prevailed throughout the world during the Fordist era. The international division of labour and political order were relatively stable, with wide consensus about the role of the leading power, the USA, in the capitalist zone. International institutions (World Bank, IMF, GATT) which helped to ensure the stability and expansion of the world economy made their presence felt within the framework of the United Nations. US political and economic hegemony gave the dollar its role as the undisputed 'world currency'.

The Taylorist organization of work entailing the progressive separation of planning and execution, the parcellization and mechanization of the labour processes, and the technical-bureaucratic control of the worker ran up against its limits at the end of the 1960s. The resistance of workers to the intensification of labour grew steadily, which, measured against the Taylorist productivity boom, resulted in a significant decline in the rate of growth of productivity, while the increasing organic composition of capital as a result of mechanization was no longer compensated for by the increase in the rate of surplus value. The result was a falling rate of profit.

Transformations in international relationships represent another dimension of the crisis of Fordism. The process of economic 'catch-up' experienced by Western Europe and Japan, and later by a few newly industrialized countries (NICs), led to considerable over-capacity in many sectors of the economy. As a result of foreign direct investment by US corporations and the increasing competitiveness of West European and Japanese capital, the US balance of payments progressively deteriorated, leading finally to the devaluation of the dollar and the collapse of the international system of fixed exchange rates. The transition to flexible exchange rates and the structural over-accumulation of capital gave rise to a considerable short-term speculative accumulation of money capital. This in turn fundamentally changed the conditions for the valorization of industrial capital. The shift in the balance of power between finance and industrial capital was a significant development in the rise of neo-liberalism, which has dominated the political arena since the end of the 1970s and has been a driving force behind deregulation and globalization.

The current situation

Let us now turn to the question of how to characterize the current period. Are we already in a new hegemonic mode of development or are we still in a phase of crisis, a relatively open situation, a state of transition to a new era of stable capital accumulation or, by contrast, are we en route to a new mode of production? It is not possible to discuss the full range of tendencies evident in this period of capitalist development. We will therefore concentrate on a few considerations in regard to the macroeconomic stability of the accumulation process and the emerging articulation of spaces of accumulation. To address this question we begin by stating that, from our viewpoint, the present state of capitalism continues to resemble a structural crisis. Even neo-liberal ideology and politics, dominant since the end of the 1970s, cannot blind itself to the fact that a new coherent mode of development has failed to emerge thus far.

Following Leborgne and Lipietz (1992), the 'supply side' crisis of Fordism could be resolved in one of two directions: either the labour process would need to be so transformed that a dramatic increase in productivity would result, or the wage relation would need to become so flexible that decreases in wages would result in a recovery of profit margins. In light of developments since the 1970s, we find evidence of both strategies to overcome the crisis. On the one hand, there has been extensive experimentation with the organization of work, with the objective of cultivating the negotiated involvement and responsible self-organization of employees in order to increase productivity and product quality, as well as to yield savings of constant capital. On the other hand, labour relations have been flexibilized, creating downward pressure on wages, while (neo-)Taylorist forms of the organization of work have been maintained.

Only on the basis of an imaginary national 'average' of the heterogeneity of labour relations within each country would it be possible to construct a spectrum of stylized national modes of development between these two ideal-typical poles, which Leborgne and Lipietz respectively describe as 'Kalmarism' and 'neo-Taylorism'. Leborgne and Lipietz maintain that these ideal-typical strategies for overcoming the crisis are incompatible: workers are not prepared to engage fully in the service of their employers if they receive no return on their efforts or if they can be made redundant at a moment's notice.

To be more precise, the incompatibility between these management strategies applies, however, only in relation to one and the same group of workers. The division and segmentation of wage-earners enables the two strategies to be connected and put to good use in different areas of production. Further yet, it may be exactly the combination of heterogeneous, complementary labour relations and forms of production which proves to be the superior strategy in the intensified struggle for competitiveness. This would explain the apparent superiority of the Japanese model of production, much discussed in the 1980s, which is based on a pronounced segmentation of the labour market combining the negotiated involvement and responsible autonomy of a core of employees with a low-cost investment strategy in South-East Asia, a flexibilization of labour contracts, and a deterioration of labour conditions for peripheral workers in subordinate supplier firms. That is to say, the Japanese model is a combination of 'Kalmarist' and 'neo-Taylorist' elements.

The strategies for overcoming the crisis sketched here are mediated by the competition of individual capitals, and concern business calculations and the restructuring of production. The question arises as to whether these strategies are also macroeconomically coherent and can lead to a new regime of accumulation. Neo-Taylorism throws up obvious problems of effective demand and the threat of a crisis of underconsumption. The macroeconomic implications of Kalmarism are anything but clear. Since Kalmarism allows for higher levels of productivity than neo-Taylorism, it may also be associated with greater unemployment. In this respect it leads, like neo-Taylorism only in different ways, to a contraction of the wage portion and to greater income inequalities, tending to a crisis of underconsumption.

On the other side, rising productivity under Kalmarism allows for increases in real wages, which are the precondition for maintaining the balance between supply and demand. Yet a renewal of the regime of intensive accumulation presupposes the existence of a post-Fordist norm of consumption, which could secure for capital new spheres of profitable investment through a transformation of wage-earners' conditions of life which could once again lower the value of labour-power and increase the production of relative surplus value, without creating a crisis of realization (Aglietta 1979: 162–9). This raises the question of what such a post-Fordist norm of consumption might look like. To assess the outlook for a renewal of the regime of intensive accumulation, the very different circumstances of the capitalist metropolises and peripheries must be examined.

In the metropolises, one can anticipate, a phase of prosperity and growth comparable to Fordism will not be repeated. The key to Fordism's success was its reorganization of the social conditions of wage-earners, whose reproduction prior to Fordism was to a large extent still characterized by subsistence production and simple commodity production. With the transition from extensive to intensive accumulation, for the first time the reproduction of labour-power was truly subsumed under capital. Today the reproduction of wage-earners in the capitalist metropolises is almost completely dependent on the consumption of commodities produced under capitalist conditions. The pre-Fordist constellation will not return.

It is hard to imagine that productivity increases in the established mass consumer goods industries can restore rapid accumulation, as in the period of transition to Fordism. The demand for classic Fordist consumer goods tends to stagnate. It is not enough simply to invent new goods to take the place of cars, refrigerators and television sets for an upswing of capital accumulation. A transformation of the norm of consumption would have to solve not only the problem of effective demand, but also the need to lower the value of social labour-power or increase relative surplus value.

A way out of the crisis of the Fordist regime of accumulation could possibly come through the catch-up development of intensive accumulation in major countries on the capitalist periphery (such as South Korea, Brazil, China, and India). The centre of capital accumulation would then shift to these countries. Currently, few signs point in this direction. Despite impressive growth rates and industrialization processes in some areas of the capitalist periphery, the centre of global accumulation remains the triad of North America–Western Europe–Japan. The NICs are confined within an international division of labour, in terms of both continental and intercontinental frameworks. Technological and financial dependencies continue to exist. Under these imperatives the 'internal bourgeoisies' (Poulantzas 1975b) in these countries do everything they can to maintain repressive industrial relations and hold down wages. The recent bitter disputes in South Korea, which actually stands on the threshold of predominantly intensive accumulation, are evidence of this. The internal balance of forces in the NICs are overdetermined by the international balance of forces. The recent financial crises have profoundly set back the development process in these countries. Although we are clearly sceptical, on the basis of these observations, we do not completely rule out the possibility of a shift in the configuration of nation-states over the long term which could open up new development prospects for capital.

In any case, the internationalization of capital has proceeded to a point such that the problem of macroeconomic coherence should no longer be seen in national contexts, but rather in a global framework. So, for example, the US, supported by the absolute size of its economy and the international position of the dollar, currently assumes the role of global consumer. It absorbs the trade surpluses of Germany and Japan, surpluses supported by mercantilist politics. The latter countries in turn accept the role of financing the US structural balance of payments deficit by means of credit.

The real character of the internationalization of capital will become clear only if one looks at specific transnationally organized commodity chains and globalized financial markets. It is rather misleading to describe this internationalization of production as 'globalization'. A large part of the world, including most of Africa and major parts of Latin America and Asia, remain far removed from the strategic planning of international capital, and will become increasingly marginalized under the conditions of 'globalized' capitalism. On the one hand, internationalization has taken the form of continental block-building, constructed on the basis of the international division of labour and centre–periphery relations within the continental blocks. On the other hand, there is an increasing interconnectedness between the centres of the triad. The two tendencies stand in a contradictory relationship to one another, and in our opinion it is wide open as to which one will prevail.

In respect of the social, there are indications of an increasing heterogeneity of social relations within nation states. This takes place primarily through the labour market and divides wage-earners into an ever-smaller core of socially insured, long-term, full-time employees on one side and a growing periphery of unskilled, underemployed and precariously employed workers on the other. This division reinforces traditional sexist and racist divisions among wage-earners, divisions which coexisted with homogenizing tendencies during Fordism. This social heterogenization has spatial consequences as well: relations between centre and periphery are multiplied many times over within national formations and even cities. The post-Fordist spatial structure has often been described as a 'leopardskin': as social differences in the national context increase, international centres of development move closer together, causing a tendential homogenization of social groups, classes and class factions across nation-states. This process, however, develops much more quickly on the side of privileged social groups than on the side of the subalterns who, under Fordism, were accustomed to struggle within a national framework. If one takes these processes seriously, it would be necessary to rethink the concept of social formations and detach it from the nation-state.

The internationalization process has also irrevocably changed the basis of national politics. Already in the mid-1970s, Nicos Poulantzas presented the thesis that the dominant factions of the European bourgeoisie had, under the influence of the internationalization of hegemonic US capital, shifted from being a 'national bourgeoisie' to an 'internal bourgeoisie'. Although they still had an independent base of accumulation at their disposal, owing to their multiple ties of interdependence and dependence with hegemonic US capital, they were no longer autonomous in the political-ideological sense (Poulantzas 1975b: 63ff.). As the superiority of American capital dwindled and the interconnections between the centres of the triad became reciprocal, however, this process transformed the American bourgeoisie as well. Imperialist contradictions and rivalries have intensified with the hegemonic crisis of US capital and the catch-up process of Japanese and Western European capital, but these have not taken on the same confrontational logic which drove the international powers towards imperialist wars in the pre-Fordist era. Only if the dynamic of continental bloc-building decisively prevails over the dynamic of interdependence between the triadic centres, or perhaps if there is a considerable shift in the balance of power between the US and the EU, do we foresee a significant sharpening of imperialist contradictions.

It is clear then that the congruence between 'national capital' and nation state politics has disintegrated, and the term 'national economy' has lost its meaning (Hirsch 1995a: 102). Kurt Hübner identified a defining feature of the present trajectory in the discrepancy between the globalization of economies and the territorial shrinkage of politics (Hübner 1996: 55). A similar argument was made by Joachim Hirsch to the effect that in the course of internationalization, economic and political spaces drift apart (Hirsch 1995a: 133). The consequences at the level of the mode of regulation have become a prominent theme in regulationist inspired studies of the state. It appears there is increasing consensus that, under the pressure of economic globalization, nation-states tend to lose their position as centres of regulation (1995a: 98) and that a functional and territorial reorganization has ensued.

In the face of this pressure, the Keynesian welfare state is being transformed into a 'Schumpeterian workfare state' (Jessop) or a 'national competition state' (Hirsch), which attempts to attract global capital and to optimize the conditions of accumulation for 'internal' capital, which is in any case more or less internationally constituted. Bob Jessop identifies three trends in the transformation of statehood. The first is illustrated in the hollowing-out of the apparatus of the nation-state which was of central significance for the monopolistic regulation of Fordism on the basis of corporatist negotiation procedures. He characterizes this development as the *denationalization of the state*, in which its writ and decision-making authority are territorially and functionally reorganized on subnational, national, supranational and translocal levels. Tied to this is the effective decentralization of political authority (Jessop 1997b: 52ff.; see also Hirsch 1995a: 116). A second trend is found in the *destatization of political regimes* and its typical political procedures and modes of operation. Decisive here is the change from government to governance. The state apparatus loses its role as a central and commanding agent with extensive powers to mobilize resources of knowledge and power in favour of new forms of partnership with para-governmental agencies and non-governmental organizations. Third, there is a trend towards the *internationalization of the state*, with a fundamental transformation of the nationally oriented economic and social politics of the Keynesian welfare state in the direction of a 'workfare orientation', embracing the imperative of 'international competitiveness' (Jessop 1997b: 61ff.).[3]

There is no fundamental erosion of the state implied in the account of these trends. The nation-state remains, at least for the moment, the most important instance with respect to the 'general function' of securing social cohesion in a class-divided society, and the central 'terrain of struggles' for social conflicts, just as much as the point of reference for the strategies of classes and class factions (Jessop 1997b: 76; Röttger 1997: 48).

Conclusion

In summary, it can be said that the present state of capitalist development discloses a far-reaching crisis and restructuring of social relations. In this crisis, many troublesome processes are at work: multidimensional spatial shifts in the balance of forces within the ruling classes/factions (for example, the shift of power from industrial to financial factions); broken and fragmented resistance of the subaltern classes/groups; and, not least, the crisis of the national welfare state and international regulation. This is most clearly indicated in the financial sector, but also in trade and industry, as well as in the regulation of international wage relations. Exemplary too are the so-called problems of migration, that is, the control and management of the mobility of the labour force, the feminization of the labour market, and the attempts to establish an international minimum wage and abolish child labour. Furthermore, evidence of intensified competition, the heterogeneity of industrial organization and a deepening ecological crisis can be discerned. It is neither globalization nor the primacy of the nation-state, but rather the multi-scaled process of restructuring of relations of power and domination which most defines the present situation. Whether we move toward a new hegemonic mode of development or to heightened rivalry and violent confrontation – and with it intensified crises – is still open to question.

Theoretical questions remain open as well. While many issues remain unresolved in this study, we hope they have at least been clarified in the context of the continuing potential of the regulation approach. The regulation approach is an incomplete project and requires further development to confront the dangers of misplaced questions and the petrification of analytical categories. With this in mind, we would like to end with a few comments about the direction in which theoretical work must be taken.

First, theoretical explanations of crisis and attendant questions about social and economic coherence need to be made more precise. It is equally important to research further the significance and interaction of changing forms of gender domination and ecological crisis for the crisis of Fordism and the current post-Fordist restructuring. Fundamental questions remain about the construction of institutions and the social production of space on different scales. What precisely is an institution? What is an institutional form? What leads to its constitution, stabilization and decay? An inadequate approach to these questions carries the danger of explaining wrongly the nature of institutions – in an *ex post* and functionalist manner – on the basis of systemic requirements (especially those of capital accumulation). In this way the 'relative autonomy' of institutional processes, which embody real balances of social forces and constitute specific terrains of social conflict, will remain obscured from analytical view. The spatial dimension must be systematically incorporated into this analysis as well. In particular, there is need for more work on the significance of the global or international level. In what way does 'the political' emerge as a relatively independent structure and process at the global level? And at which level, or at which interpenetrating levels, can a mode of development and a social formation be defined?

We believe that critical theory must seek to explain the conditions constraining social action, conditions which themselves are reproduced or transformed by social action. This is an important precondition for the evaluation of the possibilities and limits of progressive action. Emancipatory action takes place under capitalist conditions; however, it must go beyond them. In this regard, the emancipatory horizon must remain anti-capitalist, a horizon which we believe without a doubt can be accommodated and advanced within regulation theory. To give the last word to Marx, the point of theory is to serve the objective of 'overturning all relations in which man is a defeated, servile, desolate, scornful being' (Marx, MEW, 1965, 1: 385).

Notes

For helpful discussion of an earlier version, some results of which escaped further consideration, we thank Alex Demirovic, Christoph Görg and Joachim Hirsch.

1   To put it more concretely: 'the production of space . . . becomes an integral part [of the regime of accumulation]. Each regime produces a specific mode of spatial organisation profoundly different from the previous one' (Moulaert and Swynge-douw 1989: 330). In a general sense, this was also understood by advocates of the traditional regulation approach. Esser and Hirsch (1987: 37), for example, declared 'that the carrying through of an historically dominant form of capitalist production and work relations, consumption standards and modes of societalisa-tion [produced] its own spatial structuring on international, regional and local levels.' Yet the privileged analysis of the nation state level was never called into question explicitly.

2   The ideological-discursive and political-economic constitutional and regulation processes produce new social realities and patterns of perception. The slogan 'local is beautiful', for example, emphasizes not the traditional local, but the newly constituted 'glocal'.

3   It should be emphasized that this discussion is concerned with general trends. Neither the underlying dynamic of these trends nor their range can be dealt with here. As Jessop (1997b: 54) puts it, 'these general trends – above all in their contingent articulation – can have various empirical manifestations in various European societies.'

11
Class, Contradiction and the Capitalist Economy

Stephen Resnick

Introduction

Two major contributions differentiate Marx's explanation for how a capitalist economy works. One involves theorizing its functioning from the perspective of class, namely the processes of producing, appropriating and distributing surplus labour. Adding Marx's concept of class to economic explanation provides a potential threat to capitalism, for the stark implication is that the value received by industrial capitalists exactly equals what they exploit from their workers. In direct contrast to the claims of non-Marxian economic theory, class exploitation, and not the latter's marginal productivity, determines the economic rewards of industrial capitalists as well as of the managers, merchants, state officials, landlords and bankers who live off the surplus distributed to them by those capitalists. That class exploitation supports the incomes received by such an otherwise venerated group of individuals in society tarnishes, if not makes ridiculous, non-Marxian claims of capitalism's underlying fairness and efficiency.

Placing class exploitation into the economy provides a new logic connecting how a society organizes its production and distribution of wealth – its non-class economic structure – to its production, appropriation and distribution of surplus labour – its class structure. In drawing this relation between class and non-class, Marx provides an economic explanation for what Adam Smith had missed. Capitalism, as Smith theorized and advocated, could well provide the conditions for a vast accumulation of wealth for the benefit of its citizens, but Marx added, at the cost of exploiting an entire class of those same citizens. Forevermore, this relationship between class and non-class economic structures became simultaneously a central theme within Marx's work and its political target.

Marx's other contribution involves adding the dialectic as the means – the Marxian method or logic – to connect class and non-class together to produce a completely new way to conceive of how this economy exists and develops. It becomes an ever-changing site of diverse and interacting determinations emanating from these different class and non-class structures. These conflicting determinations produce its contradictory path.

What is true for the economy also holds for the processes constituting each structure. The same logic conceives the existence of each to be an overdetermined site of combined determinations emanating from all the others. At one level, this means that no one of these economic processes within this ever- changing economy, whether it is one of non-class or class, can exist independently of any other. All of these determinations constitute each in the sense that their coming together is the existence of that process. Hence as the site of them all, the economy takes on its existence – its very being – in relationship to these combined effectivities emanating from a vast array of codetermining class and non-class economic processes (as well as non-economic processes situated elsewhere in society).

At another level, conceived in this way the economy must exhibit a profoundly uneven if not chaotic character. In adding their unique determinations, these different processes propel each other and necessarily the economy, as the site of them all, into contradictory directions. In the first example below, a rise in productivity simultaneously pushes the value profit rate and economy into expansion and decline. Further, this profit rate change necessarily affects markets, thereby setting in motion still new expansionary and contractionary consequences. In the other examples, credit and financial investment act, respectively, to enhance the capitalist class structure, even as they undermine it. Constituted in this way, the economy becomes an ever-moving field of swirling interacting and changing class and non-class economic processes whose effectivities push it here and there, continually changing its nature and motion.

In these two ways, Marx provided a frightening idea of what our lives are like under capitalism. That modern society which we depend upon and endow with mystical abilities suffers from a deep sickness. Class exploitation haunts it and a deep instability describes its functioning. Similar kinds of behaviour for any individual – exploiting others and swinging from moods of euphoria to those of depression – would suggest a needy candidate for judicial and psychological help.

This chapter is written in this Marxian tradition and spirit. Focusing on one aspect of the non-class structure, namely its markets, it shows the complex and ever changing interaction between market operations of modern industrial corporations and their class structure. No order, law of motion, or telos emerges out of this relationship between markets and class, other than contradiction itself. In this regard, chaos and instability characterize the operation of corporate enterprises and that of the capitalist economy in general.

Class, competition and chaos

Consider any representative enterprise operating either in a capital goods (Department I) or consumer goods (Department II) industry. The enterprise's class structure is represented, on the one hand, by the corporate board's appropriation of surplus labour produced by workers and, on the other hand, by its distribution of the surplus to various subsumed classes – managers, merchants, owners, lenders, landlords and so forth – who provide the non-class processes enabling that surplus to be appropriated (Resnick and Wolff 1987: chapter 4).

For simplicity, divide these distributions into two forms: the value flow to subsumed class managers to secure the non-class process of capital accumulation ($SSCP_{\Delta c + \Delta v}$) and the flow to a variety of other subsumed classes within and without the enterprise to secure non-class processes of research and development, advertizing, merchanting, lending, renting, access to means of production, and so forth ($SSCP'$) : $SV = SSCP_{\Delta c + \Delta v} + SSCP'$. Divide both sides of the equation by the total value of productive capital ($C + V$) to obtain a simplified expenditure equation: $r_{ij} = k_{ij}^* + \lambda_{ij}$, where the subscript i stands for the ith enterprise, j for either one of the two departments, r for the value profit rate, and k^* and λ for the ratios, respectively, of $SSCP_{\Delta c + \Delta v}$ to ($C + V$) and $SSCP'$ to ($C + V$).

In words, an enterprise's value rate of profit equals the sum of two different kinds of flows: surplus directed to secure the rate of growth of capital accumulation (k_{ij}^*) and to acquire supervision, product design, innovation, loans, land, and so forth (λ_{ij}). While different, both distributive strategies can serve to raise the productivity of labour. Suppose in distributing the surplus in these ways, the ith enterprise raises its labour productivity more than do competing firms. The enterprise's *private* alteration of its subsumed class expenditures (a form of class strategy) creates a new and unintended *social* result: all enterprises face a lower market exchange-value per unit. The market makes its presence felt: upon selling their commodities, more efficient firms realize more revenues than were expected in production, and less efficient firms less. Higher productivity earns the more efficient firm a new non-class revenue (NCR_{sp}) flow, namely a so-called super profit, at the direct expense of lower revenues for other firms.[1] In this way, the market has intervened to redistribute the existing and unchanged surplus value from less to more efficient enterprises.

A new set of equations illustrates this result:

More efficient enterprise: $\quad SV_{ij} + NCR_{ijsp} > (SSCP_{\Delta c + \Delta v} + SSCP')_{ij}$

Less efficient enterprises: $\quad SV_{kj} - NCR_{kjsp} < (SSCP_{\Delta c + \Delta v} + SSCP')_{kj.}$

For the jth Department, i and k stand, respectively, for a more and less efficient enterprise, and the sum of super profits across all enterprises equals zero, $(\Sigma - NCR_{kjsp}) + (NCR_{ijsp}) = 0$. A market profit rate, r_{mkt}, that combines together class exploitative and non-class revenues rises for the more efficient enterprise, $r_{mkt} = (SV + NCR_{sp})/(C + V)$, while it falls for all the others, $r_{mkt} = (SV - NCR_{sp})/C + V)$.

This differential impact on the market profit rates of different enterprises operating *within* the industry serves as the first illustration of how the market acts to destabilize their respective flows of revenues. It also unbalances their respective expenditures in that a higher (lower) market profit rate can generate a higher (lower) growth of expenditures. These inequality signs index, then, what the market has accomplished: the favourable revenue situation for the *i*th enterprise creates a revenue crisis for all other enterprises. They also signal the new social conditions for the next set of private actions to take place.

Marx focuses on one of several possible distributive strategies. Reacting to their crisis, less efficient firms alter their production methods to become more efficient. Emphasizing a strategy of raising the organic composition of capital (*occ*) to increase their labour productivity, Marx draws his well known conclusion: the value profit rate for all firms within the industry falls. In other words, the rate of expansion of the capitalist class structure in each department becomes undermined because capital becomes so efficient there. It follows that the economy's overall value profit rate becomes thrust downward. Recalling our expenditure equation, falling value profit rates translate into falling productive (k^*) and unproductive (λ) capital accumulation.

On the other hand, that same economy-wide efficiency necessarily cheapens the unit values of both departments' commodities. Consequently, as buyers of now cheapened (in value terms) commodities, the value profit rate for each department's enterprise is propelled upward, even as the within-department competitive search for super profit pushes that same rate downward. In a word, the economy's value profit rate and the health of the capitalist class structure it measures exist in contradiction. That rate is the site of conflicting determinations emanating from market interactions operating at two levels in the economy: within each department and between it and the next.

Here, then, is one of many ways class and markets overdetermine one another. The resulting change in enterprises' revenues – the positive and negative NCR_{sp} *and* the enhanced SV flows via the effect of a cheapening of commodities – enable and motivate differently impacted enterprises to take new expenditure actions, all of which impact markets and class structures in a variety of still new and unexpected ways.

Initial capitalist distributions of the appropriated surpluses have set in motion an unintended, unforeseen and radical unevenness in the economy. Moreover, it is not as if any capitalist board could minimize or avoid such distributions. Distributions are required, if the conditions of existence of the appropriated surplus are to occur and be reproduced. Capitalist surplus appropriators must try to acquire access to labour-power, means of production, supervision, credit, research and development, security, ideology, rights to own things and command individuals, merchanting, and so forth, if they are to be in the (class) position to consume labour-power. These conditions represent the non-class processes – secured by their $k^* + \lambda$ expenditures – that together overdetermine class.

Yet, the very success of each capitalist board to secure its required conditions helps to produce, via the market for the produced commodity, the described disaster for them all: the value profit rate falls. Those same market forces, however, set loose in the economy forces of hope and expansion. Cheaper means of production and labour-power become new, non-class conditions enabling that same rate and the class structure to expand and prosper. The conclusion is stark: interactions between economic processes of class (appropriation and distribution of the surplus) and non-class (the market structure) continually send the economy into the two radically different directions of contraction and expansion at one and the same time.

The point is not that inter-departmental market interactions may or may not countervail the recessionary pressures set in motion by intradepartmental market processes. Rather, it is how one understands the existence of the economy as the site of all such effects. Capitalists necessarily spend their appropriated surplus on $k^* + \lambda$, thereby setting in motion unforeseen and contradictory changes in the economy for them (and everyone else too). And that is all one can say about this point. It is not an issue of taking into account 'omitted demand factors', 'the role money may play', 'institutional and technological change' or the hundred other social variables theorists have attempted to incorporate into their models to show how and why that new consideration now produces (in the supposedly improved and/or more concrete analysis) a net expansion, decline, or even stability in the economy. It is not, because each and every one of these and other introduced changes merely adds its own unique contradictory impact to an already chaotic mix of contradictory movements. That is why for any analysis of an economy, Marx's dialectical contribution is as radical in its way as is his class theorization.

Contradictions of market prices

Yet a tension lingers. Can one not say anything more definitive about the path of the economy other than what was just concluded? Can one not identify – no matter how fleeting they may be – certain tendencies following some intended private action? The answer is 'no', and the reason once more is the dialectical process itself. Nothing arrests that process: newly introduced determinations merely beget still new determinations in a never-ending swirl of mutually interacting determinations.[2] Let us examine this key point again by extending the example to include the interaction between class and, this time, market prices.

Consider the value profit rate's conflicting impact on the three different markets of labour-power, means of production and wage goods. On the one hand, a fall in that rate, because of an assumed rise in the *occ* due to intradepartmental competition, reduces the expansion of subsumed class $k^* + \lambda$ expenditures, and therefore puts downward pressure on the market price of productive and unproductive labour-power. In turn, that depressed price of labour-power reduces the demand for wage goods, and hence pushes downward market prices there. Similarly, enterprises' reduced demand for means of production acts to reduce market prices in capital goods markets. A generalized sales crisis results for enterprises in each department: lower sales prices imply enterprises cannot realize the surplus value embodied in their produced commodities. Hence the initial rise in productivity has produced economic decline, and if firms react to their crisis by cutting back on productive and unproductive labour and capital, reduced supply and wealth production as well.

On the other hand, because this same process of intra-departmental competition cheapens the unit value of commodities, it enhances enterprises' value profit rate and expands their subsumed class $k^* + \lambda$ expenditures. The resulting rising demands for inputs put upward pressure on the respective prices of labour-power, means of subsistence and means of production. In this case, Department I and II enterprises may react to their rising sales revenues by increasing supply conditions. Here then are the different operating forces of economic expansion.

This initial analysis of markets and market prices underscores the previous conclusion: the economy – its value profit rate and demand for and supply of wealth – is driven in contradictory directions by these different and mutually interacting class (value profit rate) and non-class (market) forces. The previous value equations can and should be modified to show these contradictory market consequences for capitalist enterprises' revenues and expenditures. Because these market price effects differ by department, each needs to be specified separately.

Department I:

$$[SV_i] + [NCR_{isp} + NCR_{ilp} - NCR_{icls} + SSCR_{icgn}] \gtreqless SSCP_i + SSCP_{il}$$

$$[SV_k] + [-NCR_{ksp} + NCR_{klp} - NCR_{kcls} + SSCR_{kcgn}] \gtreqless SSCP_k + SSCP_{klp}$$

Department II:

$$[SV_i] + [NCR_{isp} + NCR_{ilp} + NCR_{icgn} + NCR_{ivgn} - NCR_{ivls}] \gtreqless SSCP_i$$
$$+ SSCP_{ilp} + SSCP_{ic}$$

$$[SV_k] + [-NCR_{ksp} + NCR_{klp} + NCR_{kcgn} + NCR_{kvgn} - NCR_{kvls}] \gtreqless SSCP_k$$
$$+ SSCP_{klp} + SSCP_{kc}$$

As before, the first bracketed category of SV stands for class exploitation. The differently subscripted categories in the second set of brackets stand for how different market changes shape the revenue flows of capitalist enterprises in each department. NCR_{isp} and NCR_{ksp} represent, respectively, positive and negative super profit flows resulting from enterprises utilizing their SV revenues to enhance the productivity of labour. Competitive winners receive positive flows whereas losers suffer negative ones. The latter set in motion a new set of market value effects – the value cheapening of commodities – that raise enterprises' rate of class exploitation and, hence, the very utilization of SV that initiated those market effects in the first place.

The second category NCR_{lp} stands for a positive non-class revenue flow received by enterprises when and if they purchase labour-power at a market price (money wage) that is lower than its value.[3] This unequal exchange, to the advantage of capitalists, appears in the equations because capitalists, following Marx's assumption, react to their own unevenly generated NCR_{sp} flows in a particular and common way. They all increase their *occ* such that the value rate of profit, and therefore $k^* + \lambda$ subsumed class expenditures, fall for all. This fall produces, in turn, an excess supply of workers in the labour market which gives rise to this price or value advantage of NCR_{lp} in favour of enterprises.

On the other hand, because workers no longer can afford to purchase the same bundle of use-values as they did before, this very labour cost advantage to Department II capitalists is counteracted by falling sales of their wage goods. In this way, the assumed fall in the price of labour-power leads to a sales crisis for all Department II capitalists, indicated by the negative sign on the last non-class revenue category of NCR_{vls} in their value equations. In summary, what Department II capitalists gain on the unequal exchange of labour-power (NCR_{lp}) is offset by what they lose in the unequal exchange on the sale of their commodities (NCR_{vls}). Without specific further assumptions, it can't be determined which of these different non-class flows is the greater.

A similar result holds for the market sale and purchase of means of production. The assumed fall in subsumed class expenditures reduces the market demand and hence prices of means of production. The third of the non-class revenue flows of NCR_c stands for the resulting unequal exchange of means of production commodities arising between differing capitalists located in the two different departments. Department I capitalists suffer from falling prices of their commodities, indicated by the negative sign on their NCR_{cls} term, while Department II capitalists gain this exact value inflow, indicated by the positive NCR_{cgn} term in their equation. Without further specific assumptions, it is impossible to determine how and in what ways these relative gains and losses in revenues produced in these different labour-power, wage good and means of production markets impact these enterprises and hence the entire economy.

This *same* process of intra-departmental competition helps to raise the rate of class exploitation in the economy, thereby setting in motion forces of expansion and increased demands for inputs. Nonetheless, a similar set of uncertainties confronts the economy. An excess demand for workers in the labour market gives rise to a price or value advantage in favour of workers. Consequently, the term $SSCP_{lp}$ on the right-hand side of the equations shows that all enterprises in the economy distribute a portion of their surplus value to workers in the form of higher wages to gain access to more expensive labour-power.[5] On the one hand, this induced rise in money wages feeds back to benefit Department II capitalists. Workers use their higher incomes to expand purchases of wage goods. Department II capitalists gain increased non-class revenue flows of NCR_{vgn} (resulting from higher market prices on goods they sell to workers). On the other hand, it nonetheless remains unclear what will be the net impact of these market changes, for capitalists' higher sales revenues in the output market are offset by their higher labour costs ($SSCP_{lp}$) in the input market.[6]

In contrast, an excess demand for means of production impacts enterprises in the two departments differently: Department I capitalists gain a price or value advantage at the direct expense of Department II capitalists. The loss to the latter is measured by the category of $SSCP_c$ that appears on the right-hand side of the equations for Department II capitalists. They distribute a greater share of their subsumed class expenditures to Department I capitalists to gain market access to more expensive raw materials and machines. Department I capitalists receive subsumed class revenues (indicated by $SSCR_{cgn}$) which equal the higher subsumed class payments made to them on the part of Department II capitalists.

It remains unclear how these different market consequences set in motion by an assumed demand expansion impact one another and hence the economy. Department I capitalists' subsumed class revenues expand, because of their receipt of higher market prices for capital goods. Their costs rise, however, because of the higher price of labour-power faced. Department II capitalists' non-class revenues rise, because of their receipt of higher prices for wage goods. Their costs rise too, however, because of higher prices paid for labour-power and, in their case, for means of production as well.

The differently posed (inequality and equality) signs on the equations summarize the impossibility of figuring out – without making very specific assumptions – for any one, any subset of enterprises in any department, or *a fortiori* for the economy in general – how these interacting revenue and expenditure flows add up to produce a definitive index of net expansion, balance or decline. It follows that any calculated profit rate (see below) for any enterprize or the economy in general based upon these various forms of value (SV, $SSCR$ and NCR) in its numerator would be measuring an ever-changing and, hence, very uncertain sum of value flows. Further, changes in revenue flows beget expenditure changes which produce still new positive and negative revenue flows, and so on and on. Perhaps the point is now clear enough: there is no way to calculate an infinity of complex effects set in motion by any one change, whether it be the one assumed here of a rise in productivity or anything else. In other words, the economy is overdetermined.

Ever-changing revenues and expenditures

Complex as it may be, the story told so far deals only with the production and circulation of commodities. Capitalists, however, seek the highest possible flow of revenues, whether or not they derive from the class process. Responding to ever-changing market conditions (signalled by the creation of and continual change in SV and various NCR and SSCR flows in the above set of equations), they alter corporate expenditures attempting to modify existing and create new revenue positions. Depending on expected profit returns, they thus shift from one revenue position to another, moving back and forth between commodity and non-commodity production. Such corporate behaviour suggests that very little if anything is irreversible or stable in the behaviour of firms. In fact, if it were, firms would likely disappear from existence because of their inability to adapt to and modify their changing economic environment.

Consider two of many possible examples. The ones chosen especially reflect the ability of capitalists to shift the boundaries of their business operations. Suppose a relatively less efficient capitalist enterprise reacts to its market-induced negative NCR_{ksp} by reallocating a portion of its expenditures from $k^* + \lambda$ to the creation of one of these new revenue positions. Unlike Marx's assumption, it decides, at least initially, not to defend directly its surplus value position, but rather to reallocate funds from, say, capital accumulation to the establishment of a loan department. At this conjuncture, the enterprise expects the return on creating unproductive capital (loans to potential commodity buyers) to be higher and even less risky than the expected return on its competitively threatened surplus value position.

The capitalist enterprise establishes for itself a new *SSCR* position, if the interest received is paid by surplus appropriating capitalists, and an *NCR* position, if it is paid by other kinds of borrowers.[7] Becoming a financial capitalist in these ways may well enable an otherwise inefficient commodity producing enterprise to prosper and perhaps expand. It is unclear, however, in which direction lies its future prosperity. Less relative risk and higher relative returns on its newly created subsumed and/or non-class-lending positions might induce a full transition out of commodity production and into full-time banking. Alternatively, continuing to occupy its class exploitative position, it may bide its time, waiting for the right moment to reallocate funds from its relatively profitable banking business to improve its competitiveness in commodity production. Such a strategy suggests how less-efficient enterprises can work to become more efficient, not immediately responding to market competition by raising their *occ* to improve productivity, but rather by this kind of circuitous route, by securing new forms of revenues to help secure a threatened surplus value position.

Yet, the emergence of consumer and producer debt only adds to the contradictions and uncertainty in the economy. Not only is this strategy open to all enterprises in the economy, whatever their level of efficiency or line of business, but once any firm – industrial or financial – creates or adopts a successful credit operation, that success draws the attention of potential competitors within or without its industry. Their entry serves to reduce the SSCR and NCR returns to lending.

Even if the substitution of unproductive for productive capital has no net effect on employment, so that the demands for wage and means of production commodities remains unaffected *from this change alone*, it nonetheless remains unclear what will happen to the economy and its capitalist class structure. On the one hand, that structure is threatened, the more industrial firms in each department decide – for competitive or whatever other reason – to move out of productive and into unproductive capital. On the other hand, it also is strengthened. Consumer and producer credit facilitate the purchase of wage and means of production commodities, thereby countering both departments' potential sales crises. Additionally, credit-fed demands help enterprises expand the capitalist class structure; the mass of surplus rises as more of both kinds of commodities are produced and sold.

Yet, such an expansion is always problematic, for credit undermines borrowers' ability to sustain their purchases. Unless they receive higher revenue flows to finance interest charges, their demands for commodities must fall.[8] At that point, the resulting sales crisis for enterprises in Departments I and II would produce the respective value losses – the negative NCR_{vls} and NCR_{cls} – already analyzed.

In the second example, an enterprise – irrespective of its efficiency ranking within a department – purchases the common stock of a different enterprise in its own or another department. To finance that purchase, it issues bonds. A variety of reasons may motivate its behaviour including using its new ownership position to acquire an existing or potential competitor, gaining access to new technologies, product lines, or selling regions, or purchasing needed inputs at lower costs.

If the investing enterprise receives dividends, the stock purchase creates a new subsumed class revenue position for itself.[9] Two new items appear on the expenditure side of its value equation: the purchase of common sock and the annual interest paid on the new debt. The new equation becomes:

$$SV + SSCR_{div} + NCR_{debt} \gtreqless SSCP + X + (i \times NCR_{debt})$$

where $SSCR_{div}$ stands for the dividends received, NCR_{debt} the corporate debt issued, X the purchase of the common stock (equal to NCR_{debt}), and i the interest rate on that debt. Because NCR_{debt} and X represent flows for one period only, the final value equation becomes:

$$SV + SSCR_{div} \gtreqqless SSCP + (i \times NCR_{debt})$$

The different possible signs on the equations index once more the uncertainty in regard to how this financial transaction affects this or any enterprise.

If an investing enterprise looks only at the new dividends received and if that return is less than the required interest cost, then the financial investment clearly was not successful. Investing in another company produces a contraction, measured by the need to reduce subsumed class $k^* + \lambda$ expenditures, unless the affected enterprise can raise class exploitation sufficiently to offset the difference between these added interest charges and the smaller dividends received. However, comparing the dividend return only to the interest costs of acquiring it is hardly the sole calculation made by investing enterprises. It scarcely explains why such financial investments are so pervasive in the economy today. Nor are they easily explained by the possible capital gain earned by selling the stock at some future date. In fact, firms undertake such financial investments despite facing much higher interest costs than their revenues of SV and $SSCR$ can tolerate. They seem purposefully to place their class exploitative position in jeopardy.

Visions of the future motivate such risky behaviour. Acquiring an ownership position is expected in one way or another to create a future stream of added revenues that more than compensates for the added interest costs on the initial debt. In Marxian terms, what drives such financial investments is the expectation of earning a higher value and/or market rate of profit, because of favourable access to cheaper means of production, gaining new super profits via acquiring new production technologies, or obtaining new masses of surplus value via acquiring other companies' commodities (popular product lines). To the degree capitalists realize such expectations, the left-hand side of this equation exceeds the right, enabling subsumed class $k^* + \lambda$ expenditures to expand.

Corporate institutional arrangements also adjust to such investments. At any point, the acquiring enterprise may eliminate the distinction between the two corporations, merging them into one combined enterprise. Mergers impact the enterprises' revenues and expenditures: the subsumed class ownership position is eliminated, while the acquired company's surplus value (and corresponding SSCP) is added to the acquiring company's existing surplus value (and SSCP). Additionally, such investments also can lead to partial sales of newly acquired assets. At any point, the investing enterprise may decide to keep what it conceives to be the most profitable part of the acquired business (or that portion with which it is most comfortable) and sell the rest. It even could sell its existing business in order to specialize fully in the newly acquired one. Whatever is the choice, sales of such assets earn capitalists non-class revenues, the availability of which makes feasible the development of still new corporate strategies.

Conclusions

Because all capitalist enterprises are linked together by commodity and money markets, no one of them can be immune from the private actions taken by another irrespective of its location. Such actions both threaten and strengthen affected enterprises. Their ever-impacted categories of SV, SSCR, and NCR confirm this susceptibility to market influences. Changes in the latter make every enterprise vulnerable, put at risk of disappearing from the economy, even as they improve that enterprise's financial health. Markets always have presented this kind of contradiction to capitalists and their economist supporters. The history of non-Marxian economic thought reflects this tension. It oscillates between the fear of markets, and hence controls over them, and their celebration, and hence unfettered operation.

Each of the well-known capitalist developments examined so far – from enterprises' attempts to increase the productivity of labour to their expansion into finance capital to their more recent frenzy in the purchase of each other's common stocks – illustrates the dynamic and instability of capitalism. A common theme is a truly dizzying and seemingly never-ending change in each and every capitalist enterprise's class (*SV* and *SSCR*) and non-class (*NCR*) revenues. Caught in this swirl of effectivities, capitalists continually alter their expenditures, aiming to modify their class and non-class revenue positions, moving to eliminate some and expand others, even while seeking ever-new ones. Their private actions add yet again to those effectivities.

Capitalists create both subsumed and non-class revenue positions by loaning money to, respectively, other industrial capitalists and workers, managers, bankers, merchants, landlords, nation states, and so forth. Still other subsumed and non-class positions of ownership arise as they purchase corporate stock of, respectively, productive and unproductive capitalists. Capitalists continually seek to secure their sales revenues via advertizing and product design, hoping thereby to establish subsumed and/or non-class monopoly positions for themselves.[10] They aim for this kind of market security even as they destabilize markets by entering new ones seeking non-class super profit revenues there.

Capitalists subsumed class expenditures on research, development and design give rise to ever-new kinds of commodities that serve to strengthen and expand the capitalist class structure. Newly invented commodities signify new sources of surplus value and, therefore, still new subsumed class expenditures in the economy. Capitalists engage in and expand commodity production in this way even while they take on other subsumed and non-class positions, some of which seem hardly connected or ostensibly threatening to their commodity operation. For example, they may move into retail trade, earning new subsumed class market fees from other capitalists by selling their commodities to final buyers.[11] They also may lease owned patents, trademarks and new technologies to other industrial capitalists. It is not merely the returns on such subsumed class positions that attract them. Rather, it is also the opportunities such positions provide to expand their commodity sales and hence class structure. Such is the case when their commodities serve as complements to others.

These multiple forms of revenues identify the multiple personalities taken on by capitalists. They exploit labour, while lending money to that exploited labour; ruthlessly fight one another for market shares, even while providing one another with new technologies, finance and merchanting; seek to expand productive capital, even as they seek ways to expand unproductive capital. Their diverse activities make it literally impossible to figure out what exactly is or will become the business of a capitalist enterprise or by extension of the entire economy. Should it not follow, then, that any measure of profitability and hence movement needs to reflect or capture this complexity and instability of revenues (and expenditures)?

Consider the following profit measure. Constructed as a site of class and non-class net revenues, it measures the combined net profitability of a many faceted capitalist enterprise (Resnick and Wolff 1987: 207–13). Adding together the multiple revenues of such an enterprise yields its gross profits: $\pi = SV + SSCR + NCR$. To discover its net profits π_n, subtract specific expenditures (costs) aimed at producing these different gross profits:

$$\pi_n = (SV - SSCP') + (SSCR - X') + (NCR - Y')$$

where $SSCP'$ represent the subsumed class expenditures accounting practice and tax laws of the day designate as necessary costs, and X' and Y' stand for similarly designated costs to generate, respectively, subsumed and non-class gross revenues.[12] To derive the enterprise's net profit rate r_n, first divide each equation's component by capital expenditures, $C + V$, and then multiply and divide subsumed and non-class revenues only by the corporate expenditures, X' and Y', that respectively produce each:

$$r_n = \pi_n/C + V = [(SV - SSCP')/C + V]$$
$$+ [(SSCR - X')/X' \times X'/C + V] + [(NCR - Y')/Y' \times Y'/C + V]$$

Rewriting this equation in terms of rates of return yields:

$$r_n = (r_{sv}) + (r_{sc} \times a_{sc}) + (r_{nc} \times a_{nc}),$$

where r_{sv} stands for the enterprise's net *value* profit rate, $[(SV - SSCP)/C + V]$; r_{sc} for its net *subsumed* class profit rate, $[(SSCR - X')/X']$, weighted by a_{sc}, its ratio of unproductive (X') to productive $(C + V)$ capital expenditures; and r_{nc} for its net *non-class* profit rate, $[(NCR - Y')/Y']$, weighted by (a_{nc}), its ratio of unproductive (Y') to productive $(C + V)$ capital expenditures.

No one of these differently specified profit rates – r_{sv}, r_{sc}, r_{nc} – is more central than are the others in determining the success (failure) of this enterprise and by extension the economy of enterprises. Hence the overall net profit rate cannot be reduced merely to the partial profitability of one of its interacting, constituent parts. To do so would give only a partial and perhaps quite misleading view of its complex operation. Measuring only one or another of its profitable directions that singular rate might well miss the emergence or development of entirely new directions. A number of examples were provided showing why a rise (fall) in any one need not necessarily imply a rise (fall) in the others, starting with how intra-departmental competition may drive r_{sv} down, even as it unleashes value consequences that drive up that same rate and changes in market forces that propel r_{sc} and r_{nc} in contradictory directions as well. In other words, a change in any rate affects both itself and the others in contradictory ways. Because the weighted sum – the complex net profit rate r_n – is the site of such conflicting determinations, it too exists in contradiction. From this perspective, no inherent tendency possibly can exist for it and the economy to rise, fall or stay in equilibrium (Cullenberg 1994).

Finally, consider one of several possible new expenditure equations derived from this kind of analysis. It especially demonstrates the risk of essentializing only one form of capitalist expenditures to deduce developmental tendencies in the capitalist economy. Suppose all *SSCP, X* and *Y* expenditures are considered to be costs save those on capital accumulation, research on and development of new products, and new loans and financial investments. With these assumptions and after some simple manipulation, the above equation yields:

$$r_n = k^* + \lambda_{rd} + a_{sc} + a_{nc}$$

where as before k^* stands for capital accumulation, λ_{rd} for the ratio of research on and development of new products to capital expenditures $(C + V)$, and a_{sc} and a_{nc} for the ratios of new loans and financial investments (establishing, respectively, subsumed and non-class financial positions) to capital expenditures $(C + V)$.

This new equation underscores the importance of expected net returns from very particular kinds of capitalist expenditures, and how problematic is a focus solely on k^* as the essential sign of what will happen to the economy (Norton 1992). Capitalists' reduction of k^* need not necessarily portend a recession. Besides the expansionary forces set in motion by that very decrease, the reallocation of revenues from capital accumulation to increase one or both of these other kinds of expenditures may unleash expansionary forces in the economy. Such research, development and financial expenditures may well create environments in which k^* can then take off. Indeed, many a financial pundit today looks more to some combination of $\lambda_{rd} + a_{sc} + a_{nc}$ than solely to k^* as a sign of what will happen to any enterprise or to the economy in general.

The argument presented of enterprises, their different profit rates and expenditures, and the economy all constituted in contradiction, sent into diverse directions by any considered force, implies a very fragile existence for any one of them and hence for class exploitation. No epoch-making event is required for their possible elimination. Rather, any change herein analyzed undermines them and that class structure, and by that same dialectical logic, strengthens them as well. For Marxism, the trick is to see their ever-present vulnerability as an opportunity to intervene with the aim of enhancing it, while at the same time being ever conscious of the profound uncertainty associated with that intervention.

Notes

1 An enterprise's super profits (NCR_{sp}) equal the difference between the *common* social unit value faced in the market (EV/UV) and its *private* unit value ($[EV/UV]_{PR}$) multiplied by the units (UV) sold. The less efficient face a market loss ($-NCR_{sp}$) and the more efficient a gain ($+NCR_{sp}$) when each sells at the common unit value.

2 Any concrete analysis necessarily arrests this dialectical process to communicate its story. Without this kind of intervention on the part of a theorist, no communication ever could take place. In other contexts, such an intervention has been called an 'entry point' (Resnick and Wolff 1987: 25–30). It represents the order that a theorist brings to and imposes on the ontological chaos faced. That order enables 'tendencies' to be produced.

3 In value terms, $NCR_{lp} = (V - P_{lp} \times l)$ where P_{lp} stands for the market price of labour-power and l for the productive workers hired.

4 In this case, Department II enterprises sell their commodities at a market price of P_v that is less than the unit value. Hence $NCR_{Vls} = (EV/UV - P_v) \times UV$ where UV stands for the quantity of wage good sold in the market.

5 The favourable position workers occupy in a tight labour-power market enables them to receive a price for their labour-power that exceeds its value: $P_{lp} = V + SSCR$, where P_{lp} stands for the price of labour-power and $SSCR$ stands for the received subsumed class revenues.

6 The net impact of these different market changes on the value of workers' labour-power is unclear. A fall in the unit value of wage goods drives workers' V down. However, how much, if at all, it falls depends on what is assumed about workers' ability to demand higher real wages.

7 An enterprise that makes a loan to a surplus-appropriating capitalist and receives in return a distributed share of the latter's surplus value occupies a subsumed class

position. The interest received on the loan counts as subsumed class revenue. All other interest received on loans to borrowers who are non-surplus appropriating capitalists counts as non-class revenues. In these loans, the borrowers pay interest but not out of surplus value.

8 Workers use the value of their labour-power to purchase a mass of consumer goods, uv, at their unit values, ev/uv: $V = ev/uv \times uv$. Loans of NCR_{debt} enable them to expand their consumer purchases: $NCR_{\text{debt}} + V < ev/uv \times uv' + (i \times NCR_{\text{debt}})$, where uv' indicates the larger bundle of consumer goods purchased, and $i \times NCR_{\text{debt}}$ stands for interest (i) payments on that debt per period. Even if loan repayments are ignored, workers will undergo a crisis (signalled by the inequality sign), unless V rises sufficiently and/or new sources of revenues are found to offset the required interest payments. If one or the other does not occur, consumer expenditures (demand) fall.

Corporate debt poses a different situation. Suppose industrial capitalists receive loans of NCR_{debt} to expand their subsumed class expenditures: $SV + NCR_{\text{debt}} \geq$ or $< SSCP' + (i \times NCR_{\text{debt}})$, where the $SSCP'$ stands for the expanded subsumed class expenditures, and $i \times NCR_{\text{debt}}$ equals the interest payments on that debt per period. Because corporate, unlike consumer, debt expands subsumed class expenditures, it creates additional SV for the borrower. Because the size of this class effect is unknown, the sign on the value equation remains indeterminate.

9 Purchasing common stock enables the buyer to own the assets (means of production) of another corporation. The latter distributes a share of its appropriated surplus in the form of a dividend to gain access to those owned assets. Because the dividends received are paid out of surplus value, they create a subsumed class revenue position for the investing enterprise.

10 A Department I enterprise that gains monopoly power and sells its commodity to other industrial capitalists at a price higher than its unit value earns a subsumed class revenue. In contrast, a Department II enterprise that gains monopoly power but sells its wage commodity to buyers at a price higher than unit value earns non-class revenue. In the first case, a buying capitalist makes a distribution (a subsumed class payment) out of surplus value to gain access to the needed capital input. In the second case, the commodity buyer by definition has no surplus value out of which a distribution can be made.

11 These fees represent subsumed class payments on the part of the producing capitalist, for the commodities are assumed to be sold to the merchant at a market sum ($P \times UV$) which is less than what the commodities are worth in value terms (W). That difference (equal to $W - P \times UV$) is the capitalist subsumed class fee paid to the merchant. When merchants sell the commodities to final consumers at their value (W), they realize this difference as a subsumed class revenue. Capitalists pay such a fee in order to sell the goods sooner than they would otherwise, thus turning their capital over more quickly and avoiding risks associated with retail trade.

12 Several different forms of net profits could be calculated, depending on which expenditures are included in the set subtracted from gross revenues. Hence the very notion of profitability itself is unclear. Differently calculated net profits have their respective adherents within the business community, depending on which of these differing measures they claim portends corporate success.

12
Has the Empire Struck Back?

Alan Freeman

> One can reject in advance the attempts by Professor Kontrat'ev to assign to the epochs that he calls long cycles the same 'strict rhythm' that is observed in short cycles. This attempt is a clearly mistaken generalization based on a formal analogy. The periodicity of short cycles is conditioned by the internal dynamic of capitalist forces, which manifests itself whenever and wherever there is a market. As for those long (fifty-year) intervals that Professor Kontrat'ev hastily proposes also to call cycles, their character and duration is determined not by the internal play of capitalist forces, but by the external conditions in which capitalist development occurs. The absorption by capitalism of new countries and continents, the discovery of new natural resources, and, in addition, significant factors of a 'superstructural' order, such as wars and revolutions, determine the character and alternation of expansive, stagnating or declining epochs in capitalist development.
>
> Trotsky[1]

The idea of this chapter is to ask what is happening to the world market. This is an innocent enough question and, as orthodox economics often approaches it, the only difficulties seem to be technical and empirical: get the data, make the model, feed the computer and churn out the result. I will argue that the real difficulty is not the answer but the question. The problem is not one of models or techniques; it is to understand what a market actually consists of. In particular, we need to understand what a capitalist market consists of.

Since 1970, the world market has undergone one of the most protracted phases of decline and instability it has yet known. To know whether, or how, this will end, we must establish what conditions are required for its ending. Is there a process *endogenous* or internal to the world capitalist market which can restore its stability after such a long period of stagnation? Alternatively, if the conditions for restoration are *exogenous* or external to it, then what are they? But to answer these questions, we must first know what is inside and what is outside, that is, where the boundary lies: we must know what this market *is*.

I am going to suggest that:

1. Decline is endogenous. A regular process repeatedly leads, over a period of 20 to 30 years, to 'generalized crisis', by which I mean a prolonged period of slow growth, mass unemployment, and political and economic instability.
2. Restoration is not endogenous. Exit from generalized crisis arises from political intervention, up to and including dictatorship and war, on an ever more barbaric and brutal scale; it depends on the conscious actions of classes and the political power they wield.
3. Polarization is endogenous. The growing inequality between a small group of rich nations and a large group of poor ones is a secular trend which accelerates when the world market extends and slows down when it retreats. History has reversed Adam Smith's dictum that the wealth of nations increases with the extent of the market.
4. The two processes are linked. It has been possible to restore market stability *because* of the impoverishment of three-quarters of the world, by placing the labour of the poor countries at the service of the rich. The principal goals of the 'Reagan–Thatcher' offensive, the destruction of the USSR, the opening up of world markets to US capital, the construction of the WTO and the triumph of neo-liberalism were to recreate the conditions for such a restoration.
5. History has seen two quite distinct patterns of recovery from generalized crisis. The industrial revolution, and the post-war boom, yielded high global profit rates under a single hegemonic power (the UK in 1845, the US in 1945) which fuelled a general expansion even of its rivals, yielding rising (if unequal) prosperity, relative peace and political stability. 1890–1914 was different. The profit rate did not recover to previous levels, and there was the absence of a clear hegemon, growing misery and barbarity over the immiserated parts of the world, and intense great-power rivalry leading to the wars and revolutions that bestrode the twentieth century.

I will argue that the evidence suggests the only possible basis of a new wave of economic expansion is a recovery of this second type, more comparable with 1890–1914 than with 1945–65. I call this a return to 'classical imperialism'.

Can the market heal itself?

The market as it now exists is a definite historical phenomenon which spread out from its birthplace in Europe and conquered the world in the last century: the capitalist market. Almost every society has had market activities and institutions such as trading and money, but only under modern conditions has the market become both the principal organizer of all other social relations and institutions, and an entity distinct from them. Does this market require nothing of these institutions except that they place no limits upon it?

Trotsky, cited at the start of this chapter, opened the 1923 debate around the law of motion of such a society in these terms. Responding to Kondratiev's assertion that beside the 7-to-10-year business cycle there was a longer cycle of 50 to 60 years, he did not dispute Kondratiev's facts, and almost a century of further experience has empirically confirmed his assertion; the discussion then as now concerns its causes and laws of motion. The key issue is whether this periodic variation is the outcome of factors distinct from, and independent of, the institutions in which capital is embedded.

In asserting it is not, Trotsky explicitly contrasts it with the short cycle which is 'conditioned by the internal dynamic of capitalist forces, which manifests itself whenever and wherever there is a market'. The long cycle is determined 'not by the internal play of capitalist forces, but by the external conditions in which capitalist development occurs'.

But what *is* the difference between the 'internal dynamic of capitalist forces' and 'the external conditions in which capitalist development occurs'? Where does the boundary lie between the capitalist market itself, and the non-market conditions for its existence? In studying the distinction I am only trying to make explicit what all others take for granted. By blaming 'government interference' for market failure, neo-liberal economics for example is already, in its very language, distinguishing government from the market.

The distinction has profound policy implications. The idea that the market stabilizes itself endogenously is, when one thinks about it, the core claim of neo-liberalism. The basic idea is that the market cures its own disorders. Left to its own devices it is perfect and by definition cannot produce such unfortunate episodes as financial crashes, famines, permanent unemployment and national destitution. These must therefore result from the imperfect conditions under which it operates (such as bad government, monetary incompetence, union intransigence, cultural or historical backwardness), from the technological régime, the regulatory framework or the prevailing entrepreneurial spirit. That is, they result from circumstances exogenous to the market.

Neo-liberal policy conclusions are quite logical given these premises: remove all restrictions on the market so that it can achieve the perfection intrinsic to it. But if the capitalist market destabilizes *itself* – and if, moreover, it cannot restabilize itself – we are led to entirely different conclusions. Not only is it foolish to leave the market to its own devices; actually its failure will call exogenous forces into being whether we like it or not, whether in the form of popular or national resistance directed against market freedom, or political and military measures designed to enforce it.

There is then a sphere for conscious human choice distinct from, and superior to, the market. Precisely because they are exogenous to the market, these forces are not governed or dominated by it; precisely because the market endogenously fails, they are a necessary part of life. Politics and social intervention are legitimate, necessary and autonomous spheres of activity, not limited as in the neo-liberal vision to simply maintaining the conditions for the market to attain its perfect state.

Moreover, if the market is ultimately incapable of sustaining itself, then the task facing any responsible individual, rather than simply shielding society from the market's side-effects, is to save society from the wreckage of its failure. The problem for Brazil, South Korea or Russia was to defend themselves not against the onward march of the world capital market, but against its violent withdrawal.

What does an 'endogenous' theory look like?

Despite the substantial implications of this issue, and although very insistent that the market is a social institution distinct from all others, economics is extraordinarily vague about where boundaries actually lie. It defines what is 'endogenous' algebraically, asking which variables can be determined mathematically if other variables have been fixed by the economist. On closer examination, this begs the question. If one economist's equation makes prices a function of preferences, then that economist has defined these preferences as exogenous. But another can rewrite the same equation so that the preferences are a function of prices. This is an arbitrary choice. *Why* treat preferences as external to the market? What is it about the nature of the capitalist market that puts prices inside it, and preferences outside it?

One reaction is to say, in essence, that the market in principle contains everything. Many attempts to explain unexpected market behaviour begin by 'internalizing' things which orthodox theory treats as external. Thus Goodwin (1982) explains the business cycle as an interaction between employment and wage-bargaining; endogenous-growth theory (see Stern 1996) explains national inequality by making external factors such as policy a product of market forces; real business-cycle theory says cycles propagate exogenous shocks; and many long-wave theories treat phases of expansion as if technical innovation arises more or less automatically out of a phase of decline and suffices, with no other precondition, to reverse it.

This does not really address the problem. With enough equations, we could make everything in the world a part of the market. But then we no longer have a theory of the market but a theory of the universe. The capitalist market is a social institution distinct, for example, from government, and exhibits laws which apply under all governments except those which suppress it. It must therefore be possible to express and frame these laws without reference to government.

I do not claim that the market operates independent of politics or technology. It interacts with them. But an interaction is not the same as an internal property. The market interacts with the climate; food output depends on the weather and the weather depends on the output of pollutants. This connection really exists, which however neither means the climate is part of the market, nor that economics is a branch of meteorology. The actual course of the market arises from its interaction with countless institutions; precisely in order to analyze this interaction, we have to distinguish it from them.[2]

Nor am I saying markets must necessarily have laws, on grounds of pure logic. I will to the contrary try to show that such laws *empirically* exist, in the form of patterns of market behaviour that manifest themselves under a very wide variety of external conditions. The problem is to make sense of these patterns using categories that correspond to them; I will argue that this requires the category of *value*.

In Figure 12.1, the thin line shows the rate of profit in the US economy. The thick line shows how much the economy has accumulated: it gives the stock of capital, divided by labour employed.[3] Both are represented in terms of value, measured in socially necessary abstract labour time, by transforming raw data from Duménil and Lévy (1994b),[4] using a simple algorithm explained in Freeman (1997). However, this is not the standard, equilibrium concept of value as it appears in the orthodox literature but an alternative

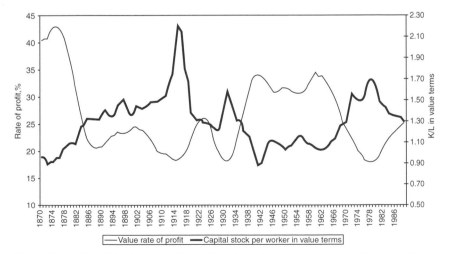

Figure 12.1 United States rate of profit and capital stock in terms of labour time, 1870–1992.
Source data: Duménil and Lévy (1994b).

which this literature systematically ignores: the *temporal single-system* (TSS) or non-equilibrium interpretation of Marx's theory of value (see Freeman and Carchedi 1995). I applied only one other transformation: I took a moving average of the profit rate over seven years to remove short-term fluctuations.

Any unprejudiced observer can verify the relation between these quantities. The rate of profit falls when capital accumulates, and vice versa. Statistical analysis confirms that 80 per cent of the variation in the value rate of profit is explained by changes in the capital–labour ratio. The only substantive exception is the period 1890–1910, of which more later. Phases of rapid accumulation – which appear on the graph as steep rises in the capital–labour ratio – invariably accompany a fall in the profit rate.

Of course this does not establish a chain of causal connection; this calls for a theoretical explanation, which I will shortly propose. However I want at this stage to draw attention to five points to which the theoretical explanation will refer:

1. Expressed in value terms, periods of crisis are clearly periods of *decline*; of negative accumulation. But even in use-value or monetary terms it is clear that periods of reduced accumulation alternate with periods of expansion.[5] This suggests that this alternation is a 'genuine' fact and not an artefact of our concept.
2. The law manifests itself. For long periods the rate of profit falls and the capital stock rises. Though not always so, this appears sufficiently often, and for sufficiently long periods, to create a prima facie case for a relation of cause that is an element of observable reality.
3. The phenomenon is largely independent of external factors. The long profit declines of 1870–90, 1902–14 and 1962–78 took place under very different regimes of regulation, technology and government but all took the same form in value terms: stock goes up, and the profit rate comes down. This suggests that the connection between growth and declining profit rates is a law *of* the market, and not of something else. It 'manifests itself whenever and wherever there is a market.'
4. Specifically, technical advance does not counteract this law. The periods of most rapid technical change, of whirlwind revolution, are precisely those periods when capital stock is rising and the profit rate is falling, which is very difficult to square with the idea that technical progress counteracts the fall in the profit rate.
5. There are two distinct types of expansionary phase. The recovery of 1890 did not re-establish the profit rate, whereas that of 1945 did. We can relate this to other facts: 1890 opened a prolonged period of extreme and violent political crisis, and 1945 closed one. A key question is whether any new upturn can be stable like 1945–1962 or would be unstable like 1890–1914. At least part of the explanation, although

stock figures from this period are less reliable, is that a significant element of the 1890 recovery was an additional source of US profits, rather than a decline in US capital stock. I will argue that this source was the appropriation of profit by the great powers from the rest of the world, for which the exogenous precondition was military and commercial conquest.

What does an endogenous law consist of?

We have presented only supporting evidence for a law that explains generalized crisis. A full justification requires a theoretical explanation, deduced from logically developed properties of the category in which the law is expressed.

Such an account does indeed follow from the concept of value applied in this chapter: it is a law linking capital stock and investment, which I call the law of accumulation.[6] Capital stock grows by exactly what is added to it by investment, over any period. Suppose, for example, an initial capital of 1000 units and a constant labour force of 300. Suppose 200 of this is profit, and of this profit, 100 is invested. Then in year 1, the capital stock must grow to $1000 + 100 = 1100$; in year 2, to $1100 + 100 = 1200$; and so on: it grows *as long as investment is positive*. Profit, to the contrary, remains fixed at 200 and even if exploitation increases, cannot possibly rise above 300, the amount of living labour worked each year.

This is *why* accumulation leads to a falling profit rate. The profit rate itself, for a given capital stock, cannot possibly rise above the total living labour worked in each year. But this is fixed independent of accumulation, by the size of the work force. The profit rate asymptotically falls.[7] The only other way that the profit rate can then be restored is if accumulation itself is suspended, that is, if profits are not invested but instead, capital is converted into revenue.

Normally, investment is positive. But when capital stock is reducing, it becomes negative – disaccumulation. This is not the same as the physical liquidation of stock. It simply means the capitalists spend their wealth in the current period, a situation that Marx describes as the conversion of capital into revenue or the release of capital (Maldonado-Filho 1997). In fact, if technical progress is taking place, disaccumulation will occur even if the capitalists *only* replace their physical stock in kind, because in each period they need to spend less money to secure the same goods.

This exceptional circumstance takes place only in crisis. Capital that ceases to expand is destroying itself, not least because it destroys the source of demand for investment goods, provoking a slump. In this sense we are dealing with a law of the capitalist market, not 'the market in general'; only under capitalism must the market expand to survive, so that accumulation becomes its form of existence. Crisis is hence not a suspension of equilibrium but a suspension of *growth*. This gives precise meaning to the idea that the fall in the profit rate is endogenous to capitalism: it can be reversed only by suspending capitalist accumulation itself. There are two ways this can happen: one is if the market in capital is eliminated and investment is removed from its sphere. The other is if the fall ends destructively as investment is hit by falling profitability: this is the source of general crisis.

A pure law of value: Distinguishing value from use-value and money

At this point we encounter a complication which I have so far kept in the background. What concepts do we presuppose, in order to speak of accumulation, profit rate and capital stock? Only one: the substance that accumulates – the 'result' of economic production, or value. Stock is the quantity of value in existence, accumulation is the value increment of this stock, profit is the excess of value produced in a given period, and the profit rate is profit divided by stock.

The law of accumulation is what I term a 'pure law'; it is expressed in terms of a single substance, value, without any external admixture. This is what makes it universal; it also makes it endogenous. It applies regardless of technology or monetary regime, just as the law of gravity applies regardless of the material of the planets. Technology may interact with this law but cannot suspend it because it cannot modify the quantity of value which a given number of workers create.

This quantitative absoluteness is not manifested by other, more common concepts of value. If we treat money as the measure of value, for example, then as assets get dearer their possessor gets richer, making them appear as a source of profit. Similarly, if we think of output as a mass of use-values, or quantities of goods, as does most of economics, then it will appear that technical progress can increase profits because more goods will be created with the same labour.

In each such case we are attempting to express a law which applies to labour alone in terms of something which is not labour. This is like using a pair of scales to tell us how big a piece of cake is; the problem is that the scales can't tell us how much air the cake contains. Nevertheless, all cakes obey empirically observable laws determined only by their weight, regardless of their size. We can understand the logical foundation of these laws only if we understand weight for what it is, a property independent of size.

The empirically observable law of accumulation is grounded only when we express it in terms of a substance – value – independent of money and technique: when we eliminate, from the definition of production, every source of new value except the producer, namely labour itself.

Then:

1. the value added by living labour is *conserved in circulation*: it is destroyed or created only in production;
2. the only source of new value is living labour.[8]

Because of (1), capital stock continues to rise unless the capitalists actually disinvest. Because of (2) the effect of this on the profit rate can be offset only by raising the amount of value the capitalists appropriate, and this is strictly limited by the growth rate of world living labour.

While the law also appears empirically in terms of other concepts of value such as use-value, it cannot theoretically be accounted for using these concepts. There is no obvious reason for the profit rate in use-value terms to fall as a consequence of accumulation; indeed Okishio's (1961) famous theorem shows it must rise indefinitely unless offset by increasing real wages.

It is a dogma of most writings on Marx that, because the profit rate in use-value terms necessarily rises with technical progress, this law cannot hold. This dogma ignores the fact, well known to Keynesians, that the profit rate varies according to the unit of account. The 'errors' which the literature attributes to Marx's law arise because in the standard equilibrium framework, value is incorrectly accounted for and is treated as being destroyed without being consumed; all rates of profit are collapsed onto a single rate, the use-value or 'material' profit rate. If, however, we interpret Marx's value concept without presupposing equilibrium – and the evidence that this was Marx's own idea is very substantial – then his own theory of the tendency of the rate of profit to fall is logically faultless (Freeman and Carchedi 1995).

Conceiving the poverty of nations

A general concept is not scientifically useful unless

1. it explains a variety of phenomena, not just a single phenomenon, and
2. it exhibits the relations between phenomena.

I will now argue that the same concept of value which explains the periodic long-term decline of accumulation also explains the long-term, secular differentiation of nations (see also Freeman 1996a).

At one time the left widely believed that a falling rate of profit was irreversible and would lead to a terminal collapse of capitalism. I think the evidence of the 1930s has settled this question. Capitalism did survive a shattering and protracted crisis and it would be imprudent to suppose it cannot do so again.

The same cannot be said for the differentiation of nations. A large body of evidence shows that the global market has produced a prolonged and irreversible divergence between the nations of the world, organizing them in two groups:

1. A small group containing around one-fourth of the world's population and comprising essentially those nations that have been rich since the start of this century, plus a tiny number of additions, mainly peripheral to the existing centres.
2. A much larger group containing three-fourths of the world population. Although this contains two groups, middle- and low-income nations, it shouldn't be forgotten what 'middle' means in this context – a living standard between a fifth and a tenth of the advanced-country average.

This secular change in market relations, unlike the decline in the profit rate, has *never* been reversed and has only been interrupted when nations protect themselves from the world market in capital.[9] Moreover it is nearly universal: a minute number of nations have risen from poor to rich since 1870. An authoritative article by Pritchett (1997: 9) sums up the results as follows:

> You cannot escape the conclusion that the last 150 years have seen divergence, big time... The magnitude of the change in the absolute gaps in per capita incomes between rich and poor is staggering. From 1870 to 1990, the average absolute gap in incomes of all countries from the leader had grown by an order of magnitude from $1,286 to $12,662.

Pritchett gives the ratio of the GDP of the richest to the poorest country as 8.7 in 1870, and 45.2 in 1990. He gives the ratio of the 'advanced capitalist' to all other countries as 2.4 in 1870, and 4.5 in 1990. This differentiation accelerated markedly after 1980, when the US opened its world trade offensive. According to Maddison (1995), Brazil grew by 4.13 per cent per year between 1960 and 1979, and actually declined by 0.54 per cent between 1980 and 1994.

How should we account for these facts? They find almost no explanation within orthodox theory. In my view, this is due to a conceptual framework which conceals the fact that distribution is a competitive struggle. It is literally inconceivable, in use-value terms, that one country might get poorer *because* another gets richer. Consider Figure 12.2, which compares the output of the major regions of the world in use-value terms.

It appears as if everyone gains, but some more than others. Since by the application of technology, output can increase in principle without limit, there is no obvious reason why anyone should fail to benefit from it. The framework of 'development' economics becomes that of obtaining access to a limitless resource, and a failure to do so must be explained not by competition but by backwardness; countries are poor not because others are rich, but because they have not 'done as well'. They are made responsible for something that has in fact been done to them.

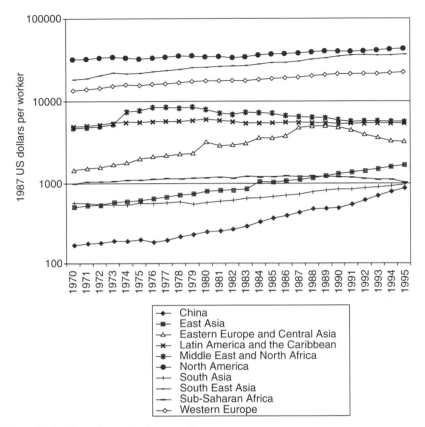

Figure 12.2   Use-value output per worker.

However, human output *is* limited, not by external resources but by human production. The world *cannot* produce for more hours than it works. If we express the outcome of the phenomenon of distribution in terms of these hours worked, precisely because this neither rises nor falls in circulation, it becomes clear that the market locks nations in a battle for a fixed magnitude, which cannot rise faster than the number of consumers. There is no such thing as comparative advantage in the acquisition of value: only a ruthless struggle to survive.

We can observe this as shown in Figure 12.3, by asking how many years of local labour are required, in each region, to acquire one year of world labour, a number I call the 'labour-appropriation ratio'. This conveys several phenomena that were not apparent in Figure 12.2. First, the competitive struggle between nations emerges clearly. When one goes up, the others go down, and vice versa.

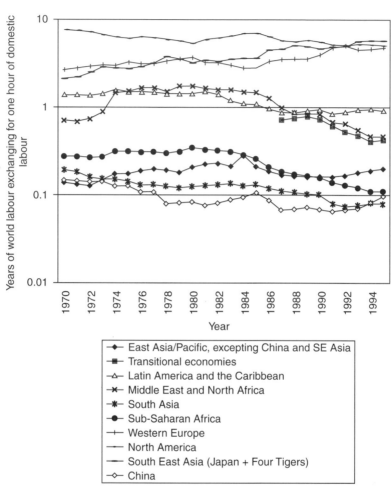

Figure 12.3   Unequal value for equal work.

Second, the graph shows that 1980 was a turning point in the structure of the world economy. The protracted downturn of the Middle East, of Latin America, of South Asia and of sub-Saharan Africa all date from this point; although the data for the transitional economies is available only from 1989, their collapse was in large degree the culmination of the US policy offensive launched in 1980.

The graph also conveys very clear information about the structure of the world economy. Three groups of countries have converged at a labour-appropriation ratio of 8, namely Western Europe, North America and South-East Asia (Japan and the Four Tigers). Among these, North America shows a clear relative decline. Though the graph does not show it because the figures are disaggregated, the industrial countries as a whole show a rising trend.

A second group bumps along the bottom at a labour-appropriation ratio between 0.2 and 0.1 and is also differentiating: China and East Asia/Pacific (a group which excludes China and the South-East Asian economies) are rising, although China's rise is quite recent and has not restored its 1970 position. South Asia – a region with nearly a quarter of the world population – and sub-Saharan Africa have suffered what Pritchett (1997) calls 'an implosive decline'.

A further 'middle' group of regions track each other at a ratio between 0.5 and 1. Of these only Latin America has held its own: Middle East/North Africa and the transitional economies are in effect converging not with the advanced countries but with the poorest.

Explaining the poverty of nations

There are fundamentally two ways to interpret inequality. Its basic explanation lies either in the market itself or else in something external such as historical backwardness or national culture. This spontaneously racist second conception lies at the heart of much sophisticated economics.

However it gives some difficulty with the data. Not least, we should notice the sheer scale of the differences. One hour of US labour was by 1995 exchanging for 80 hours of Indian labour on the world market, double what it was in 1980. South Asia contains some of the most ancient civilizations of the world. It gave the world numbers, algebra and some of its greatest mathematicians. It bequeathed material, aesthetic and spiritual riches which nourished the British Empire for three centuries. The idea that its present economic state is a consequence of productive, cultural or psychological backwardness is a mockery of science. If cultural backwardness explains inequality, what catastrophic cultural event made India in 1995 twice as backward as it was in 1980? Asia was neither born with nor achieved this status; it was thrust upon it. No other explanation makes sense.

We then confront the following problem: if there is no cultural or historical basis for inequality, why aren't the world's goods distributed equally? And why is the inequality growing? And why are so many people actually getting poorer? After all, there is actually now enough to go around. World production per head of population now stands at around $3000 in 1987 US dollars. This could house, clothe, feed and educate everyone on the planet. It could protect them from major diseases, maintain them in dignified old age, and provide for all those disadvantaged by difference. This output per head continues to grow; the equivalent figure in 1970 was $2000. Thus the principal obstacle to human progress is no longer technical. The only limit to humanity is humanity itself. There is no absolute need for the human race to produce more in order to survive. In consequence it is not empirically sustainable to explain national differentiation in terms of factors exogenous to the market. The differentiation is a *product* of the capitalist market – not inadequate absorption of the market, nor resistance to the market, nor even late adoption of the market.

This is particularly clear in the period that opened in 1980. This unleashed a marked acceleration in differentiation; but it was precisely the period of greatest extension of the market, of 'globalization'. It came at the end of the only period when inroads of any kind were made in the gap between nations, namely the period 1950–80 during which the developing nations secured concessions within GATT setting at least some limits on the penetration of the world market into their economies (see Freeman 1998). The gap started to open up again at the precise point when these barriers crumbled before the US onslaught. If inequality results from factors exogenous to the market, why did it accelerate so markedly when the barriers to the market were removed?

The point is also emphasized by the economic performance of China; when we compare its performance in use-value terms with the same performance in exchange-value terms, we begin to get some glimmering of what might be going on. Between 1980 and 1995, in constant 1987 dollars, Chinese per capita output rose by 7.65 times while its monetary value grew by less than the US. This is reflected in a declining labour-appropriation ratio. Its technical performance thus directly contradicts its status in the world market. Yet it was China that most strongly resisted and controlled the impact of the world market on its domestic economy during the IMF reforms, in contrast to Russia and Eastern Europe which accepted orthodox 'shock therapy' recipes.

The case of China demonstrates that two competing standards of efficiency are at work. By one standard – human need – all production is useful which diminishes the labour needed to meet human requirements. By the other standard – profitability in the world market – only that production is useful which makes a money profit. Orthodox theory predicts that these two standards of efficiency are *mutually compatible*: that if investment is governed by the principle of money efficiency, technical efficiency must follow. But the actual facts show precisely the reverse; it is only when a principle other than that of money efficiency is applied that national differentiation is reversed.

Combined and uneven accumulation: How value interacts with technical change

Distribution, expressed in value terms, is a competitive process. But why should the outcome be uneven? Much literature from the 1960s challenges the orthodox dogma of convergence, but to explain divergence falls back on exogenous factors such as historical specificity. The empirical evidence shows that inequality arises 'whenever and wherever there is a market'. The real problem, therefore, is to understand how it arises from market relations alone.

The key to this understanding is the form in which capital organizes technology, which is both exogenous to the capitalist market and a prerequisite of it.[10] Science is 'produced' non-capitalistically. But, as technology, it is embodied in definite processes of production requiring definite amounts of capital investment. Access to technology in the capitalist market demands access to capital.

The world market in capital imposes a constraint on the *quantity of capital*, which is what a nation needs in order to avail itself of technology. This sets a fundamental limit on the expansion of the world market, precisely because it cannot be altered in circulation – for example, through credit, which may make more money available to purchase capital goods, but cannot increase the capital goods themselves. The problem of national inequality then reduces to the following: why does capital accumulation distribute capital unevenly?

I can now clarify an important methodological point. A 'pure law' of value applies, independent of all other factors: it is always true. But the form in which it appears certainly does depend on other factors. National inequality arises from the *interaction* of accumulation with technical change. Specifically it arises from the way technical changes takes place under the free movement of capital. A market where the bulk of investment decisions are not dictated by the capital market, as China shows, obeys different laws. The law of uneven accumulation is endogenous to the capitalist market in the following sense: when investment is organized by the market in capital, technical change cannot escape the limits placed on it by the requirement that it produce value.

The reason is as follows: different sellers of the same product are obliged to accept a single world price, and appropriate different amounts of world value depending on their productivity. A technically superior producer makes an above-average profit, yielding an investment fund which amplifies the original advantage that led to the excess profit rate. Sources of consistently high profit rates are therefore *self-reinforcing*; the process of innovation itself polarizes the world into technical haves and have-nots; one small group possesses, maintains and single-mindedly cultivates a near monopoly of the means of technical innovation, harnessing the labour of the remainder to fuel this dominance.

The unequal distribution of profit rates is the actual motor of capital movement, as first discussed by Marx (for example, 1976: 1024) but more recently by Ernest Mandel (1975; compare Freeman 1996b). Capital pours into those places where it can reach a higher than average profit rate; it thirstily spearheads technical revolution upon technical revolution in the process. The most dynamic sectors, which also yield the highest profits, are those which innovate the fastest.

Accumulation is therefore intrinsically uneven. Uneven accumulation is an endogenous law of the capitalist market, overcome only when the capitalist investment mechanism is itself suspended, that is, when the market in capital is exogenously overridden.

What happened in 1980?

We are now in a position to return to the question that opened this chapter. Since 1970, the world economy, as reported by many observers, has been in a state which we call generalized crisis: low accumulation, low general profit rates, mass unemployment, and economic instability. Is there a possible exit from this crisis for the market, and if so, what?

There is little doubt that the US economy has staged a partial recovery although it is far too early to say whether this is stable, and the recovery certainly has not communicated itself to the rest of the world. Nevertheless it is important, in order to identify what future options are open, to assess what this recovery, as far as it has gone, is based on.

The historical evidence is reasonably plain: the date of the turnaround clearly associates it with the political offensive of 1980. This was not an endogenous process of the market: it was the outcome of a political reorganization of the world economy initiated in the USA. The process began with the 'neo-classical counterrevolution' (Todaro 1994: 85) which advocated 'the privatization of public corporations in developed nations and called for the dismantling of public ownership, statist planning, and government regulation of economic activities in developing countries' and secured controlling votes on the World Bank and the IMF. Its core argument was that '[by] promoting free trade and export expansion, welcoming investors from developed countries, and eliminating the plethora of government regulations and price distortions in factor, product, and financial markets, both economic efficiency and economic growth [would] be stimulated.'

The World Bank and IMF used the lever of debt to secure market reform packages in line with free-market principles. This also involved a conscious reorganization, not just of national markets but also of the regulatory framework of world trade. The 1986 formation of the World Trade Organization (WTO) was the outcome of a six-year round of trade negotiations held under the auspices of the General Agreement on Trades and Tariffs (GATT), the principal post-war world trade regulatory body. The cornerstones of the new order were:

1. A mandatory framework for world trade with economic sanctions as an automatic penalty for violation. Countries could no longer choose

whether or not to accept the market; it was now imposed upon them with full binding force.

2. GATS (General Agreements on Trade and Services) covering one-fifth of all world trade (1 trillion US dollars), which liberalized trade in services, including notably financial services. Because this encapsulated a legal obligation to free capital movement, it imposed, as part of the free-trade framework, full participation in the market in capital.

3. GATS extended the definition of exports to include production by foreign-owned subsidiaries in the host country. Trade regulation was thus extended to the internal market regimes of member states; subsidized state social provision is a technically criminal violation of the rights of foreign private providers. The offensive to open up capital markets, overriding national sovereignty through treaty obligations, continued with the drive to secure the MAI (Multilateral Accord on Investment).

4. A new trade category of Intellectual Property Rights (IPRs), an absolute monopoly of advanced countries: 0.16 per cent of world patents are currently owned by Third-World residents (Mihevc 1995). Transforming technological know-how into a marketable instrument, IPRs formalize the unequal exchange mechanism and provide formal permanent guarantees of advanced country dominance.

The WTO's agenda was the culmination of the aggressive US practice of mandatory unilateral sanctions to enforce GATT-agreed arrangements. Bhagwati (1993) records new legislation which

> required the US Trade representative to prepare an inventory of foreign trade barriers, establish a priority list of countries and their unreasonable practices, and then set deadlines for their removal by the foreign countries, and, should they fail to comply, for decisions on retaliation by the United States ... [It] is characterized by the (wholly distinct) fact that it enables the United States to unilaterally make demands for trade concessions by others without offering any matching, reciprocal concessions of its own that others might demand in turn.

The market was thus dramatically extended, as it has been on previous occasions, notably 1890–1914 when it reached a comparable extent, and in contrast to the onset of the 1945 Golden Age, which was characterized by a contraction of the world market, not an expansion. This extension of the world market was nevertheless restricted in a number of decisive ways:

5. A system of trading blocs – 'free trade areas' around the dominant capitalist countries – the EC, NAFTA and APEC – gave specific exemption from the measures imposed on all other WTO members.

6. Large-scale anti-dumping (AD) actions as the preferred protectionist device of the US, EEC and Australia/New Zealand. Before 1986, these were exceptional events. By 1992 they were universal for the advanced countries, which initiated 1,040 AD actions between 1985 to 1992, over half directed against either Eastern Europe (132), the Third World (137) or the developing Asian countries (297). The non-industrialized countries – three-quarters of the world's people – initiated 91.

7. The specific new development of IPRs manifests a new, explicit contradiction in the commodity form, since trade in knowledge can be achieved only by the *restraint* of trade in products embodying this knowledge. The WTO's harmonization offensive against India, for example, began by outlawing Indian production of pharmaceutical products whose patents were less than 20 years old, overriding Indian legislation providing for a 7-year patent period.

This total package constitutes a new world-political framework for trade. It is an extension of the market, but also a systematic manipulation of it to restore US profitability. Anti-dumping is baldly described by the World Bank as 'a packaging of protectionism to make it look like something different' (Hoekman and Kostecki 1995). As Hoekman and Kostecki remark: 'AD is not about fair play. Its goal is to tilt the playing field' (1995: 178). Though Article xxiv of the GATT proposes stringent conditions that a free trade area must satisfy, these are never applied. The enthusiastic dismantling of Third-World barriers to Northern goods has not been reciprocal. What has actually been established is a world market into which the advanced countries can sell with the necessary freedom to restore their own profitability at the expense of everyone else's. In particular, the central focus of US and European policy, epitomized by the MAI (Multinational Accord on Investments), has been to create a world market in capital; free capital movement is the central tenet of the new offensive. The US, running the largest trade deficit in history, is financing its recovery by draining the rest of the world.

Endogenous recovery, or a new phase of imperialism?

A genuine recovery of US productivity would be marked, first and foremost, by a US trade surplus. The absence of a surplus is the surest indicator that recovery is not grounded in an intrinsic product of the market but an exogenous intervention: the subordination of the political world order to US profitability.

At the very least we have to admit the following: this mechanism has little in common with the expansive wave of 1945–65. We confront two distinct processes. The crisis itself was a direct endogenous consequence of accumulation. There was no evidence, however, of endogenous recovery. Not only did the US recovery arise from an exogenous intervention that kicked in when accumulation broke down, but also it has completely failed to establish the golden-age conditions of 1945, in which US hegemony was accompanied by a US surplus that financed world recovery.

This has practical conclusions. It means that the price of recovery from general crisis necessarily includes a *further* general reorganization of the world market, including all that goes with this: a reorganization of its territories, wars of intervention, the forcible imposition of the market relations where necessary against the will of the nations concerned, and so on. It means that the exit from one kind of catastrophe is, in the last analysis, another kind of catastrophe. The idea that the market itself, if 'left to itself' will simply restore the conditions for its own existence, does not hold.

The evidence confirms Marx's original judgement of 130 years ago: capital sets the limits on its own existence. To this we must add that there is, however, no evidence of any intrinsic limit on the barbarism and destructiveness of which capital is capable: on the contrary, each new exit from general crisis reaches previously inconceivable heights of it. As a 'way out' therefore, what is now happening can only be regarded by the human race with the most extreme distrust.

Notes

1 Trotsky (1923: 9), cited in Day (1981: 8–9).
2 Even tight linkages do not abolish the distinction, in Marx's terminology, between formal subordination where an external institution conditions another, and real subordination in which each is a condition of existence of the other. Labour, as a huge reserve of non-waged direct producers, initially existed as an external condition of existence of the market. Relative surplus value made the market a condition of existence of labour, creating a new totality containing and transforming both. Cf. Marx (1976: 1019–49).
3 In symbols K/L, where $L = S + V$, K is capital stock, S is surplus value and L is total labour. I graphed K/L rather than the more usual K/V, the organic composition of capital, to differentiate strictly between effects of distribution (variations in S) and of accumulation (variations in K). Steindl (1952) points out that Marx himself poses his sharpest arguments in terms of K/L.
4 Data are taken from Duménil and Lévy, *Sources and Construction of the Series* (available from the authors at levy@cepremap.msh-paris.fr).
5 For empirical evidence see Freeman (2000).
6 See Harrod (1937), Steindl (1952: 262). The law is actually satisfied by money, as well as TSS value, but not by the standard interpretation of value: this is why most of the literature alleges that Marx made an error in asserting this law.
7 Let $r_{max} = L/K$ be the maximum profit rate. Then $r'_{max} = (KL' - LK')/K^2$. This will be negative until $KL' = LK'$, that is, $r = L'/L$, the growth rate of the labour force. For profit rates higher than this floor, the maximum rate falls asymptotically towards this floor and the actual rate fluctuates under this ceiling.
8 Note that (2) is only (1) expressed another way, since all economic activity falls either into production or into circulation. Note also that production includes the reproduction of the commodity labour-power, and of the capitalist class itself.

9 I distinguish between isolation from the world market – that is, the products of capital – and separation from the world market in capital itself, that is, the capitalist mechanism for allocating investment resources. The decisive strategic question for any nation is how to take investment decisions without being required to make a competitive money profit in an open world market. The decisive tactical question is preserving access to the world's products while so doing.

10 By analogy with labour, technology is formally but not really subsumed by capital. The present phase has introduced a new unique element, which is the attempt, by means of universal intellectual property rights, to subsume science *really* into capital. This enterprise is in itself fraught with contradiction; for example, it actually involves *restraining* trade in normal commodities, by making it illegal to produce something whose technology is owned by another.

13
Imperialist Contradictions at the Threshold of the Third Millennium: A New Phase?

Guglielmo Carchedi

Debates on whether capitalism has entered a new phase are not new to Marxism and have coincided with periods of deep social, economic and political transformations. Not by chance, then, has the same question emerged again after the fall and disintegration of the Soviet Union. What follows argues that this momentous event has ushered in a new phase of inter-imperialist relations. The focus will be on EU imperialism versus US imperialism. The thesis will be that this new phase differs from the previous one only quantitatively – in other words, because of the strengthening of tendencies already long present.

Let us begin by characterizing EU imperialism. When the official story of the EU is told, emphasis is placed on the following factors:

1. The realization that European nations were no longer large enough to hold their own in world markets.
2. The desire to avoid economic protectionism which had characterized inter-war Europe and was widely thought to have been one of the causes of the Second World War.
3. The desire to contain the expansion of the Soviet Union and the European communist parties.[1]
4. The desire, especially by France, to contain a possible resurgence of German expansionism by integrating the German economy in a European context.[2]

These four points highlight the motives behind the birth of the EU (at that time, the European Economic Community).[3] They represent the view of European capital, its preoccupation with economic and political competitors, both from other capitalist countries and from non-capitalist ones. However, this view, while illuminating some real reasons, is at the same time ideological. It suggests that capitalist integration is based upon, and reinforces, European capital's common interests (*vis-à-vis* both non-European capital and non-capitalist nations). From the perspective of class analysis, however, given the imperialist past and nature of the countries founding the European Economic Community, the body emerging from their integration could not but contain the same seeds and develop into the same weed. It is hard to believe that colonial (imperialist) nations could join into a supranational body of a different nature. From this point of view, capitalist integration arises from, and reinforces, capital's internal contradictions (vis-à-vis both non-European capital and non-capitalist nations). Such a perspective casts the official story of European integration in a different light:

1. The argument concerning the relatively small size and uncompetitiveness of European nations (that is, of European firms especially relative to US companies), while reflecting a real situation (Mandel 1970), conceals the expansionary nature of the European project after decolonization (in the post-war period) had reduced Europe's international weight[4] and after the weight of the dominant nation, Germany, had been further reduced through its splitting into West and East Germany.
2. The thesis concerning the desire to avoid protectionism carefully avoids mentioning EEC's own protectionism *vis-à-vis* non-EEC (including Third-World) countries, especially in the Common Agricultural Policy.
3. The view stressing the urge to contain the ex-Soviet Union reveals the desire to destroy it not only for ideological and political reasons but especially for reasons of economic expansionism.
4. The claim that France wished to contain German expansionism barely disguises France's own expansionist project, a project which (due to France's insufficient economic weight) could be realized only within a new context of 'cooperation' with other ex-colonial powers, that is, within a united Europe. This project was facilitated by the 'Cold War context, in which the United States and the USSR effectively checked German ambitions, and which empowered France to act as an arbitrator of European integration' (Holman and van der Pijl 1996: 71).

These are so many facets of a process moved by the interests of (inter)national capital[5] in which, not by chance, popular participation (not to speak of real democratic decision-making power) has been remarkably absent. Irrespective of the intentions of the major players, the essence of this process has been from the very beginning that of constituting a major power capable of challenging US world domination, in Marxist terms a new imperialist pole. The question, then, is: what is EU imperialism?

First of all, imperialism means basically systematic appropriation of value from one nation by another.[6] Traditionally, research on imperialism has centred on the relation between the 'mother' countries and their colonies.

In this *colonial* type of imperialism, the colonies must deliver raw materials to, and import manufactured products from, the colonial centre, and because of this, the colonies undergo little if any capitalist economic growth and diversification. But there is also a newer type of imperialist relation (holding, for example, for some South American and Asian countries). In this case, the dependent countries can achieve a (sometimes remarkable) degree of capitalist economic growth and diversification. This is *dependent development and capital accumulation*, in that:

1. Capital in the dependent countries adapts its production and more generally its economic activity to the markets in the centre, while the centre exports to the dependent countries what these latter need (including capital as aid and infrastructures) for this process of dependence to continue.
2. The dependent countries produce what the imperialist centre needs (wants) through the use of more labour-intensive techniques than those in the centre (even though those techniques might be relatively advanced), so that there is a transfer of value from the dependent to the imperialist countries (Carchedi 1991: chapter 7).
3. Given that they cannot compete with the centre on the basis of more advanced technologies, the dependent countries must 'save' on labour costs. This means that wages in terms of use-values can be relatively high in the centre and (sometimes absolutely) low in the dependent countries.[7]

In traditional colonialism it is the market of the colonies which is important as an outlet for the manufactured goods of the imperialist centre. The colonies export raw materials to the centre. In the dependent development type of imperialism, it is the market of the centre that is important for the dependent countries as an outlet for these latter's production, 'commissioned' as it were by the imperialist centre itself. In the colonial type of imperialism, the colonies' resources are squeezed and their markets used as long as it is convenient. Subsequently, they are abandoned without any substantial process of industrialization and capitalist development having taken place. Actually, local industries are often destroyed by the imperialist nations.[8] In the new type of imperialism, some dependent countries can undergo even a substantial process of capitalist development, but of a dependent type. Of course, the distinction between these two types of imperialism is analytical. In real life, they can coexist in hybrid forms in which one of the two types of imperialist relations is more pronounced.

The EU countries have a colonial type of imperialist relation with the African, Caribbean and Pacific countries (ACP), but could establish a different type of imperialist relation (dependent development) with some of the Central and Eastern European Countries (CEEC). But, besides this, the EU *as a whole* also has a set of imperialist relations with these two sets of (as well as with other) countries. To see this, consider the following. From a class analysis perspective, to say that a country has imperialist relations with another country is only a short cut to indicate that capitalist enterprises in some country have such relations with (that is, they appropriate value systematically from) enterprises (or 'independent' producers) in another country; and these relations need a set of national institutions handing down a set of legally binding relations and military instruments making (the continuation of) those relations possible.

Nowadays, imperialist relations exist not only between some imperial powers and some dominated countries. They also exist between the imperialist block (the centre of capitalism, the developed countries) and the dominated block (the periphery, the underdeveloped countries). This systematic appropriation of value is made possible by a set of international institutions, like the IMF, the World Bank, the WTO and the NATO. But it would be improper to refer to these institutions as pursuing their own imperialist policies. They only represent the interests of the centre *vis-à-vis* the dominated block and mediate those interests within the dominant block.

The case is different for the EU. Here, EU institutions not only represent and mediate common (but contradictory) national interests. They also formulate in a relatively independent way those common interests because the member states have relinquished part of their sovereignty to these institutions. While the EU is not (yet) a state entity, it has the legal instruments to legislate and thus to regulate sections of the economy and of other spheres of a member state's society. Through the formulation of these common interests, these institutions make it possible for all member states to participate in the systematic appropriation of value from non-EU countries. The imperialism of the EU's member states thus acquires new frontiers. One implication is that those member countries which, taken separately, would not enjoy the privileges of belonging to the centre, participate (even if in a subordinate position) in these privileges when they join the EU. Thus, strictly speaking, *EU imperialism* refers to this latter dimension:

1. to the imperialist relations between the capitalist enterprises of the EU countries and those of the non-EU countries;
2. to the unequal shares in which this value is split up among the EU countries;
3. to the EU institutions, and thus to the legally binding sets of rules and laws handed down by those institutions (for example the Lomé Conventions with the ACP countries and the Association Agreements with the CEEC), which make those relations possible; and
4. to the military might needed to enforce compliance with these rules and laws upon reluctant countries.

Once imperialist relations have been established in the industrial sphere (as being either a colonialist or a dependent development relation), all other relations can be seen in the same light. Thus, the Common Agricultural Policy emerges as a policy aimed at imposing on the weaker countries outside the EU a dependent type of agricultural development. The Schengen System can be seen as regulating the reproduction of EU labour-power according to the need of the EU itself. And the Western European Union can be seen as an attempt by the EU to develop its own military arm in order to fulfil entirely its own imperialist urge. The former two points will not be dealt with here (see Carchedi and Carchedi 1999). The latter will be examined below.

Of course, the imperialism of the EU as a whole (EU imperialism proper) is strictly interconnected with the imperialism of the EU member countries (national imperialisms). As of now, EU imperialism proper might still be less relevant than national imperialisms, but this situation is bound to change as the process of European unification proceeds. Here it is not necessary to distinguish between the separate effects of these two aspects of EU imperialism.

Up to very recently, the EU had posed no real threat to US imperialism. While some European nations (capitals) had managed to become powerful competitors of US capital in some sectors, the US economy as a whole had been vitally challenged in its world-dominant role neither by any single EU country nor by the EU as a whole. The first such challenge has occurred with the introduction of the EMU and thus of the Euro. The reasons for this are basically two. First, it can be shown that technological leaders appropriate part of the surplus value produced by technological laggards. This is called unequal exchange. The mechanism by which unequal exchange occurs is through the objectively determined appreciation/revaluation of the currencies of the former and depreciation/devaluation of the currencies of the latter. This increments the capital accumulation of the technological leaders at the cost of the technological laggards (Carchedi 1991: chapter 7).

The second advantage of being the dominant imperialist country, that is, the country hosting the technological leaders in those sectors that are of strategic importance for capital growth and accumulation, is that its currency becomes the world currency. That country appropriates international value simply by printing (within limits) non-convertible paper money. This is the role of the US dollar today. But this privilege could be threatened by the Euro (Carchedi 1991: chapter 7). Quite obviously, the US is quite keen to check this from happening for as long as possible. The point is that, to become a veritable rival to the US dollar, it is not sufficient for the Euro to be the currency of a powerful economic block (the EU). The EU needs something more. First, this currency has to be managed as if it were a world currency and second, it has to be backed by the military strength to support the EU's new imperialist role. While the EU as a whole has the economic strength to challenge the US and attempts to manage the Euro as if it were a world currency, it lacks the necessary military power. It is precisely on the military level that the US tries to contain the emergence of the Euro as a formidable challenger of the dollar. This is one important element explaining the recent war by NATO against Yugoslavia.[9] Before dwelling on these two aspects (the managing of the Euro and the military might), let us consider how the imperialist project behind the EMU/Euro features both contradictions among the EU countries and the uneven distribution among those countries of the advantages deriving from the EU's emerging imperialist role. In other words, the imperialist nature of the EU emerges also in the relations among the EU member countries. To see this, consider the ECU as the predecessor of the Euro.

When it was introduced in 1978, the ECU was composed of nine currencies. Of these, the Deutschemark (DM) weighted far more than any other currency, about 33 percent of ECU 1. This overpowering monetary weight both reflected and further fostered the greater weight of the German economy within the EU. To see this, suppose ECU 1 had been set equal to DM 1 (that is, the DM would have been weighted at 100 per cent of ECU 1). The ECU being only a copy of the DM, the demand and supply of the former would have been moved only by the factors affecting the demand and supply of the latter and ultimately by Germany's economic power. A change in the exchange rate of the DM would have been reflected in an equal change in that of the ECU. The fluctuation of the ECU on the exchange rate markets would have been caused only by Germany's 'fundamentals' and thus would have been functional only for Germany's economic policy. Since the DM weighted more in the composition of the ECU than any other currency, the value of the ECU reflected the interests and economic position of German capital more than those of other national capitals. This situation has remained basically unchanged up to the transformation of the ECU into the Euro.

Once the internal composition of the ECU had been fixed, a system for restricting the fluctuations of the ECU around this level had to be devised in order for this privileged situation for German capital not to be dented. Up to 1992, the member states undertook to keep their currencies' fluctuations within relatively narrow limits, 2.25 per cent above and 2.25 per cent below the cross rates (Italy was allowed a ± 6 per cent band but adopted the ± 2.25 per cent band in 1990). After the 1993 crisis, these bands were widened to ± 15 per cent (except for Germany and the Netherlands, which retained the ± 2.25 per cent band). The way in which these narrow fluctuations were functional for Germany's interests is revealed in the following.

Take Germany (a higher-productivity country) and Italy (a lower-productivity country). Germany, given her higher productivity, was more competitive on foreign markets. Also, greater productivity allowed German labour's greater material welfare.[10] Germany's pursuance of higher profits, then, was relatively independent from high inflation. Moreover, inflation would have dented price competitiveness thus requiring devaluation, something Germany was reluctant to use because, as we shall see shortly, this would have checked Germany's aim to make the DM an international currency. Inflation, then, was Germany's enemy number one. Italy's situation was the opposite. Lower productivity levels created the conditions for inflationary policies as a means to reduce the level of real wages (that is, to increase the rate of surplus value and thus the rate of profit). To safeguard her international competitiveness, Italy had to resort to devaluation. But the possibility of its resort to competitive devaluation was limited by the relative fixity of the exchange rates within the ERM.

This seemingly neutral mechanism fostered specific economic policies and interests, those of the dominant country, that is, Germany, and within it of the German oligopolies. Technological laggards had to compete basically through higher rates of surplus value. This could be done in one of the following two ways. It could be done at the point of production, that is, through longer working days and higher intensity of labour. The extraction of absolute surplus value increased. This was fostered by the dismantling of social security systems and by labour 'flexibility'. Alternatively, higher rates of surplus value could be achieved through redistribution, that is, inflation. The ERM forced technological laggards to renounce inflation and devaluation, and to extract more absolute surplus value at the point of production rather than through redistribution mechanisms (inflation). This made it possible for Germany as well to raise its rate of absolute surplus value, as German entrepreneurs too demanded more 'freedom' to deal with labour.

The introduction of the EMU/Euro froze this situation of privilege for Germany. Six common advantages for European capital followed.

First, Germany advanced capital's leading role in the interests of all European advanced capitals and not only of the German oligopolies, since it forced all capitals to extract higher rates of surplus value. This is basically the reason why the advanced capitals of other nations accept that role.

Second, in post-war Europe, high rates of inflation have been a means to increase the rate of surplus value, and thus the rate of profit, in periods of heightened labour militancy. But inflation erodes not only labour's income but also that of all other classes, including those which are traditional allies of capital, thus being a possible cause of generalized dissatisfaction with the national governments' economic policies. High rates of absolute surplus value at the point of production avoid this drawback.

Third, while inflationary measures increase the average rate of profit by redistributing the value produced, higher rates of absolute surplus value at the point of production increase both that rate and the economic base (the production of value and commodities).

Fourth, contrary to inflationary measures, high rates of absolute surplus value at the point of production foster an increased direct control of labour within the labour process itself and the (ideological, political and organizational) weakening of labour's organizations.

Fifth, high rates of inflation in Europe might have called for successive rounds of competitive devaluations and these would have left the relative competitive positions of the European currencies unaltered while weakening their international strength. This becomes impossible after the introduction of the single currency. In short, the Euro, and thus German leadership, is accepted by the other European countries because the bill is paid by labour.[11]

This all occured under a double deception. In the first place, an anti-labour policy desired by national governments (and by the multinationals) is disguised as if it were an economic policy imposed by some distant bureaucracy, for whom the member states are not responsible, and reflecting some socially neutral rationality. In the second, an economic policy ultimately in the interest of (the technologically advanced) industrial capital appears as if it were imposed by (German) financial capital. In reality, financial capital forces industrial capital to renounce the competitive instruments of the poor countries (inflation and devaluation). It calls industrial capital to task, and thus is functional for the greater creation of (surplus) value rather than simply for a more favourable redistribution of the (surplus) value created. Supra-national financial capital (the European Central Bank, ECB) enjoys a measure of relative autonomy in the interest of the expanded reproduction of the most advanced European industrial capital. Without this 'independence' the ECB cannot perform this basic task, and it is for this reason that so much fuss is made of the issue concerning the ECB's 'independence'.

The sixth common advantage is at present only potential and will materialize if the Euro becomes the new world currency. It has often been said that the Euro would become the currency used in the whole community, in a market comparable to that of the US, served by an efficient and technologically advanced production system. This would propel a volume of Euro-denominated international transactions such that the demand for the Euro would be equal to or surpass that for the dollar. This, in turn, would facilitate the placing of Euro-denominated financial instruments on non-EMU markets, thus increasing the demand for the currency. Inasmuch as this process would be successful, the world's central banks and other institutional investors would adjust their portfolios from dollar-denominated to Euro-denominated instruments, thus reinforcing this virtuous circle. The initial fixing of the Euro 1 at 1.1712 US dollars has been a propagandistic move aimed at impressing upon international financial circles the idea that the Euro was worthier than the dollar.

But the economic basis is not sufficient. A second condition for the Euro to become a world currency is that it will have to be, and thus it will have to be managed as, an international reserve currency. This coincides with

Germany's interests. For Germany there will be an advantage in having transformed the DM into the Euro and this into a world currency only if the Euro is managed according to German capital's interests (even though in a mediated and negotiated way[12]); that is, according to a relatively strict interpretation and application of the Maastricht convergence criteria (at least, as long as Germany retains its dominant position within the EU[13]). This means an anti-inflationary and revaluation-bound economic and monetary policy. These are also the criteria functional for the Euro to become an international reserve, and thus a world, currency. But, as we have seen, it is through these criteria that the other member countries' interests are subordinated to those of Germany.[14] The single currency erases even the restricted possibility offered by the ERM to resort to devaluation (realignments) while the stability criteria tie even more the weaker countries' economic policies to that of Germany.[15]

The dominated countries within the EU accept this disadvantage for a number of reasons. Aside from those reasons common to all EU countries mentioned above, there are four reasons specific to the dominated countries. First, given that their currencies have been converted into the Euro, these currencies too will be able to participate in the gains derived from seignorage, inasmuch as the Euro does become a rival to the dollar. Second, in a common market, given the free movement of goods, the effects of demand stimulation through inflation might be lost to other member states. Thus, the disadvantage of renouncing inflation might be smaller than otherwise. Third, the EMU/Euro makes generalized competitive devaluations impossible. These would leave all countries concerned with an unchanged competitive position relative to each other, would create commercial and political tensions with Germany, and would ultimately endanger their membership in the European project. Fourth, a common currency eliminates by definition the monetary crises of, and the speculative movements against, the weaker currencies. These crises can have a disruptive effect on the real economy of every country as well, but even more so on that of the laggard ones.

Up to here the analysis has focused on the EMU as the manifestation of the contradictory relations within this emerging imperialist block. Let us now consider the EMU/Euro as the manifestation of the inter-imperialist relations between EU and US. To begin with, both the EU and the US have a common interest, that of dominating the rest of the world. This implies a measure of cooperation, especially in dealing with the dominated countries through international agencies such as the IMF, the World Bank, the WTO and NATO. However, the EU is still in a dominated position, as the role of the Euro *vis-à-vis* the dollar shows. It is clear that the US will resist as much as possible developments in the EU which challenge this dominance. The best way for the US to do this, perhaps at present the only one, is through military power. A currency will be accepted as a world currency only if it is backed by the military power needed to conquer and subject to imperialism's yoke those countries with an economic or geo-political import (to 'protect investments'). The US disposes of such power, the EU does not. The question then is: why doesn't the EU develop its own military arm? The process of emergence of a European imperialist might is deeply contradictory. Let us review some of its salient features.

While, within the EU, one nation (Germany) is predominant in economic power, the same cannot be said of military power. On a military plane, not only is there no clear-cut predominance of one nation over the other, but each member state still has its own military means to advance its interests. This is a first important factor accounting for Europe's weakness in the military sphere. This has been the case from the very beginning, that is, from the first post-war defence treaty. In 1948, the Brussels Treaty was signed establishing the West European Union (WEU). Its members were Belgium, France, Luxembourg, the Netherlands and the United Kingdom. Its purpose was collaboration in economic, social and cultural matters and collective self-defence but in a position of subordination to the NATO (that is, the US). This situation has basically remained the same ever since. It is true that the Petersberg Declaration of 1992 extends the scope of the operations to 'humanitarian and rescue tasks; peacemaking tasks; tasks of combat forces in crisis management, including peacemaking'. This indicates a considerably wider scope for the WEU than simply defence. Intervention (that is, aggression) anywhere in the world can thus be legitimated as 'humanitarian and rescue tasks; peacemaking tasks; tasks of combat forces in crisis management, including peacemaking' whenever such intervention is perceived as being in the interest of the EU. NATO's 1999 'humanitarian' aggression against Yugoslavia shows that this is a very real and even likely possibility. However, as the Maastricht Declaration adds, 'The objective is to develop WEU as a means to strengthen the European pillar of the Atlantic Alliance ... WEU will act in conformity with the positions adopted in the Atlantic Alliance.' The WEU is developing its own imperialist act, but within the limits of a persisting *de facto* subordination to NATO and thus to the US.[16] It is within these limits that the US favours a strengthening of the WEU. In the immediate future, the EU will remain a second rate imperialist power. But this need not be the case in the longer term. Power relations might become more favourable to the EU. This new state of affairs might be a harbinger of a new world conflict.

Two factors help to explain this persisting weakness. The first is the division within the WEU itself, that is, among its member states, concerning the role of the WEU and its relation to NATO. The key aspect of this divergence of opinions is British reticence to develop an autonomous European military power. The UK has always been for military cooperation but against military integration. There are historical and ideological reasons for this: for example, Britain's fear of losing its national sovereignty; or its 'choice, made at the end of the Second World War, to try to retain a status as close as possible to that of a great power by finding a genuine great power to influence' (Chuter 1997: 114). These and similar factors should be explained in terms of conscious economic policies and interests. Thus, attachment to the notion of national sovereignty, and fear of losing it, is a residue of a historical phase when Britain was a great imperial power. This is an example of how ideologies can survive the economic situation that determined them. The reason this ideology has survived the imperial age is that it defended, and still defends, the interests of the weakest sectors of British capital. These are the sectors which stand to lose the most from ever-stricter forms of European economic integration and which use the argument of a loss of national sovereignty as an ideological weapon against joining (before 1973) or deepening (after that date) the scope of European economic integration.

As for Britain's attempt to retain the status of a great power, Britain wants to restrict the scope of economic integration because full integration would mean that the pound would be absorbed into the Euro, into a currency managed according to the criteria reflecting, even though in a mediated way, the interests of German oligopoly capital.[17] London would have to play a subordinate role both economically in general and in the financial markets more specifically. An independent European military force would be a strong factor pushing towards some sort of a (federalist) European state and thus towards a full economic integration of the UK within the EU. This explains Britain's opposition to making the WEU an incisive military force.[18] It is doubtful, however, whether this policy will be sustainable in the long run.

The second reason for the WEU's weakness is the obvious superior military might of the US. Rather than imposing their will directly, the US manifests its military superiority through NATO. NATO was founded in 1949, officially to contain Soviet expansionism but actually to contribute, through its military power, to the destruction of the Soviet Union. In 1991, with the fall and dissolution of the Soviet Union, NATO found itself suddenly without an enemy. It would seem that this would have provided an opportunity for the WEU to grow in importance. In fact, it can be reasonably argued that, before the fall of the Soviet Union, such a growth would have weakened NATO, and this was something which the European nations did not want, given that only the US had the military power to face the USSR. Thus, after the dissolution of the USSR, one would have expected an increased interest in a stronger role for a European military power. Yet, NATO's influence has increased rather than decreased. The US welcomes a European military force, provided it remains subordinated to the US, both for military and for economic–financial reasons. The 1999 US attack on and destruction of Yugoslavia (through NATO) was meant (among other things) to keep Euro's ambitions under control.

US military predominance, through NATO, over the WEU is also visible in other areas, as in the recent agreement between NATO and Russia to start cooperation in the political and military spheres. In May 1997, the 'Founding Act on Mutual Relations, Co-operation and Security between NATO and the Russian Federation' was signed. This is not a binding treaty (something Russia had hoped for) but simply a commitment between heads of state and of government. Russia and NATO sit on a permanent joint committee but NATO will take decisions on its own in situations of emergency and crisis. Clearly, Russia has accepted a subordinate position relative to NATO. This reduces the influence of OSCE, which both Russia and many European states would like to see strengthened. The reason is that the US has greater influence within NATO than within OSCE. Obviously, the point is to prevent a military alliance between the EU and Russia.[19]

Finally, NATO and thus the US reveal their military superiority also *vis-à-vis* the CEEC on the one hand and the Arab countries on the other. Concerning the CEEC, Poland, the Czech Republic and Hungary have already become NATO members. Other CEEC will follow suit. The specific aim of this policy is to extend the US sphere of influence from the military to the economic one, thus countering the EU's (and especially Germany's) economic ties with these countries. The means through which this is being accomplished is military procurements. In fact, NATO membership implies that the new member states renew their armaments to make them compatible with those used by NATO. For example, the new member countries have already begun acquiring F-16 fighter-bombers to replace the Soviet Mig. A new, colossal business is thus being opened for the American military-industrial complex, which already controls half of the world trade in armaments. Moreover, once these weapons have been acquired, more will have to be spent on maintenance, spare parts and more replacements. Given that these countries lack the funds for such huge expenditures, they will have to resort to US credit, thus increasing their economic dependence upon the US (Dinucci 1998: 26). The same will hold for Russia, as soon as its huge, 'obsolete', weaponry will have to be replaced.

As for the Arab countries, US policies are aimed at oil reserves in the Gulf. Even though the US is the second oil producer after Saudi Arabia, it has reserves which, at the present pace of consumption, are estimated to last only 10 years. Saudi Arabia's reserves, on the contrary, can last 80 years and Iraq's 10 years. But this is not the only factor. About 57 per cent of Middle East oil exports goes to the Asian countries (of which 25 per cent to Japan only) and 25 per cent to Western Europe. Control of these reserves, thus, is of fundamental strategic importance for the US to retain economic and military leadership over all countries, including its allies (Dinucci 1998: 27). This explains NATO's policies in the Middle East, including the effort to replace 'communism' with 'Arab fundamentalism' as the new menace to world peace and democracy.

As a result of these developments, NATO's political role has undergone a considerable change. Up to the end of the 1980s, its basic function was perceived as 'defence' against the 'communist threat'. With the fall of the Soviet Union NATO's new image is that of providing global 'security' for the 'international community', including protection against 'Islamic fundamentalism'. This includes preventing wars between states, reinstituting democratic governments that have been overthrown, and facilitating the downfall of 'undemocratic governments'. Of course, NATO itself decides which wars should be prevented, which governments are democratic, and which wars should be waged (if need be, contravening rules of international law). NATO is now being projected in the world's collective consciousness as the guarantor of world democracy, peace, order and human rights. It has emerged in the 1990s stronger than ever. This strength of NATO and the inner weakness of the WEU are the two elements blocking projects, like the WEU and the OSCE, which aim to build an alternative centre of military power outside the dominance of the US.

To the strength of the expansionary drive of US imperialism there corresponds the weakness of the European working class that has yet to recover from the series of debacles since the defeat of the mass social movements of the 1970s. The enthusiastic participation of European social democracies in the 1999 war against Yugoslavia is only history's last brushstroke to an abysmal picture. It is the interrelations of these factors which allow us to speak of a new phase in capitalist development, more specifically of inter-imperialist transatlantic relations, at the threshold of the new millenium. This new phase is fraught with grave dangers and could be the harbinger of a new world conflict.

Notes

1 The US had an interest of its own in, and contributed to, the economic reconstruction of Europe, which it saw as a precondition for Europe to play the role of the anti-communist bastion.
2 This has been a constant of French policy: starting in 1951, when the European Coal and Steel Community was thought as a means towards Franco-German reconciliation, up to 1992, when an important motivation in negotiating the Treaty on European Union (the Maastricht Treaty) was to contain Germany's economic predominance after the 1990 reunification.
3 The *European Economic Community* (EEC), founded in 1958, became the *European Community* (EC) in 1965, when it was merged with the European Coal and Steel Community (ECSC) and the Euratom, and this became the *European Union* (EU) in 1992.
4 Even nowadays Europe's role in forming the elites of the dependent countries is far smaller than that of the US. European universities host 50 000 Asian students as opposed to the 215 000 Asian students admitted at US universities.
5 Beyen, the Dutch foreign minister who first proposed the Common Market 'was not an elected politician but a former executive for Philips and director of

Unilever parachuted straight from the IMF into the Dutch cabinet' (Anderson 1997: 63) and Monnet, the 'father' of European integration was an international banker by profession.

6   There might be appropriation of wealth that does not have the social form of value (because it has been produced in a non-capitalist system). However, this wealth changes its social form and becomes value as soon as it is brought into the capitalist market.

7   The role of the IMF is that of forcing the dependent countries to compete through lower labour costs (wages) while fostering at the same time a dependent form of industrialization.

8   This does not imply that the fortunes of those countries improve automatically if foreign capital inflows stop. Systematic plunder of natural resources makes development (in whatever form) impossible. Moreover, the alternative to forced under-development is a different type, a socialist type, of development.

9   This is only one of the causes. Even though the war against Yugoslavia cannot be properly dealt with here, a few comments are in order. First, it is said that this war was not caused by inter-imperialist contradictions. The above argues to the contrary: the US tries to prevent the rise of an imperialist competitor. It cannot be ruled out that inter-imperialist contradictions similar to those between the US and the USSR might emerge again, this time between the US and other blocs, including the EU. Second, it is said that, with the fall of the USSR, NATO has changed from a defensive to an offensive organization. A different view will be submitted below. Third, it is said that this was a 'humanitarian' war, to defend the Albanian Kosovars from Serbia's aggression and ethnic cleansing. This assertion is unbelievable, given the countless examples of both NATO and the US not only ignoring but also actually supporting gross and massive violations of human rights. But even more unbelievable is the readiness of public opinion to swallow this lie, even though crimes against humanity did occur in that country (both against Kosovars and against Serbs).

There are at least three real reasons, besides the one just mentioned, for NATO's intervention in Yugoslavia. First, the US/NATO wanted to show the rest of the world that the US military machine reigns supreme and that it would be unwise to challenge it. This holds particularly for Russia, just in case the critics of Russia's subordination to Western imperialism might be tempted to reverse the course. Second, both the US and the EU have economic interests in the Balkans, namely a safe corridor for the pipeline needed to transport the oil of the rich Caspian fields to the Mediterranean through Bulgaria, Macedonia and Albania. It is for this reason that the Balkans had to fall within the US and the EU sphere of influence. And third, the US/NATO wanted to create a precedent for future interventions in the name of 'humanitarian' interests (for example, the defence of ethnic groups or of human rights) and anti-terrorist measures. Future action against 'rogue states' such as Cuba (on the basis of supposed violations of human rights or international terrorism), or even Russia or China (both multi-ethnic countries where ethnic strife can be fomented deliberately through covert actions or propaganda), might find in the destruction of Yugoslavia a test case, justification and rationale (B. Carchedi 1999).

10   Which does not necessarily mean that Germany's rate of surplus value is lower than that of the other less advanced countries.

11 Within labour, some strata, such as women, children, foreign workers, racial and other minorities, are penalized more than others. This important point cannot be pursued here. See Gill (1998).

12 Contrary to the opinion of some commentators (for example, Bladen-Hovell and Symons 1994: 337), the 'German leadership hypothesis' does not imply Germany's absolute power to impose its policies.

13 These criteria are: deficit must not be greater than 3 per cent of GDP, debt must not be greater than 60 per cent of GDP, inflation cannot be higher than 1.5 per cent of the average of the inflation rates of the three countries with the lowest rates, long-term interest rates cannot be higher than 2 per cent of the rates of the three countries with the lowest rates, and the exchange rates must be within the ERM. While these criteria are meant to transform the future Euro into the new form of the DM, as many others have pointed out, quantitatively, these targets are arbitrary (why 3 per cent and not any other figure?) and irrational (Japan would not be allowed membership in the EMU due to its high level of debt). These criteria are not limited to the accession to the EMU. They are meant to continue to play a role also after its inception. On 8 November, 1995, the German Minister of Finance Waigel spelled out his proposal for a 'stability pact'. This has been recently approved at the Dublin summit of 13 and 14 December 1996. Basically, after joining the EMU, member countries will have to aim at a budget deficit of 1 per cent in normal times and no more than 3 per cent in difficult times. Countries failing these requirements will have to pay a deposit (of between 0.2 per cent and 0.5 per cent of GDP) which, in case the deficit is not corrected within two years, will be turned into a fine. There are also escape clauses (*Europa van Morgen* 1996).

14 This is the meaning of article 3a(3) of the EC Treaty, which lays down the EMU's guiding principles: stable prices, sound public finances and monetary conditions, and a sustainable balance of payments.

15 Within the EMU, the ERM has not disappeared, but ties the non-EMU members to the Euro. The difference is that the Euro replaces the ECU as the pivot of the central rates of non-Euro currencies (European Council 1996). This will tie the economic policy of the non-Euro members to that of the Euro area and thus of its dominant country, Germany.

16 At present, the WEU has 10 full European members, 5 observers, 3 associate members and 10 associate partners.

17 Carchedi (1997) argues that it is in the interest of the advanced capital sector (the oligopolistic one, under the leadership of German oligopolies) to make of the ECU first and then the Euro a strong currency.

18 There are of course differences between the major political players. In the 1970s and 1980s, the Conservative Party leaned towards policies in tune with the Community's restrictive monetary and fiscal policies as *the* way to stimulate the European economies. The Labour Party, on the other hand, leaned more towards import controls, state intervention, and subsidies for declining industries (Newman 1989).

19 NATO's greater influence has been strengthened by France's realization that progress towards a stronger WEU has been lacking and by her decision, announced on 5 December, 1995, to re-enter NATO (at least partially). France left NATO in 1966, knowing that such a hegemonic project behind a united Europe necessitated a strong, independent military organization.

14
Periodizing Capitalism and Analyzing Imperialism: Classical Marxism and Capitalist Evolution

Alex Callinicos

Marx's *Capital* selects as its main object a singular phenomenon – the capitalist mode of production. The habit of going further and distinguishing between different species of capitalism became, however, well entrenched in the classical Marxist tradition. In particular, Hilferding's *Finance Capital*, Lenin's *Imperialism* and Bukharin's *Imperialism and World Economy* all sought to analyze the specific characteristics of the particular phase of capitalist development which the authors agreed had emerged around the turn of the twentieth century, and, in particular, to identify the respects in which these characteristics differed from those of the mid-Victorian capitalism that provided the context of Marx's great work. As a result, an opposition between 'classical' or 'competitive' capitalism and imperialism or 'monopoly' capitalism was established in Marxist theoretical writing.

The revival of Marxist political economy in the 1960s continued the tendency to distinguish between phases of capitalist development. Baran and Sweezy's *Monopoly Capital* (1966) and Ernest Mandel's *Late Capitalism* (1975) represent particularly distinguished attempts to analyze the structural features of the capitalism of their time. More recently, both the Regulation School and the Social Structures of Accumulation (SSA) theorists breathed new life into the stadial approach to capitalism, even if the phases they identified and the mechanisms they claimed were responsible were significantly different from those conceptualized by earlier Marxist economists. In particular, thanks to the influence of Michel Aglietta's seminal *A Theory of Capitalist Regulation* (1976), a new contrast moved to the centre of attention, that between post-war Fordism, an 'intensive regime of accumulation' and, on the one hand, the 'extensive regime of accumulation' that preceded it and, on the other, the 'post-Fordism' emerging from the economic crisis of the 1970s.

Both the specific claims made by these various writers and the very idea of distinct phases of capitalist development have come under increasing attack.[1] These attacks arise ultimately from a tension inherent in that idea. Marx (1973: 101) famously described his method as that of 'rising from the abstract to the concrete'. *Capital* is not a concrete historical description of Victorian capitalism. Rather, it seeks to identify the constitutive structures and inherent tendencies of the capitalist mode of production as such. As we shall see in more detail below, the discourse of *Capital* accordingly proceeds on the basis of the formulation of abstract propositions and concepts intended to delineate these structures and tendencies: specific, less fundamental factors are progressively introduced at appropriate points in the argument where their context makes clear their particular and relatively subordinate role. The massive empirical detail that Marx provides at various points in *Capital* Volume I and Part V of Volume III (devoted to money capital and the working of financial markets) offers evidence of the inner structures of the capitalist mode, and illustrations of Marx's arguments. Nevertheless, 'classical' capitalism is not the main object of *Capital*; at most one can say that *Capital* has two objects – the capitalist mode of production as such, as Althusser puts it, 'an object that has no existence in the strong sense (in the strong sense, the capitalist mode of production does not exist, but only social formations dominated by the capitalist mode of production)', and the 'actually existing' capitalism of Marx's day (Althusser (1990: 47).

This duality of objects posed a specific problem for later Marxist economists – namely, how to distinguish those aspects of *Capital*'s discourse that identify constitutive features of the capitalist mode from those chiefly of contemporary significance? This question is, of course, inseparable from the related problem of how to extend Marx's analysis, with respect to both the general theoretical understanding of the capitalist mode and the more concrete analysis of capitalism as an historically evolving system. One reason why Hilferding's *Finance Capital* is such a distinguished work of Marxist political economy is that it undertakes both – developing a value-theoretical analysis of the operation of financial markets and identifying the structural features of finance capital, conceived as the fusion of industrial and money capital as a result of the concentration and centralization of capital.

It is inherent in the nature of Marxism as a scientific research programme that the work of extending *Capital* in these two ways may rebound back on Marx's analysis by requiring its modification. One obvious point of difficulty concerns the applicability of Marxist value theory to monopoly capitalism. To the extent that the concentration of economic power that Lenin, Hilferding and Bukharin all agreed was producing a 'higher stage of capitalism' implied a suspension of the competitive processes responsible for the social equalization of labour on which the law of value depended, surely the labour theory of value and the various propositions derived with its aid (most importantly the law of the tendency of the rate of profit to fall, hereinafter TRPF) no longer applied to capitalism in its 'organized' phase?

Part of the significance of Baran's and Sweezy's *Monopoly Capital* was that it explicitly drew and systematically explored this inference.

This apparent contradiction between the law of value and monopoly capitalism was, however, felt less directly by the Marxists of the Second and Third Internationals. It is a well known, but to my knowledge unexplained, anomaly in the history of Marxist political economy that the TRPF figured little in crisis theory before the Second World War. Most of the main figures – notably Hilferding, Bukharin and Preobrazhensky – all accepted some version of disproportionality theory: in other words, they explained economic crises as consequences of the imbalances between different sectors of the economy. They disagreed, however, over the implications of the development of monopoly capitalism for crises. Hilferding believed that the emergence of what he was the first to call 'organized capitalism' meant that state planning could, in principle, prevent the development of disproportions between the main departments of production, and therefore eliminate economic crises without the need for socialist revolution. Bukharin agreed, but argued that the contradictions of capitalism were displaced onto the military and political rivalries among nationally organized 'state capitalist trusts'. Preobrazhensky argued that monopoly capitalism actually made sectoral imbalances worse: in conjunction with dysfunctions arising from a tendency to underconsumption and the turnover of fixed capital these were driving towards systemic crisis.[2]

One of the major advances of Marxist political economy over recent decades has been to restore the TRPF to its proper place at the centre of Marxist crisis theory.[3] The effect was to locate the source of capitalist crises deep in the relations of production themselves, rather than to treat them as a relatively contingent consequence of disequilibria between different sectors.[4] This shift in analytical focus has, of course, been accompanied by intense disagreement over the internal coherence of the theory of the TRPF closely related to the more general Sraffian assault on Marx's theory of value. One consequence of these controversies, in conjunction with the debates provoked by Althusser's critique of Hegelian Marxism, has been to direct attention towards the conceptual structure of *Capital* and the epistemological status of Marx's principal propositions. It is against this background that a specifically Marxist scepticism about the idea of phases of capitalist development has emerged. This is not to say that more empirical doubts have not played their part. The notion of 'monopoly capitalism' has attracted increasing critical scrutiny: in particular, its implication that concentration and centralization of capital has led to an attenuation of competition between capitals has rightly come under fire. No doubt the fact that the present period has witnessed an intensification of competition on a global scale has contributed to this scepticism. But there are more methodological concerns at work as well, and it is on these that I concentrate here.

The limits of regulation theory

The sources of this scepticism can be brought out by considering regulation theory. Aglietta's initial formulation of this theory explicitly broke with earlier theorists of what Lenin called 'the monopoly stage of capitalism': 'We reject the idea that the concentration of capital is the most fundamental process in the history of 20th century capitalism. The key theoretical process lies rather lies in a radical change in the conditions of reproduction of capital in general.' This claim depends on what amounts to a disproportionality theory of crisis. Department I (production of means of production) tends to develop more rapidly than Department II (production of means of consumption). But, without an increase in relative surplus value, which in turn depends on Department II being able to absorb more means of production and transform them into constant capital invested in the production of cheaper consumer goods and on the existence of effective demand for these commodities, the general rate of profit will fall. 'The uneven development of Department I' therefore ... 'meets a barrier in the course of accumulation. This barrier, which is always latent, can be raised only if *capitalist production revolutionizes the conditions of existence of the working class*' (Aglietta 1979: 20–1, 61).

In the absence of such a transformation, the devalorization of capital caused by rising labour productivity in Department I 'is expressed in a recurrent movement formed by successive phases of massive increase in gross fixed capital and phases of deep depression'. The great slump of the 1930s represented the climax of these oscillations. Taylorism eroded working-class autonomy within production, but 'the disproportion between expansion in Department II and accumulation in Department I rapidly increased, since the forces that were revolutionizing the labour process were also those reducing effective demand for commodities from Department II' because of the resulting fall in the share of wages in national income. Fordism overcomes these contradictions by combining further transformations in the labour process – in particular, the development of '*semi-automatic assembly-line production*' – with 'the formation of a social consumption norm' based in particular on the intensive commodification of everyday life and the underwriting of mass consumption by the welfare state, thereby ensuring that Departments I and II would develop in relative harmony (Aglietta 1979: 104, 94, 117, 116).

Fordism thus illustrates the main function of regimes of accumulation, namely to achieve a stable articulation of Departments I and II. As Alain Lipietz puts it, '[A] *regime of accumulation* describes the fairly long-term stabilization of the allocation of social production between consumption and accumulation'. It must be 'materialized in the shape of norms, habits, laws and regulating networks which ensure the unity of the process and which guarantee that its agents conform more or less to the schema of

reproduction in their day-to-day behaviour and struggles'. This institutionalized 'set of internalized rules and social procedures' is the mode of
regulation (Lipietz 1987: 14–15).

Aglietta does not openly embrace a disproportionality theory of crises. On
the contrary, he gives his account a gloss which appears to accord explanatory primacy to the relations of exploitation: 'The root of these crises is
always the upsurge of the class struggle in production, which jeopardizes
the expanded creation of surplus value on the basis of the prevailing organization of the labour process.' A more accurate description of his position
would be that an appropriate organization of the labour process is a necessary condition for the establishment of equilibrium between Departments I
and II. Nevertheless, the attainment of such an equilibrium is, according to
Aglietta, the overriding problem of the capitalist mode of production: 'There
is an overaccumulation of capital when the constraint of the full realization
of the value newly created by society can no longer be effected by way of
organic exchanges between the two departments of production' (Aglietta
1979: 352, 356). At most one can say that, on this model, what Robert
Brenner calls a 'supply-side crisis' arising from distributional conflict
between capital and labour is a symptom of a breakdown of the mode of
regulation harmonizing Departments I and II (Brenner 1998: 10–24).

The emergence of the Regulation School in the 1970s and 1980s was
marked by its proponents' elaboration of a sophisticated conceptual apparatus drawing on a distinctive interpretation of Marxist value theory.[5] This
dazzling surface glitter concealed, however, a substantive analysis which
drew little on the main concepts and propositions of *Capital*. Consider, for
example, the spin Aglietta gives to the TRPF: 'The law of the tendency of the
rate of profit to fall thus has the following meaning. It asserts that a phase of
apparently regular accumulation does not contain self-correcting mechanisms that can perpetuate it indefinitely' (Aglietta 1979: 357). One does not
have to be a sign-up supporter of the TRPF theory to see that it asserts more
than *that* – a proposition that any orthodox Keynesian could cheerfully
endorse. Bruce Norton's comment on SSA theory could indeed be applied
unaltered to the Regulation School: 'One might conclude simply that the
framework links an appreciation of social structure to a Keynesian sort of
instability hypothesis, thereby producing an interesting but not necessarily
radical approach to economic theory' (Norton 1992: 179).

The similarities between regulation theory and Keynesianism indeed
turned out to go considerably deeper. By the later 1980s, Lipietz, rejecting
what he called the 'pessimistic functionalism' of world systems theory, was
stressing that the nation-state was the privileged site of economic regulation: 'The state is the archetypal form of all regulation. It is at the level of the
state that the class struggle is resolved' (Lipietz 1987: 19). He presented the
world economy as a congeries of autonomous national capitalisms. Another
decade or so on, Aglietta summarized his book thus:

The essential idea of *A Theory of Capitalist Regulation* is that the dynamism of capital represents an enormous productive potential but that it is also a blind force. It does not contain a self-limiting mechanism of its own, nor is it guided in a direction that would enable it to fulfil the capitalists' dream of perpetual accumulation.

Enter the mode of regulation, 'a set of mediations which ensure that the distortions created by the accumulation of capital are kept within limits which are compatible with social cohesion within each nation.' The breakdown of Fordism has created a situation where a 'diversity of modes of regulation' coexist:

> It was possible, for example, to distinguish an Anglo-Saxon form of capitalism, in which the markets and the state interacted within a framework of active economic policies, and a so-called Rhenish-type capitalism, where collective interests were organized and social compromises were negotiated and capable of making accumulation of capital and social progress consistent.
>
> (Aglietta 1998: 49, 44, 77)

The focus of Aglietta's analysis has thus shifted from the diachronic succession of regimes of accumulation to the synchronic coexistence of rival modes of regulation. It is plain that his sympathies now lie with the 'Rhenish' mode, as the best way of ironing out the 'distortions' of capital accumulation. In both this political conclusion and its larger analytical framework Aglietta's position now bears a remarkable resemblance to Michel Albert's *Capitalism Against Capitalism* (1993), which argued that world history would continue after the collapse of the Stalinist states in the struggle between rival kinds of capitalism, and in particular that between the Anglo-American and Rhenish models. This work in turn influenced the development by Will Hutton and other left-Keynesian intellectuals in Britain of the concept of 'stakeholder capitalism' as an alternative to Tory *laissez faire* – an idea Tony Blair toyed with in opposition before rejecting it as too radical (Callinicos 1996).

These considerations suggest that the concept of 'Fordism', of which Aglietta offered the most influential theorization, at best has a certain descriptive value in identifying some characteristics of capitalist production and consumption during the Long Boom of the 1950s and 1960s. It may have helped stimulate some fruitful work – notably Mike Davis' (1986) brilliant studies of American capitalism in the Reagan era – but lacked any satisfactory theoretical account of the driving forces of boom and slump. Of far less utility even at the descriptive level is the concept of 'post-Fordism', often used to characterize the economic epoch supposedly corresponding to the advent of postmodernism, since it was typically derived through a contrast with what was at best a very partial account of capitalism after the Second World War (Callinicos 1989: 132–44).

Scepticism about periodizing capitalism

Another way of putting the difficulty with regulation theory is that in the often valuable analyses it offers of nationally specific institutional complexes, any understanding of the structures and tendencies common to all forms of capitalism vanishes. The laws of motion of the capitalist mode of production that Marx sought to uncover are trumped by the institutional forms characteristic of particular modes of regulation. It is hardly surprising therefore that many committed to continuing Marx's project should conclude by rejecting the attempt to differentiate between species of the genus capital. A relatively simplistic version of this response is provided by followers of the 'capital-logic' approach, but since they tend to follow the metaphysical procedure of deducing the concrete behaviour of capitalist economies from features postulated as intrinsic to the concept of capital, attacks from this quarter are hardly likely to discredit the very idea of studying types of capitalism and isolating phases of capitalist development.

Much more consequent is the position defended by Robert Brenner and Michael Glick. At the end of their lengthy, detailed, and devastating critique of the theoretical arguments and historical claims advanced by the Regulation School, they cast doubt on the latter's attempt 'to develop a set of historically founded concepts as intermediate links between high theory and economic history', notably those of regimes of accumulation and modes of regulation:

> [S]ince each mode of development must represent a phase within the evolution of, and thus a variation upon, the capitalist mode of production per se, it would appear necessary to understand the emergence, the reproduction, and the effects of the modes of regulation that guide each regime of accumulation at least *partly* in terms of the general constraints constituted by capitalist social-property relations. This is, first of all, because capitalist social-property relations, once established, impose on the individual economic units or actors certain necessary forms of economic behaviour – maximization of the price–cost ratio for the sale of their goods by appropriately specializing, by accumulating surpluses, and bringing in the latest technique, on pain of going out of business under the pressure of competition. The aggregate developmental tendencies that result – tendencies for medium-run prices to reflect costs of production, for rates of profit in different lines of production, to equalize, for obsessive capital accumulation, and for the unprecedented development of the productive forces – distinguish capitalism from all other types of economy. Secondly, capitalist social-property relations, once established,

form a sort of field of natural selection for the emergence and reproduction of historically specific economic institutions themselves. The failure of the Regulationists, in practice, to take adequate account of these general and distinctive features of the capitalist mode of production, lies behind many of the central conceptual and empirical weaknesses of the theory.

(Brenner and Glick 1991: 105–6)

I have cited this passage at length because it represents a most carefully framed argument for asserting the priority of the laws of motion of the capitalist mode over its historically variable forms. The thought is that each set of 'social-property relations' (Brenner's preferred expression for referring to the relations of production) impose on economic actors certain 'rules of reproduction'; in the case of capitalism, the patterns of behaviour enjoined by these rules override whatever tendencies might otherwise have been generated by the historically specific institutional forms on which regulation theorists focus.[6] Although there is no explicit argument for this conclusion, the upshot is to enjoin a generalized scepticism about the value of distinguishing between historical variants and stages of capitalist development. Certainly Brenner's own substantive work on both the origins of capitalism and its current development tends to move directly from analysis of capitalist rules of reproduction to study of how these rules' effects are manifested empirically.[7]

Despite the force of Brenner's and Glick's critique of regulation theory, it seems to me that there is still an important role for what they call 'intermediate' concepts that seek, in particular, to specify different phases of capitalist development. My reasons for taking this position may be brought out by considering an even more radically sceptical take on any stadial conceptualization of capitalism. In a skilful critical survey of some versions of Marxist political economy, Bruce Norton argues that all – the 'stagnationist' approach of Steindl, Baran and Sweezy, Mandel's variant of long-wave theory, and the SSA approach – suffer from the common fault of 'essentialism'. That is, 'each argument is constructed as if the process of accumulation is shaped by an essence, an originating force thought to produce the behavioural characteristics of the whole by manifesting itself inevitably in particular ways' (Norton 1988a: 203). Thus each phase of capitalist development distinguished by the various theorists follow ineluctably from their version of capitalism's laws of motion, and is therefore bound eventually to go into crisis till either a new historically specific kind of capitalism emerges or a socialist society is installed in its place. Furthermore:

Bound up with such reasoning is a particular use of abstract propositions. Each of the schools considered here proposes a general hypothesis about

238 Phases of Capitalist Development

the determination of accumulation and utilizes that proposition to structure the ensuing analysis... these initially-posited causal links are not
rethought and transformed as the arguments are developed more concretely and additional processes and relationships considered. Instead
they are treated as fixed, once established at an abstract level of analysis.
(Norton 1988a: 203; compare 1992)

Norton contrasts this treatment of abstraction, in which the actual history
of capitalism is reduced to mere exemplifications of certain theoretical
propositions, to what he calls 'the current view' of the kinds of crisis identified by Marx in *Capital*:

these are possible rather than necessary outcomes of periods of rapid
accumulation: they are ways in which Marx suggested that accumulation,
by changing the rate of profit may influence its own continuation.
Whether it will or not cannot be deduced from the mere existence of
the analytical possibilities. Not, that is, unless one adds the additional
assumption that the accumulation of capital is an essence – a separately
constituted aspect of social life determined by its own internal nature.
(Norton 1988a: 216)

What Norton announces to be the 'current view' is (as so often) in fact
that shared by a particular group of Marxist theorists – in this case the post-
Althusserians associated with Stephen Resnick, Richard Wolff and the journal *Rethinking Marxism*. This position represents the opposite extreme to that
of Brenner and Glick. While the latter assert that capitalist production
relations are so powerful as to overwhelm all specific institutional forms,
Norton and his co-thinkers espouse a pluralist conception of social explanation in which a multiplicity of different factors are responsible for any given
phenomenon. Marxist concepts merely provide one optional 'entry point'
for social analysis.[8] Yet, like Brenner and Glick, though from very different
premises, Norton effectively discredits the entire enterprise of distinguishing
between phases of capitalist development.

Abstract and concrete in *Capital*

Norton's criticisms of established schools of Marxist political economy are
often shrewd. But they do not necessarily validate the alternative approach he
espouses. The worry with it is, quite simply, that analysis based on it
will amount to an undifferentiated mush. Thus another post-Althusserian
theorist, Stephen Cullenberg, seeks to recommend the merits of the approach
of 'decentred totality' (his version of Norton's 'current view') in economic
theory by telling us: 'An analysis of a decentred capitalist enterprise and its
conditions of existence, is never complete. It is always the case that the

conditions of existence complexly [*sic*] overdetermine each other, in a never-ending contradictory process of uneven development' (Cullenburg 1994: 103). Reality is, in other words, infinitely complex.

It is hard to see how this truism, on its own, will get us to the formulation of definite theories sufficiently determinate to admit of critical assessment with respect to their internal consistency and empirical corroboration. Norton complains that 'essentialist' theorists tend to treat certain general propositions as 'fixed, once established at an abstract level of analysis'. But how can any theory generate testable hypotheses unless some of its assertions are treated, at least for some purposes, as simply given? The distinction which Imre Lakatos drew between the unrevisable 'hard core' of a scientific research programme and the testable and dispensable hypotheses generated on its basis reflects this requirement. Without some such distinction, the impact of any empirical counter-example on a research programme will be completely indeterminate (Lakatos 1978).

When we turn to *Capital* itself, we see Marx proceeding neither as Brenner and Glick do, by constructing an abstract model of the capitalist mode which is then applied directly to historical cases, nor as Norton suggests, by outlining a set of 'abstract possibilities' whose implications for actual capitalist economies are left quite open. Gérard Duménil's important study of Marx's discourse in *Capital* offers an illuminating picture of his method of theory-construction. Its main thesis is very well summarized by Althusser:

> Far from proceeding by *self-production* of concepts, the thought of Marx proceeded rather by *position* of concepts, inaugurating the exploration (analysis) of the theoretical space opened and closed by this position, then by position of a new concept enlarging the theoretical field, and so on: until the constitution of theoretical fields of extreme complexity.
> (Althusser 1978: 17–18)

Duménil himself describes the 'system' of *Capital* as that of 'a dosed abstraction or, if you prefer, of a concretization constructed element by element'.[9] This is a method of progressive complication, in which new determinations are introduced at appropriate stages in the analysis. Within this procedure, certain general propositions initially affirmed by Marx *are* modified in the course of the argument: most obviously, he drops the assumption that commodities exchanged at their values when, in Part II of *Capital*, Volume III, he introduces the equalization of the rate of profit. But this is not, as Norton claims, playing the variations of a matrix of abstract possibilities. Rather these modifications occur when dictated by the enterprise of conceptually reconstructing the structure and tendencies of the capitalist mode of production as a totality. As Marx himself writes at the start of Volume III, 'The various forms of capital, as evolved in this book, *thus approach step by step* the form which they assume on the surface of society, in the action of different capitals on one another, in competition, and in the ordinary consciousness of the agents of production themselves' (Marx 1971: 25, emphasis added).

This method of what Duménil calls 'concretization' establishes the pertinence of certain abstract concepts and propositions for the understanding of actual capitalist economies, as Marx puts it, 'through a number of intermediate stages' (Marx 1963–72, II: 174). The relationship between abstract and concrete here is not a deductive one: rather, it involves, in Althusser's felicitous formulation, the *position* of concepts. In other words, concepts specifying some new determination are introduced where it becomes necessary to analyze an aspect of the capitalist mode hitherto excluded from consideration. Thus it is only in Part II of *Capital*, Volume II, when studying the circulation process, that Marx considers the turnover of capital, a concept which has important implications (not properly integrated into the analysis of Volume III) for the determination of the general rate of profit (Duménil 1978: 281ff.). Such new determinations are not somehow contained in the 'concept' of capital, as capital-logicians claim: their introduction adds new content to the theory and allows it better to reconstruct the capitalist mode, in Marx's words, 'as a rich totality of many determinations and relations' (Marx 1973: 100). As Jacques Bidet puts it, summarizing Marx's hard-won development of a method across the successive drafts from the *Grundrisse*, across the *1861–3 Manuscript*, to *Capital* itself,

> within a determinate structural level, categories are introduced whose legitimacy does not derive from the fact of their 'deduction' starting from anterior categories, but from their connection in a global intelligible structure which they together constitute; ... *the passage to another* level is constituted by the introduction of a new category ... which thus 'opens' a new categorial whole.[10]

This method is used in *Capital* to construct a theory of the capitalist mode as such. But there is no reason why the process of 'concretization' should not be extended to the study of more concrete objects. The Althusserian reconstruction of historical materialism focused attention on the distinction between modes of production, and social formations, specific combinations of modes of production that actually exist 'in the strong sense'. Whatever the merits of the concept of social formation, it represents merely one direction in which concretization might proceed. Another is precisely that of developing a theory of the different phases of capitalist development.

The theory of imperialism

The critical 'intermediate stage' here is a level of analysis largely ignored by those influenced by Althusser, including the Regulation School, namely the world economy. Brenner and Glick rightly argue that the regulationist 'project of conceptualizing the history of capitalism as a progression of institutionally determined, nationally situated modes of development' is undermined by

> the manner and degree to which, not only the broader framework of social-property relations, but also the nature of the world economy, shapes local process of capital accumulation . . . This is because the given international distribution of productive power will have a central role in determining what institutions are even viable within national economies at a given historical juncture, as well as what will be their effect on capital accumulation, since, unless they are shielded in some way, these institutions must directly respond to international competition.
>
> (Brenner and Glick 1991: 111)

This criticism poses the demand for a theory of the world economy. Brenner has been famously critical of world systems theory as practised by Wallerstein and Gunder Frank, essentially for positing an undifferentiated, trans-historical 'capitalism' from which the distinctive features and consequences of capitalist production relations have been effaced (Brenner 1977). The point is well taken, but it does not remove the need to conceptualize the interrelationship between patterns of international competition and forms of capital accumulation. The significance of the classical theory of imperialism is precisely that it seeks to meet such a need by constructing a model, more concrete than that of *Capital*, of a distinctive phase of capitalist development on a world scale.

Bukharin offers the most rigorous version of that theory (and, partly in consequence, the most problematic), in which this phase is defined by, on the one hand, the internationalization of the productive forces, and on the other, the progressive national organization of capital, of which the emergence of finance capital is one form, but whose highest expression is the formation of 'state-capitalist trusts'. As a result, competition between capitals increasingly develops on a global rather than a national arena, and takes the form, not merely of economic rivalries among firms, but of military and diplomatic conflicts between states. Both these tendencies constitutive of imperialism are conceived as consequences of the process of centralization and concentration of capital. In this sense, Bukharin's theory may be considered a 'concretization' of Marx's analysis in *Capital*, which proceeds through the position of new concepts, notably those of the world economy and the distinctive forms of capitalist organization and competition characteristic of this phase of development (Bukharin 1972; 1971).

The weaknesses of the theory may be quickly stated. Bukharin tends to assume that the tendency towards state capitalism is fully realized, so that the world economy is now divided into nationally organized blocs of capital that compete militarily rather than economically. In conjunction with his acceptance of a disproportionality theory of crisis, this then leads him to predict that state capitals will, in effect, be able to organize themselves out of the boom–slump cycle. On this basis he denied the possibility of the kind of global depression which gripped the world economy at the end of the 1920s (Callinicos 1987a: 84–8). Preobrazhensky's (1985) more complex and sophisticated version of disproportionality theory better equipped him to analyze the slump (before, of course, both were swept away by the Stalinist terror).

These defects do not necessarily entail the abandonment of Bukharin's theory. They stem in large part from his propensity (for which Lenin taxed him) to think undialectically in terms of finished tendencies rather than structural contradictions. For if imperialism is defined by the coexistence of *two* tendencies, namely those towards *both* the internationalization *and* the statization of capital, it follows that each tendency must set limits to the other. Even when the tendencies towards autarky were at their highest in the 1930s, the most closed economies continued to depend on access to the world market. Thus one of the driving forces of the Stalinist forced collectivization of agriculture was the need to maximize grain exports in order to finance imports of plant and equipment required by the new industries, while shortages of foreign exchange required to purchase raw materials helped to push the Nazi regime towards the *Blitzkrieg* strategy of obtaining these resources through military expansion and rapid conquest.

Once both the tendencies which Bukharin holds to be constitutive of imperialism are given their proper weight, they throw a distinctive light on the twentieth century. One might distinguish three periods within the imperialist epoch that reflect the changing balance between the national organization and the global integration of capital: 1914–45, in which the statization of capital predominates in the context of military conflicts among the imperial powers so intense that they threaten the very survival of the system; 1945–73, when both tendencies are held in check against the background of the Long Boom and the cold war partition of the world; 1973 to the present, where the tendency towards globalization of capital comes to prevail amid successive world recessions and growing political instability. Naturally, such a periodization requires substantiation by careful supporting analysis involving what Bukharin's account manifestly lacks, namely an adequate theory of crises.[11]

Nevertheless that account has one decisive merit, namely that it places at the centre of the understanding of contemporary capitalism the relationship between private capital and the nation state and, correlatively, that between economic and military competition. Too often among both Marxists and their opponents, the state and military conflict are conceived as the 'outside' of capital (Barker 1978). Thus Michael Mann conceives the evidence he provides of the role of military competition in the development of the modern system of nation-states as a refutation of Marxism. Bukharin's theory of imperialism suggests, by contrast, that, at least once the capitalist mode becomes dominant on a world scale, inter-state conflict must be conceptualized as a specific form of competition among capitals.[12]

To develop this suggestion would require a reformulation of Marx's theory of competition (in any case an underdeveloped and largely implicit aspect of *Capital*) in more general terms in order to distinguish between the cases of economic and military competition, as well as a non-reductive conceptualization of each of these cases. But some such theorization is any case necessary if Marxism is to confront one of the brute realities of the twentieth-century world – namely the manifest, but complex interconnections between military power and capital accumulation. Understanding these interconnections is not merely theoretically important, but politically urgent.[13]

It follows from the approach thus sketched out that imperialism itself should not be conceived as a simple 'stage' of capitalist development, but rather as a process arising from the centralization and concentration of capital on a global scale that itself undergoes significant internal transformations and reorganizations. Nevertheless, the existence within each phase of imperialist development of certain common features defined by the tendencies towards the statization and the internationalization of capital is of critical importance in helping to immunize analysis from the temptations of 'globalization theory', and in particular the belief, common to many contemporary accounts of 'post-Fordism' and 'multinational capitalism' that capital has broken free from any anchorage in the nation state. Such belief leads to a dangerous underestimation of the extent to which the leading economic actors in the contemporary world – multinational corporations, investment banks, even hedge funds – depend on the assertion of state power in order effectively to prosecute their interests.[14]

From this perspective, the weakness of the kind of approach pursued, for example, by Brenner and those influenced by him is that it relies on an abstract model of capitalist property-relations and the rules of reproduction they entail for individual actors which is applied to a wide range of historical cases. Those social practices and institutions that fail to correspond to the requirements of the model are treated as instances of non-capitalist property-relations (Callinicos 1995: 128–40). The method of 'concretization' used by Marx in *Capital* by contrast leaves open the possibility that these apparently aberrant cases may turn out, through the position of intermediary concepts, to be aspects of the capitalist mode of production, conceived now not as an abstract model, but as a historically evolving system that takes on a succession of different concrete forms.

Is not thus conceptualizing capitalism inherently liable to the essentialism and evolutionism with which Norton taxes much of Marxist political economy? As I have noted above, any scientific research programme has certain propositions that are treated as its irrefutable hard core. It is hard to see what would be the point of calling an economic theory Marxist if it did not affirm, for example, that the capitalist mode of production is constituted by the exploitation of wage labour and the competitive accumulation of capital, and that it is inherently liable to crises. But it does not follow from these assertions either that capitalism is bound to collapse by virtue of its economic contradictions or that any such collapse will usher in socialism. Equally (and it is at this apparent implication of any stadial approach to capitalism that Norton directs much of his fire), it does not follow that capitalism will necessarily evolve any stable (if temporary) solution to these contradictions. Merely, as Marx does in Part III of *Capital*, Volume II, to specify the conditions under which a capitalist economy may reproduce itself is not to offer any guarantee that it will succeed in doing so. Economies and the social formations in which they are imbricated sometimes fail to meet their functional requirements and therefore collapse, as the inhabitants of large parts of Africa have melancholy reason to know.

Nevertheless, it remains the case that the advanced capitalist economies at least have succeeded in evolving relatively stable and historically specific patterns of reproduction that have coped, at least for quite long stretches of time, with the system's crisis-tendencies. It is the merit of regulation theory to have recognized this fact, though, as we have seen, the resulting conceptualizations tended to disengage themselves from any theoretical understanding of capitalism's constitutive structures and tendencies. It is against this background that the more classical attempt to connect up this understanding with a more concrete analysis of evolving patterns of reproduction that the theory of imperialism assumes its importance.[15]

There can in the nature of things be no guarantee that this theory, amended in the ways indicated above, will succeed in capturing the main course of capitalist development. Ultimately even the hard core of a research programme whose predictions consistently fail will turn out not to be irrefutable after all. But it seems to me that, at least when set against the background of Marx's larger theory of the capitalist mode of production, the theory of imperialism does ask many of the right questions. In particular, as noted above, it poses more sharply than any rival approach the question of the interrelationship between economic and politico-military power. The classical Marxist project of analyzing the phases of capitalist development thus still has plenty going for it.[16]

Notes

1   For example, see Brenner and Glick (1991) and Norton (1988a).
2   For an important study of Bolshevik political economy, see Day (1981).
3   *Pace* Simon Clarke, one of the main objects of whose *Marx's Theory of Crisis* (1994) is to play down the significance of the TRPF for Marx's own crisis theory and to tax its current adherents with economic determinism.

4 See Callinicos (1999).
5 See, for example, de Vroey (1979).
6 See Brenner and Glick (1991: 108). For a broader theoretical background, see Brenner (1986).
7 See, in addition to Brenner (1998), the articles reprinted in Ashton and Philpin (1986).
8 Norton (1988a: 221). The *fons et origo* of this kind of post-Althusserian economic theory is Cutler *et al.* (1977–78).
9 Duménil (1978: 89); see also ibid. (373ff). The merits of this interpretation survive the extraordinary error Duménil commits when he claims that '[t]he theory of value makes abstraction of the material determinations characteristic of use-value: concrete labour, productive force of labour...' and that consequently use-value and associated concepts have a 'specific logic... external to that of political economy' (1978: 43). This astonishingly wrong-headed view, contemplation of which should not have survived a reading of the *Critique of the Gotha Programme*, as Jacques Bidet puts it, 'transforms the theory of *Capital* into pure formalism on the side of value, apprehended in strictly tautological terms, into pure empiricism on the side of use-value, presented as simple contingency' (Bidet 1985: 133).
10 Bidet (1985: 154–5). See more generally ibid. (chapters vi and vii).
11 See Harman (1984, new edition 1999) for an important attempt to provide such an analysis, and also Callinicos *et al.* (1994).
12 See, on the challenge to Marxism of Mann's historical sociology, Callinicos (1987b: 157–72).
13 I wrote this chapter as the new, expanded NATO waged its first war in the Balkans.
14 Peter Gowan (1999: especially part I) offers an important (if occasionally excessively conspiratorial) analysis of the interrelationship between economic and strategic interests in US foreign policy since the end of the cold war. For effective critiques of 'globalization theory', see Hirst and Thompson (1996); Harman (1996); Marfleet (1998).
15 From the Lakatosian viewpoint in the philosophy of science, the theory of imperialism might be seen as constituting an important part of the belt of 'auxiliary hypotheses' through which a research programme's hard core is articulated and rendered liable to empirical corroboration or refutation.
16 I approach the problem of periodizing capitalism from the somewhat different angle presented in Robert Brenner (forthcoming) under the title 'The indeterminary of Perry Anderson'.

15
Growth and Change in the World Economy Since 1950

Michael J. Webber and David L. Rigby

The world economy has grown and changed since 1950. It is six times larger and more integrated than then, though growth has been uneven through time. Rates of profit, GDP growth and capital formation were greater before the early 1970s than since. While poverty, famine and the dominance of the industrial market economies are constants, other features of the global economy have changed – financial markets have become global (Corbridge *et al*. 1994) and increasingly dominate productive capital, while multinational corporations have entangled more and more countries ever more tightly into a network of intra-corporate links (Dicken 1992). Despite the events of the last few years, the emergence of Japan and the newly industrialized economies as economic powers represents another important structural change.

Many theorists and commentators more or less concur with this general history: see, for example, Freeman and Perez (1988), Lipietz (1986a), Mandel (1975) and Piore and Sabel (1984). However, there has been insufficient evidence with which to distinguish the explanations adduced by different theories. The empirical information presented in this chapter permits us to reinterpret what has happened to the industrial and industrializing economies of the world since the Second World War: the chapter reviews the historical record, assesses how existing interpretations stack up against that record and finally sketches a reinterpretation of post-war historical geography. The evidence is drawn primarily from the manufacturing sectors of Australia, Canada, Japan and the USA and the newly industrialized economies of Brazil, South Korea and Taiwan, essentially for the period 1950–90. The chapter provides a non-technical review of the results of a long running research program; details of methods and sources are to be found in the papers cited and in Webber and Rigby (1996).

Existing alternatives

Why have rates of growth slowed in the advanced industrial economies since the mid-1970s? A variety of schools of thought – orthodox, technological, regulatory and falling-rate-of-profit views – have proposed answers to this question.

Orthodox attempts to understand the exceptionalism of the so-called Golden Age rest on the neo-classical theory of economic growth (following Solow 1957), or on theories of endogenous economic growth (Grossman and Helpman 1991; Lucas 1988; Romer 1994). Neo-classical theory predicts that long-run rates of growth of output depend on the rate of saving and the rate of population growth (de Long and Summers 1991; Mankiw *et al.* 1992), with variables added to hold other things constant (Barro 1991).[1] Endogenous growth theories (Grossman and Helpman 1994) model external economies (Romer 1986; Lucas 1988; Young 1991) or improvements in technology (Grossman and Helpman 1991; Rivera-Batiz and Romer 1991). However, the intellectual appeal of endogenous growth theories is not matched by their substantive empirical backing (Maddison 1987; Griliches 1988; Chandler 1990; Pack 1994). The orthodox, then, largely explain the slowdown in terms of investment in physical and human capital and investment in research and development (and such accidents as the OPEC oil price rises).

Freeman and Perez (1988) identify fluctuations in rates of growth as Kondratieff waves (see too Kleinknecht 1987: 19–51; contrast Berry 1991). Freeman and Perez view long waves as alternating periods of accord and discord between new technologies (Mensch 1979) and social institutions. Freeman and Perez (also Freeman *et al.* 1982) thus explain the slowdown in terms of a reduced rate of productivity growth. In turn, they ascribe the productivity slowdown to the standardization of new products and intensified cost competition. As process innovations become subject to diminishing returns, they yield progressively smaller improvements in productivity and generate diminishing increases in demand. Thus overcapacity, together with the productivity slowdown, explains the reduction in profitability.

In the regulatory account of Piore and Sabel (1984), the problem is one of markets. In the mass production economy of the 1950s and 1960s, firms had to stabilize their markets in order to achieve economies of mass production and social institutions sought to match aggregate supply and demand. The mechanism that performed this role was wage contract bargaining, which worked so that the increase in wages equalled the economy-wide increase in productivity plus the rate of inflation. When the search for economies of scale drove the mass production economy to become international, without any international mechanism to regulate demand and supply, a shortfall in demand became inevitable. Piore and Sabel argue that in the event demand failed because of market saturation and international competition from the newly industrializing countries. The falls in profitability and in the rate of productivity growth are consequences of that failure. Thus, underconsumption is a cause; the slowdown in productivity growth is a consequence.

More radical regulatory accounts have been presented by some French scholars (Aglietta 1979; Boyer and Mistral 1978; Lipietz 1986a). Lipietz, for example, conceives the 1950s and 1960s as a period of Fordist accumulation, when the production of goods was increasingly standardized, productivity increases equalled increases in fixed capital per worker, output increases were matched by increases in consumption, and wage and price setting encouraged productivity growth. However, by the late 1960s, the rate of productivity increase fell, because of a (naturally) reduced rate of learning by doing and the effects of the Fordist exclusion of workers from management. Slower productivity growth is thus a cause. Given the pattern of wage increases, the rate of profit consequently fell. Finally, therefore, the rate of accumulation slowed as firms reacted by internationalizing production (to save on wages), and the state by austerity.

The most radical account of post-war economic history has been advanced by such Marxists as Mandel (1975) and Harvey (1982). Mandel describes a recent phase that began during the Second World War in the USA and later elsewhere, after wages had been suppressed and the rate of surplus value was high. In this phase, technological rents became the primary source of surplus profits, leading to a high rate of innovation and a reduced turn-over time of fixed capital. However, as that technical revolution spread through the economy, it raised the organic composition of capital. By the mid-1960s, the reserve armies of labour in Western Europe and the USA had been used up; so the rate of surplus value could no longer be increased to compensate for changes in the organic composition of capital. Therefore the rate of profit began to fall and the desired rate of accumulation of capital declined (capital had been overaccumulated). The slowdown in the rate of growth of productivity is thus a consequence of the fact that the fall in profitability limited opportunities for the profitable accumulation of capital.

Why, then, did accumulation slow? The answer depends on who one reads: rising organic composition of capital; rising power of labour and wage patterns; inflationary shocks; deflationary policies; deregulation of financial and exchange markets; market saturation; competition from the newly industrializing countries; slowed productivity change; reduced rates of saving; changing patterns of innovation; internationalization of production; and technical changes (in microelectronics, transport and communication). To disentangle cause and effect, this chapter examines evidence about changes in rates of profit and their determinants, variations in rates of technical change and their determinants, and changes in location and their determinants.

Profitability and its determinants

The first issue concerns the manner in which capital–output ratios, wage increases, changes in demand and productivity change are related to the rate of profit.

Firms compete in two arenas to raise their rate of profit. Within the chaotic arena of the market, firms compete by minimizing the costs of inputs and by maximizing the price of their outputs (Farjoun and Machover 1983). If firms obtain inputs below average prices or if they sell output at prices above the market average, they capture additional profit – at the expense of firms that are weak in the market. Within production, firms compete by raising productivity – adopting the most efficient techniques at their disposal. To measure the impact of the two forms of competition, the price rate of profit is defined as

$$\pi_p = M\pi_v \tag{1}$$

where M measures the ability of firms to compete in the market and π_v is the value rate of profit.

The value rate of profit measures performance on the assumption that all firms exchange commodities at the same average price. Differences in the value rate of profit therefore depend on differences in the techniques of production rather than in market characteristics. The value rate of profit is defined, as usual, by

$$\pi_v = \frac{S}{C+V} \tag{2}$$

where S is surplus value, C is constant capital (the annual equivalent of the capitalized value of plant, equipment and machinery advanced in production) and V is variable capital (the value of labour-power applied in production each year).

Dividing equation (2) by V,

$$\pi_v = \frac{S/V}{C/V + 1} = \frac{e}{(q+1)t} \tag{3}$$

where e is the rate of exploitation (measuring the distribution of the value added in production to capital and labour), q is the value composition of capital (the ratio of the value of constant capital advanced in production to the value of variable capital advanced) and t is the turnover time of capital. In turn, equation (3) may be expanded to reveal the basic components of the value rate of profit (values of commodities, the real wage and input–output coefficients).

Thus changes in the price rate of profit can be decomposed into the effects of changes in market competitiveness and changes in production efficiency. Variations in market performance show how spatial and sectoral variations in prices influence profitability. Changes in the value rate of profit can be decomposed similarly: into the effects of changes in the rate of exploitation, in the value composition of capital and in the turnover time of capital (Webber 1987). Production characteristics reflect the impacts of technical change on the rate of profit. In aggregate – at the level of the national economy – value and price rates of profit are equal; so the effects of price differences on profitability are revealed only at the industry and regional level.

In Australia, Canada, Japan and the USA the rate of profit in manufacturing tended to fall into the early or mid-1980s. However, the history of profitability has differed in the four countries (Figure 15.1). In the USA (and perhaps Australia) profitability climbed until the mid-1960s then fell until the early 1980s and has since recovered slightly. Only in the USA was there anything like a boom in profit rates that lasted until the mid-1960s to be followed by a decline during the 1970s. In Canada the rate of profit in manufacturing declined consistently from the mid-1950s until the early 1980s. In Japan the rate of profit continued to rise until the mid-1970s, has fallen since then and has not yet begun to recover. The timing and the extent of the decline in profitability are different in the four countries: the decline began earliest in Canada and latest in Japan; slight recovery began in the early 1980s in the three Anglo economies but has not appeared in Japan.

The decline in profitability was loosely associated with reduced rates of growth. In all four countries rates of growth of capital and of output have declined as profitability fell, though the mechanism and the strength of

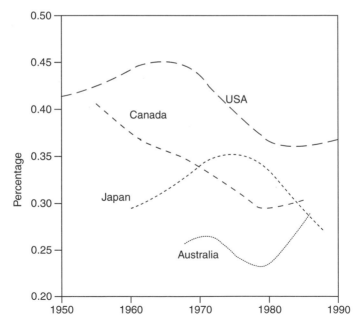

Figure 15.1   Rate of profit in manufacturing: Australia, Canada, Japan and the USA. (Dates differ between countries, depending on the availability of data. The data are smoothed.)
Source: Webber and Rigby (1996: figure 8.25).

these relationships differ between the four countries. So the slowdown of the late 1970s and 1980s was indeed accompanied by reduced rates of profit. As such, this history is compatible with the accounts of Freeman and Perez, Mandel and Lipietz as well as orthodox theorists. The fact that rates of profit were falling from at least the mid-1960s in Australia, Canada and the USA seems to argue against the account of Piore and Sabel (in which falling profit rates are a consequence of the slowdown).

The determinants of changes in the rate of profit in Australia, Canada, Japan and the USA are indicated in Table 15.1. The first column of data reveals the change in the rate of profit in each country and period. The second, third and fourth columns indicate the effects on profitability of changes in respectively, the rate of exploitation, the value composition of capital and turnover times. For example, in the USA between 1981 and 1989 the rate of profit rose by 5.8 percentage points; of that rise, 2.4 percentage points were contributed by increases in the rate of exploitation, 2.0 by falls in the value composition of capital and 1.1 by reductions in the time taken to turn capital over. In all four countries through most of the 1970s the rate of profit fell; those falls were driven essentially by increases in the value composition of capital. That is, profit rates fell because increases in the

Table 15.1 Determinants of changes in the rate of profit: Australia, Canada, Japan and the USA

Country	Period	Change in Value rate of profit	Effect of		
			Exploitation	*Value composition of capital*	*Turnover time*
Australia	1969–79	−0.028	0.011	−0.054	0.021
	1979–85	0.042	0.085	−0.062	0.033
Canada	1956–79	−0.111	−0.021	−0.204	0.065
	1979–85	0.013	0.036	−0.075	0.049
Japan	1961–74	0.048	−0.061	0.032	0.103
	1974–87	−0.077	0.050	−0.536	0.251
USA	1963–65	0.024	0.033	−0.008	−0.000
	1965–81	−0.159	0.019	−0.262	−0.002
	1981–89	0.058	0.024	0.020	0.011

Note: The data are estimated from differential equations derived from (1) and (3). Time series are smoothed by three-year moving averages. The actual changes in profitability and the sum of the effects differ because calculations ignore interactions between the variables. The differentials and effects are measured as discrete annual changes and summed over periods indicated. The periods reflect changes in the rate of profit: for example, in Australian manufacturing, profitability was tending to fall to 1979 and to rise thereafter.
Source: Webber and Rigby (1996: table 8.4).

amount of plant, equipment and raw materials per worker led to a decline in the productivity of capital. When rates of profit were falling, the rate of exploitation and the speed at which capital is turned over both tended to raise profitability (except in Canada). There is little evidence that labour costs were rising faster than productivity when rates of profit were falling. These observations are compatible with Marxist accounts of the falling rate of profit (including Mandel). While the apparent role of slower gains in efficiency accords with the story of Lipietz, the fact that changes in the rate of exploitation have not driven rates of profit down is incompatible with his argument.

In Australia and Canada subsequent increases in the rate of profit have been fuelled by increases in the rate of exploitation, predicated on stagnant real wages rather than improvements in efficiency. In the USA, by contrast, the value composition of capital has exerted little effect recently, because the technical composition has changed only slowly. The change in regime in Japan from rising to falling rates of profit depended essentially on a shift from falling to rising value composition of capital once efficiency gains could no longer offset changes in the technical composition of capital. In none of these countries had there appeared by the end of the 1980s a form of development that could yield long-run growth and rising real wages: in Japan, profit rates had not started to recover; and in the other economies the recovery was fuelled by deeper exploitation or stagnant technique rather than by high rates of investment that carry new techniques.

The aggregate picture fails to do justice to the diversity of histories of profitability in different industries. In the USA some (two-digit) industries' price rates of profit rose despite the aggregate decline in profitability: increases in the price–value ratio more than offset the effect of changes in the value rate of profit in the food and kindred products and tobacco industries, for example. In other industries the price rate of profit was more or less unchanged during the aggregate decline – petroleum, for example. In the remaining industries price rates of profit followed aggregate profits down; but in the rubber and plastics products and stone, clay and glass products industries the primary cause of decline was a fall in market power. In the fabricated metals products industry, the effects of market power and the value rate of profit were equal. The transport industry has a history all of its own, which is ironic since the Regulation School identifies transport as the hegemonic industry in the US during the long boom. So in 13 of the 20 industries the price rate of profit fell basically because the value rate of profit fell and that happened because the value composition of capital was driven upwards by the technical composition of capital. Similar diversity is apparent in the history of profitability in Canada's industries and regions.

The variety of history is disturbing for accounts of the long boom (Lipietz and Piore and Sabel). The history of rates of profit is not the same in the four countries: only in the USA was there a boom in profit rates that lasted until the mid-1960s to be followed by a decline during the 1970s. In Japan, changes in turnover times have exerted a greater influence on profitability than changes in the rate of exploitation. Furthermore, while the crisis in US manufacturing has been spread widely over its manufacturing sectors the histories of profitability in different industries are diverse. Similarly in Canada: there are wide variations about the aggregate story among the individual industries and regions of the country. Variety and difference in timing and cause argue against the concept of an overarching long boom.

Also problematic are the links between profitability and accumulation. Rates of profit and accumulation are clearly correlated. However, the lag structure of the data does not indicate whether profitability drives accumulation or conversely. Nor is it clear why changes in profitability are at some times but not at others associated with changes in the rate of accumulation. Models of accumulation must attend to this link.

In addition, the theory of the falling rate of profit needs to be extended. The theory is usually explained in terms of the value composition of capital and the rate of exploitation. Yet turnover times of capital and unequal exchanges in the market between industries and regions affect rates of profit. In about one-third of Canadian and US industries the ability of firms to compete in the market has a greater effect on the rate of profit than does the value rate of profit. Clearly theories of the rate of profit need not only to be couched in terms of a formal, dynamic model but must also examine controls over turnover times and market power.

Productivity change

The history and sources of productivity change in US manufacturing also help to arbitrate between competing accounts of the slowdown. The main contenders are Freeman and Perez (1988) and Lipietz (1986a), who regard the slowdown in productivity growth as a cause of the failure of the Fordist regime of accumulation, and Mandel (1975) and Piore and Sabel (1984), who claim that the observed slowdown in aggregate productivity is a consequence rather than a cause of slower accumulation. So the issue concerns the relations between profitability, rates of economic growth and productivity change. Was there a slowdown in technical change and if so when? What can be deduced about the determinants of a slowdown? Is the aggregate history common to individual industries?

Webber *et al.* (1992) proposed a method for calculating the sources of technical change. Productivity change is identified as the change in costs of production, measured at constant prices. The components of productivity change are:

1. innovation within individual plants, as firms develop new techniques or imitate competitors;

2. selection, as the market differentially rewards firms with different levels of productivity;
3. the entry of plants to and their exit from an industry, as price changes permit or prevent less productive plants from entering the market.

The first term represents productivity increases due to changes in the technical and social relations within plants. The second and third terms represent changes in an industry's productivity that arise from changes in the composition of the industry. This method is used to estimate the rate, direction and sources of technical change in US manufacturing between 1962 and 1990 (see Webber and Rigby 1996: Appendix A9).

Between 1962 and 1973 there was steady productivity change in US manufacturing (see Figure 15.2). On average, costs of production (at constant prices) declined at an annual rate of 2.07 per cent. This progress was largely neutral (that is normal to the ratio of prices), though with occasional bouts of labour saving bias. Then until 1981, capital was substituted for labour and costs of production increased: energy price increases prompted at least some firms to invest in new, energy-efficient plant and equipment; paradoxically, that period was therefore one of increases in both the prices of and the investment in fixed capital. Since that time technical change has returned to its role of reducing costs of production (at an average annual rate of 2.96 per cent).

Productivity change was consistently reducing costs of production well after profitability began to fall in US manufacturing (the mid-1960s) and after the onset of the slowdown in growth and investment in the early 1970s. The slowdown in productivity change must therefore have been a consequence rather than a cause of the slowdown in growth and of the falling rate of profit. Furthermore, the slowdown in productivity change was not caused by a failure of labour productivity: rather the capital–output ratio rose between 1973 and 1981. These results contradict the claims that slower productivity progress caused by a failure of labour productivity was one of the reasons for the falling rate of profit. Actually capital was oversubstituted for labour.

The slowdown in productivity gains is better understood as a consequence of changes in rates of profit and investment (Table 15.2). When the rate of profit and rate of investment were still relatively high, innovation and imitation (technical changes within plants) were both high also. When profitability and investment fell in the 1970s so innovation and imitation fell too – because investment carries the new technologies that are central to these forms of productivity change. Since 1981 the rate of investment has remained low, but imitation has been spurred by widening cost differences between best- and worst-practice firms. By contrast, the effects of selection on productivity change have grown gradually stronger as the variance of production costs has increased. Finally the inflation of the middle and late

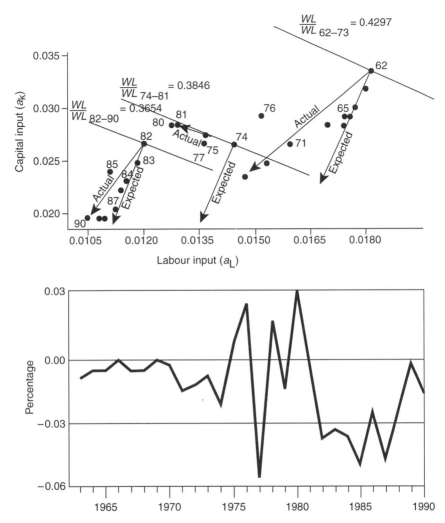

Figure 15.2 Technical change within US manufacturing industry, 1962–90. (The upper part of the figure indicates the change in input output coefficients, as compared with the changes that would be normal to the ratio of prices; the lower diagram indicates the annual rate of cost reduction due to technical change.)
Source: Webber and Rigby (1996: figures 9.1 and 9.2).

1970s induced many new firms to enter US manufacturing; these firms tended to raise costs. In the 1960s and 1980s, when prices were more stable, fewer firms entered US manufacturing industry and their effect on costs of production was correspondingly weaker. In other words, the slowdown in productivity change after 1973 was caused as (1) reduced rates of investment

Table 15.2   Sources of technical change in US manufacturing industry, 1962–90

Period	Technical change	Innovation and imitation	Selection	Entry/Exit	Drift and error
1965–73	−0.0054	−0.0021	−0.0068	0.0020	0.0015
1974–81	0.0037	0.0005	−0.0118	0.0148	0.0003
1982–90	−0.0222	−0.0042	−0.0252	0.0099	−0.0026
1965–90	−0.0084	−0.0020	−0.0147	0.0087	−0.0003

Note: The data represent the annual average changes in costs of production (at constant prices) and in the components of the cost of production. A negative sign implies that the cost was tending to fall or the component was tending to push costs down.
Source: Webber and Rigby (1996: table 9.2).

cut both innovation and imitation; and (2) rapid price increases induced new, marginal firms to enter manufacturing. Since 1981 the pace of productivity change has recovered as (1) imitation has picked up because intra-industry cost differences have widened; and (2) stable prices have deterred additional marginal firms from entering manufacturing. That is, changes in the structure of markets have been far more important than the productivity change within firms emphasized by orthodox views.

Again, though, the history of individual (two-digit) industries has been varied. Only the history of the effects of the entry and exit of firms has been common to virtually all industries. A quarter of the industries experienced no slowdown in productivity growth after 1974. Selection has tended to raise production costs in some sectors and dominates other sources of productivity change in the chemicals and petroleum industries. Innovation and imitation have exerted the largest effect on productivity change in three industries: food and kindred products, tobacco and instruments. In only about half the sectors did the pace of innovation and imitation slow after 1974. Furthermore, the history of innovation and imitation and difference in them between sectors are correlated with inter-sectoral differences in profitability.

The theoretical accounts offer two different interpretations of the relations between productivity growth and accumulation. Freeman and Perez and Lipietz, like the orthodox, regard lower rates of productivity growth as a cause of lower profitability and slower accumulation. Mandel and Piore and Sabel, by contrast, regard the history of productivity change as a consequence rather than a cause of changes in profitability and accumulation. The evidence broadly accords with the views of Mandel and Piore and Sabel: (1) productivity slowed in the 1970s, after profitability had already begun to fall and after rates of accumulation had tumbled; (2) the productivity slowdown originated in lower rates of investment (which slowed innovation and imitation) and in inflation (which spurred the entry of inefficient firms);

(3) productivity and innovation or imitation are positively correlated across different industries; (4) faster gains in productivity since 1981 have not been reflected in rates of profit. Freeman and Perez and Lipietz seem to have their pattern of causation wrong and so their timing.

The international location of production

The third issue concerns the international location of production – specifically the growth of newly industrializing countries. When did they grow? What forces underlay growth? Was growth a matter of comparative costs or did local conditions and agency have more effect? The crucial question is: how is the growth of the newly industrializing countries related to the history of growth and profitability in the advanced industrial countries? We take as examples Brazil, (the Republic of) Korea and Taiwan.

The growth of Brazil, Korea and Taiwan had little to do with wage costs. The first steps to growth in all three countries were independent of cost advantages. Brazil started industrializing when world trade was interrupted by the depression of the 1930s and the Second World War (see Deyo 1990; Evans 1979; Foot and Webber 1990a). In Korea and Taiwan infusions of US aid – related to political strategy not to costs – provided the first growth impulses (Amsden 1989; Hamilton 1987; Wade 1990; Webber 1994; Woo 1991). All three took advantage of world conditions, but for domestic political and strategic reasons. The goal in Brazil was domestic capital accumulation, subject to the constraints of the power of landowners and workers. In Korea and Taiwan, capital accumulation has been a means to achieve independence and economic power in the face of perceived threats. Since industrialization began, the states have been deeply involved in directing it (Foot and Webber 1990b; Webber 1994). The state affects prices and determines market conditions by protecting domestic markets and supporting exporters. Prices have been manipulated and are not international; cost advantage does not determine outcomes. The countries had choices which they exercized in a way that depended on local class forces and their perceptions of the global environment.

Furthermore, the relation between the growth of Brazil, Korea and Taiwan and the slowdown in the industrial market economies is less cause than consequence. One index of this relationship is the level of capital inflow into the three economies (Webber and Rigby 1996: table 10.6). The inflow of foreign capital to all three countries sharply increased in the early 1970s. The years of sharpest increase in capital inflows were 1972 in Brazil, 1975 in Korea and 1974 in Taiwan. By 1975 net capital flows to Brazil were more than five times larger than in 1966–70; and in Korea and Taiwan more than twice as large. Nor were capital flows to these newly industrialized countries exceptional: in 1970 the net flow of foreign capital to all developing countries was 1.71 times the 1961 level; by 1980 the net flow was 3.20 times as large as a decade earlier (Stallings 1990). To the extent that there has been an increase in outflows of capital from developed to developing countries, it has occurred at the same time as (or after) the slowdown rather than before it. These data are consistent with the view that the increase in foreign capital inflows to developing countries was a response to rather than a cause of the slowdown in the industrialized countries.

The international geography of production has also been affected by the extent to which newly industrializing countries have relied on financial rather than production capital. Financial capital was commonly lent to governments or their banks during the heyday of cheap money, after the onset of the slowdown in 1974 (as again in the 1990s). It was lent under government guarantees to repay, that relied upon the continued expansion of the economy as a whole, not on the profitability of individual industries. The industries financed in this way did not have to be competitive with their international rivals even in domestic markets. To the extent that industries in newly industrialized countries were financed by international banks, newly industrialized countries were not necessarily least-cost locations for those industries (as, for example, the Brazilian steel industry: Foot and Webber 1990b; Webber and Foot 1988). They may have later become least-cost locations, by learning, exporting and economizing with scale. By contrast, direct foreign investors require newly industrialized countries to be maximum-profit locations. International financial capital offered the newly industrialized countries freedom to plan industrial growth without the constraints of competitiveness; long-term success has depended on acquiring competitiveness not starting with it.

Wages, then, do not explain development. Nevertheless, even if wage levels do not sufficiently explain development they are connected to development. If industrialization substitutes for imports then domestic demand provides the only market for industry: wages become a source of demand as well as a cost. If industrialization promotes exports, wages are purely a cost: demand can grow by wage rises in other countries. In this sense, export promotion permits firms to avoid paying sufficient wages to absorb supply.

Interpretations of post-war economic history offer two broad accounts of the relations between the internationalization of production (including the growth of newly industrialized economies) and profitability and accumulation in the industrially mature economies. (The agnostics are Freeman and Perez and Mandel.) Piore and Sabel regard the internationalization of the world's economies as a deep cause of the instability that eventually wrought the end of the long boom; competition from newly industrialized economies is an immediate reason why demand failed in Europe and North America. The evidence seems to favour the other camp (of Lipietz), which maintains that internationalization and growth of the newly industrialized economies have been mainly consequence rather than cause of the slowdown in advanced capitalist economies: export-oriented industrialization really began in newly industrialized economies in the 1970s; and capital flowed most strongly into newly industrialized economies after profit rates had fallen in Europe and North America. However, the argument from the theories of regulation and of the new international division of labour does seem to overemphasize the significance of low wages and other production costs in stimulating growth and exports – growth in newly industrialized economies was not merely structural but reflected their strategic exploitation of global economic conditions.

So what did happen?

Most existing accounts of the slowdown in the world economy have not explained this history well. Theorists of the long boom (Piore and Sabel, and Lipietz) overemphasize the homogeneity of the 1960s and early 1970s and err in seeking external reasons for falling rates of profit. Freeman and Perez and Lipietz mistakenly seek to explain falling rates of profit by referring to slower rates of growth of productivity rather than regarding productivity changes as driven by investment and profitability. Piore and Sabel misread the newly industrialized economies as a cause of slower rates of accumulation in advanced capitalist economies rather than as exploiting the new global conditions. The error of interpreting the locational changes in the light of costs of production has been common. While the account of Mandel is broadly compatible with the evidence, it remains incomplete. A full account of the historical geography of the post-war years requires a far deeper investigation of the political economy of individual countries and a more concrete history of the global political economy than we can provide. But a sketch is possible.

The underlying change was a fall in profitability in the advanced industrial economies. The declines in rates of profit were driven by increases in the value composition of capital. Profit rates fell because increases in the amount of plant, equipment and raw materials per worker were not offset by improvements in efficiency even though the rate of exploitation and the speed at which capital is turned over were both tending to raise profitability. This fall was underway by the mid-1960s in Australia and North America, and by the mid-1970s in Japan. Investment subsequently slowed – more than profitability – and by the early 1970s rates of growth of output had faltered too.

This much is clear, even though we have measured rates of profit in manufacturing rather than in the economy at large. Once rates of profit had risen sufficiently after the Second World War, the rate of capital accumulation began to exceed the rate of growth of the labour force, putting pressure on wages. Furthermore, in a largely closed economy the market into which firms could sell depended on the wages paid to workers, and corporations at large had an incentive to raise wages (even if individual corporations sought to pay less than their competitors). For both reasons, the real wage was bid up and the rate of capacity utilization approached its effective upper bound. Under these circumstances, demand and supply grow at the same pace and the rate of profit is subject to the classic constraints. Productivity change raises the capital–labour ratio. But if all the output that is produced is to be sold then the real wage must rise, for otherwise some capital has to shift into unproductive uses. In practice, both effects occurred: real wages continued to rise, limiting corporations' capacity to raise the rate of exploitation, and some capital became surplus. Therefore rates of profit began to fall under the impetus of increases in the technical composition of capital.[2]

The history of profitability differs between places and sectors. The fall in rates of profit was delayed in Japan because of particular conditions there; was delayed or hastened in some industries and regions and was subject to particular influences; and never appeared in a few industries. Market power, the ability to exclude competitors, policies towards labour, investment in process innovations and the capacity to capture consumers' dollars have all modified the history of profits in individual industries and regions. That is, at the level of individual industries and regions, external influences on rates of profit prove important. But at the level of the aggregate economy the rate of profit is driven largely by internal effects.

Two effects followed the aggregate fall in rates of profit.

First, in the advanced industrial economies productivity change slowed. The pace of productivity change in US manufacturing has been slower in 1974–81 than before or since. There are two reasons for this slowdown. As investment slowed, so there were fewer new plants and machines to carry innovations and to permit firms to imitate. Furthermore, as inflation got underway in the aftermath of the oil shock of 1974 so new, relatively inefficient firms were induced to enter manufacturing – and they dragged productivity down too. More recently, as inflation has fallen so fewer firms are entering the market, and as the differences between firms have grown so imitation has once more emerged. In general, productivity seems to follow investment and therefore profits rather than to initiate a virtuous cycle of productivity and investment.

Second, since rates of investment had fallen far more than rates of profit there was a sea of surplus capital by the early 1970s that was seeking profitable avenues for investment. Some of it was creamed off by the OPEC countries after 1974, but most of that was eventually invested by the banks of the advanced industrial economies. Both the internal and the OPEC surpluses have contributed much to the capacity of banks and other financial institutions to range over the globe seeking new outlets for locally unproductive capital. Much surplus capital was invested in the newly industrialized economies – commonly as financial capital rather than as direct investment – spurring their rapid growth. The locational pattern of investment had little to do with relative cost differences between the newly industrialized economies and the industrially mature economies and a lot to do with the availability of capital, the development of global financial markets and state strategies.

The newly industrialized economies were investing in new plant and equipment during an interval when productivity change in the advanced industrial economies had slowed. They were also learning and achieving economies of scale. The companies in the newly industrialized economies were therefore gradually reducing the technological lag between themselves and more established corporations, so their capacity to compete in global markets improved and exports from the newly industrialized economies could grow faster than their imports from advanced market economies. The export boom from the newly industrialized economies was a matter of their relative improvement in technology, not of an absolute advantage in production costs.

The past fifty years has witnessed the expansion of industrial capitalism to a new set of countries. The major impetus for this spread has been the existence of a capital surplus since the mid-1970s. In the last decade Eastern Europe, China and the ASEAN Four have shown evidence that they are about to enter this realm too – again using surplus capital from Japan, Europe, North America and some of the dragons. However or wherever the industrially mature economies discover a new source of growth, that club now includes the newly industrialized economies. This is a larger group than formerly of industrial capitalist countries to which the constraint on capital accumulation applies. As capital has sought to unbind itself from the constraints of labour and demand in industrial capitalist countries so it has brought additional economies into the bounds of those constraints.

Today, however, we face an entirely different world. After successive increases in the scale of financial capital flows and successive deregulations of the world's financial sectors, the recent events in East Asia demonstrate that financial capital has come to dominate productive capital (Webber forthcoming). Partly, this is a matter of scale: official and private financial flows to developing countries trebled between 1990 and 1997 (Howell 1998). Partly, it is a matter of widespread financial and currency crises in the 1980s and 1990s, affecting Australia, Italy, Latin America, Russia, Scandinavia, the UK, the USA and, most recently, East Asia. But most importantly, large capital inflows fuel rising asset prices, which tend to stimulate currency revaluations even as they tend to increase the trade deficit. Currency values and trade deficits are thus increasingly moving in nonorthodox directions, tending to increase disequilibrium. The implications of this new world economy, that has emerged gradually as the old economy slowed, will become increasingly obvious during the twenty-first century.

Notes

1   On the robustness of such statistical explanations, see Levine and Renelt (1992); Grossman and Helpman (1994).
2   In Japan exports provided a means by which demand could be raised even though real wages grew only slowly and it was not until the mid-1970s that the links between productivity change, real wages and excess capital forced rates of profit down.

16
Globalize, Globa-lize, Global Lies: Myths of the World Economy in the 1990s[1]

John Weeks

Introduction

Major changes occurred in the world economy during the last twenty years of the twentieth century, but there was considerable disagreement as to what those changes were and who gained and who lost from them. In the opinion of the business establishment in the developed countries, the changes created an integrated international economy that benefited all. This sanguine view was summarized in the US *Economic Report of the President* of 1999:

> Economies that are open to international trade and investment are more likely to experience a rising standard of living than are economies with significant barriers to cross-border economic activities. Consumers in open economies benefit from a wider variety of goods at lower prices than do consumers in economies that resist competition from foreign suppliers. The economy as a whole benefits from an increased ability to devote its scarce resources to economic activities that it performs relatively efficiently. Over time, through both international trade and international investment, open economies benefit from higher rates of productivity growth and innovation that result from increased participation in international markets.
>
> (CEA 1999: 260)

The foregoing statement, typical of the eulogies to 'free markets', incorporates a number of theoretical and empirical assertions. It epitomizes what we call *the globalization hypothesis*: over some clearly defined period at the end of twentieth century, the world economy underwent a dramatic change. The quantitative aspect of this change was a substantial increase in the importance of trade and foreign investment at both the international and nation levels. The qualitative aspect was that the quantitative changes

263

ushered in a new era, in which the only viable national economic policy involved liberalization of trade, deregulation of capital flows and orthodox fiscal and monetary policy. The globalization policy package can be briefly stated. Liberalization of trade would be necessary to achieve domestic efficiency and capture welfare gains for consumers. 'Investor-friendly' policies would be required to attract capital that would embody growth-stimulating technical change and managerial skills. Low budget deficits and tight monetary policy would be the macroeconomic prerequisites for maintaining the 'confidence' of international financial markets.

This chapter deals with these assertions, summarized so confidently in the *Economic Report*, and demonstrates that they are in each case either false or half-truths. First, there is the theoretical allegation that international trade is based upon the so-called comparative advantage of countries ('benefits from ... [specialization in] activities it performs relatively efficiently'). Second, there is the empirical assertion that more 'open' markets have increased international trade more than would have been the case in its absence ('open' economies trade more). Third, and closely related to the second, is the contention that foreign investment has increased beyond what would have been the case had market liberalization not been followed. The corollary of this contention is that countries with fewer regulations on trade and foreign investment can expect to receive a disproportionate amount of said investment.

In a rather different category, and a stronger assertion, is that deregulating trade and capital flows increases the standard of living ('economies ... [more] open to international trade and investment are more likely to experience a rising standard of living ... '). This allegation has two aspects: a dynamic one (open economies grow faster); and a static one ('consumers ... benefit from a variety of goods at lower prices ... '). Not found in the CEA eulogy to open markets, but asserted with regularity (for example, World Bank 1995a), is the proposition that in more open economies unemployment is lower and wages higher than in less open economies.

Prior to considering each of these propositions of deregulation, it is necessary to clarify a few fundamental theoretical points, namely what 'openness' is and how it might be measured, and what the basis is of the trade among countries. Analysis of these two issues reveals that the international deregulation assertions rest upon extremely unstable theoretical foundations.

Myth 1: Orthodox trade theory is sound

The globalization hypothesis that less-regulated trade is inherently good rests on neo-classical trade theory, frequently called Heckscher–Ohlin–Samuelson trade theory after its principal theorists. Under extremely restrictive assumptions, this theory reaches the conclusion that free trade, in the sense of trade in the absence of private and public barriers to competition, is

optimal. Of course, trade is never 'free' in this sense. Prior to the ideologically laden 1980s and 1990s, the theory concluded that in the absence of free
trade, 'some trade is better than no trade', a conclusion that could hardly be
faulted.

The most frequent defence of unregulated trade is that it increases competition and, therefore, raises the efficiency of production and brings lower
prices to consumers. This is not based upon H–O–S theory; indeed, the
argument typically invokes no theory at all, or the most primitive partial
equilibrium analysis. In the orthodox analysis, all producers in all countries
are assumed to operate at maximum efficiency by both the technical and
economic definitions.[1] In this, the standard framework, trade increases
efficiency through altering the allocation of resources; that is, the efficiency
gains from trade refer to economy-wide allocative efficiency, not firm-level
production efficiency. To be precise, H–O–S theory concludes that moving
from 'autarky' to 'free trade' results in a reallocation of productive inputs,
such that each country *specializes*, with specialization based upon the so-
called factor endowments of each country. To put it simply, for the case of
two inputs, labour and 'capital', in a country which is 'abundant' in labour,
free trade will shift resources to 'labour-intensive' product lines (Evans 1989:
chapters 4 and 5). As a result, the country will export these 'labour-intensive'
products and import 'capital-intensive' products. This is the famous principle of 'comparative advantage'.[3]

The frequent use of quotation marks in the foregoing paragraph is necessary because of the problematical nature of the concepts of standard theory.
For consistency, a theory whose argument is based upon the concept of
input abundance and scarcity must, at the minimum, specify a theoretically
consistent method of measurement of those inputs. To put this another way,
a theory which predicts that the trade of countries will reflect the relative
supply of labour and capital (in the two-input case) must have a measure of
the supplies of labour and capital which is independent of composition of
trade. This proves possible only under extremely restrictive assumptions.
The problem arises because, in general, the 'supply of capital' is not independent of the rate of return on capital. Only in a special case, where an
output uses a capital input which is the same as that output, are the relative
supplies of capital and labour unambiguously defined (Weeks 1989:
chapter 10).

An example can demonstrate the seriousness of the problem for orthodox
trade theory. Let there be two countries with closed economies (no trade).
When trade barriers are reduced, commodities will be exchanged. As a result,
the prices of the commodities will change in each country, gravitating
towards a common price for each (net of transport costs). As a result of
changes in prices, wage rates and profit rates in each country will change.
If the traded commodities are each produced with a capital input different
from the output, the change in the wage–profit rate can result in a change in

the ordering of the commodities in terms of the capital–labour ratio. In other words, a commodity which before trade opened was relatively labour-intensive can become relatively capital-intensive after trade occurs. As a result, the country which before trade was measured as 'labour-abundant' could, after trade, export commodities which are measured as 'capital-intensive', and import commodities measured as 'labour-intensive'. Empirical evidence indicates that this outcome is not merely a theoretical possibility (Forstner and Ballance 1990). Given the theoretical and methodological problems in the application of orthodox trade theory to actual trade, it should not be a surprise that empirical studies show that its explanatory powers are extremely weak. For example, two studies by Yeats, a World Bank economist, conclude that the observed pattern of developing country exports differs substantially from what H–O–S theory would predict (Yeats 1989 and 1992; see also White 1978).

Orthodox theory claims to explain not only the pattern of trade among countries, but also the macroeconomic aspects of trade, determination of the exchange rate and the aggregate balance of trade. These were central issues in the defence of globalization, because they related to the stabilizing or destabilizing nature of unregulated trade. In the orthodox approach, unregulated trade should reduce the instability of the real exchange rate, and foster a sustainable trade balance. On these issues, the orthodox theory is even less successful than in its attempts to explain the pattern of trade. In a review of the literature on exchange rates, Harvey concludes:

> [N]eoclassical economists have expressed increasing frustration over their failure to explain exchange rate movements . . . Despite the fact that this is one of the most well-researched fields in the discipline, not a single model or theory has tested well. The results have been so dismal that mainstream economists readily admit their failure.
>
> (Harvey 1996: 567)

In the same vein, Stein refers to 'why economists have been so disappointed in their ability to explain the determination of . . . capital flows' (Stein 1995: 182). Indeed, the most successful attempt to explain the movement of exchange rates has been within a Marxian theoretical framework, in the work of Shaikh and Antonopoulos (1998). The globalization advocates would have one believe that a grand corpus of high theory provides support for the conclusions that (1) unregulated trade fosters an efficient allocation of resources; (2) unregulated trade ensures less exchange rate volatility; and (3) unregulated trade will promote equilibrium of the balance of payments. These are the myths of globalization. The theoretical support for the first is weak at best; empirical evidence provides little support for any of the three.

Myth 2: Globalization has increased international trade and investment

Central to the globalization hypothesis is the allegation that trade and foreign investment increased dramatically towards the end of the twentieth century. The hypothesis maintains that this increase represented an inevitable and irreversible process, to which governments throughout the world had to adjust. It is further maintained that failure to adjust to the globalization of markets would exclude countries from the benefits of this process. Prior to assessing alleged benefits, we consider the empirical question: did foreign investment and trade grow dramatically over some period one might justifiably define as the era of globalization? The globalization hypothesis is not necessarily supported by evidence that either of these indicators increased towards the end of the century. Since the Second World War, both foreign investment and trade showed an upward trend. What must be demonstrated is that for a specifically defined 'globalization period' there was a significant upward shift in these indicators.

Table 16.1 inspects the fundamental quantitative assertions of the globalization hypothesis, the trends in foreign direct investment and trade. It is based upon the following test. To take investment, for each major region of the world foreign direct investment was calculated as a portion of gross domestic product. The trend in this indicator was calculated, using regression analysis (ordinary least squares). Within this trend analysis, it was tested whether over various years that might be defined as 'globalization periods' the share of foreign investment differed significantly from its longer-term trend. The cells in the table report whether for the period in question, the values of the indicator were significantly above the longer-term trend, significantly below, or not significantly different. The test is then repeated for the share of exports in gross national product. Because there is no consensus as to when 'globalization' began, four periods are tested: 1985–97, and the sub-periods 1985–89, 1990–95, and 1990–97.

For foreign direct investment, the results are mixed, with limited support for the allegation that the importance of the variable increased. For all groups except the developed ('high-income' OECD) countries, there was a long-term positive trend in the percentage over 1970–97. For two of the six groups, the Middle East and North Africa, and South Asia, no period that might be defined as globalization shows a significant increase. For the developed countries, there was a significant increase for 1985–97. However, when the period is disaggregated, one finds that the increase was significant for the second half of the 1980s, but not for the 1990s; that is, the increase was not sustained. East Asia and the Pacific did show a significant increase for the 1990s (both 1990–95 and through 1997), but this was almost entirely explained by foreign investment flows to China, which rose from 0.5 per cent of GDP in 1985 to 5 per cent in 1997. For the other important

Table 16.1   Foreign investment and international trade in the era of 'globalization', 1970–97

A. *Foreign direct investment as a percentage of GDP*

		Period shifts:			
	Trend	1985–97	1985–1989	1990–95	1990–97
High-income: OECD	pos, nsgn	pos, sgn	pos, sgn	neg, nsgn	neg, nsgn
Latin America and Caribbean	pos, sgn	neg, nsgn	neg, sgn	neg, nsgn	pos, sgn
Middle East and North Africa	pos, sgn	pos, nsgn	pos, nsgn	pos, nsgn	neg, nsgn
East Asia and Pacific	pos, sgn	neg, nsgn	neg, sgn	pos, sign	pos, sign
South Asia	pos, sgn	neg, nsgn	neg, sgn	neg, nsgn	pos, nsgn
Sub-Saharan Africa	neg, sgn	neg, nsgn	neg, sgn	pos, nsgn	pos, sgn

B. *Exports as a percentage of GDP*

		Period shifts:			
	Trend	1985–97	1985–1989	1990–95	1990–97
High-income: OECD	pos, sgn	neg, sgn	neg, sgn	neg, sgn	neg, sgn
Latin America and Caribbean	pos, sgn	neg, nsgn	pos, sgn	neg, sgn	neg, nsgn
Middle East and North Africa	no data	no data	no data	no data	no data
East Asia and Pacific	pos, sgn	neg, nsgn	neg, sgn	pos, nsgn	pos, sgn
South Asia	pos, sgn	neg, nsgn	neg, sgn	pos, nsgn	pos, sgn
Sub-Saharan Africa	pos, sgn	neg, nsgn	pos, nsgn	neg, sgn	neg, nsgn

Notes: The trends in all cases are for 1970–97.
pos = positive relationship
neg = negative relationship
sgn = statistically significant at 10% probability or less
nsngn = not statistically significant
Source: World Bank, *World Development Indicators 1999* (CD-ROM).

economies in the region, the share of foreign investment flow in GDP did not deviate significantly from the longer-term trend.[4] For the sub-Saharan countries, foreign investment flows were significantly above trend for 1990–97, but this disappears if 1996 and 1997 are excluded, as is the case for Latin America and the Caribbean.

Overall, there is little compelling evidence that levels of foreign direct investment in the late 1980s and 1990s represented anything other than a continuation of previous trends. In other words, the shift of policy in developed and underdeveloped countries to be more accommodating of the interests of international business seems to have had no significant impact on aggregate flows. It is possible that competition among countries for foreign investment, for example *via* the lowering of labour and environmental standards, shifted flows among countries. If so, this probably reduced the host country's benefits, such that the positive impact of foreign investment was less in the 1990s than previously.

If globalization increased the importance of trade in the world economy, one would expect this to be manifest in an increase in the share of exports across countries. Part B of Table 16.1 tests this issue. After the Second World War, world trade grew consistently faster than world output, so, again, the question is whether in the 1980s and 1990s the share of exports in gross domestic product shifted above its long-term trend. The table reveals that this was not the case. For the high-income countries, export shares were significantly *below* their trend value in the late 1980s and 1990s. That is, for the world's largest trading countries, the period of globalization was associated with significantly *lower* export shares than would have been the case had previous trends continued. For Latin American and the Caribbean, the export share rose above its trend in the 1980s, but fell below it in the 1990s (though the decline is non-significant if 1996 and 1997 are included). The significant increase in the export share in the late 1980s resulted from that region's stagnation of output, not rapid export growth.

There was an increase above the trend for East Asia and the Pacific, but its significance was dependent upon the inclusion of 1996 and 1997. If these two years are excluded, the deviation is non-significant. It may be that subsequent years will confirm that these two regions have shifted to a significantly larger export share, but this cannot be concluded on the basis of data through 1997.

At the end of the century the evidence for a more 'globalized' world economy was extremely weak. For most groups of countries, the levels of direct foreign investment and exports were close to what one would have predicted on the basis of long-term trends. The allegation that the world economy experienced a dramatic change in the degree of integration in trade and investment was another myth of globalization.

Myth 3: Globalization has improved growth performance

The allegation that there was a dramatic increase in foreign investment and trade towards the end of the century (which we have shown to be unconfirmed) was accompanied by the normative judgement that this was a good thing, because it fostered faster growth of countries that adopted the globalization policy framework. This judgement had little theoretical support. In as far as increased trade and investment flows would foster allocative efficiency of labour and capital, there is no theoretical reason to think that this would increase growth. Orthodox theory concludes that such efficiency gains, if they are realized, provide once-and-for-all increases in welfare, and need have no impact on growth (Weeks 1998).

The arguments that globalization would increase growth were *ad hoc*: by facilitating the transfer of technology, stimulating innovation under competitive pressure and making economies more 'flexible' in adapting to external 'shocks'. Thus, the hypothesized pro-growth effect of globalization was an empirical issue that would rise or fall on the evidence. Figures 16.1 to 16.5 show the growth rates of the world's major groupings of countries. In each figure, the growth rate for the 1960s through to 1980 is calculated, along with the rate for 1985–98. The years 1980–84 were excluded, because they covered a world-wide recession, affecting most regions severely. Their inclusion, therefore, would seriously distort and bias the calculations. For the OECD (developed) countries, the evidence is clear. The average growth rate was 2.3 per cent per annum after 1984, compared to 3.8 per cent for 1961–80. While both periods show pronounced cyclical movements, the level of growth rates shifts *downwards* from 1985 onwards. This downward shift can be seen clearly by inspecting the derivations from the long-term average, which were negative for only 4 years out of 20 before 1980, and negative for 8 years out of 14, 1985 through 1998. The result is similar for the Latin American countries (Figure 16.2), an average of 5.1 per cent per annum for 1961–80, and 3.2 per cent for 1985–98. For these two groups the slower growth after 1984 is particularly significant, for they included the countries that adopted neo-liberal policies most fervently. This is especially the case for the Latin American countries. In the 1960s and 1970s, these countries, with few exceptions (Chile after 1973) pursued protectionist trade regimes, with strong capital controls. After 1985, all the Latin American countries, with the exception of Cuba, deregulated markets, liberalized trade and abandoned capital controls. Growth rates were significantly higher in the earlier period.

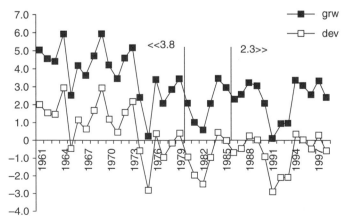

Figure 16.1 OECD countries: annual growth rate and deviations from the period average, 1961–98.

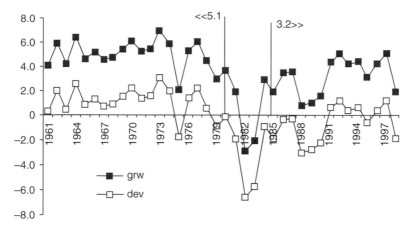

Figure 16.2 Latin American countries: annual growth rate and deviations from the period average, 1961–98.

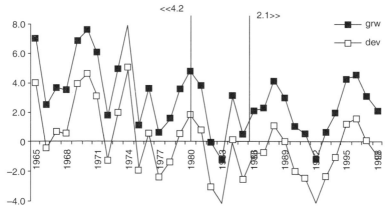

Figure 16.3 Sub-Saharan countries: annual growth rates and deviations from the period average, 1965–98.

Declining growth rates after 1985 also afflicted the countries of the sub-Saharan region (Figure 16.3). In the second half of the 1980s and in the 1990s a great wave of deregulation, trade liberalization and decontrol of capital accounts swept the region, fostered by stabilization and structural adjustment programs in virtually all of the forty-odd continental sub-Saharan countries (World Bank 1994). Whatever the achievements of these dubious programs, improved growth rates were not among them. From 1965 through 1980, the sub-Saharan countries grew at 4.2 per cent, and at half that rate after 1984. Though a rise in growth rates occurred during 1992–96, reaching a rather modest peak of 4 per cent, the data for 1997 and 1998 suggest that this was merely part of a cyclical movement, not to be sustained.

East and South-East Asia show a more complex pattern (Figure 16.4). This group includes the famous 'miracles' of growth (World Bank 1993), as well as China, one of the fastest-growing countries in the world in the 1980s and 1990s, which had tight capital controls. For these countries, growth rates were higher on average after 1984 than before 1980 (7.5 compared with 6.8). However, beginning in 1992, the cross-country growth rate declined in every year, falling below zero in 1998. It would appear that after having weathered the instability of the world economy in the 1980s, the East and South-East Asian countries fell victim to those instabilities in the 1990s. Their crisis of the late 1990s reflected many of the problems that afflicted the Latin American countries in the previous decade, exacerbated by the capital account liberalization that was central to the policy agenda of the globalizationists.[5]

Of the five charts, perhaps the most instructive is that for the South Asian countries (Figure 16.5). Of all the groups reviewed, this is the one whose countries adhered least and most tardily to the globalization policy agenda. This is especially the case for India and Pakistan, the two largest economies in the region. Taken as a group, the South Asian countries grew substantially faster in the 'globalization' period than before 1980, that is, by 5.6 per cent per annum compared with 3.6 per cent.

Looking back over the five groups of countries, one can summarize as follows: the country groups that introduced the globalization policies to the greatest degree fared least well in the 1990s relative to previous decades (the OECD, the Latin American and the sub-Saharan countries); the best performing group since 1960, East and South-East Asia, entered into a severe

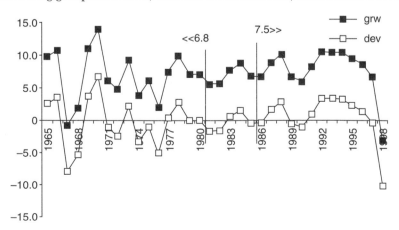

Figure 16.4 East and South-East Asia: annual growth rates and deviations from the period average, 1965–98.

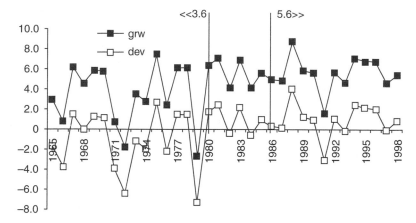

Figure 16.5 South Asia: annual growth rates and deviations from the period average, 1965–98.

recession in the 1990s; and the group whose growth improved in the 1990s without recession, South Asia, was that which least adopted polices of deregulation, trade liberalization and decontrol of the capital account. The hypothesis that those policies foster growth is unconfirmed; that is, it is a myth of globalization.

It should not be surprising that it is a myth. Were it the case that freer trade fostered growth, one would expect to find a positive correlation between growth rates and the share of trade in gross domestic product: if liberalization stimulates trade, then the trade share should rise; if trade stimulates growth, then the rise in the trade share should be associated with faster growth. Inspection of the statistics reveals quite the opposite, as Table 16.2 shows. For the five country groups, the simple correlation between the export share and the rate of growth was estimated,[6] for 1965–97. For none of the groups of countries was the relationship positive and significant, and for two groups (the OECD and Latin American groups) the

Table 16.2 Simple correlations between the export share in GDP and the GDP growth rate, 1965–97

Region	Export share	Shift (1985)
OECD, high-income	Negative, *significant*	nonsignificant
Latin America and the Caribbean	Negative, *significant*	nonsignificant
Africa, South of the Sahara	Positive, nonsignificant	Negative, *significant*
South Asia	Positive, nonsignificant	nonsignificant
East Asia and Pacific	Positive, nonsignificant	nonsignificant

relationship was significant and *negative*; a rise in the export share was associated with a slower rate of growth.

Notwithstanding the negative or non-significant relationship between the trade share and growth, a number of studies purport to demonstrate a positive interaction between 'openness' of an economy and growth performance. These studies do not use a direct and common-sense measure of openness (the trade share), but rather some esoteric proxy which allegedly measures the degree of liberalization of the trade and capital accounts.[7] In addition to the interpretation of these statistical exercises suffering from serious ambiguities, Pritchett (1996) showed that the various measures of openness are not correlated with trade performance.

Myth 4: Consumers have gained from trade liberalization

Of all the myths of globalization, perhaps the most ideologically potent is the argument that freer trade brings lower prices for consumers. Therefore, it is in the general interest of society, while trade protection reflects special interests. This argument is so powerful that opponents of trade liberalization frequently concede it, and argue that costs associated with freer trade, such as the environmental impact, outweigh the gain from lower prices. The argument need not be conceded, for it is essentially ideological with little empirical support.

In trade theory, all members of society are treated as utility maximizers, and they are all consumers. Thus, the desire of agents to improve the conditions of consumption is a *general interest* of society. On the other hand, as producers, people work in different sectors and occupations, and their desire to improve their conditions of work is a *special interest*. The trade policy debate is presented as a tension between the general interest of society as consumer and the special interest of producers. It is on the basis of this interpretation of society that free trade is viewed as beneficial to all, and any restraint on private trading, domestic or international, as a manifestation of anti-social special interests. In this context, it can be asserted that 'international trade brings immediate gains through cheaper imports' (World Bank 1995a: 10).

However, the functioning of society is considerably more complex than this. It ignores the possibility that unequal bargaining power among people as producers can reduce the incomes of some and increase the incomes of others, such that gains from consumption (lower prices) are rendered trivial by the gains and losses of income from production. Treating all agents primarily as consumers also ignores the welfare effect of working conditions. In the short run, the 'working conditions of capital' are improved by a deterioration of the working conditions of labour, because longer hours, more intense work, and reduction of workplace safety and hygiene tend, in general, to reduce operating costs.

Once the ideological nature of the 'lower prices' argument is recognized, it must be defended on purely empirical grounds: do the lower prices offset the welfare losses from trade liberalization? The necessary condition for price gains to offset other welfare losses is that it be demonstrated that price gains occur. To demonstrate that trade liberalization has given consumers lower prices is not straightforward. Inflation during the 1990s was lower throughout the world than during the 1980s, but this could neither be attributed to globalization nor did it imply that 'prices are lower'. Since prices are the source of money incomes, a lower price level implies lower purchasing power in an economy as a whole.

If the freer trade associated with globalization benefited consumers, this would be manifest in a change in *relative* prices. If one divides products between traded goods and services and non-traded goods and services (a standard analytical division), then one would expect prices of the former to fall or rise slower than prices of the latter. A comparison of import and export prices to the prices of domestic goods and services not exported, when such data are available, does not accurately capture the price ratio of tradables to non-tradables. The great majority of domestic goods and services would be products which to some degree substitute for imports, and, therefore, their prices would be correlated with import prices. A standard measure to avoid this is to compare a country's consumer price index (CPI) with the producer price index (PPI). The former includes a range of non-traded inputs, principally transport and marketing services. In algebra, for an economy with two traded commodities, a consumer commodity (1) and an input to the consumer commodity (2),

$$p_1 = \{[p_2 m + wn][1 + \pi]\}[1 + \beta]$$

Where p is price, m is the unit materials requirement, w is the wage, n is the unit labour requirement, π is the manufacturer's profit margin, and β is proportion of all retailing costs in the price of the consumer commodity; and

$$p_1 = CPI$$

$$p_1^* = [p_2 m + wn][1 + \pi] = PPI$$

For computation purposes, one could set both indices to 100 in some base year. We can now consider the impact of trade liberalization. If less regulated trade resulted in cheaper imports of consumer goods and material inputs, then p_1 and p_2 would fall. If both prices fell by an equal amount, there would be a fall in the manufacturer's profit margin. If retailing costs remained the same, or fell less than import prices, then the CPI would fall less than the PPI. The PPI can also fall as a result of an increase in labour productivity (the parameter n), which may be independent of the change in trade policy. Thus, the necessary condition for evidence of gains to consumers from trade deregulation is that the CPI fall less (rise more) than the PPI falls (rises). The sufficient condition is either (1) that the fall in the PPI not be the result of faster productivity growth in the production of goods and services than in distribution, or (2) that this faster productivity growth be demonstrated to be the result of the trade liberalization itself.

For the United States, the globalization prediction would appear confirmed: after moving virtually in step for 1960–84, from 1985 onwards the consumer price index rose faster than the producer price index (Figure 16.6). However, this is only the *necessary* condition for trade to bring lower prices, not a sufficient condition. Figure 16.7 shows the relationship between the US producer price index and an index of nominal wage costs in manufacturing. Inspection of the chart shows that the two were highly correlated, as one would expect. Figure 16.6 showed that the CPI and the PPI diverged after 1985. If this reflects that globalization tended to bring lower prices to consumers, one would expect to find that producer mark-ups were lower after 1985. That is, one would expect to find that the divergence was not merely the result of productivity change (lower increases in nominal wage costs), but also the result of lower profit margins, due to import competition. As a simple test for this, we regressed changes in nominal unit labour costs against changes in the producer price index, with a shift variable for various periods after 1985. No series of years with 1997 as the last (the last year for which there were data on costs) was significant. Two earlier time periods did yield significant negative shift coefficients, 1967–72 and 1981–87. The implied downward shift in manufacturing mark-ups during these periods could probably be explained as a cyclical phenomenon.

If there is no evidence that greater openness to trade benefited consumers by reducing profit margins, is it possible that the import pressure stimulated faster growth of productivity, such that labour costs rose less than would have been the case in a less 'globalized' environment? The evidence is quite

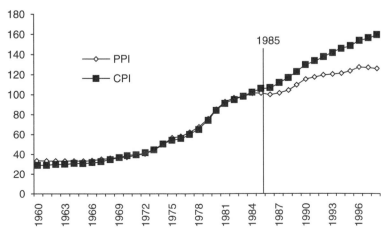

Figure 16.6   United States: consumer price index and producer price index, 1960–98.

to the contrary. Over 38 years, there was a statistically significant long-term decline in the rate of productivity increase,[8] and the rates for the 1990s did not differ significantly from this trend. We can conclude that the rise in the consumer price index relative to the producer price index is apparently explained by a faster rate of productivity change in production compared to distribution, rather than to competitive pressures associated with trade liberalization. And the faster rate of growth of productivity increase *was relative*: in absolute terms, production productivity grew more slowly in the 1990s than in any previous decade after 1960. There is no evidence that consumers in the United States gained from trade liberalization via lower prices.

Figures 16.8 to 16.10 present the consumer and producer price indices for three other countries generally recognized as 'trade liberalizers': the United

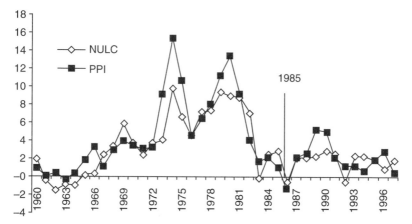

Figure 16.7 United States: changes in nominal unit labour costs and the producer price index, 1960–97.

Table 16.3 Annual percentage change in non-farm labour productivity, United States, 1960–97

Time periods	Non-farm productivity
1960–64	3.3
1965–69	2.3
1970–74	2.1
1975–79	1.7
1980–84	1.2
1985–89	1.0
1990–94	1.0
1995–97	0.9

Source: CEA (1998).

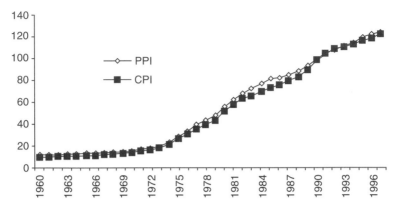

Figure 16.8   United Kingdom: consumer price index and producer price index, 1960–97.

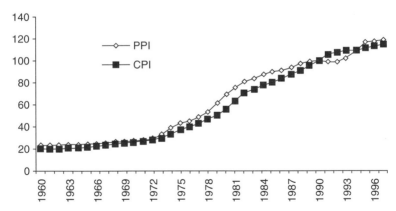

Figure 16.9   Canada: consumer price index and producer price index, 1960–97.

Kingdom, Canada and Mexico. For Mexico, the rate of change of the two indices is shown, to accommodate the country's high rate of inflation during 1981–89 on the chart. For these countries no further investigation is required, for none shows any significant or systematic divergence between the producer and consumer price indices. While we have presented evidence for only four countries, these four are the ones that would be expected to show evidence of consumer gains were the gains there to be shown. In the absence of other evidence, one can conclude that the assertion that consumers gain from liberalization of trade is yet another myth of globalization.

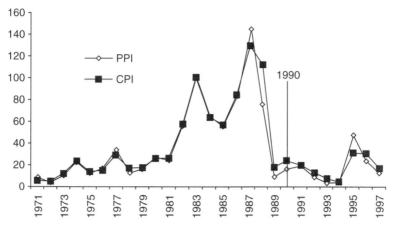

Figure 16.10 Mexico: changes in the producer price index and the consumer price index, 1971–97.

Myth 5: Workers gain from globalization

Of all the myths of globalization, perhaps the least convincing is the allegation that increased trade and investment flows stimulated higher real wage growth. Even the *Economic Report of the President* (CEA 1998) floundered on this issue:

> Throughout the first half of the postwar era, real average hourly wages for US production and nonsupervisory workers increased at an average rate of about 2 per cent per year. Between 1974 and 1996, however, this measure of real wages fell by roughly 10 per cent, retreating to 1965 levels... the coincidence of increasing trade and falling real average hourly earnings suggested to many that international forces were the source of this decline. (p. 239)

The reader is assured that 'this inference is *probably* wrong' (emphasis added). In the view of the report the probability of falsehood derives from several considerations. First, 'it is more appropriate to focus on the level of total compensation', which included 'health care benefits, pension costs, and other fringe benefits'. When these were included, the reader is told that 'total real compensation has increased by almost 8 per cent since 1974'. A quick calculation shows that an increase of 8 per cent over 22 years implies an annual rate of increase of 0.4 per cent, *one-fifth* of the rate for the post-war years before 1974. Perhaps in recognition of the lameness of the 'total compensation' argument, the report asserts, 'this slowdown is more appropriately explained by factors other than international trade'.[9]

The principal 'other factor' offered in explanation is 'a slowdown in productivity growth'. This is a rather strange defence of the trade impact on real wages, for two pages previously one read, 'by encouraging continuous productivity improvements, international trade can increase an economy's growth rate' (p. 237). Thus, a *non-sequitur* seems to be lurking here:

1. trade encourages 'continuous productivity improvements';
2. 'growth in trade exceeded growth in output by approximately 3.5 percentage points per year following 1974' (p. 239);
3. there was a 'coincidence of increasing trade and falling real hourly earnings' (p. 239); and
4. the fall in real earnings is explained 'by a slowdown in productivity growth' (p. 239).

In other words, increased trade *did not* encourage productivity growth, and real wages fell. It would seem safe to conclude that if an 'appropriate' (much less convincing) argument for a positive link between real wages and trade cannot be made by the advisers to an enthusiastically pro-trade president then it did not exist.

A rigorous analysis of the impact of globalization on wages in the other developed countries is beyond the scope of this chapter.[10] There is evidence for the Latin American countries (Weeks 1999a). During the globalizing 1990s, real urban wages rose in most Latin American countries. This was to be expected after the severe depression of the 1980s, when per capita income fell in virtually every country. The defenders of globalization argued that an important gain from greater openness to trade would be increased employment generation for any rate of growth. This would occur because 'comparative advantage' would induce use of more labour-intensive techniques (see Myth 1, above). Evidence shows that, to the contrary, in the 1990s growth was less employment-generating (Weeks 1999b: 160–2). Further, neither for the 1990s nor for the two previous decades were real wage changes correlated with measures of openness to trade (ibid.). These results are particularly damaging to the globalization advocates, because of the dramatic shift in Latin America from import substitution to trade liberalization in the 1980s and 1990s.

It may have been that some workers in some countries gained from the deregulation of trade, but this remained conjecture. The lack of evidence for labour's gain was hardly surprising, given the strong bias in favour of capital in the globalization policy agenda. Especially damaging to the welfare of workers was the growth of job insecurity (Standing 1999: chapters 5–8). The assertion that workers gained from increased trade was another myth of globalization.

Conclusion

The so-called globalization process at the end of the twentieth century was not inevitable. It resulted from a set of clear and purposeful policies, motivated by the interests of capital, with little regard to its impact on the welfare of the vast majority of the world's population. Clearly, it could not be presented as such, so the advocates of globalization produced a set of myths to induce the belief that the allegedly inevitable was also desirable. One central purpose of the myths was to convince people that they had little choice but to be passive observers of the process, but could look forward to the spread of its benefits.

The myths were exactly that: myths of globalization, fairy tales of welfare gains constructed upon weak theoretical arguments with little empirical support. As part of the construction of the mythology, public reaction against the costs of globalization policies was treated as irrational fear generated by special interest groups bent upon denying 'consumers' the gains from trade and countries the benefits of specialization. This argument, that fears about the negative impact of trade and investment flows are irrational,[11] is particularly ironic coming from the globalizationists, for their supporting theory treats economic agents as rational decision makers who are rationally informed. It would appear that people throughout the world are rational: they can distinguish between the myths and realities of globalization.

Notes

1 The title of this chapter originates from Rob Davies of the University of Zimbabwe.
2 Production is technically efficient if a producer achieves a level of output with the minimum inputs. Production is economically efficient if, given technical efficiency, the producer choice of the level of output results in producing that output at the lowest unit cost. The latter implies, under the typical assumption of perfect competition, that the price of output is equal to the marginal cost of output, and (implied by $P = MC$) that each input is employed in a quantity such that the 'marginal' unit's contribution to output is equal in value to that input's market price.
3 In the *Economic Report of the President*, one reads:
   The primary source of static gains from trade is specialization... Such trade can be beneficial even in cases where one country could produce both goods more efficiently. This notion, commonly referred to as comparative advantage, is straight forward when applied to individuals – each of us sometimes purchases from others some goods or services that we could make or perform even better ourselves, because be realize that our time is most profitably spent doing those things we do best. But the principle applies equally well to countries. (CEA 1998: 236)
   Shaikh (1979) demonstrated that this principle *cannot* be applied to countries.

4   We refer to Indonesia, Malaysia, the Republic of Korea, the Philippines and Thailand. The foreign investment share across these countries was 0.9 in 1980, 2.0 in 1990 and 2.4 in 1997.

5   For a comparison of the growth performances of the Latin American countries and the so-called high-performing Asian economies, see Weeks (1999).

6   The export share is used because the other obvious measure of the importance of trade would give theoretically ambiguous results. The import share might be positively related to growth because an economy is import-constrained. That is, growth may be dependent upon imported inputs in the short run, and imported machinery in the medium term. This would not indicate that trade stimulates growth in the sense of the globalization hypothesis, which refers to the alleged benefits of *liberalized* trade. If an economy were import-constrained, an appropriate policy response might be protection of domestic producers, to stimulate domestic production (so-called import substitution policies). The rate of growth of exports is also ambiguous, since a positive correlation could reflect that the economy is demand constrained. Were this the case, the appropriate policy might be export subsidies, which are judged as inefficient by the globalizationists.

7   For example, Sachs and Warner (1997), in an exercise in cross-country regression analysis, use an index of openness which includes tariff levels, impact of quotas and whether or not a country had a 'socialist' economic system. Collier and Gunning (1999) measure openness by the difference between a country's official exchange rate and the black market or 'parallel' market rate. It is unclear what either set of authors is measuring.

8   The fall from an average rate of change of about 3 per cent in the 1960s to less than 1 per cent in the 1990s implies a long-term trend of about minus 9 per cent per year.

9   An expert in textual analysis might wish to pursue the implications of the phrase 'more appropriately explained', rather than 'more correctly explained', which would seem more precise if an empirical argument is being made. All the quotations in this paragraph are from page 239 of the *Report*.

10 For example, it would require a relevant measure of policy changes, to compare with the movement in wages.

11 From the *Economic Report of the President*:
    [P]ublic opinion polls continue to reveal a low sense of job security among American workers. This is surprising... *Rightly or wrongly*, workers may associate much of their concern about job security with the expansion of trade. (CEA 1999: 244, emphasis added.)

17

What Follows Fordism? On the Periodization of Capitalism and Its Regulation

Bob Jessop

This chapter addresses three issues: the general nature of periodization; alternative criteria for periodizing capitalism; and the contradictions of Atlantic Fordism and after-Fordist economies. My analysis rests on a 'strategic-relational' approach.[1] Emphasizing the interplay of structure and strategy, this implies that, within broad limits set by the abstract logic of capitalism, its structural contradictions and its strategic dilemmas, capitalist development is nonetheless open. Particular trajectories and sequences of capitalist development are always mediated and transformed through specific social forces acting in specific institutional contexts or conjunctures. This openness invalidates attempts to periodize capitalism's past development or predict its destiny as if these were connected by a pregiven logic. But it does not mean that the succession of stages (or phases) is purely accidental. My task below is to explore the contingent necessities of capitalist development.

On periodization

The primary purpose of any periodization is to interpret an otherwise undifferentiated 'flow' of historical time by classifying events and/or processes in terms of their internal affinities and external differences in order to identify successive periods of relative invariance and the transitions between them. Alongside any practical concerns, such exercises have general ontological, epistemological and methodological aspects. Their basic ontological assumption is the paradoxical simultaneity of continuity/discontinuity in the flow of historical time. For, if nothing ever changed, periodization would be meaningless in the face of the self-identical repetition of *eternity*; if everything changed at random all the time, however, so that no sequential ordering was discernible, then *chaos* would render periodization impossible (Elchardus 1988: 48). It is possible only when relative continuity alternates with relative discontinuity. Relative continuity does not presuppose the stasis of identical self-repetition – only that relevant changes do not disrupt the structural coherence typical of this period (for example, the widening and deepening of mass production in the Atlantic Fordist accumulation regime). Nor does relative discontinuity presuppose random variation and hence a total absence of structure – only that relevant changes disrupt the previous structural coherence (for example, the hypermobility of global financial capital versus the Atlantic Fordist mode of regulation). This disruption may itself have a distinctive logic (for example, neo-liberal structural adjustment programmes imposed on developmental states) and/or serve as an experimental transitional phase with different forces struggling over future patterns of structural coherence (for example, new accumulation strategies after the 'Asian crisis'). What matters for present purposes is not the content of this sequential ordering but its grounding in the alternation of relative continuity and discontinuity.

Thus the three keys to periodization from a critical realist perspective are the extents to which, first, a differentiated and stratified real world creates the possibility of relative invariance and sequential order (Elchardus 1988: 47); second, these possibilities are actualized in specific conjunctures; and, third, one can empirically identify continuity in discontinuity and/or discontinuity in continuity. Clearly the scope for such an exercise depends on the 'objects' being periodized and the levels of abstraction and complexity at which they are studied. It is most appropriate where a distinctive temporality is an inherent property of the object under investigation rather than an accidental one.

Capitalism has just such a naturally necessary temporal structure. This is based on its organization as an 'economy of time'. The expanded reproduction of capitalism is never based, as Marx's simple reproduction schemas might suggest, on purely self-identical repetition. Instead it involves an ever-changing balance among repeated cycles of self-valorization, continuous self-transformation, bouts of crisis-induced restructuring, and other modalities of change. These are often linked to new patterns of time–space distantiation and time–space compression as well as to shifts in dominant spatio-temporal horizons and in the leading accumulation spaces. These different spatio-temporal aspects provide solid ontological grounds for attempts to periodize capitalism.

Epistemologically, the simultaneity of relative invariance and sequential change means that, just like individual 'events', periods do not exist in themselves before their identification. A participant or observer must first abstract some features from time's flow that permit her to identify sequential periods of relative continuity and relative discontinuity (or vice versa) relevant to the practical and/or intellectual task in hand. The appropriate criteria to establish when the transition from competitive to monopoly capitalism occurred in England, for example, differ from those useful for identifying a suitable alliance strategy in a critical election. The chosen levels of abstraction and complexity also affect whether more emphasis is given to continuity or discontinuity. Thus one might emphasize the survival of the generic features of capitalism in a shift from industrial to post-industrial society; or, alternatively, the changes in 'late Fordism' compared with 'high Fordism'. Periodizations always refer to particular problems and units of analysis. There can be no master periodization that captures the essence of a period and reveals its coherence for all purposes.

Methodologically, a strategic-relational approach would examine how a particular relatively invariant structure may privilege some actors, some identities, some strategies, some spatial and temporal horizons, some actions over others; and the ways, if any, in which actors (individual and/ or collective) consider this differential privileging in 'strategic-context' analyses when deciding how to act. It involves studying relatively invariant structures in terms of their structurally inscribed strategic selectivities and studying actions in terms of actors' (differentially reflexive) structurally oriented strategic calculation. In so far as reflexively reorganized structural configurations and recursively selected strategies and tactics *co-evolve* to produce a relatively invariant order, we can describe it as structurally coherent. This co-produced (and always tendential) structural coherence involves a structurally inscribed strategic selectivity that differentially rewards actions (including attempts to transform it) that are compatible with the recursive reproduction of the structure(s) in question.

The implications of a strategic-relational approach can be seen in three features that distinguish a periodization from a chronology. First, a chronology orders actions, events or periods on a unilinear time scale that serves as a neutral parameter (for example, clock times from nano seconds to geological time or beyond). Conversely, a periodization uses several time scales that include the temporalities of the phenomena being periodized. It orders actions, events or periods in terms of multiple time horizons (for example, *l'évènement* [the event], trends, the *longue durée* [long duration]; business versus political cycles; the temporalities of different fractions of capital). Second, a chronology recounts temporal coincidence or succession. It groups actions, events or periods into successive stages according to their occurrence in given time intervals (demarcated simply through the calendar and/or other socially relevant markers, such as government changes). A periodization, on the other hand, focuses on conjunctures. It classifies actions, events and periods into stages according to their conjunctural implications (as specific combinations of constraints and opportunities) for different social forces over different time horizons and/or for different sites of social action. Third, a chronology typically provides a simple narrative explanation, that is, it refers to the temporal coincidence or succession of a single series of actions and events. Conversely, a periodization presupposes an explanatory framework oriented to the contingent necessities generated by more than one series of events that unfold over different time horizons; it can therefore provide the basis for a complex narrative. In short, the key feature of a strategic-relational periodization is its concern with the strategic possibilities any given period provides for different actors, different identities, different interests, different coalition possibilities, different horizons of action, different strategies, different tactics.

There are many bases of periodization, and the criteria adopted will vary according to its object. Progressively more concrete-complex criteria are needed, for example, to establish the internal unities of capitalism as a pure mode of production, state monopoly capitalism as a stage of capitalism, Fordism as an accumulation regime, 'flexi-Fordism' in Germany as a mode of growth, the crisis of the Keynesian welfare national state in post-war Britain as a mode of regulation, or successive steps in the emergence and consolidation of Thatcherism as a neo-liberal response to that crisis. Substantive purposes also make a difference. Sometimes class struggle is crucial, sometimes it is less relevant. Thus, whereas Albritton (1986) claims that class struggle is wholly irrelevant to the analysis of pure capitalism and its division into stages, Cleaver (1979), following the Italian 'operaist' school, which focuses on the self-organization of workers, emphasizes just this aspect.

Four sets of complications must be noted before moving to Fordism, its crisis and the prospects of post-Fordism. First, periodization is not the only method of studying history. Others include chronicles, which merely record events or list statistics in calendric time; narratives, which emplot selected past events and forces in a sequential order with a beginning, middle and end, with an overarching structure that permits causal and moral lessons to be drawn; chronologies (see above); and genealogies, which trace the differential, fragmentary origins of various elements that are later combined into a structurally coherent pattern marking a new period of relative invariance. *Capital* provides a genealogy of capitalism as well as an analysis of its developed logic (Marx 1976).

Second, if capitalist development has no telos, transitions are moments of disjunction and relative openness. They involve relatively unstructured complexity as the preceding structural coherence decomposes and new institutional fixes are sought. This is seen in responses to the crisis of Atlantic Fordism. Thus states acted not only to end the crisis-induced state interventions of the 1970s but also to cut back the 'normal' forms of intervention at national and local level that emerged in the heyday of Atlantic Fordism. States also tried to establish new forms of intervention favouring the emergence of a new accumulation regime. Some of these were purely transitional, concerned to establish the preconditions of a post-Fordist 'take-off'. Others were precursors of the 'normal' forms of intervention held suitable for post-Fordist modes of growth in the 1990s or beyond (Jessop 1994). How such superficially confusing initiatives consolidate, if at all, to produce a new structural coherence as a basis for renewed capital accumulation depends on continuing social struggles in a complex conjuncture.

Third, since transitions between periods never involve a total rupture, path-dependent 'conservation-dissolution' effects can occur. Change can transform and refunctionalize earlier social relations, institutions or discourses, conserving them in the new pattern; or, alternatively, can dissolve them into elements that are selectively articulated into the new relations, institutions or discourses. Failure to note these effects can easily lead one to misread relative continuity or discontinuity across different periods. Thus the fact that Sweden had active labour market policies during Atlantic Fordism and still does so now does not mean that nothing has changed. For in the earlier period they were tied to full employment and redistributive regional policies; today they serve international competitiveness and labour market flexibility.

Fourth, if temporal prefixes (such as 'proto-', 'pre-', 'neo-', 'late-', or 'post-') are to be more than chronological markers, more detailed support is needed than reference to the calendar. In the case of post-Fordism, for example, one could show how it emerges from tendencies originating in Fordism but nonetheless marks a break with it; and/or indicate how the articulation of old and new elements in post-Fordism resolves or displaces one or more of the contradictions, dilemmas or crises that decisively weakened Fordism. In either case this would demonstrate the primacy of discontinuity over continuity needed to justify the term post-*Fordism*. Otherwise, it might be better to talk of high Fordism, late Fordism or neo-Fordism.[2] But without at least some continuity, a label that shows merely that the new system is *not* Fordist would be sufficient (examples include Sonyism, Toyotism and Wintelism). At best the notion of 'after-Fordism' would then indicate that such non-Fordist alternatives first arose and/or became dominant after the period of high Fordism, but that this sequencing is accidental.

A strategic-relational approach to capitalist periodization

In his 1857 *Introduction*, Marx said that neither production in general nor general production existed: only particular production and the totality of production. But one could still theorize production in general as a rational abstraction that enabled one to fix the elements common to all forms of production. In specific conjunctures, however, 'a definite production' existed and this 'determines a definite consumption, distribution, and exchange as well as *definite relations between these different moments*' (1973: 85, 99). Thus periodization could address not only the specificity of capitalism relative to pre-capitalist modes of production but also what gives coherence to these definite relations in particular phases of capitalism. A good starting point here is the commodity as the cell form of the capitalist mode of production.

Marx located capitalism's defining feature in the generalization of the commodity form to labour-power. Only when the commodity form was imposed on labour-power did the self-valorization of capital became possible. And only then did the sole source of value acquire a commodity form, economic exploitation acquire its distinctive capitalist mediation through exchange relations, and the disposition of labour-power become subject to capitalist laws of value. This last result was reinforced when labour-power was directly subsumed under capitalist control through machine-pacing in the factory system. These conditions enabled (but did not ensure) capital's repeated metamorphosis as it passes through the successive stages in the circuit of capital. Commodification of labour-power and its direct subsumption under capitalist control also make labour markets and the labour process sites of class struggle. For it shapes the forms of economic exploitation, the nature and stakes of class struggle between capital and labour in production, and the competition among capitals to secure the most effective valorization of labour-power.

Attempts to valorize capital and contain class struggles in these conditions are the source of capitalism's dynamism. Even at the most abstract level of analysis, capitalism depends on an unstable balance between its economic supports in the various expressions of the value forms and its extra-economic supports beyond the value form. This excludes the eventual commodification of everything and, hence, a pure capitalist economy. Instead we find uneven waves of commodification, decommodification and recommodification as the struggle to extend the value moments of the capital relation encounters real structural limits as well as increasing resistance and then seeks new ways to overcome them (Offe 1984). Such structural limits and contradictions (often expressed ideologically as 'market failure') offer chances to shift direction in so far as capitalism is constantly oriented, under pressure of competition, to new opportunities for profit. This spurs innovation – in techniques, production, organization, products, markets, finance and so on – in the hope of getting temporary competitive advantages, producing 'rents' beyond the average level of profit (Schumpeter 1937; Mandel 1975). Successful innovation then pushes other capitals to adopt the same, similar or superior innovations. This helps explain capitalism's technically and socially revolutionary character, its drive to extend capitalism around the world, and its uneven and combined development. But there is no fixed end point to this general trajectory, which, within broad limits, remains open.

Marx identified a fundamental contradiction in the commodity form between exchange-value and use-value. On this basis he dialectically unfolded the complex nature of the capitalist mode of production and its dynamic; and showed the necessity of periodic crises and their role in the forcible reimposition of the relative unity of capital accumulation (compare Albritton 1986; Harvey 1982; Postone 1993). My concern here is not to reconstruct the dialectical logic of Marx's *Capital*, but to build on its account of the basic contradictions in capital. Specifically, I argue that all forms of the capital relation embody different versions of the contradiction between exchange-value and use-value and that these impact differently on (different fractions of) capital and labour. These contradictions are reproduced as capitalism itself is reproduced. Changes in their articulation provide one base for periodization.

Let me enumerate some forms of this contradiction. The commodity is both an exchange-value and a use-value; the worker is both an abstract unit of labour-power substitutable by other such units (or, indeed, other factors of production) and a concrete individual with specific skills, knowledge and creativity; the wage is both a cost of production and a source of demand; money functions both as an international currency and as national money; productive capital is both abstract value in motion (notably in the form of realized profits available for reinvestment) and a concrete stock of time-and-place-specific assets in the course of being valorized; and so forth. Such structural contradictions and their associated strategic dilemmas always exist but assume different forms and primacies in different contexts. They can also prove more or less manageable, depending on the specific 'spatio-temporal fixes' and institutionalized class compromises with which they are associated.

One way to distinguish periods of capitalism (or accumulation regimes and modes of regulation) is in terms of the relative primacy of these different contradictions. Thus Petit suggests that, for any accumulation regime, the overall mode of regulation is organized around one dominant structural form. For Fordism, this was the wage relation; in the emerging post-Fordist regime, competition. Other structural forms that might fill this position in other contexts are money, the state and international regimes (Petit 1999). But Petit himself concedes there is no good theoretical reason to assume that only one structural form at a time plays this role. Hence it would better to leave this issue open to further theoretical and empirical analysis. Mao's remarks on contradiction are useful here, especially as read by Althusser (1970). Thus one could examine changes in the principal and secondary contradictions and shifts in their respective primary and secondary aspects. This is the approach developed below.

A strategic-relational approach emphasizes the dialectical interplay of structure and strategy. This is illustrated by Poulantzas's claim that 'the reproduction of these contradictions with their contradictory effects and their impact on the historical tendency of capitalist development depends on the *class struggle*' (1975a: 40–1). Poulantzas tended to essentialize class struggle, but his argument can be made less reductionist by referring to two general features of capital accumulation. The first provides a basis for introducing agency into the analysis of accumulation regimes, the second for considering agency's role in modes of regulation.

First, the complex internal relations among the different moments of the value form have only a formal unity, that is, they are unified only as modes of expression of generalized commodity production. They do not give it substantive unity or guarantee crisis-free accumulation. From a strategic-relational perspective, any such unity (or structural coherence) that exists is coproduced through structurally inscribed strategic selectivities and actors' (differentially reflexive) structurally oriented strategic calculation. Accumulation strategies and institutionalized class compromises play key roles here in framing attempts to manage capitalism's contradictions and dilemmas. Accumulation strategies elaborate an account of the general interest in a feasible mode of growth together with its economic and extra-economic conditions, build support around its realization and seek to institutionalize the compromise that underpins it (Jessop 1990b: 193–247). Whatever its form and content, this general interest is imaginary. For it always marginalizes some forces, identities and interests; and always defers and/or displaces the costs involved in tackling the contradictions and dilemmas of a given accumulation strategy. No such strategy can ever be completely coherent or fully institutionalized, of course, owing to the opacity and indeterminacy of the conditions necessary to accumulation and the need to develop and build support for them despite continuing competition and conflict. Nonetheless, in so far as one accumulation strategy becomes dominant or hegemonic and is institutionalized within a specific spatio-temporal fix, it will help consolidate an accumulation regime within the economic space linked to this fix. Because the underlying contradictions and dilemmas still exist, however, any such regimes are always partial, provisional and unstable. The circuit of capital can still break at many points. Economic crises then serve to reimpose the always relative unity of the circuit of capital through its restructuring. If the latter matches the prevailing accumulation regime, growth will be renewed within its parameters. If not, a crisis *of* – and not just *in* – the accumulation regime will develop, provoking the search for new strategies, new institutionalized compromises and new spatio-temporal fixes.

Second, despite the capacity for self-valorization facilitated by the commodification of labour-power, the capitalist economy is not wholly self-contained. It also depends on social relations that are not subordinate to the value form. Even labour-power itself, despite its commodification, is largely reproduced outside any immediate capitalist labour process[3] – which means that the sole source of value and its bearers, the working class, are placed outside as well as inside the logic of capital. It is also becoming increasingly apparent, as Polanyi noted, that 'land' (in the broad sense of nature) is also a fictitious commodity whose reproduction times do not coincide with those of the capital relation (Polanyi 1957; also Altvater 1993; O'Connor 1996; Stahel 1999). In addition, outside a purely imaginary 'pure capitalist economy', capitalism is 'structurally coupled' to other systems with their own operational logics or instrumental rationalities and to the 'lifeworld' formed by various social relations, identities, interests and values not otherwise anchored in specific systems. At least some of these extra-economic conditions and forces must be integrated into accumulation strategies for the latter to be feasible. Thus accumulation regimes are usually associated with modes of regulation that regularize the extra-economic as well as economic conditions required for their expanded reproduction. Attempts to subordinate other systems and to colonize the lifeworld by extending the value form typically face resistance – with a corresponding impact on the trajectory of capital accumulation. This is also why the more successful accumulation strategies are often connected to hegemonic projects that link economic success to the national-popular (or some equivalent) interest that aims to mobilize a broader social constituency behind the growth strategy. This extends in turn the influence of accumulation via its modes of regulation to the overall mode of societalization in a given social formation (see Jessop 1997a).

Thus an adequate account – and adequate periodization – of the capitalist economy and its dynamic should explore how it is embedded in a wider nexus of social relations and institutions; how its evolution is linked to environing, embedding institutions; and how the latter help or hinder the overall reproduction, regularization and governance of the economy. This is especially significant today as capital becomes increasingly innovation- and information-driven, more closely linked to so-called 'post-industrial' processes, and more global in scope – with major implications for embedding, disembedding and re-embedding. In short, as social embeddedness changes, it produces a path-dependent structural coupling affecting the economy and its environments. Attempts to coordinate capitalist development are inevitably prone to failure. But, in so far as modes of coordination change, they too can inform periodization. This is illustrated by the importance now attached to networking as opposed to the role of mixed economy in Atlantic Fordism.

Overall, this approach implies that there is no single and unambiguous 'logic of capital' but, rather, several such logics with a family resemblance. For, given the underdetermination of capitalism's dynamic at the level of its generic but inevitably abstract logic, each accumulation regime and/or mode of regulation imparts its own distinctive structure and dynamic to the circuit of capital – including distinctive forms of crisis and breakdown. This can provide the basis for typologies for comparative and/or historical analysis. Moreover, if different regimes and/or modes of regulation succeed each other, it can also inform a chronology (simple succession in a unilinear timeframe) or a periodization (succession generated through the contingently necessary realization of the open-ended dialectical logic of capital as a social relation).

Atlantic Fordism and the KWNS

I now illustrate this approach with comments on Atlantic Fordism. A full account of post-war capitalism should examine modes of growth elsewhere in the world system – including state socialist economies, economies undergoing dependent development, emerging East Asian economies, etc. – and their complex articulation with the dominant Atlantic Fordist regime. This requires a far more complex analysis and periodization than is offered here. Nor do I consider the genealogy of Fordism, the reasons for the eventual triumph of the US variant of Fordism, and its subsequent diffusion to create Atlantic Fordism. Instead I focus on the structural coherence of this system, the factors behind its breakdown and the scope that the latter offers for a coherent post-Fordism.

Fordism and post-Fordism can be analyzed in regulationist terms on four different levels: the labour process, the accumulation regime, the mode of regulation and the mode of societalization (Jessop 1992). But this analysis is best undertaken by analyzing the structural contradictions and strategic dilemmas of capitalism. For these enable us to reassess the crisis of Fordism by stressing the limits to accumulation and regulation and the problems they pose for any post-Fordist regime. They also enable us to address the changing spatio-temporal dynamics of capital accumulation.

Atlantic Fordism was an accumulation regime based on a virtuous auto-centric circle of mass production and mass consumption secured through a distinctive mode of regulation that was institutionally and practically materialized in the Keynesian welfare national state (hereafter KWNS) (see Jessop 1992; 1994). Its distinctive contribution to Atlantic Fordism was to manage, at least for a while, the contradictions in the different forms of the capital relation. The Atlantic Fordist economies benefited from a spatio-territorial matrix based on the congruence between national economy, national state, national citizenship and national society; and from institutions relatively well adapted to combining the tasks of securing full employment and growth and managing national electoral cycles. This spatio-temporal fix enabled a specific resolution of the contradictions of accumulation as expressed under Atlantic Fordism. Thus, within relatively closed national economies which had been institutionally–discursively constituted as the primary objects of economic management, national states aimed to achieve full employment by treating wages primarily as a source of (domestic) demand and managed their budgets on the assumption that money circulated primarily as national money. The diffusion of mass production (and its economies of scale) through expanding Fordist firms as well as collective bargaining indexed to productivity and prices helped bring wages as a cost of production under control. And the Bretton Woods monetary regime and GATT trade regime helped ensure that the (still limited) circulation of free-floating international currencies did not seriously disturb

Keynesian economic management based on state control over the national money. Welfare rights based on national citizenship helped to generalize norms of mass consumption and to promote full employment levels of demand; and they were sustained in turn by an institutionalized compromise involving Fordist unions and Fordist firms. Full employment and welfare rights were in turn important themes in party-political competition.

Some costs of the Fordist compromise and KWNS were borne within Fordist societies by the relative decline of small and medium firms, by workers employed in disadvantaged parts of segmented labour markets and by women performing both paid and domestic labour. Other costs were exported to other economic and political spaces integrated into international regimes (such as those for cheap oil or migrant labour) necessary to Atlantic Fordism's continued growth but not included in its Fordist compromise. Atlantic Fordism was also enabled through a Janus-faced temporal fix. On the one hand, it depended on the rapid exploitation of non-renewable resources laid down over millennia; and, on the other, it produced environmental pollution and social problems which it either ignored or hoped to resolve in the indefinite future (see, for example, Altvater 1993: 247–78; Brennan 1995; Stahel 1999).

Crises *in* and *of* Fordism are inevitably overdetermined. The typical manifestation of the crisis *in* Fordism was stagflation – reflecting the grounding of its mode of regulation in the wage and money forms. This crisis-tendency was usually overcome through crisis-induced economic restructuring and incremental institutional changes. The crisis *of* Fordism emerged with the breakdown of these crisis management mechanisms. A major contributing factor here was the undermining of the national economy as an object of state management – notably through the internationalization of trade, investment and finance. This inverted the primary aspects of its two main contradictions and gave renewed force to other contradictions of capitalism. Thus the wage (both individual and social) was increasingly seen as an international cost of production rather than a source of domestic demand; and money increasingly came to circulate as an international currency, weakening Keynesian demand management on a national level. This shift in the primary aspect of the monetary contradiction is related to the tendential subordination of industrial capital to the hypermobile logic of financial capital and the tendency for returns on money capital to exceed those on productive capital. The relative exhaustion of the Atlantic Fordist growth dynamic also posed problems of productivity growth and market saturation (which contributed to an emerging fiscal crisis of the state) and problems of how to manage the transition to the next long-wave upswing (a task which entails changes in the temporal horizons as well as forms of state economic intervention). The crisis of US hegemony is also reflected in struggles over new international regimes and how far they should serve American interests rather than capitalism more generally.[4] In addition, new conflicts and/or forms of struggle have emerged that escape stabilization within existing structural forms: two major examples are the crisis of corporatism and the rise of new social movements. New problems have also arisen, such as pollution and new categories of risk, which are not easily managed, regularized, or governed within the old forms. Finally, relative to Atlantic Fordism's growth phase, some contradictions have increased in importance and/or acquired new forms.

Towards post-Fordism?

The problem of reregulating accumulation after the Fordist crisis is irreducible to finding new ways of managing old contradictions within the same spatio-temporal matrix. This is not just because the primary and secondary aspects of the principal structural forms in Atlantic Fordism (the wage relation and money form) have been reversed. Other contradictions and their associated dilemmas have also become more dominant and the spatio-temporal contexts in which all the above-mentioned contradictions are expressed have become more complex. The wage relation and money forms of after-Fordist economies have been widely discussed elsewhere. I would simply add that they have not successfully resolved Fordism's crisis tendencies, but have deferred and/or displaced them, thereby creating new forms of international and national disorder. This is especially clear in the dominant neo-liberal form of after-Fordist restructuring. This reinforces the abstract-formal moment of exchange-value in different structural forms at the expense of the substantive-material moment of use-value. It is capital in these abstract moments that is most easily disembedded from specific places and thereby freed to 'flow' freely through space and time. However, in each of its more concrete moments, as noted above, capital has its own particular productive and reproductive requirements. The relative neglect of these in the neo-liberal model at the international and national levels is partly compensated by more interventionist policies at the regional, urban and local levels (Gough and Eisenschitz 1996; Brenner 1999), as well as by capital's own increasing resort to various forms of partnership to secure these requirements. The rescaling of politics and the changing forms of coordination with which these counter-tendencies to neo-liberalism are linked also indicate the continuing movement away from Fordist regulation. But they have not yet produced a stable post-Fordist mode of regulation, because this must address other problems too.

I now discuss three newly important contradictions that hinder the search for a stable post-Fordist accumulation regime and mode of regulation. They comprise: first, a dissociation between abstract flows in space and concrete valorization in place; second, a growing short-termism in economic calculation versus an increasing dependence of valorization on extra-economic factors that take a long time to produce; and, third, the contradiction between the information economy and the information society as a specific expression of the fundamental contradiction between private control in the relations of production and socialization of the forces of production. In addition, though it is not as such a structural contradiction, major problems surround the ideal spatio-temporal fix, if any, within which the principal contradictions of Atlantic Fordism and today's newly important contradictions might prove manageable.

The first contradiction reflects the fact that 'the new economy operates in a "space" rather than a place, and over time more and more economic transactions will migrate to this new space' (Kelly 1998: 94). This is a complex, non-propinquitous, multidimensional, cyberspace with novel spatial dynamics grounded in the possibilities that cyberspace offers for simultaneous colocation of myriad entities and relationships. Yet cyberspace is not a neutral, third space between capital and labour, market and state, public and private: it is a new terrain on which conflicts between these forces, institutions and domains are fought out. Its best-known expression is the separation of hypermobile financial capital from industrial capital – with the former moving in an abstract space of flows, the latter still needing to be valorized in place. The same contradiction also appears in the individual circuits of financial, industrial and commercial capital and their interconnections. For, in different ways, each circuit depends on a complex relation between a physical marketplace and a conceptual marketspace (Kelly 1998: 96). However much economic activity migrates into cyberspace, territorialization remains essential to capital. The grid of global cities provides this territorial 'fix' for financial capital and international producer services (Sassen 1996). For industrial capital, it could be innovation milieux, industrial districts, and so on, as well as physical infrastructure (see Harvey 1982). Even e-commerce needs such an infrastructure. Thus, an emerging globalizing, knowledge-driven after-Fordism does not signal the final transcendence of spatial barriers but effects 'new and more complex articulations of the dynamics of mobility and fixity' (Robins and Gillespie 1992: 149).

The second contradiction is rooted in the paradox that '(t)he most advanced economies function more and more in terms of the extra-economic' (Veltz 1996: 12). The paradox rests on the increasing interdependence between the economic and extra-economic factors making for structural or systemic competitiveness. This is linked to new technologies based on more complex transnational, national and regional systems of innovation, to the paradigm shift from the Fordist concern with productivity growth rooted in economies of scale to concern with mobilizing social as well as economic sources of flexibility and entrepreneurialism, and to the more general attempts to penetrate micro-social relations in the interests of valorization. It is reflected in the growing emphasis given to social capital, trust and communities of learning as well as the enhanced role of competitiveness based on entrepreneurial cities, an enterprise culture and enterprising subjects. This is where Petit's suggestion that competition is the dominant axis of post-Fordist regulation finds most justification (Petit 1999).

The changing nature of competition generates major new contradictions that affect the spatial and temporal organization of accumulation. Thus, temporally, there is a major contradiction between short-term economic calculation (especially in financial flows) and the long-term dynamic of 'real competition' rooted in resources (skills, trust, heightened reflexivity, collective mastery of techniques, economies of agglomeration and size) that may take years to create, stabilize and reproduce. Spatially, there is a funda-mental contradiction between the economy considered as a pure space of flows and the economy as a territorially and/or socially embedded system of extra-economic as well as economic resources and competencies. The latter moment is reflected in varied concepts to describe the knowledge-driven economy – national, regional and local systems of innovation, innovative milieux, systemic or structural competitiveness, learning regions, social capital, trust, speed-based competition and so on. This poses new dilemmas if the capital relation is to be stabilized over more scales as well as increasingly compressed and/or extended temporal hori-zons of action.

A third contradiction that becomes important once again in the after-Fordist (or, at least, the post-industrial) accumulation regime is the so-called 'fundamental contradiction' of capitalism, namely, that between the increasing socialization of the productive forces and private control in the relations of production. Networked knowledge-driven economies heighten this contradiction from both sides. Thus the socialization of productive forces is enhanced, first, by the 'economies of networks' that are generated in and through multi-actor, polycentric and multiscalar networks rather than by single (or quasi-vertically integrated) organizations, which are better able to realize economies of scale; and, second, by the almost exponentially increasing returns to network size, such that 'each additional member increases the network's value, which in turn attracts more members, initiat-ing a spiral of benefits' (Kelly 1998: 25). These two features pose a number of collective action problems around socialization and private appropriation linked to the tendencies to market failure noted even in orthodox studies of the 'economics of information'. In particular, they make it 'difficult legally to distinguish between different firms' intellectual property, since all intel-lectual property is a mixture of innovations arising from different places' (Kundnani 1998–99: 56). This reinforces the tendency for network econom-ies to be captured by the network – albeit often asymmetrically – rather than by a particular firm (Kelly 1998: 26–8). This suggests the need for new forms of enterprise able to capture network economies without destroying the broader network(s) that generate them. 'Virtual' and/or networked firms are said to correspond to this need (Castells 1996: 151–200). However, unless the 'virtual' firm becomes coextensive with the collective labourer, the contradiction remains. For every capital wants free access to information, knowledge and expertise, but wants to charge for the information, knowledge and expertise that it can supply (see Frow 1996: 102).

A fourth site of problems concerns the appropriate horizons of action for the spatio-temporal fix, if any, within which Atlantic Fordism's principal contradictions and those of the current period might prove manageable. This is closely related to a new complexity in informational capitalism due to new forms of 'time – space distantiation' and 'time – space compression'. Time – space distantiation stretches social relations over time and space so that they can be controlled or coordinated over longer periods of time (including into the ever more distant future) and over longer distances, greater areas, or more scales of activity. Conversely, time – space compression involves the intensification of 'discrete' events in real time and/or increased velocity of material and immaterial flows over a given distance. This is linked to changing material and social technologies enabling more precise control over ever-shorter periods of action as well as 'the conquest of space by time'. Differential abilities to stretch and/or compress time and space shape power and resistance in the emerging global order. Thus hyper-mobile forms of finance capital have a unique capacity to compress their own decision-making time (for example, through split-second computerized trading) while continuing to extend and consolidate their global reach. New developments in both respects, promoted by certain fractions of capital and some states, helped significantly to erode Atlantic Fordism's spatio-temporal fix. This occurred because of the growing incongruence between proliferating scales of economic action and because new forms of time-space compression undermined the preferred temporalities of Atlantic Fordist accumulation and regulation.

This is now reflected in a 'relativization of scale' (Collinge 1996). This involves a proliferation of discursively constituted and institutionally embedded spatial scales (whether terrestrial, territorial or telematic), their relative dissociation in complex tangled hierarchies (rather than a simple nesting of scales), and an increasingly convoluted mix of scale strategies as economic and political forces seek the most favourable conditions for insertion into a changing international order. The national scale has lost its taken-for-granted primacy in Atlantic Fordism; but no other scale of economic, political or social organization (whether the 'global' or the 'local', the 'urban' or the 'triadic') has yet won a similar primacy. Indeed, there is intense competition between different economic and political spaces to become the new primary anchorage point of accumulation. The new politics of scale is still unresolved – although I suspect that 'triads' will eventually replace the nation as the primary scale in an eventual post-Fordist spatio-temporal fix.

As yet, however, these four newly important problems have prevented a stable post-Fordist regime from emerging either in the old space of Atlantic Fordism or on some wider scale. I suggest that the principal contradictions around which a new accumulation regime would crystallize comprise the *forms of competition* (notably the growing importance of the extra-economic conditions of competitiveness and hence their colonization by the value form and, tied to this as well as to the new knowledge-driven technological paradigm, the emergence of the networked firm as the dominant organizational paradigm) and the *forms of the state* (notably its restructuring in the light of the relativization of scale and of the incapacity of traditional state forms to govern the new economy). I have addressed both sets of issues in recent work on the shift from the Keynesian welfare national state typical of Atlantic Fordism to an emerging Schumpeterian workfare post-national regime (SWPR) that could help reregularize an after-Fordist accumulation regime.

The ideal-typical SWPR can be described as follows. First, it tries to promote permanent innovation and flexibility in relatively open economies by intervening on the supply side and to strengthen their structural and/or systemic competitiveness by rearticulating the extra-economic and economic conditions bearing thereon. Second, it subordinates social policy to the demands of labour market flexibility and/or employability and the perceived imperatives of structural or systemic competitiveness. This includes putting downward pressure on the social wage *qua* cost of international production. Third, compared with the earlier primacy of the national scale, the SWPR is '*post-national*' because the increased significance of other spatial scales and horizons of action makes national territory less important as a 'power container'. This is associated with transfers of economic and social policy-making functions upwards, downwards and sideways. International agencies (such as the IMF, World Bank, OECD and ILO) play an increased role in shaping the economic and social policy agendas; in Europe, the European Union also has a growing role. But there is a simultaneous devolution of some economic and social policy-making to the regional, urban and local levels on the grounds that policies intended to influence the microeconomic supply side and social regeneration are best designed close to their sites of implementation. Such arguments also justify cross-border cooperation among regional, urban or local spaces. Yet, paradoxically, this leads to an enhanced role for national states in controlling the interscalar transfer of these powers – suggesting a shift from sovereignty to a *primus inter pares* role in intergovernmental relations. Finally, public – private networks have an increased role in state activities on all levels in delivering economic and social policies and compensating for market failures and inadequacies. But here, too, states have a key role through their involvement in *meta*-governance, that is, designing governance regimes on different scales and moderating their operations and mutual repercussions (on the SWPR, see Jessop 1993; 1994).

Concluding remarks

My general conclusions are easily stated. The abstract logic of capitalism is the best *starting point* for theorizing accumulation regimes and their modes of regulation and, a fortiori, for distinguishing and periodizing phases of capitalist development. Thus my analysis starts from the basic contradiction between exchange-value and use-value and its relation to different but cognate structural contradictions and strategic dilemmas in all expressions of the value form. I then introduce strategic-relational concepts to examine how the capital relation may acquire an always-relative substantive (as opposed to merely formal) unity as the basis for expanded reproduction. This relative unity can be analyzed in a concretization-complexification spiral to reveal its structural and strategic moments. These include the institutionalized compromises, spatio-temporal fixes and spatial and temporal horizons of action that help to secure the relative stabilization and structural coherence of accumulation regimes and modes of regulation. They do this in part by displacing and/or deferring certain contradictions, dilemmas and costs onto social spaces and forces beyond the internal and external boundaries of the compromise and its spatio-temporal fix. I also argue that different compromises and spatio-temporal fixes involve different relative weights for these contradictions and dilemmas and suggest how this may serve as one basis for periodizing capitalism.

Two general methodological conclusions can now be drawn. First, no particular scale or space (such as the national) or particular periodicity (such as long waves, product cycles or business cycles) should be privileged a priori in analyzing phases of capitalism. For the relative importance of different scales, spaces or time horizons is a key variable in the structural coherence of accumulation regimes and modes of regulation. The key role of the national scale in Atlantic Fordism, for example, contrasts with the more multiscalar patterns that preceded it and are now succeeding it. Temporal horizons have likewise shifted, owing to the rearticulation of time–space distantiation and compression, especially given new information and communication technologies. Second, my approach rejects the dichotomous choice of qualitatively different capitalisms in history versus one overriding structure since capitalism began. The same abstract logic of capital certainly shapes all forms of capitalism; but this logic can be expressed in different forms. The dynamic of capital accumulation on a world scale depends on diverse complementarities among accumulation regimes and modes of regulation on different scales and on the ways these provide the requisite variety for capital to experiment, to respond to new forms of crisis and obstacles to accumulation, to displace the leading growth centres as new regimes and modes of regulation emerge, and to establish buffer zones and sinks for absorbing the costs of capital's uneven development outside the spatio-temporal fixes of the leading regions.

Notes

1 A need for brevity means my views below are often oversimplified, if not self-caricatured, versions of arguments presented elsewhere. Readers can consult the references for more developed arguments.
2 Many early comments on Fordism in crisis saw a revamped Fordism (neo-Fordism) as the solution.
3 In this sense it is a 'fictitious commodity'.
4 In contrast the new post-war international regimes established under US hegemony served broader interests in capital accumulation.

18
Phases of Capitalism and Post-Capitalist Social Change

Richard Westra

Introduction

Concomitant to the searching re-evaluation of the socialist predicament that followed in the wake of the 1989 'Fall of the Wall' were discussions by Marxists over the apportioning of blame for the Soviet-style disappointments (Blackburn 1991; Cox 1991). My immediate concern here is with the directing of blame towards Karl Marx himself and a 'Marxism' as his theoretical progeny. To fault Marx I believe is deeply problematic, because not only did Marx pass away long before the first experiment was embarked upon, but during his lifetime he consistently eschewed the advancing of any sort of 'blueprint' for socialist construction. Now while some may view this omission itself as blameworthy, as Marx made the case to his 'utopian socialist' contemporaries, the priority for his generation was to produce knowledge of that peculiar transformatory force that had enveloped the world they lived in, that is, *capital*, and it would probably fall into the hands of future generations to channel such knowledge into creative initiatives at remaking the world. Unfortunately, death interrupted even Marx's ability to see that initial task brought to fruition.

This brings me to the next point regarding *Marxism*. As Marxology confirms (Haupt 1982), that very designation (Marxism) referring to the existence of a systematic body of thought with political imperatives emerged in the hands of Second International doyen Karl Kautsky. From the outset, therefore, what has constituted Marxism involved the interpreting and purported elaboration of Marx's work: in short, efforts which can be succinctly referred to as *reconstructions* of Marxist theory. And, of course, Kautsky's system was but the first in a succession of such endeavours. Hence, while certain reconstructions of Marxism may have propelled social actors in Soviet-style directions, I see absolutely no basis for holding Marxism *per se* accountable for the unpalatable Soviet-style politico-economic outcomes.

Nevertheless, if in fact there exist reconstructions of Marxism which contain theoretical cues that support Soviet-style adventures, or propound future directed action with questionable socialist substance, or for that matter, in some fashion continue to trammel the sort of creative thinking that Marx surely would have desired to see emanate from his research agenda, then these must be identified and exorcized from Marxism. It is to such an undertaking that this chapter contributes. In keeping with the questions animating this anthology, the intended focus is the relationship between the theory of capital's inner logic and the theorizing of phases of capitalist development, and how such theorization most felicitously contributes to creative future-directed thinking. The position taken here is that the development of this domain of Marxism has suffered from serious misapprehensions, the resolution of which will be required for the reinvigoration of the socialist project.

The chapter will be structured in the following manner. The second section presents the 'conventional Marxist' approach to phases of capitalism and discusses its implications for future-directed thinking. I do admit that it is with a certain trepidation that I use a term such as conventional Marxism, lest I be accused of erecting a 'straw Marxism'. However, I believe the case can be made that there persists a core disabling convention in the theorization of phases of capitalism cutting across otherwise diverse reconstructions of Marxism for which the appellation is appropriate. In the third section the Uno approach[1] to Marxism will be introduced. This school, originating in Japan, offers a reconstruction of Marx's work that takes the theorization of phases of capitalism in distinctly different directions from conventional Marxism; directions, I shall contend in the fourth section, that open the door to a hitherto unrealized creative deployment of Marxism in the making of a genuine socialist world. Finally, the chapter will be concluded.

Conventional Marxism and phases of capitalism

Thematic in the development of conventional Marxism has been the equation of Marxism and historical materialism, with the latter conceptualized as an overarching theory of history the validity of which is linked to its ability to produce knowledge supporting at least the possibility of a socialist historical outcome. Now I would agree with objections that the foregoing is quite stark and elides the richness and diversity of the field. And space considerations certainly preclude anything approximating an authoritative review of the literature from which the characterization was derived. Nevertheless, in my view it is definitely defensible as capturing generally accepted (though rarely interrogated) assumptions in Marxist theory.

Within the conventional Marxist apprehension of historical materialism as the master environment for the elaboration of Marxist theory, the political economic study of capitalism is viewed as a *sub-theory*. To be sure, there exist a host of variations on this theme such as historical materialism delineated as the 'general theory' and the study of capitalism as the 'special' theory, yet the messages devolving from such are similar enough to justify the blanket expression 'sub-theory.' However, what is most pertinent at this juncture is to adequately grasp the precise ramifications of appending the political-economic study of capitalism, commencing with its formative work – Marx's *Capital* – to historical materialism as a sub-theory. Given that the crux of Marxism was purportedly its theorizing of historical directionality, *Capital* and the project of Marxian political economy was conscripted in this design in order to demonstrate the unfolding historical tendencies of capitalism portending a socialist historical outcome.

In the earliest exposition of the foregoing, conditioning the thinking of the immediate post-Marx and Engels generation of Marxists, Kautsky (1936) claimed that the journey of capital commenced in a historically existent era of simple commodity production. That period, however, as the narrative goes, was soon to be supplanted by capitalism proper, itself driven by an inexorable 'law' of accumulation – advancing the concentration and centralization of capital and a concomitant proletarianization – responsible for propelling capitalism towards its demise. Socialism thereby, was conceived as essentially a product of the necessitarian 'socializing' laws of capitalism, making a historical contribution to human development largely through its amelioration of the supposed ills of capitalism (such as the latter's unequal distributional consequences).

To be sure, this schema of socialism as the outcome of the laws of accumulation captured in *Capital* did not go unchallenged for long, as exemplified by the renowned 'revisionist controversy' it sparked. Abstracting from the crude empiricist matrix, what the famous debate did ultimately spotlight was the vulnerability of the conventional statement to the vicissitudes of history. Thus, it was in an attempt to nullify this weakness that the Marxist project of theorizing phases or 'stages' of capitalism was inaugurated. Interestingly, as recounted in the masterful study by Jukka Gronow (1986), the primary architects of the theory of the stage of 'imperialism' (Hilferding and Lenin) accepted much of Kautsky's take on *Capital* – that it charted the historical course of capitalism from a petty-commodity society to capitalism and ultimately towards the socialization of production. Where they saw their intervention however, was in specifying the precise modalities of the latter process that Marx himself did not survive to witness. Capitalism as such was considered essentially a short-lived formation wedged between its petty-commodity precursor and imperialism. Imperialism for its part embodied the 'truth' about capitalism; its divergence from the pristine world of *laissez-faire* portrayed in bourgeois mythology to one of rampant monopolization which, in wielding vast worker collectivities, prefigured socialism.

Recent scholarship (McDonough and Drago 1989, McDonough 1995) suggests the theorizing of imperialism resolved the 'first crisis of Marxism' (where crisis refers to the situation in which history appears to be throwing unmanageable curves at the *theory* of history's trajectory). In this specific instance, *Capital* was purportedly unable to deal with the challenge of explaining the persistence of capitalism or the precise modalities of its new historical configuration. However, we have to ask how imperialism so theorized really extricated Marxism from the problems it faced. After all, in theorizing imperialism it was accepted that *Capital* demonstrated the historical tendencies of capitalist development. In the end therefore, imperialism provided a mere supplementation to these, emphasizing the increasing 'complexity' of the transformatory process, and in this sense at best bought Marxism some time. Also, in perpetuating the view that the contours of the socialist economy would be shaped by capitalism – in this case its monopolistic form – the theory of imperialism hardly provided an inducement for creative thinking about socialism. In fact, it set the course for the agonizing Soviet-style experience. Finally, there is the issue of what sort of Marxism was being saved. The conventional edifice – with the study of capitalism and its phases appended to a theory of history validated by its ability to produce knowledge confirming at least the possibility of a socialist historical outcome – remained intact. This version of Marxism, poised to quake at the aporias of history, certainly does not offer a robust foundation for future-directed action.

Following the events of 1989, it is precisely such issues that were revisited in the outpouring of Marxist commentary. Analysts (Altvater 1993; Dirlik 1994) were quick to point out how the social economy of the Soviet-style societies behind the 'Wall' seemed oddly reminiscent of imperialist, turn-of-the-century Western capitalism. What made this observation particularly noteworthy was the fact that after the Second World War, the capitalist economies of the West underwent a distinct socio-economic transformation to a so-called 'Fordist' type of capitalism pivoting upon a unique mass consumption dynamic. It was concurrently suggested that the latter indirectly contributed to the downfall of the Soviet-style regimes. For while expectations were that capitalism would be outperformed in an historic race, the reality was that Sovietized societies continued to stagnate in a pre-Fordist time warp.

But the key question here is this: how is it possible to reconcile the claim that socialism is prefigured by the monopoly 'socializing' capitalism of the imperialist phase (with, of course, experiments having already been embarked upon predicated on just such a premise), when capitalism itself had experienced further development and transformation towards but another phase, beyond the borders of the socialist world? One answer that sustains the claims of historical materialism and confirms the legacy of *Capital* as per the conventional paradigm, is that Fordist mass consumption is but the obverse of the monopolistic production coin (Altvater 1993).

However, the defence of that monopolization/socialism nexus was soon challenged by evidence of a purported further transmutation of capitalism into what has been dubbed a 'post-Fordist' or 'post-industrial' phase. As culled from statements of that position (Dirlik 1994; Therborn 1992), reasons why Marxism found itself under threat are briefly as follows: first, the new stage allegedly involves the 'disorganization' of capitalism (Lash and Urry 1987), a historical reversal of the tendency towards the aggregation of the production structure, accompanied by the reinstatement of markets and diminution of state involvement in the economy. The second disruptive feature of the new stage is the supposed drift towards 'globalization'. Simply put, the inference here is that the geographical dispersal, disaggregation and mobility of capital has undermined the nation-state as the locus for capital accumulation (and its management) upon which socialist strategy had been predicated.

Arising in response to this latest indictment has been a virtual growth industry in a 'crisis of Marxism' literature. One contingent of this writing (Callari and Ruccio 1996a) contends that what bedevilled Marxism *qua* historical materialism all along has been the reduction and centering of its understanding and vision of socialist change in the historical trajectory of the *economic* in general and the capitalist economy in particular. Even the theorizing of capitalist phases, notwithstanding its recent incarnations, it is asserted (Gibson-Graham 1996), has been unable to escape from the determinist web spun in Marx's *Capital*. The solution which now appears to have gained acceptance among divergent affiliates of the 'crisis' contingent, then, is a Marxism *qua* historical materialism that has exorcized the economic!

To sum up, one need not buy into the periodizing of post-war capitalism expressly in terms of Fordism/post-Fordism which in their common rendering, as I argued elsewhere (Westra 1996), have questionable theoretical credentials, or for that matter, accept the hyperbole of the globalization literature, to acknowledge that in the hands of conventional Marxism, the heritage of Marx is being leeched of all substance. And there should be agreement with the prescription of this chapter, that the modality of theorizing capital's logic and capitalism's phases of development and the implications of such for post-capitalist social change be rethought.

The Unoist reconstruction of Marxist theory

Breaking fundamentally with the conventional paradigm, the Uno approach opposes the view of historical materialism as the master environment for the elaboration of Marxist theory. Rather for Unoists, Marxist theory is divided into *two* distinct research projects – historical materialism *and* the political economic study of capitalism – each with very different subject-matters. Historical materialism is the study of human history *in toto*. The concern of the political economic study of capitalism, on the other hand, is solely with the *modus operandi* of a very peculiar kind of economy. And, Unoists maintain, it is the latter project, embarked upon by Marx in *Capital* (though left incomplete by him), that constitutes the *sine qua non* of Marxism. The Uno approach in effect reverses the cognitive sequence that has pervaded Marxist thought since Kautsky. What permitted Marx's work to flow in the direction that Unoists claim will become clear following the discussion of the Uno approach to Marxian political economy.

The undergirding for the project of the political economic study of capitalism is Uno and Sekine's recasting and completion of Marx's *Capital* as *the theory of a purely capitalist society.*[2] Being cognizant of the compass of this chapter, I will outline just two of the principal ways in which this theory taps the potential of Marx's research agenda.

First, the theory of a purely capitalist society establishes the definitive *economic theory*. It is certainly no accident that economic theory initially arises in the age of capital. For it is only with capitalism that economic or material life appears 'transparently';[3] that is, 'disengaging' from and set above the social, in the sense that it tends to manage the social with a peculiar self-directed, self-serving automaticity. In exploring this phenomenon, it was a reflection of his genius that Marx perceived how as commodity-economic marketization increasingly mediated the material intercourse of human beings, it tended not only to impersonalize or objectify sociomaterial relationships (converting them into 'relations among things'), but led in effect to the governing of material life by an extra-human principle or 'logic' (Marx dubbed this the *law of value*). What the Uno approach contributes here is that it renders explicit the precise conditions under which it is possible to conclusively demonstrate the inner workings of this commodity economic logic of capital. To this effect, the core assumption of the reconstruction of *Capital* as the theory of a purely capitalist society is a full-fledged commodity economy: where all inputs and outputs of the production process including labour-power are commodified, all subject positions are class positions personifying economic categories and all economic activity is completely regulated by society-wide self-regulating markets. And though it is true that such a stark social order as envisaged in the theory has never existed, what the theory effectively accomplishes is that it extrapolates to a hypothetical conclusion the marketizing tendency of capital that purifies or purges its environment of extraneous non-capitalist, non-economic interferences. In this sense, it constitutes the definitive economic theory of an 'economic' society; a society moreover, in which economic or material life is governed according to the dictates of the objective commodity-economic law of value and human material reproduction subordinated to the abstract principle of value augmentation.

The second significant way in which the theory of a purely capitalist society realizes the potential of Marx's political economic research agenda is its constituting of a genuine *social science*. Through the disengaging of the economic from the social as discussed above, the economic or material basis of social life is revealed with the advent of capitalism for the very first time in the history of human society. However, the economic substructure that appears here with such transparency does so only in its specifically capitalist commodity-economic form. From this unique state of affairs springs a particular tendency understood by Marx as the 'fetishism' of capital, which conflates the specifically commodity-economic with the substantive economic or material life *per se*. Or, what amounts to the same thing, it advances the historically constituted characteristics of the commodity economy as eternal features of human material existence. It is precisely to deal with such mystifications as capital engenders that there arises the need for a science of society. In regard to this point, Unoists make it abundantly clear that in their reconstruction of Marxist theory, the term *science* is utilized only in relation to the study of a subset of purposive human activity where human beings are entered into social relationships reproducing their material livelihood as determined by the commodity-economic logic of capital. What the theory of a purely capitalist society as a genuine social science unravels is the complex of objective interrelations of the commodity economy, ultimately illustrating how it is possible for human economic existence to be organized by an impersonal, extra-human force. And most vitally, given how the process of theory construction is 'guided' by the very logic of this force, we can be assured with the highest degree of objectivity attainable in a social scientific enterprise, that our knowledge of capital is complete and robust.[4]

The time has arrived to turn the focus upon how the theory of a purely capitalist society unleashes the revolutionary future directed power of Marxism. In this regard I will first discuss the means through which the theory constitutes the revolutionary kernel of Marxism. Next, the way the theory advances the conceptualizing and study of phases of capitalism will be explored. The fourth substantive section of this chapter will examine the contribution to creative thought about socialist construction that is furnished by the Uno approach to Marxian political economy. Of course, given space considerations, none of this will be exhaustive.

It was argued above that the condition of possibility for economic theory or the systematic scientific study of material life, is the tendency of the commodity-economy to purify or purge such life of extra-economic interferences and contingencies. Consequently, the theory of a purely capitalist society, which produces complete knowledge of economic life as governed by the objective principles of the commodity economy, constitutes a prism through which it is possible to study the economic substructure of other human societies. For in conclusively demonstrating how the extra-human logic of capital reproduces the economic life of an entire society, the theory of a purely capitalist society simultaneously elucidates what Uno innovatively characterized as the '*general norms*' of material life (1980), the satisfaction of which must be undertaken for any human society to survive. According to Unoists, it is precisely this cognitive procedure that Marx sought to capture with the statement: 'the anatomy of man is key to the anatomy of the ape' (1970: 211). It is upon the understanding of the foregoing then, that Unoists substantiate the argument that the theory of a purely capitalist society constitutes the *sine qua non* of Marxism, with the discrete project of historical materialism clearly rendered dependent upon the science of Marxian economics for any claims it has to validity. And further, by establishing in such a robust fashion the means by which the operation of an historically constituted extra-human commodity-economic logic actually satisfies the general norms of material life, the theory of a purely capitalist society proves the *feasibility* of socialism (Uno 1980), a society where the satisfaction of those very norms will be ensured by the conscious decision-making of freely associated human beings. It is precisely this – the production of robust knowledge of human material existence and material reproduction – that Marx intended as the scientific foundation of socialism. And it is upon this point according to Unoists that the most fundamental revolutionary claims of Marxism are predicated.

The Uno approach therefore anchors Marxism and the socialist enterprise far more securely than ever before in the timeless knowledge of material life supplied by the theory of a purely capitalist society. It also frees historical materialism to deploy knowledge drawn from economic science to study material existence in human history without any obligation to account for extra-human 'tendencies', 'laws', and so on that do not exist in that subject-terrain. Conversely, Unoists recognize the fact that, singularly in human history, capitalism *does* manifest an objective extra-human inner logic, and that this saddles the distinct project of Marxian political economy with a unique challenge. It is to this we now turn.

Though yielding rigorous and systematic knowledge of all the logical inter-relations of the commodity-economy, the theorizing of a purely capitalist society opens a wide gulf between the study of capital's inner logic and that of actual capitalist history. However, in order to display how it was even possible for capital to subordinate the reproduction of the material life of an entire society to the abstract goal of value augmentation, the theory necessarily assumed that the use-value dimension of such life could easily be neutralized or subsumed by capital's marketizing chrematistic. In this circumstance, which as I will again emphasize, emanates from the ontological peculiarity of the subject-matter, Unoists argue that the theoretical move to the study of capitalist history – requiring the complete reinstatement or reactivation of the use-value dimension of socio-material life in all its empirical richness and potential intractability – must be mediated. Therefore, according to the Uno approach, the Marxian project of the political economic study of capitalism is to be necessarily undertaken as three *levels of analysis* – the theory of a purely capitalist society, *stage theory* and *historical analysis of capitalism*.

Stated succinctly, as a genuinely mediating level of analysis, stage theory captures the *modus operandi* of capital as it strives to manage the production of use-values most characteristically capitalist and idiosyncratic to world-historic phases of capitalist development. Drawing upon the important Unoist contribution of Albritton (1991), I will now outline three signal facets of such theorization. First, stage theory periodizes capitalism according to four stages – mercantilism (1700–50), liberalism (1840–70), imperialism (1890–1914) and consumerism (1950–70). Following from the fact that stage theory is *synchronic*, theorizing predominant world-historic structures or types of accumulation, the dates signify the 'golden age' of each capitalist stage from which stage-specific features are abstracted.[5] Also, given the geographical unevenness of capitalist development, each golden age is theorized at the most advanced and representative accumulatory sites. These are: Britain for mercantilism and liberalism; Germany and the US for imperialism; and the US in the stage of consumerism.

Second, and of high consequence for the discussion in the next section of the chapter, stage theory turns the focus of Marxian political economy onto the use-value dimension of socio-material life, doing so through the preliminary introduction of use-value in its controlled environment. Interestingly, if capital could manage the production of all use-values unproblematically – that is, solely according to commodity-economic principles – it could materialize a purely capitalist society as a bourgeois utopia in history! What stage theory instead confirms in this regard, is firstly the extent to which key historical use-values deflect the logic of capital, requiring it to meet different techno-organizational imperatives. Thus, the capitalist production of *wool*, the typical stage-specific use-value of mercantilism, was managed by *merchant capital;* the *cotton* manufacturing of the stage of liberalism, by *industrial capital;* the production of the use-value *steel* characteristic of imperialism, necessitated *finance capital*; and the demands of the production of the *automobile*, the complex stage-specific use-value typical of consumerism, are met by *corporate capital*. In this context, stage theory suggests that the grip of value on human material existence is compatible only with a relatively narrow range of use-value production. And, in fact, it was the 'light' use-value complex typical of liberalism that proved most amenable to commodity-economic subsumption as evidenced by capital's *laissez-faire* superstructure in that stage. Commencing with the stage of imperialism however, the logic of capital becomes increasingly compromised.

This latter point leads us to the third facet of stage theory. To fully expose capital for what it is, the theory of a purely capitalist society hypothetically consummated the logic of capital in a thought experiment of a world unencumbered by non-economic non-capitalist elements. Again, testifying to the historical transience of capital, such is never the case in historical capitalism. Stage theory therefore is drawn to the study of the predominant types of political, ideological, and legal supports which capital receives in each stage. (In fact Uno argued stages of capitalism should be named according to stage-specific *state policy*.)

To sum up, the theorizing of phases of capitalist development in the Uno approach is counterposed to that of conventional Marxism in the most profound fashion. Appending political economy to historical materialism, itself conceived as a theory of historical directionality, conventional Marxism regarded *Capital* as demonstrating the existence of laws concurrently socializing capitalism as they propelled it towards its demise. The theorizing of phases of capitalism was inaugurated to supplement the foregoing with an account of transformations undergone by capitalism since Marx's passing. However as capitalism continued to transmutate, with the tendencies purportedly driving it towards its demise appearing increasingly diluted and the socialism they foreshadowed considered highly unpalatable as a current social alternative, some conventional Marxists concluded that the time had arrived to jettison *Capital* and the political economic edifice constructed upon it.

According to the Uno approach, the mission of the distinct project of political economy is to produce knowledge of capitalism, a very peculiar human society. The theory of a purely capitalist society, the scientific undergirding of the project, displays how such a thing as an extra-human logic reproducing the material existence of an entire society is possible. What the theory unearths is the law of value as the fundamental inner principle of capital, simultaneously organizing material reproduction for the purpose of value augmentation while satisfying the general norms of economic life required of any human society. Stage theory, for its part, far from confirming a historical teleology of capitalism (or even the threads of such, buttressed with qualifications about new complexities), establishes that use-value obstacles thwart the logic of capital. From the perspective of the Uno approach, *no stage of capitalist development constitutes a prefiguration of socialism!* Rather, while the logic of capital if unobstructed generates a purely capitalist society, phases of capitalism represent specific configurations of capital and accumulatory supports necessary for the capitalist management of particular types of use-value production. In the end, it is historical analysis as a level of analysis in the Marxian political economic study of capitalism that is charged with examining the impact of capitalism upon modern history and determining the extent to which capitalism has shaped and continues to shape it. The fact is, however, that such determinations must be based upon a precise understanding of capital and its predominant accumulatory modalities. Also, the Uno approach underscores Marx's argument that challenges to capitalism must be predicated upon comprehensive knowledge of that which is to be superseded. Therefore, to jettison the Marxian project of the political-economic study of capitalism, or to collapse the rigor of the theory of capital's inner logic into an all-embracing theory of history (however ingeniously configured), is to subvert forever our ability to transform the world.

The use-value dimension of socio-material life and post-capitalist social change

In the second section above, 'Conventional Marxism and phases of capitalism', I contended that in fixating upon questions of historical directionality and assuming that the contours of socialism would be set by an organized capitalism as the outcome of such, conventional Marxism not only precluded creative thought about post-capitalist social change but actually provided very little basis for even the most rudimentary considerations on socialist construction. In contrast, the Uno approach constitutes a fecund ground for producing knowledge useful for building a post-capitalist future. Below I will discuss first how the Uno approach generates the most fundamental conceptualizations of socialism. And second, I will outline the way the Uno approach points to key structural directives for organizing material reproduction in a distinctly socialist fashion.

Because our grasp of what socialism entails is dependent upon knowledge of capitalism, it makes sense that the basic understanding of socialism should be derived from the clearest and most precise expression of capitalism. As such, I will now set forth the three cardinal principles of what I have dubbed an *ontology of socialism*, that emanate from the theory of a purely capitalist society. To begin, the theory of a purely capitalist society captures an abstract, 'upside-down', *reified* order in which responsibility for material reproduction is abdicated to an extra-human force. Thus, the first principle of an ontology of socialism which springs from it, is that *socialism constitutes a non-reified economy in which the responsibility for organizing material life is vested in human beings themselves*. Socialism accordingly is not as conventional Marxism suggests, an amelioration of the ills of capitalism, but its diametrical opposite.

Next, characteristic of material life in a purely capitalist society is the effacement of direct person-to-person relationships including those involving interpersonal domination and subordination. Premised upon this is capitalism's claim to be the embodiment of individual freedom, and to be a social order which suspends class conflict. The theory of a purely capitalist society establishes that capitalism is in fact a very peculiar class society, where on the basis of the commodification of labour-power, the direct producers are compelled to work solely by *economic* means. Socialism therefore demands the de-commodification of labour-power. But this must not be allowed to occur through the revival of extra-economic coercion, as was the case in Soviet-style societies, for capitalism already represents an historical advance over that. Hence the second principle of an ontology of socialism is that *socialism requires the de-commodification of labour-power without the reinstatement of extra-economic compulsion*.

Finally, if in a genuine socialist society work is to be compelled by neither economic nor extra-economic means, workers must become *self-motivated*.

Paradigmatically at least, such is impossible in capitalist society no matter how handsome the remuneration or benefits accruing to labour. For in recruiting workers as commodity-economic inputs to produce *any* good deemed appropriate for the satisfaction of its chrematistic of value augmentation, capital renders labour *indifferent* to use-value in production. Work, that most essential human activity upon which social life itself rests, therefore becomes, in capitalist society, something with which to secure only *future* enjoyment; that is, a disutility or 'alienated' (Sekine 1997, II: 217). The surmounting of alienation or worker indifference and the enabling of self-motivation in even the most arduous forms of work, demands what is here set forth as the third principle of an ontology of socialism: *the re-entrenchment of the use-value dimension of socio-material life*.

With Soviet-style centralized state planning discredited as the paradigm for future material existence, Marxists have divaricated into two grand camps of combatants on the question of the post-capitalist economic physiognomy: advocates of market socialism and defenders of democratic or participatory planning. The literature here is voluminous and even a cursory review of it would excede the bounds of this chapter.[6] However the debate provides a useful backdrop to the showcasing of the future directed power of the Uno approach. Hence I will briefly explore some of its central tenets referring to specific players only when necessary.

Advocates of market socialism can lay claim to the high ground, given how their arguments dovetail nicely with the perception that capitalism is transmutating towards a post-industrial society. In other words, working with the conventional Marxist view that socialism is prefigured by advanced capitalism, it could be said that Soviet-style actors jumped the gun and a disorganized capitalism is the wave of the socialist future. The high ground can be commanded as well on the basis of the dismal economic showing of Soviet-style socialism. At the dawn of the millennium it is argued, capitalism continues to 'deliver the goods'. Responsible for this state of affairs is purportedly 'the market' with its properties of efficiency and incentive – the former referring to the transmission of information to economic actors through price signals, the latter to the motivational effect of reaping the rewards of one's price-taking actions. Market socialism professes to harness the wellspring of capitalist success, yet decouple markets from capitalism proper, embedding them in a decentralized though non-private institutional matrix. The last-mentioned is the remedy for the unpalatable distributional outcomes of capitalism decried by those socialists.

Confronted with arguments for market socialism, defenders of economic planning have been pressing their case in several directions. The first is extolling the merits of as yet untested democratic or participatory forms of planning. The second is analyzing the elements of market operations celebrated by enthusiasts as the root of capitalist success in order to produce models of socialist planning that simulate or even trump them. Thirdly, the planning contingent continues to remind market socialist proponents of the social and ecological 'externalities' plaguing markets despite the glittering facade.

Strikingly, at no point is the debate forthcoming with a clear and consistent definition of what is actually meant by 'the market'. In fact, as suggested by Boyer (1997), such a lacuna tends to be endemic to much political economic writing! In any case, when a market socialist declares: 'We need an economy that will allow us to get on with our lives without having to worry so much about economic matters' (Schweickart 1998: 19), it is evident that what is being referred to is the self-regulating integrated market system of capitalism. The notion that the capitalist market can be decoupled from the capitalist mode of production reflects the unfolding of the debate over socialism within the parameters set by neo-classical economics which views the market as a transhistorical 'economic' institution. Marxian economics as discussed in section three regards capitalism as an historically transient order and problematizes its tendency to dissolve the direct face-to-face material relationships characteristic of past societies. The culmination of its enterprise is the theory of a purely capitalist society which exposes how market self-regulation involves the governance of the commodity-economic law of value that ensures the viability of capitalism as a historical society while pursuing its abstract chrematistic of value augmentation. Hence, though the redistributive goals of market socialists are commendable, models advocating the surrendering of control over material reproduction to an extra-human power (which necessarily requires the commodification of labour-power) must be disqualified as socialist.

Neo-classical influenced misapprehension of the *capitalist* market can also be detected in the wholesale occlusion of use-value in the discussion of socialism. Marxian economics demonstrates that a fully marketized or purely capitalist society can operate only on the assumption that all use-values are inactivated or neutralized. What the study of phases of capitalism in stage theory demonstrates however, is that real activated use-values place demands upon capital, forcing it to reconfigure its techno-economic structure of accumulation and enlist an array of non-economic and even non-capitalist supports to manage their production. The stage of liberalism, with cotton production as the characteristic form of use-value production around which capital accumulates, approximates most closely the market chrematistic exemplified in the theory of a purely capitalist society. The heavy and more complex use-values characteristic of imperialism and consumerism increasingly compromise the logic of capital, reinforcing the view that the utility of capital as the governing principle of human material reproduction is delimited to a relatively restricted range of possible human use-value wants. What is certain is that the use-value complexes beckoning humanity at the threshold of the twenty-first century – mass transportation systems, renewable energy sources, restructured urban and rural infrastructure, and so on – all explode the possibility of capitalist purveyance and by association that of market socialism.

Unfortunately, defences of democratic or participatory planning have not been immune to the effects of the neo-classical impelled neglect of use-value. This appears most glaringly through the very reduction of the question of economic planning to the simulation of the market 'calculation' of equilibrium prices. Within the context of neo-classical thought that holds the market to be suprahistoric, the technical or abstract bent of the issue appears unremarkable because the purpose of material reproduction in capitalist society – the production and augmentation of value – is itself abstract. Conventional Marxism for its part, expecting socialism to be prefigured by an organized capitalism and, moreover, never developing the potential of Marxian economic theory, never flagged this fact. In a genuine socialism, however, the society-wide commodity-economic sundering of production and consumption engendered by the capitalist market cannot be countenanced. The fact is that the marketized disinterest of the direct producers in use-value in production, their marketized indifference to the wherewithal and modalities of use-value production as consumers, the sum total enabling daily production of use-values with the potential to even destroy life on the planet itself, could actually be exacerbated by economic planning fixated largely upon the abstract and technical question of economic calculation. Instead, genuine socialist planning demands the *re-connection* of production and consumption that must develop around a concern over use-value and engender respect for the earth. This will necessarily entail the creative redesign of communities as well as creative thought about various forms of socio-material exchange and communication.[7]

Simulation of society-wide market coordination as the goal of socialist economic planning also undermines the fostering of genuine socialist forms of incentive. For example, in the attempt by Cockshott and Cottrell (1997) to solve the neo-classical inspired problem of economic calculation, democratic central planning is to achieve an optimal (equilibrium) balancing of inputs and outputs *vis-à-vis* information derived from direct calculation of labour time, transmitted through computer networks. However, without the economic compulsion of the capitalist market there exists a slip towards a sort of quasi-feudal arrangement deploying a 'poll tax', which 'establishes that all have the same *obligation* to work for the common good *before* they work for themselves' (Cockshott and Cottrell 1997: 345, emphasis added). In the model of Albert and Hahnel (1991; 1992), equilibration of supply and demand is to be effectuated through an iterative participatory planning process where decentralized micro-level consumers' and workers' councils make allocatory demands that are subject to revision according to information transmitted from relevant meso-and macro-level bodies. Again, in this universe of market-simulating abstract calculation, incentive to work and participate is to derive from 'peer pressure' (Albert and Hahnel 1992: 62), a fact aptly referred to as 'Orwellian' (Ticktin 1998a: 75). As intimated above, this sort of regression to forms of extra-economic coercion would be untenable for those with the historical experience of capitalism and the peculiar commodity-economic freedom that it offers. To constitute a genuine advance over capitalism work in a socialist society must become self-motivated; that is, compelled by neither extra-economic nor economic means. Accomplishing that requires the extirpation of the capitalist sundering of production and consumption and the indifference to use-value in production engendered by such. Thus if the notion of planning is to have a socialist substance, the *plan* must be to construct a society where material reproduction will be undertaken according to the principles of socialism.

Finally, recent efforts within the framework of bourgeois economics (Stiglitz 1994) have questioned the standard neo-classical account of the information transmitting property of markets and suggested that socialist models founded upon its unassailability would, if actually applied in the real world, never produce the desired outcome. Adding to this kind of work, has been argumentation from the perspective of the 'Austrian approach' to bourgeois economics (Kirzner 1997), to the effect that what constitutes the mainspring of capitalist vitality and innovativeness is not price-informed action, but economic *'discovery'* engaged in by entrepreneurs motivated by private gain and operating in an environment of competition. And that it is this entrepreneurial discovery process which stands as the ultimate test that a viable post-capitalist society must pass. Now it is not necessary (nor possible, given space limitations) to enter into discussion of how the theory of a purely capitalist society deals with the questions of capital's dynamic and equilibrative tendencies that have bifurcated bourgeois economics.[8] What needs to be said here, however, is this: first, like their neo-classical confederates, the Austrians never problematized use-value. Hence the 'horizons' that the Austrian entrepreneur is purportedly forever 'scanning' on the lookout for discoveries (Kirzner 1997: 72) are, as the Unoist study of phases of capitalism suggests, necessarily delimited to horizons of use-value production tractable for commodity-economic value. Second, I am in agreement with the important work of Adaman and Devine (1997: 75), that the 'tacit knowledge' of the discovery process is not the sole prerogative of an entrepreneurial cohort but actually quite widespread. And that its dynamic mobilization could be facilitated through socialist transformation that endows the wider social element with the appropriate capacities. My point is that this demands the reconnecting of production and consumption and re-embedding of material existence in use-value, the de-reification of socio-material communication, the creative redesign of communities, and the self-motivation of direct producers that such will engender.

Conclusion

I do not intend to recapitulate each point made in this chapter. Several however, do demand re-emphasis. To begin, in tethering Marx's project in *Capital* as well as the later study of phases of capitalism to a theory of historical directionality, conventional Marxism occluded that which was most valuable in Marx's research agenda: the production of knowledge of the logical inner workings of a peculiar reified society; knowledge that would provide the undergirding for the study of capitalism's historical accumulatory modalities as required, and which would constitute a prism for the study of material life *per se*. Standing at the cusp of the millennium, with the existence of Soviet-style socialism becoming ever more a distant memory, the claim that history evinces any kind of telos with a socialist outcome will certainly ring hollow in the ears of all but the most isolated cabals of paleo-Marxists. If the socialist enterprise is to be reinvigorated and have any purchase at the current conjuncture, it will have to be grounded on a fundamentally different and far more robust basis. My contention is that the Uno approach offers this. The Uno approach maintains that socialism does not spring from historical tendencies *deus ex machina*, nor will it be prefigured by some 'final stage' of capitalism. Rather, socialism will be the result of social action that is predicated upon the scientific understanding of material life flowing from the theory of a purely capitalist society which establishes the feasibility of socialism. I have further confirmed the future directed power of the Uno approach to political economy demonstrating how from its conceptual architecture of levels of analysis emanates an ontology of socialism and a set of concrete imperatives for its viable construction.

One final comment: critics are certain to argue that the far-reaching socio-material transformation required of a genuine socialism such as I have depicted is far too disruptive to induce a meaningful social constituency to strive for its realization. My response is simply to remind all, of the devastation and dislocation of the depression and wars punctuating the periods of transition between the capitalist phases of liberalism and imperialism and imperialism and consumerism. And for what did Western publics countenance this? Without entering into discussion over the degenerative tendencies of the current phase of capitalist development or whether there exists a use-value complex on the horizon able to sustain the march of value in history, the foreboding I have is that the human exertions and tumult involved in the making of the socialist future today will pale in comparison to that entailed in a non-socialist one tomorrow.

Notes

1 The defining monographs of the Uno approach are: Uno (1980 [1964]), an English version of Uno's abridgement of a two-volume work written in 1950–52; Sekine

(1997), a condensed version of idem (1986); and, Albritton (1991). The article literature is substantial. For a selection under one cover, see Albritton and Sekine (1995). Recent efforts include Albritton (1998); Westra (1999).

2 Sekine (1997) is the most up-to-date rendition of this theory.

3 What follows draws upon Sekine (1986, I: 37ff.).

4 Space allotments preclude a full defence of this controversial question. While there is no substitute to careful study of Sekine (1997; 1986), succinct defences of the nexus between the dialectic and social science include: Sekine (1980; 1998). On the scientific truth claims of the theory, see Albritton (1998; 1999).

5 Again, given the compass of the chapter, it is not possible to step too far into the thorny epistemological thicket here. See, for example, Albritton (1991; 1992; 1999).

6 Adaman and Devine (1997) offer what in my view is the most sophisticated overview of all the central questions regarding post-capitalist social change. Ollman (1998) provides an interesting introduction to the debate over market socialism.

7 As elaborated upon in the work of Itoh (1995), markets in the form in which they existed prior to the dawn of capitalism – in the 'interstices' of the ancient world, as extra-community, supplementary forms of material communication – may persist benignly in a socialist society.

8 Required reading here is Sekine (1997, II).

Bibliography and Select Readings

Achcar, G., ed. (1999) *Le Marxisme d'Ernest Mandel* (Paris: Presses Universitaires de France). Forthcoming in English as *The Legacy of Ernest Mandel* (London: Verso).

Adaman, F. and Devine, P. (1997) 'On the Economic Theory of Socialism', *New Left Review*, 221.

Aglietta, M. (1974) *Les Principaux Traits contemporains de l'internationalisation du capital* (Paris: INSEE).

Aglietta, M. (1979) *A Theory of Capitalist Regulation* (London: New Left Books).

Aglietta, M. (1998) 'Capitalism at the Turn of the Century: Regulation Theory and the Challenge of Social Change', *New Left Review*, 232.

Albert, M. (1993) *Capitalism Against Capitalism* (London: Whurr).

Albert, M. and Hahnel, R. (1991) *Looking Forward* (Boston: South End Press).

Albert, M. and Hahnel, R. (1992) 'Socialism as It Was always Meant to Be', *Review of Radical Political Economics*, 24(3/4).

Albritton, R. (1986) *A Japanese Reconstruction of Marxist Theory* (Basingstoke: Macmillan).

Albritton, R. (1991) *A Japanese Approach to Stages of Capitalist Development* (Basingstoke: Macmillan).

Albritton, R. (1992) 'Levels of Analysis in Marxian Political Economy: An Unoist Approach', *Radical Philosophy*, 60.

Albritton, R. (1995) 'Regulation Theory: A Critique', in Albritton and Sekine, *A Japanese*, op cit.

Albritton, R. (1998) 'The Unique Ontology of Capital', in L. Nowak and R. Panasiuk, eds, *Marx's Theories Today* (Amsterdam: Rodopi).

Albritton, R. (1999) *Dialectics and Deconstruction in Political Economy* (London: Macmillan).

Albritton, R. and Sekine, T., eds (1995) *A Japanese Approach to Political Economy: Unoist Variations* (London: Macmillan).

Althusser, L. (1970) *For Marx* (London: New Left Books).

Althusser, L. (1978) 'Avant-propos', in G. Duménil, *Le Concept de loi économique dans 'Le Capital'* (Paris: Maspéro).

Althusser, L. (1990) 'On Theoretical Work', in idem, *Philosophy and the Spontaneous Philosophy of the Scientists and Other Essays*, edited by G. Elliott (London: Verso).

Altvater, E. (1993) *The Future of the Market* (London: Verso).

Amin, A., ed. (1994) *Post-Fordism: A Reader* (Oxford: Blackwell).

Amin, S., Arrighi, G., Frank, A.G. and Wallerstein, I. (1982) *Dynamics of Global Crisis* (New York: Monthly Review Press).

Amineh, M. (1999) *Towards the Control of Oil Resources in the Caspian Region* (Muenster: Lit Verlag).

Amsden, A.H. (1989) *Asia's Next Giant* (New York: Oxford University Press).

Anderson J.L. (1991) *Explaining Long-Term Economic Change* (Basingstoke: Macmillan).

Anderson, P. (1997) 'Under the Sign of the Interim', in P. Anderson and P. Gowan, eds, *The Question of Europe* (London: Verso).

Armstrong, P., Glyn, A. and Harrison, J. (1991) *Capitalism since 1945*, second edition (Oxford: Blackwell).

Arrighi, G. (1978) *The Geometry of Imperialism* (London: New Left Books).

Arrighi, G. (1982) 'A Crisis of Hegemony', in Amin *et al.*, *Dynamics*, op cit.

Arrighi, G. (1989) 'Custom and Innovation: Long Waves and Stages of Capitalist Development', in Di Matteo *et al.*, *Technological*, op cit.

Arrighi, G. (1990a) 'Marxist Century – American Century: The Making and Remaking of the World Labor Movement', *New Left Review*, 179.

Arrighi, G. (1990b) 'The Three Hegemonies of Historical Capitalism', *Review*, 1990, 13(3).

Arrighi, G. (1994) *The Long Twentieth Century* (London: Verso).

Arrighi, G. (1996) 'Workers of the World at Century's End', *Review*, 19(3).

Arrighi, G. and Silver, B. (1999) *Chaos and Governance in the Modern World System* (Minneapolis: University of Minnesota Press).

Ashley, R.K. (1986) 'The Poverty of Neorealism', in R.O. Keohane, ed., *Neorealism and its Critics* (New York: Columbia University Press).

Aston, T.H. and Philpin, C.H.E., eds (1986) *The Brenner Debate* (Cambridge: Cambridge University Press).

Augelli, E. and Murphy, C.N. (1988) *America's Quest for Supremacy and the Third World: A Gramscian Analysis* (London: Pinter).

Awan, A. (1985) 'Marshallian and Schumpeterian Theories of Economic Evolution', *Atlantic Economic Journal*, 14.

Bairoch, P. and Kozul-Wright, R. (1998) 'Globalization Myths', in Kozul-Wright and Rowthorn, *Transnational Corporations*, op cit.

Baker, D., Epstein, G. and Pollin, R., eds (1998) *Globalization and Progressive Economic Policy* (Cambridge: Cambridge University Press).

Baran, P. (1957) *The Political Economy of Growth* (New York: Monthly Review Press).

Baran, P. and Sweezy, P. (1966) *Monopoly Capital* (New York: Monthly Review Press).

Bardhan, P.K. and Roemer, J.E., eds (1993) *Market Socialism* (Oxford: Oxford University Press).

Barker, B. (1978) 'The State as Capital', *International Socialism*, Second Series, 1.

Barr, K. (1979) 'Long Waves: A Selective Annotated Bibliography', *Review*, 2.

Barro, R.J. (1991) 'Economic Growth in a Cross Section of Countries', *Quarterly Journal of Economics*, 106.

Berger, S. and Dore, R., eds (1986) *National Diversity and Global Capitalism* (Ithaca: Cornell University Press).

Berle A and Means G. (1932) *The Modern Corporation and Private Property* (London: Macmillan).

Berry, B.J.L. (1991) *Long-Wave Rhythms in Economic Development and Political Behavior* (Baltimore: Johns Hopkins Press).

Bhaduri, A. (1998) 'Implications of Globalization for Macroeconomic Theory and Policy in Developing Countries', in Baker, *et al.*, *Globalization*, op cit.

Bhagwati, J. (1993) 'Aggressive Unilateralism: An Overview', in J. Bhagwati and H. Patrick, eds, *Aggressive Unilateralism* (Ann Arbor: University of Michigan Press)

Bidet, J. (1985) *Que faire du Capital?* (Paris: Klincksieck).

Bihr, A. (1989) *Entre Bourgeoisie et prolétariat: L'Encadrement capitaliste* (Paris: L'Harmattan).

Binns, P. (1975) 'The Theory of State Capitalism', *International Socialism*, First Series, 74.

Blackburn, R. (1991) 'Fin de Siècle: Socialism after the Crash', in R. Blackburn, ed., *After the Fall* (London: Verso).

Bladen-Hovell, R. and Symons, E. (1994) 'The EC Budget', in M. Artis and N. Lee, eds, *Economics of the European Union* (Oxford: Oxford University Press).

Block, F. (1977) *The Origins of International Economic Disorder* (Berkeley: University of California Press).

Block, F. (1990) *Postindustrial Possibilities* (Berkeley: University of California Press).

Boccara, P., ed. (1976) *Le Capitalisme monopoliste d'État* (Paris: Éditions Sociales).

Bonefeld, W., Gunn, R. and Psychopedis, C., eds (1992–95) *Open Marxism*, 3 volumes (London: Pluto).

Bonefeld, W. and Holloway, J. (1991) *Post-Fordism and Social Form* (London: Macmillan).

Bottomore, T., ed. (1991a) *A Dictionary of Marxist Thought*, second edition (London: Blackwell).

Bottomore, T. (1991b) 'Organized Capitalism', in idem, *A Dictionary*, op cit.

Bowles, S. (1985) 'The Production Process in a Competitive Economy: Walrasian, neoHobbesian and Marxist Models', *American Economic Review*, 75.

Bowles, S., Gordon, D. and Weisskopf, T. (1983) *Beyond the Waste Land* (Garden City: Anchor Press).

Bowles, S., Gordon, D. and Weisskopf, T. (1990) *After the Wasteland* (Armonk: M.E. Sharpe).

Boyer, R. (1986) *La Théorie de la regulation* (Paris: edition La Découverte).

Boyer, R. (1990) *The Regulation School* (New York: Columbia University Press).

Boyer, R. (1997) 'The Variety and Performance of Really Existing Markets', in Hollingsworth and Boyer, *Contemporary Capitalism*, op cit.

Boyer, R. (1998) 'The Pyrrhic Victory of Anglo-Saxon Capitalism', *Thesis Eleven*, 53.

Boyer, R. and Mistral, J. (1978) *Accumulation, Inflation, Crises* (Paris: Presses Universitaires de France).

Brand, U., and Görg, C. (1998) 'Nachhaltige Widersprüche: Die Rolle von NRO in der internationalen Biodiversitätspolitik', *Peripherie*, 71.

Braudel, F. (1981) *Civilization and Capitalism*, Volume I. *The Structures of Everyday Life* (New York: Harper and Row).

Braudel, F. (1982) *Civilization and Capitalism*, Volume II. *The Wheels of Commerce* (New York: Harper and Row).

Braudel, F. (1984) *Civilization and Capitalism*, Volume III. *The Perspective of the World* (New York: Harper and Row).

Braverman, H. (1974) *Labor and Monopoly Capital* (New York: Monthly Review Press).

Brennan, T. (1995) 'Why the Time is Out of Joint', *Strategies*, 9–10.

Brenner, N. (1999) 'Beyond State-Centrism? Space, Territoriality, and Geographical Scale in Globalisation Studies', *Theory and Society*, 28(1).

Brenner, R. (1977) 'The Origins of Capitalist Development: A Critique of Neo-Smithian Marxism', *New Left Review*, 104.

Brenner, R. (1986) 'The Social Basis of Economic Development', in J. Roemer, ed., *Analytical Marxism* (Cambridge: Cambridge University Press).

Brenner, R. (1998) 'Economics of Global Turbulence', *New Left Review*, 229.

Brenner, R. and Glick, M. (1991) 'The Regulation Approach: Theory and History', *New Left Review*, 188.

Brewer, A. (1990) *Marxist Theories of Imperialism*, second edition (London: Routledge).

Bryan, D. (1995) *The Chase Across the Globe: International Accumulation and the Contradictions for Nation States* (Boulder: Westview).

Bukharin, N.I. (1971) *The Economics of the Transformation Period* (New York: Bergman).

Bukharin, N.I. (1972) *Imperialism and World Economy* (London: Merlin).

Burnham, J. (1945) *The Managerial Revolution* (Harmondsworth: Penguin).

Burnham, P. (1991) 'Neo-Gramscian Hegemony and the International Order', *Capital and Class*, 45.

Callari, A. and Ruccio, D.F. (1996a) 'Introduction' in idem, *Postmodern*, op cit.

Callari, A. and Ruccio, D.F., eds (1996b) *Postmodern Materialism and the Future of Marxist Theory* (Hanover: Wesleyan University Press).

Callinicos, A. (1987a) 'Imperialism, Capitalism, and the State Today', *International Socialism*, Second Series, 35.

Callinicos, A. (1987b) *Making History* (Cambridge: Polity).

Callinicos, A. (1989) *Against Postmodernism* (Cambridge: Polity).

Callinicos, A. (1995) *Theories and Narratives* (Cambridge: Polity).

Callinicos, A. (1996) 'Betrayal and Discontent: Labour Under Blair', *International Socialism*, Second Series, 72.

Callinicos, A. (1999) 'Capitalism, Competition and Profits: A Critique of Robert Brenner's Theory of Crisis', *Historical Materialism*, 4.

Callinicos, A., Rees, J., Harman, C. and Haynes, M. (1994) *Marxism and the New Imperialism* (London: Bookmarks)

Cameron, R. (1991) *Economische wereldgeschiedenis* (Utrecht: Spectrum).

Carchedi, B. (1999) 'Colpirne uno per educarne cento', *Alternative Europa*, Giugno, 13.

Carchedi, B. and Carchedi, G. (1999) 'Contradictions of European Integration', *Capital and Class*, 67.

Carchedi, G. (1991) *Frontiers of Political Economy* (London: Verso).

Carchedi, G. (1997) 'The EMU, Monetary Crises and the Single European Currency', *Capital and Class*, 63.

Carchedi, G. (1999) 'A Missed Opportunity: Orthodox Versus Marxist Crises Theories', *Historical Materialism*, 4.

Castells, M. (1996) *The Rise of the Network Society* (Oxford: Blackwell).

Castells, M. (1998) *End of Millennium* (Oxford: Blackwell).

Chandler, A.D. (1977) *The Visible Hand* (Cambridge: Harvard University Press).

Chandler, A.D. (1990) *Scale and Scope* (Cambridge: Harvard).

Chase-Dunn, C. (1985) 'Interstate System and Capitalist World-Economy: One Logic or Two?', in W. Hollist and J. Rosenau, eds, *World-System Structure* (Beverly Hills: Sage).

Chauvel, L. (1995) 'Inégalités singulières et plurielles', *Revue de l'OFCE*, n. 55, Oct.

Chomsky, N. (1998) 'Power in the Global Arena', *New Left Review*, 230.

Chuter, D. (1997) 'The United Kingdom', in J. Howorth and A. Menon, eds, *The European Union and National Defence Policy* (London: Routledge).

Clarke, S. (1983) 'State, Class Struggle, and the Reproduction of Capital', *Kapitalistate*, 10/11.

Clarke, S. (1988a) *Keynesianism, Monetarism and the Crisis of the State* (Cheltenham: Edward Elgar).

Clarke, S. (1988b) 'Overaccumulation, Class Struggle and the Regulation Approach', *Capital and Class*, 36.

Clarke, S. (1989) 'The Basic Theory of Capitalism: A Critical Review of Itoh and the Uno School', *Capital and Class*, 37.

Clarke, S. (1990a) 'New Utopias for Old: Fordist Dreams and Post-Fordist Fantasies', *Capital and Class*, 42.

Clarke, S. (1990b) 'The Crisis of Fordism or the Crisis of Social-Democracy?', *Telos*, 83.

Clarke, S. (1990c) *The State Debate* (London: Macmillan).

Clarke, S. (1992) 'The Global Accumulation of Capital and the Periodisation of the Capitalist State Form', in Bonefeld *et al.*, *Open Marxism*, op cit., volume I.

Clarke, S. (1994) *Marx's Theory of Crisis* (Harmondsworth: Macmillan).

Clarke, S. (1999) 'Capitalist Competition and the Tendency to Overproduction: Comments on Brenner's "Uneven Development and the Long Downturn"', *Historical Materialism*, 4.

Clarke, S., Fairbrother, P., Burawoy, M. and Krotov, P. (1993) *What about the Workers?* (London: Verso).

Cleaver, H. (1979) *Reading Capital Politically* (Brighton: Harvester).

Cliff, T. (1974) *State Capitalism in Russia* (London: Pluto).

Clifton, J. (1977) 'Competition and the Evolution of the Capitalist Mode of Production', *Cambridge Journal of Economics*, 1(2).

Coates, D. (2000) *Models of Capitalism* (Cambridge: Polity).

Cockshott, W.P. and Cottrell, A.F. (1997) 'Value, Markets and Socialism', *Science and Society*, 61(3).

Collier, P. and Gunning, J. (1999) 'Explaining African Economic Performance', *Journal of Economic Literature*, 37(1).

Collinge, C.J. (1996) 'Self-Organisation of Society by Scale: A Spatial Reworking of Regulation Theory', *Society and Space*, 17(5).

Coombs, R.W. (1983) 'Long Waves and Labour Process Change', in Freeman, ed., *Long Waves*, op cit.

Corbridge, S., Martin, R. and Thrift, N., eds (1994) *Money, Power and Space* (Oxford: Blackwell).

Council of Economic Advisers to the President of the United States (CEA) (1999) *Economic Report of the President, 1999* (Washington: Government Printing Office).

Cowling, K. (1982) *Monopoly Capitalism* (New York: John Wiley).

Cowling, K. and Sugden, R. (1987) *Transnational Monopoly Capitalism* (New York: St Martin's).

Cox, R.W. (1987) *Production, Power and World Order* (New York: Columbia University Press).

Cox, R.W. (1991) '"Real Socialism" in Historical Perspective', *Socialist Register 1991* (London: Merlin).

Cox, R.W. (1999) 'Civil Society at the Turn of the Millennium', *Review of International Studies*, 25(1).

Crotty, J. (1990) 'Keynes on the Stages of Development of the Capitalist Economy', *Journal of Economic Issues*, 24(3).

Crouch, C. and Streeck, W. (1997) *Political Economy of Modern Capitalism* (London: Sage).

Cullenberg, S. (1994) *The Falling Rate of Profit* (London: Pluto).

Curry, J. (1993) 'The Flexibility Fetish', *Capital and Class*, 50.

Cutler, A., Hindess, B., Hirst, P. and Hussain, A. (1977–78) *Marx's 'Capital' and Capitalism Today*, 2 volumes (London: Routledge & Kegan Paul).

Davis, J.B., ed. (1992) *The Economic Surplus in Advanced Economics* (Brookfield: Edward Elgar).

Davis, M. (1978) 'Fordism in Crisis: A Review of Michel Aglietta's *Regulation et crises du capitalisme*', *Review*, 2(2).

Davis, M. (1986) *Prisoners of the American Dream* (London: Verso).

Day, R.B. (1976) 'The Theory of Long Waves: Kondratiev, Trotsky, Mandel', *New Left Review*, 99.

Day, R.B. (1981) *The 'Crisis' and the 'Crash'* (London: New Left Books).

de Long, J.B. and Summers, L.H. (1991) 'Equipment Investment and Economic Growth', *Quarterly Journal of Economics*, 106.

de Vroey, M. (1979) 'Value, Production, and Exchange', in I. Steedman *et al.*, *The Value Controversy* (London: New Left Books).

de Vroey, M. (1984) 'A Regulation Approach Interpretation of the Contemporary Crisis', *Capital and Class*, 23.

DeMartino, G. (1993) 'The Necessity/Contingency Dualism in Marxian Crisis Theory: The Case of the Long-Wave Theory', *Review of Radical Political Economics*, 25(3).

Demirovic, A. (1997) 'Nachhaltige Entwicklung, Transformation der Staatlichkeit und globale Zivilgesellschaft', in A. Demirovic, ed., *Demokratie und Herrschaft* (Münster: Westfälisches Dampfboot).

Deyo, F.C. (1990) 'Economic Policy and the Popular Sector', in G. Gereffi and D.L. Wyman, eds, *Manufacturing Miracles* (Princeton: Princeton University Press).

Di Matteo, M., Goodwin, M. and Vercelli, A., eds (1989) *Technological and Social Factors in Long Term Fluctuations* (New York: Springer-Verlag).

Dicken, P. (1986) *Global Shift* (London: Harper & Row).

Dicken, P. (1992) *Global Shift*, Second Edition (London: Paul Chapman).

Dinucci, M. (1998) 'La Nuova Strategia della NATO', *L'Ernesto*, March-April.

Dirlik, A. (1994) *After the Revolution* (Hanover: Wesleyan University Press).

Dosi, G., *et al.*, eds (1988) *Technical Change and Economic Theory* (London: Pinter).

Drucker, P. (1986) 'The Changed World Economy', *Foreign Affairs*, 64(4).

Duménil, G. (1978) *Le Concept de loi économique dans 'Le Capital'* (Paris: Maspéro).

Duménil, G. and Lévy, D. (1993) *The Economics of the Profit Rate* (Aldershot: Edward Elgar).

Duménil, G. and Lévy, D. (1994a) 'The Emergence and Functions of Managerial and Clerical Personnel in Marx's Capital', in N. Garston, ed., *Bureaucracy* (Boston: Kluwer Academic).

Duménil, G. and Lévy, D. (1994b) *The U.S. Economy since the Civil War* (Paris: CEPREMAP).

Duménil, G. and Lévy, D. (1996) *La Dynamique du capital: Un siècle d'économie américaine* (Paris: Presses Universitaires de France).

Duménil, G. and Lévy, D. (1998) *Au-delà du Capitalisme?* (Paris: Presses Universitaires de France).

Duménil, G. and Lévy, D. (1999a) 'Structural Unemployment in the Crisis of the Late Twentieth Century: A Comparison between the European and the US Experiences', in R. Bellofiore, ed., *Global Money* (Aldershot: Edward Elgar).

Duménil, G. and Lévy, D. (1999b) 'Pre-Keynesian Themes at Brookings', in L. Pasinetti and B. Schefold, ed., *The Impact of Keynes on Economics in the 20th Century* (Aldershot: Edward Elgar).

Duménil, G. and Lévy, D. (1999c) *Costs and Benefits of Neoliberalism: A Class Analysis* (Paris: CEPREMAP). Forthcoming in *New Left Review*.

Duménil, G. and Lévy, D. (1999d) 'Brenner on Distribution', *Historical Materialism*, 4.

Duménil, G., Glick, M. and Lévy, D. (1997) 'The History of Competition Policy as Economic History', *The Antitrust Bulletin*, xlii(2).

Duncan, C.A.M. (1996) *The Centrality of Agriculture* (Montreal: McGill-Queen's University Press).

Dunford, M. (1990) 'Theories of Regulation', *Society and Space*, 8(3).

Economic Commission for Europe (1959) *Long-term Trends and Problems of the European Steel Industry* (Geneva: United Nations).

Economic Report of the President (various years) (Washington: United States Government Printing Office).

Elchardus, M. (1988) 'The Rediscovery of Chronos', *International Sociology*, 3(1).

Esser, J. and Hirsch, J. (1987) 'Stadtsoziologie und Gesellschaftstheorie', in W. Prigge, ed., *Die Materialität des Städtischen* (Basel: Birkhäuser).

Europa van Morgen (1996), Number 16, October 23.

Evans, D. (1989) *Comparative Advantage and Growth* (London: Macmillan).

Evans, G. and Newnham, J. (1992) *The Dictionary of World Politics*, Revised Edition (New York: Harvester Wheatsheaf).

Evans, P. (1979) *Dependent Development* (Princeton: Princeton University Press).

Fairley, J. (1980) 'French Developments in the Theory of State Monopoly Capitalism', *Science and Society*, 44(3).

Farjoun, E. and Machover, E. (1983) *Laws of Chaos: A Probabilistic Account of Political Economy* (London: Verso).

Financial Times, September 18, 1995.

Fine, B. (1984) *Macroeconomics and Monopoly Capitalism* (Brighton: Wheatsheaf).

Fine, B. and Harris, L. (1979) *Rereading Capital* (New York: Columbia University Press).

Fine, B., Lapavitsas, C. and Milonakis, D. (1999) 'Addressing the World Economy: Two Steps Back', *Capital and Class*, 67.

Fischer, S. (1988) 'Symposium on the Slowdown in Productivity Growth', *Journal of Economic Perspectives*, 2(4).

Foot, S.P.H. and Webber, M.J. (1990a) 'State, Class and International Capital 1: Background to the Brasilian Steel Industry', *Antipode*, 22.

Foot, S.P.H. and Webber, M.J. (1990b) 'State, Class and International Capital 2: The Development of the Brasilian Steel Industry', *Antipode*, 22.

Forrester, J. (1976) 'Business Structure, Economic Cycles and National Policy', *Futures*, 8.

Forstner, H. and Ballance, R. (1990) *Competing in a Global Economy* (London: Uwin Hyman).

Foster, J.B. (1986) *The Theory of Monopoly Capitalism* (New York: Monthly Review Press).

Foster, J.B. (1988) 'The Fetish of Fordism', *Monthly Review*, 39.

Foster, J.B. and Szlajfer, H. (1984) *The Faltering Economy: The Problem of Accumulation under Monopoly Capitalism* (New York: Monthly Review Press).

Frank, A.G. (1998) *ReOrient* (Berkeley: University of California Press).

Frantzen, D.J. (1990) *Growth and Crisis in Post-War Capitalism* (Dartmouth: Gower House).

Freeman, A. (1988) 'The Crash of '87: The Crash', *Capital and Class*, 34.

Freeman, A. (1996a) 'The Poverty of Nations', *Links*, 7.

Freeman, A. (1996b) 'Ernest Mandel's Contribution to Economic Dynamics', Presented to the International Institute for Research and Education, Amsterdam, November. (CONTACT a.freeman@greenwich.ac.uk)

Freeman, A. (1997) 'Time, the Value of Money and the Quantification of Value', Presented to the 1997 Conference of the Eastern Economic Association (available at http://www.greenwich.ac.uk/~fa03).

Freeman, A. (1998) 'The Emperor's Tailor: The Economists and the Crash of '98', Presented to the 1998 Conference of the Eastern Economic Association (available at http://www.greenwich.ac.uk/~fa03).

Freeman, A. (2000) 'Crisis and the Poverty of Nations: Two Market Products Which Value Explains Better', *Historical Materialism*, 5.

Freeman, A. and Carchedi, G. (1995) *Marx and Non-Equilibrium Economics* (Cheltenham: Edward Elgar).

Freeman, C., ed. (1983) *Long Waves in the World Economy* (London: Frances Pinter).

Freeman, C., ed. (1996) *Long Wave Theory* (Cheltenham: Edward Elgar).

Freeman, C. and Perez, C. (1988) 'Structural Crises of Adjustment: Business Cycles and Investment Behaviour', in Dosi, *et al.*, *Technical Change*, op cit.

Freeman, C., Clark, J.A. and Soete, L. (1982) *Unemployment and Technical Innovation* (London: Pinter).

Friedman, A. (1977) *Industry and Labour* (London: Macmillan)

Frobel, F, Heinrichs, J. and Kreye, O. (1980) *The New International Division of Labour* (Cambridge: Cambridge University Press).

Froud, J., *et al.* (1999) 'The Third Way and the Jammed Economy', *Capital and Class*, 67.

Frow, J. (1996) 'Information as Gift and Commodity', *New Left Review*, 219.

Fukuyama, F. (1992) *The End of History and the Last Man*, 2 volumes (Tokyo: Mikasashobo).

Funke, R. (1978) 'Sich durchsetzender Kapitalismus', in *Starnberger Studien*, vol. 2 (Frankfurt: Suhrkamp).

Galbraith, J.K. (1967) *The New Industrial State* (Boston: Houghton Mifflin).

Galtung, J. (1972) *De EEG als Nieuwe Supermacht* (Amsterdam: van Gennep).

Gannage, C. (1980) 'E.S. Varga and the Theory of State Monopoly Capitalism', *Review of Radical Political Economics*, 12(3).

Gibson-Graham, J.K. (1996) *The End of Capitalism (as We Knew It): A Feminist Critique of Political Economy* (Oxford: Blackwell).

Gill, S. (1990) *American Hegemony and the Trilateral Commission* (Cambridge: Cambridge University Press).

Gill, S., ed. (1993) *Gramsci, Historical Materialism and International Relations* (Cambridge: Cambridge University Press).

Gill, S. (1995) 'The Global Panopticon? The Neoliberal State, Economic Life, and Democratic Surveillance', *Alternatives*, 20(1).

Gill, S. (1998) 'European Governance and the New Constitutionalism', *New Political Economy*, 3(1).

Goldstein, J. (1987) *Long Cycles* (New Haven: Yale University Press).

Goodwin, R. (1982), *Essays in Economic Dynamics* (London: Macmillan).

Gordon, D. (1978) 'Up and Down the Long Roller Coaster', in URPE, eds, *U.S. Capitalism in Crisis* (New York: Union for Radical Political Economics).

Gordon, D. (1980) 'Stages of Accumulation and Long Economic Cycles', in Hopkins and Wallerstein, *Processes*, op cit.

Gordon, D. (1988) 'The Global Economy: New Edifice or Crumbling Foundations?', *New Left Review*, 168.

Gordon, D., Edwards, R. and Reich, M. (1982) *Segmented Work, Divided Workers* (Cambridge: Cambridge University Press).

Gottdiener, M. and Komninos, N., eds (1989) *Capitalist Development and Crisis Theory* (Basingstore: Macmillan).

Gough, J. and Eisenschitz, A. (1996) 'The Modernization of Britain and Local Economic Policy: Promise and Contradictions', *Society and Space*, 14(2).

Gowan, P. (1999) *The Global Gamble: Washington's Faustian Bid for World Dominance* (London: Verso).

Graham, J. (1991) 'Fordism/Post-Fordism, Marxism/Post-Marxism', *Rethinking Marxism*, 4(1).

Gramsci, A. (1977) *Selections from Political Writings 1910–1920* (New York: International Publishers).

Griliches, Z. (1988) 'Productivity Puzzles and R&D: Another nonExplanation', *Journal of Economic Perspectives*, 2(4).

Gronow, J. (1986) *On the Formation of Marxism* (Helsinki: Finnish Society of Sciences and Letters).

Grossman, G.M. and Helpman, E. (1991) *Innovation and Growth in the Global Economy* (Cambridge: MIT Press).

Grossman, G.M. and Helpman, E. (1994) 'Endogenous Innovation in the Theory of Growth', *Journal of Economic Perspectives*, 8.

Gulalp, H. (1989) 'The Stages and Long-Cycles of Capitalist Development', *Review of Radical Political Economics*, 21(4).

Hall, H.D. (1971) *Commonwealth* (London: Van Nostrand Reinhold).

Hall, P. and Preston, P. (1988) *The Carrier Wave* (London: Unwin Hyman).

Hall, S. and Jacques, M., eds (1989) *New Times* (London: Lawrence & Wishart).

Hamilton, C. (1987) 'Price Formation and Class Relations in the Development Process', *Journal of Contemporary Asia*, 17.

Harman, C. (1978) 'Mandel's *Late Capitalism*', *International Socialism*, Second Series, 1.

Harman, C. (1984) *Explaining the Crisis* (London: Bookmarks, New Edition 1999).

Harman, C. (1996) 'Globalization: A Critique of a New Orthodoxy', *International Socialism*, Second Series, 73.

Harris, L. (1991) 'Monopoly Capitalism', in Bottomore, *A Dictionary*, op cit.

Harris, L. (1991a) 'Periodization of Capitalism', in Bottomore, *A Dictionary*, op cit.

Harris, L. (1991b) 'State Monopoly Capitalism', in Bottomore, *A Dictionary*, op cit.

Harrison, B. (1987) 'Cold Bath or Restructuring? An Expansion of the Weisskkopf–Bowles–Gordon Framework', *Science and Society*, 51(1).

Harrison, B. and Bluestone, B. (1988) *The Great U-Turn* (New York: Basic Books).

Harrod, R.F. (1937) *An Essay on Dynamics* (London: Macmillan).

Harvey, D. (1982) *The Limits to Capital* (Chicago: Chicago University Press).

Harvey, D. (1989) *The Condition of Postmodernity* (Oxford: Blackwell).

Harvey, D. (1995) 'Globalization in Question', *Rethinking Marxism* 8(8).

Harvey, J. (1996) 'Orthodox Approaches to Exchange Rate Determination: A Survey', *Journal of Post-Keynesian Economics*, 18(4).

Haupt, G. (1982) 'Marx and Marxism', in E. Hobsbawm, ed., *The History of Marxism*, volume 1 (Bloomington: Indiana University Press).

Helleiner, E. (1994) *States and the Reemergence of Global Finance* (London: Cornell University Press).

Hexner, E. (1943) *The International Steel Cartel* (Chapel Hill: University of North Carolina Press).

Hilferding, R. (1981) *Finance Capital: A Study of the Latest Phase of Capitalist Development* (London: Routledge & Kegan Paul).

Hirsch, J. (1991) 'Fordism and Post-Fordism – The Present Social Crisis and its Consequences', in Bonefeld and Holloway, *Post-Fordism*, op cit.

Hirsch, J. (1993) 'Internationale Regulation', *Das Argument*, 198.

Hirsch, J. (1995a) *Der nationale Wettbewerbsstaat* (Berlin: Edition ID-Archiv).

Hirsch, J. (1995b) 'Nation-State, International Regulation and the Question of Democracy', *Review of International Political Economy*, 2(2).

Hirst, P. and Thompson, G. (1996) *Globalization in Question* (Cambridge: Polity).

Hirst, P. and Zeitlin, J. (1991) 'Flexible Specialization versus Post-Fordism', *Economy and Society*, 20(1).

Historical Materialism (1999), 'Symposium: Robert Brenner and the World Crisis (Part 1)', 4.

Hobsbawm, E. (1987) *The Age of Empire 1875–1914* (New York: Pantheon Books).

Hobson, J. (1938) *Imperialism: A Study* (London: Allen & Unwin).

Hoekman, B. and Kostecki, M. (1995) *Political Economy of the World Economy* (Oxford: Oxford University Press).

Hollingsworth, J.R. and Boyer, R. (1997) *Contemporary Capitalism: The Embeddedness of Institutions* (Cambridge: Cambridge University Press).

Holloway, J. and Picciotto, S., eds (1978) *State and Capital* (London: Edward Arnold).

Holman, O. (1998) 'Integrating Eastern Europe: EU Expansion and the Double Transformation in Poland, the Czech Republic, and Hungary', *International Journal of Political Economy*, 28(2).

Holman, O. and van der Pijl, K. (1996) 'The Capitalist Class in the European Union', in G. Kourvetaris and A. Moschonas, eds, *The Impact of European Integration* (Westport: Praeger).

Hoogvelt, A. (1997) *Globalisation and the Postcolonial World* (Basingstoke: Macmillan).

Hopkins, T. and Wallerstein, I., eds (1980) *Processes of the World-System* (Beverly Hills: Sage).

Hough, J. (1990) *Russia and the West* (New York: Simon & Schuster).

Houweling, H.W. (1999) 'The Limits to Growth na ruim 25 jaar', *Transaktie*, 28(1).

Howard, M.C. and King, J.E. (1992) *A History of Marxian Economics*, 2 volumes (Princeton: Princeton University Press).

Howell, M. (1998) 'Asia's 'Victorian' Financial Crisis', Presented to the East Asia Crisis workshop at the Institute of Development Studies, http://www.ids.ac.uk/ids/research/howell.pdf.

Howorth, J. (1997) 'National Defence and European Security Integration', in J. Howorth and A. Menon, eds, *The European Union and National Defence Policy* (London: Routledge).

Howorth, J. and Menon, A. eds (1997) *The European Union and National Defence Policy* (London: Routledge).

Hübner, K. (1990) ' "Wer die Macht hat, kann sich alles erlauben!" Anmerkungen zu den Konzepten Hegemonie – Dominanz – Macht – Kooperation in der globalen Ökonomie', *Prokla*, 81, 20(4).

Hübner, K. (1996) 'Globalisierung, Hegemonie und die Aufwertung des Regionalen', in M. Bruch and H-P. Krebs, eds, *Unternehmen Globus* (Münster: Westfälisches Dampfboot).

Husson, M. (1996) *Misère du capital* (Paris: Syros).

Hutton, W. (1996) *The State We're In*, revised edition (London: Vintage).

Hyman, R. (1988) 'Flexible Specialization: Miracle or Myth?', in R. Hyman and W. Streeck, eds, *New Technology and Industrial Relations* (Oxford: Blackwell).

International Monetary Fund (1998) *International Financial Statistics, Second Quarter* (Washington: IMF, CD-ROM).

Itoh, M. (1980) *Value and Crisis* (New York: Monthly Review Press).

Itoh, M. (1988) *The Basic Theory of Capitalism* (London: Macmillan).

Itoh, M. (1990) *The World Economic Crisis and Japanese Capitalism* (London: Macmillan).

Itoh, M. (1995) *Political Economy for Socialism* (London: Macmillan).

Jameson, F. (1984) 'Postmodernism, or The Cultural Logic of Late Capitalism', *New Left Review*, 146.

Jameson, F. (forthcoming) 'The Indeterminacies of Perry Anderson', forthcoming in a collection edited by Robert Brenner.

Jenkins, R. (1987) *Transnational Corporations and Uneven Development* (London: Methuen).

Jessop, B. (1982) *The Capitalist State* (Oxford: Blackwell).

Jessop, B. (1983) 'Accumulation Strategies, State Forms, and Hegemonic Projects', *Kapitalistate*, 10/11.

Jessop, B. (1990a) 'Regulation Theory in Retrospect and Prospect', *Economy and Society*, 19(2).

Jessop, B. (1990b) *State Theory* (Cambridge: Polity).

Jessop, B. (1991a) 'Polar Bears and Class Struggle: Much Less than a Self-Criticism', in Bonefeld and Holloway, *Post-Fordism*, op cit.

Jessop, B. (1991b) *The Politics of Flexibility* (Aldershot: Edward Elgar).

Jessop, B. (1992) 'Fordism and Post-Fordism: A Critical Reformulation', in Storper and Scott, *Pathways*, op cit.

Jessop, B. (1993) 'Towards a Schumpeterian Workfare State', *Studies in Political Economy*, 40.

Jessop, B. (1994) 'Post-Fordism and the State', in Amin, *Post-Fordism*, op cit.

Jessop, B. (1997a) 'Capitalism and its Future: Remarks on Regulation, Government, and Governance', *Review of International Political Economy*, 4(3).

Jessop, B. (1997b) 'Die Zukunft des Nationalstaates: Erosion oder Reorganisation?', in S. Becker, T. Sablowski and W. Schumm, eds, *Jenseits der Nationalökonomie?* (Hamburg: Argument).

Jessop, B. (1997c) 'Twenty Years of the Regulation Approach: The Paradox of Success and Failure at Home and Abroad', *New Political Economy*, 2(3).

Kautsky, K. (1936) *The Economic Doctrines of Karl Marx* (New York: Macmillan).

Kelly, K. (1998) *New Rules for the New Economy* (London: Fourth Estate).

Kenney, M. and Florida, R. (1993) *Beyond Mass Production* (New York: Oxford University Press).

Kenwood, A.G. and Lougheed, A.L. (1971) *The Growth of the International Economy 1820–1960* (London: Allen & Unwin).

Kidron, M. (1970) *Western Capitalism since the War* (Harmondsworth: Penguin).

Kindleberger, C.P. (1973) *The World in Depresession 1929–1939* (London: Allen Lane).

Kirzner, I.M. (1997) 'Entrepreneurial Discovery and the Competitive Market Process: An Austrian Approach', *Journal of Economic Literature*, 35.

Kleinknecht, A. (1987) *Innovation Patterns in Crisis and Prosperity* (London: Macmillan).

Kleinknecht, A., Mandel, E. and Wallerstein, I., eds (1992) *New Findings in Long-Wave Research* (New York: St Martin's).

Kondratiev, N.D. (1935) 'The Long Waves in Economic Life', *Review of Economic Statistics*, 17.

Kotz, D. (1987) 'Long Waves and Social Structures of Accumulation', *Review of Radical Political Economics*, 19(4).

Kotz, D. (1990) A Comparative Analysis of the Theory of Regulation and the Social Structure of Accumulation Theory', *Science and Society*, 54(1).

Kotz, D., McDonough, T. and Reich, M., eds (1994) *Social Structures of Accumulation* (Cambridge: Cambridge University Press).

Kotz, D., with Weir, F. (1997) *Revolution from Above: The Demise of the Soviet System* (London: Routledge).

Kozul-Wright, R. and Rowthorn, R., eds, (1998) *Transnational Corporations and the Global Economy* (New York: St Martins's).

Krüger, S. (1986) *Allgemeine Theorie der Kapitalakkumulation* (Hamburg: VSA).

Kundnani, A. (1998–9) 'Where do you want to go Today? The Rise of Information Capital', *Race and Class*, 40(2–3).

Kurth, J. (1979) 'The Political Consequences of the Product Cycle', *International Organization*, 33(1).

Kuczynski, T. (1985) 'Marx and Engels on Long Waves', in Vasko, *The Long Wave*, op cit.

Kuznets, S. (1930) *Secular Movements in Production and Prices* (New York: Houghton Mifflin).

Kuznets, S. (1952) *Income and Wealth of the United States* (Baltimore: Johns Hopkins Press).

Labergott, S. (1996) 'Labour Force and Employment, 1800–1960', in NBER, *Output, Employment, and Productivity in the United States after 1800* (New York: Columbia University Press).

Laibman, D. (1991) *Value, Technical Change, and Crisis* (New York: M.E. Sharpe).

Lakatos, I. (1978) *Philosophical Papers*, 2 volumes (Cambridge: Cambridge University Press).

Landes, D.S. (1969) *The Unbound Prometheus* (Cambridge: Cambridge University Press).

Lane, C. (1995) *Industry and Society in Europe* (Aldershot: Edward Elgar).

Lash, S. and Urry, J. (1987) *The End of Organized Capitalism* (Cambridge: Polity Press).

330 *Bibliography and Select Readings*

Leborgne, D. and Lipietz, A. (1991) 'Two Social Strategies in the Production of New Industrial Spaces', in G. Benko and M. Dunford, eds, *Industrial Change and Regional Development* (London: Belhaven Press).

Leborgne, D. and Lipietz, A. (1992) 'Conceptual Fallacies and Open Questions on Post-Fordism', in Storper and Scott, *Pathways*, op cit.

Lebowitz, M. (1985) 'The Theoretical Status of Monopoly Capital', in Resnick and Wolff, *Rethinking Marxism*, op cit.

Lebowitz, M. (1999) 'In Brenner, Everything is Reversed', *Historical Materialism*, 4.

Lefebvre, H. (1976) *De l'Etat*, 4 volumes (Paris: Union Generales).

Lefèbvre, Henri (1991) *The Production of Space* (Oxford: Blackwell).

Lenin, V.I. (1952) 'Imperialism: The Highest Stage of Capitalism', in *Selected Works*, volume I (Moscow: Foreign Languages Publishing House).

Lenin, V.I. (1965) *Imperialism: The Highest Stage of Capitalism* (Peking: Foreign Languages Press).

Levine, D. (1975) 'The Theory of the Growth of the Capitalist Economy', *Economic Development and Cultural Change*, 23.

Levine, R. and Renelt, D. (1992) 'A Sensitivity Analysis of Cross-Country Growth Regressions', *American Economic Review*, 82.

Lipietz, A. (1986a) 'Behind the Crisis: The Exhaustion of a Regime of Accumulation. A "Regulation School" Perspective on some French Empirical Work', *Review of Radical Political Economics*, 18.

Lipietz, A. (1986b) 'New Tendencies in the International Division of Labour', in A.J. Scott and M. Storper, eds, *Production, Work, Territory* (London/Sydney: Allen & Unwin).

Lipietz, A. (1987) *Mirages and Miracles: Crises in Global Fordism* (London: Verso).

Lipietz, A. (1988) 'Accumulation, Crisis, and Ways Out: Some Methodological Reflections on the Concept of "Regulation"', *International Journal of Political Economy*, 18(2).

Lipietz, A. (1992a) 'Allgemeine und konjunkturelle Merkmale der ökonomischen Staatsintervention', in A. Demirovic, *et al.*, eds, *Hegemonie und Staat* (Münster: Westfälisches Dampfboot).

Lipietz, A. (1992b) *Towards a New Economic Order: Postfordism, Ecology, Democracy* (New York: Oxford University Press).

Lipietz, A. (1996) *La Société en sablier* (Paris: La Découverte).

Lipietz, A. (1997a) 'Die Welt des Postfordismus', Supplement der Zeitschrift Sozialismus, 7–8/97.

Lipietz, A. (1997b) 'The Post-Fordist World: Labour Relations, International Hierarchy and Global Ecology' *Review of International Political Economy*, 4(1).

Lipietz, A. (1999) 'Working for World Ecological Sustainability: Towards a New Great Transformation', in OECD, *The Future of the Global Economy: Towards a Long Boom* (Paris: OECD).

Louca, F. (1997) *Turbulence in Economics* (Cheltenham: Edward Elgar).

Louca, F. and Reijnders, J., eds (1999) *The Foundations of Long Wave Theory* (Northampton: Edward Elgar).

Lucas, R.E. (1988) On the Mechanics of Economic Development', *Journal of Monetary Economics*, 22.

Lum, S. and Yuskavage, R. (1997) 'Gross Product by Industry, 1947–96', *Survey of Current Business*, 77(11).

Maddison, A. (1971) *Twee modellen van economische groei* (Utrecht: Spectrum).

Maddison, A. (1987) 'Growth and Slowdown in Advanced Capitalist Economies', *Journal of Economic Literature*, 25.

Maddison, A. (1991) *Dynamic Forces in Capitalist Development* (Oxford: Oxford University Press).

Maddison, A. (1995) *Monitoring the World Economy, 1820–1992* (Paris: OECD).

Magdoff, H. (1969) *The Age of Imperialism* (New York: Monthly Review Press).

Magdoff, H. (1975) *Imperialism* (New York: Monthly Review Press).

Maldonado-Filho, E. (1997) 'The Circuit of Industrial Capital, Price Changes and the Profit Rate', Presented to the 1997 Conference of the Eastern Economic Association (available at http://www.greenwwich.ac.uk/˜fa03).

Mandel, E. (1967) 'The Labor Theory of Value and "Monopoly Capitalism"', *International Socialist Review*, 29(4).

Mandel, E. (1969) *The Inconsistencies of 'State Capitalism'* (London: International Marxist Group).

Mandel, E. (1970) *Europe vs. America: Contradictions of Imperialism* (New York: Monthly Review Press).

Mandel, E. (1975) *Late Capitalism* (London: New Left Books).

Mandel, E. (1980) *Long Waves of Capitalist Development* (Cambridge: Cambridge University Press); second edition, London, Verso, 1995.

Mankiw, N.G., Romer, D. and Weill, D.N. (1992) 'A Contribution to the Empirics of Economic Growth', *Quarterly Journal of Economics*, 107.

Marfleet, P. (1998) 'Globalization and the Third World', *International Socialism*, Second Series, 81.

Marglin, S. and Schor, J., eds (1990) *The Golden Age of Capitalism* (Oxford: Clarendon Press).

Marshall, M. (1987) *Long Waves of Regional Development* (Cambridge: MIT Press).

Martin, R. (1989) 'Industrial Capitalism in Transition', in D. Massey and J. Allen, eds, *Uneven Re-Development* (London: Hodder & Stoughton).

Martin, R. (1989) 'The Reorganization of Regional Theory: Alternative Perspectives on the Changing Capitalist Space Economy', *Geoforum*, 20(2).

Marx, K. (1959) *Capital*, 3 volumes (Moscow: Foreign Languages Publishing House).

Marx, K. (1963–72) *Theories of Surplus-Value*, 3 volumes (Moscow: Progress).

Marx, K. (1965) *Das Kapital, Volume III*, in *Marx-Engels Werke*, vol. 25 (Berlin: Dietz, 1965–).

Marx, K. (1965–) *Marx-Engels Werke* (MEW) (Berlin: Dietz)

Marx, K. (1970) *A Contribution to the Critique of Political Economy* (Moscow: Progress).

Marx, K. (1971) *Capital, Volume III* (Moscow: Progress).

Marx, K. (1973) *Grundrisse* (Harmondsworth: Penguin).

Marx, K. (1973) 'Introduction to the Contribution to the Critique of Political Economy', in idem, *Grundrisse*, op cit.

Marx, K. (1976) *Capital, Volume I* (Harmondsworth: Penguin Books).

Marx, K. (1981) *Capital, Volume III* (New York: Vintage).

Marx, K. and Engels, F. (1998) *The Communist Manifesto* (London: Verso).

Marx, K. and Engels, F., *Werke* (cit. MEW.) (Berlin: Dietz), various years.

McDermott, J. (1991) *Corporate Society* (Boulder: Westview Press).

McDonough, T. (1995) 'Lenin, Imperialism, and the Stages of Capitalist Development', *Science and Society*, 59(3).

McDonough, T. and Drago, R. (1989) 'Crises of Capitalism and the First Crisis of Marxism', *Review of Radical Political Economics*, 21(3).

McMichael, P. (1990) 'Incorporating Comparison within a World-Historical Perspective', *American Sociological Review*, 55.

McMichael, P. and Myhre, D. (1991) 'Global Regulation vs. the Nation-State', *Capital and Class*, 43.

McMurtry, J. (1999) *The Cancer Stage of Capitalism* (London: Pluto).

Meeus, M. (1989) *Wat betekent arbeid?* (Assen: Van Gorcum).

Mensch, G. (1979) *Stalemate in Technology* (Cambridge: Ballinger).

Menshikov, S. (1997) 'Indicators and Trends of Economic Globalization', unpublished paper.

Menshikov, S. and Klimenko, L. (1989) 'Long Waves in Economic Structure', in Di Matteo, *et al.*, *Technological*, op cit.

Mihevc, J. (1995) *The Market Tells them So* (London: Zed Books).

Minsky, H.P. (1964) 'Longer Waves in Financial Relations: Financial Factors in More Severe Depressions', *American Economic Review*, LIV(3).

Mistral, J. (1986) 'Régimes international et trajectoires nationales', in R. Boyer, ed., *Capitalismes fin de siècle* (Paris: Presses Universitaires de France).

Miyazaki, Y. (1990) *Kawariyuku Sekai-Keizai* [The Changing World Economy] (Tokyo: Yuuhikaku).

Modelski, G. (1987a) *Long Cycles and World Politics*, (Seattle: University of Washington Press).

Moseley, F. (1992) *The Falling Rate of Profit in the Post-War United States Economy* (New York: St Martin's).

Moulaert, F. and Swyngedouw, E. (1989) 'A Regulation Approach to the Geography of Flexible Production Systems', *Society and Space*, 7.

Newman, M. (1989) *Britain and the EEC*, European Dossiers Series (London: PNL Press).

Norton, B. (1987) 'Steindl, Levine and the Inner Logic of Accumulation: A Marxian Critique', *Review of Radical Political Economics*, 13(4).

Norton, B. (1988a) 'Epochs and Essences: A Review of Marxist Long-Wave and Stagnation Theories', *Cambridge Journal of Economics*, 12.

Norton, B. (1988b) 'The Power Axis: Bowles, Gordon and Weisskopf's Theory of Postwar U.S. Accumulation', *Rethinking Marxism*, 1(3).

Norton, B. (1992) 'Radical Theories of Accumulation and Crisis: Developments and Directions', in B. Roberts and S. Feiner, eds, *Radical Economics* (Boston: Kluwer Academic).

O'Hara, P.A. (1994) 'An Institutionalist Review of Long Wave Theories: Schumpeterian Innovation, Modes of Regulation, and Social Structures of Accumulation', *Journal of Economic Issues*, 28(2).

O'Connor, M. (1996) *Natural Causes* (New York: Guilford).

Offe, C. (1984) *Contradictions of the Welfare State* (London: Hutchinson).

Offe, C. (1985) *Disorganized Capitalism* (Cambridge: MIT Press).

Okishio, N. (1961) 'Technical Changes and the Rate of Profit', *Kobe University Economic Review*, 7.

Ollman, B., ed. (1998) *Market Socialism: The Debate Among Socialists* (New York: Routledge).

Overbeek, H.W. (1990) *Global Capitalism and National Decline* (London: Unwin Hyman).

Overbeek, H., ed. (1993) *Restructuring Hegemony in the Global Political Economy* (London: Routledge).

Pack, H. (1994) Endogenous Growth Theory: Intellectual Appeal and Empirical Shortcomings', *Journal of Economic Perspectives*, 8.

Pakulski, J. and Waters, M. (1996) *The Death of Class* (London: Sage).

Palloix, C. (1975) *L'Internationalisation du capital: Éléments critiques* (Paris: Maspero).

Panitch, L. (1994) 'Globalisation and the State', *Socialist Register 1994* (London: Merlin).

Parsons, T. (1954) *Essays in Sociological Theory*, (Glencoe: The Free Press).

Peck, J. and Tickell, A. (1994) 'Searching for a New Institutional Fix: The *After*-Fordist Crisis and the Global-Local Disorder', in Amin, *Post-Fordism*, op cit.

Perez, C. (1983) 'Structural Change and the Assimilation of New Technologies in the Economic Social Systems', *Futures*, 15(5).

Perez, C. (1985) 'Micro-electronics, Long Waves and World Structural Change', *World Development*, 13(3).

Perraton, J., Goldblatt, D., Held, D. and McGrew, A. (1999) *Global Transformations* (Stanford: Stanford University Press).

Petit, P. (1999) 'Structural Forms and Growth Regimes of the Post-Fordist Era', *Review of Social Economy*, 66(2).

Pevsner, Ya. (1982) *State-Monopoly Capitalism and the Labour Theory of Value* (Moscow: Progress).

Pgano, U. (1999) 'Information Technologies and Diversity of Organizational Equilibrium', translated into Japanese by M. Nishibe, in N. Yokokawa, M. Noguchi and M. Itoh, eds, [*Capitalism in Evolution*] (Tokyo: Nihon-hyoronsha).

Phillimore, A.J. (1989) 'Flexible Specialisation, Work Organization and Skills: Approaching the "Second Industrial Divide"', *New Technology, Work, Employment*, 4.

Piore, M.J. and Sabel, C.F. (1984) *The Second Industrial Divide* (New York: Basic Books).

Polanyi, K. (1957) *The Great Transformation* (Boston: Beacon).

Pollin, R. (1996) 'Contemporary Economic Stagnation in World Historical Perspective', *New Left Review*, 219.

Postone, M. (1993) *Time, Labor, and Social Domination* (Cambridge: Cambridge University Press).

Poulantzas, N. (1975a) *Classes in Contemporary Capitalism* (London: New Left Books).

Poulantzas, N. (1975b) *Klassen im Kapitalismus heute* (Berlin: VSA).

Preobrazhensky, E.A. (1985) *The Decline of Capitalism* (Armonk, NY: M.E. Sharpe).

Pritchett, L. (1996) 'Measuring Outward Orientation in LDCs: Can it be Done?', *Journal of Development Economics*, 49(2).

Pritchett, L. (1997) 'Divergence, Big Time', *Journal of Economic Perspectives*.

Reich, M. (1997) 'Social Structure of Accumulation Theory: Retrospect and Prospect', *Review of Radical Political Economics*, 29(3).

Reijnders, J. (1990) *Long Waves in Economic Development* (Aldershot: Edward Elgar).

Resnick, S. and Wolff, R., eds (1985) *Rethinking Marxism: Struggles in Marxist Theory. Essays for Harry Magdoff and Paul Sweezy* (New York: Autonomedia).

Resnick, S. and Wolff, R. (1987) *Knowledge and Class* (Chicago: University of Chicago Press).

Resnick, S. and Wolff, R. (1996) 'The New Marxian Political Economy and the Contribution of Althusser', in Callari and Ruccio, *Postmodern*, op cit.

Rifkin, J. (1995) *The End of Work* (New York: G.P. Putnam's Sons).

Rigby, D.L. (1991a) 'The Existence, Significance and Persistence of Profit Rate Differentials', *Economic Geography*, 67.

Rigby, D.L (1991b) 'Technical Change and Profits in Canadian Manufacturing: A Regional Analysis', *The Canadian Geographer*, 35.

Rivera-Batiz, L.A. and Romer, P.M. (1991) 'International Trade with Endogenous Technical Change', *European Economic Review*, 35.

Robins, K. and Gillespie, A. (1992) 'Communication, Organization and Territory', in K. Robins, ed., *Understanding Information* (London: Belhaven).

Robinson, W.L. (1996) *Promoting Polyarchy* (New York: Cambridge University Press).

Robles, A. (1994) *French Theories of Regulation and Conceptoins of the International Division of Labour* (London: Macmillan).

Romer, P.M. (1986) 'Increasing Returns and Long-run Growth', *Journal of Political Economy*, 94.

Romer, P.M. (1994) 'The Origins of Endogenous Growth', *Journal of Economic Perspectives*, 8.

Roobeek, A.J.M. (1987) 'The Crisis in Fordism and the Rise of a Technological Paradigm', *Futures*, 19(2).

Rosenberg, N. and Frischtak, C.R. (1984) 'Technological Innovation and Long Waves', *Cambridge Journal of Economics*, 8(1,2).

Rosenstock-Huessy, E. (1961) *Die europaeischen Revolutionen und der Character der Nationen*, Third Edition (Stuttgart: Kohlhammer).

Ross, R.J.S. and Trachte, K.C. (1990) *Global Capitalism* (Albany: SUNY Press).

Rostow, W.W. (1960) *Stages of Economic Growth: A Non-Communist Manifesto* (Cambridge: Cambridge University Press).

Rostow, W.W. (1978) *The World Economy* (Austin: University of Texas Press).

Röttger, B. (1997) *Neoliberale Globalisierung und eurokapitalistische Regulation* (Münster: Westfälisches Dampfboot).

Rowthorn, R. (1976) ' "Late Capitalism" (*Review*)', *New Left Review*, 98.

Ruigrok, W. and van Tulder, R. (1995) *The Logic of International Restructuring* (London: Routledge).

Rupert, M. (1993) 'Alienation, Capitalism and the Inter-State System: Towards a Marxian/Gramscian Critique', in Gill, *Gramsci, op cit.*

Rupert, M. (1995) *Producing Hegemony: The Politics of Mass Production and American Global Power* (Cambridge: Cambridge University Press).

Rustin, M. (1989) 'The Politics of Post-Fordism: or, The Trouble with "New Times"', *New Left Review*, 175.

Sabata, T. (1994) *Yohroppa no Hohken-Toshi* [Medieval Cities in Europe] (Tokyo: Kodansha).

Sachs, J.D. and Warner, A.M. (1997) 'Sources of Slow Growth in African Economies', *Journal of African Economies*, 6(3).

Sassen, S. (1996) *Cities in a World Economy* (Thousand Oaks: Pineforge Press).

Sawyer, M. (1988) 'Theories of Monopoly Capitalism', *Journal of Economic Surveys*, 2(1).

Sayer, A. and Walker, R. (1992) *The New Social Economy* (Oxford: Blackwell).

Scheuplein, C. (1997) 'Regulation des Raumes: Raumstrukturen in der groaindustriellen, fordistischen und postfordistischen Formation', Supplement der Zeitschrift Sozialismus, 3/97.

Schmid, C. (1996) 'Urbane Region und Territorialverhältnis – Zur Regulation des Urbanisierungsprozesses', in M. Bruch and H-P. Krebs, eds, *Unternehmen Globus* (Münster: Westfälisches Dampfboot).

Schneider, S.H. (1989) *Global Warming* (San Francisco: Sierra Club Books).

Schor, J. (1991) *The Overworked American* (New York: Basic Books).

Schumpeter, J.A. (1937) *The Theory of Economic Development* (Cambridge: Harvard University Press).

Schumpeter, J.A. (1954) *Capitalism, Socialism, and Democracy* (London: George Allen & Unwin).

Schwartz, H.M. (1994) *States versus Markets* (New York: St Martin's).

Schweickart, D. (1998) 'Market Socialism: A Defence', in Ollman, *Market Socialism*, op. cit.

Screpanti, E. (1984) 'Long Cycles and Recurring Proletarian Insurgency', *Review* 7(3).

Sekine, T. (1980) 'Appendix', in K. Uno, *Principles of Political Economy* (New Jersey: Humanities Press).

Sekine, T. (1986) *The Dialectic of Capital*, 2 volumes (Tokyo: Toshindo Press).

Sekine, T. (1997) *An Outline of the Dialectic of Capital*, 2 volumes (London: Macmillan).

Sekine, T. (1998) 'The Dialectic of Capital: An Unoist Interpretation', *Science and Society*, 62(3).

Semmler, W. (1982) 'Theories of Competition and Monopoly', *Capital and Class*, 18.

Senghaas, D. (1982) *Von Europa lernen* (Frankfurt: Suhrkamp).

Shaikh, A. (1979) 'Foreign Trade and the Law of Value: Part I', *Science and Society*, XLIII(3).

Shaikh, A. (1992) 'The Falling Rate of Profit as the Cause of Long Waves', in Kleinknecht *et al.*, *New Findings*, op. cit.

Shaikh, A. and Antonopoulos, R. (1998) 'Explaining Long Term Exchange Rate Behavior in the United States and Japan', *Working Paper no. 250* (Annandale-on-Hudson, NY: Jerome Levy Economics Institute).

Shaikh, A. and Tonak, E.A. (1994) *Measuring the Wealth of Nations* (Cambridge: Cambridge University Press).

Shannon, T. (1996) *An Introduction to the World-Systems Perspective*, second edition (Boulder: Westview Press).

Sherman, H. (1985) 'Monopoly Capital vs. the Fundamentalists', in Resnick and Wolff, *Rethinking Marxism*, op. cit.

Silver, B. (1995) 'World-Scale Patterns of Labor-Capital Conflict: Labor Unrest, Long Waves, and Cycles of World Hegemony', *Review*, 12(1).

Silver, B. and Slater, E. (1999) 'The Social Origins of World Hegemonies', in G. Arrighi, *et al.*, *Chaos*, op. cit.

Singh, K. (1999) *The Globalization of Finance: A Citizen's Guide* (London: Zed).

Smith, A. (1910) *The Wealth of Nations* (London: Dent).

Soja, E. (1989) *Postmodern Geographies* (London: Verso).

Solomou, S. (1986) *Phases of Economic Growth, 1850–1973* (Cambridge: Cambridge University Press).

Solow, R. (1957) 'A Contribution to the Theory of Economic Growth', *Quarterly Journal of Economics*, 70.

Stahel, A.W. (1999) 'Time Contradictions of Capitalism', *Culture, Nature, Society*, 10(1).

336 Bibliography and Select Readings

Stallings, B. (1990) 'The Role of Foreign Capital in Economic Development', in
G. Gereffi and D.L. Wyman, eds, *Manufacturing Miracles* (Princeton: Princeton University Press).

Standing, G. (1999) *Global Labor Flexibility* (London: Macmillan).

Stein, J.L. (1995) 'The Natrex Model, Appendix: International Finance Theory and Empirical Reality', in J.L. Stein, P.R. Allen and Associates, *Fundamental Determinants of Exchange Rates* (Oxford: Clarendon).

Steindl F. (1952) *Maturity and Stagnation in American Capitalism* (Oxford: Blackwell).

Stern, N. (1996) 'Growth Theories, Old and New, and the Role of Agriculture in Economic Development', FAO Economic and Social Development Paper no.136 (Rome: FAO).

Stiglitz, J.E. (1994) *Whither Socialism?* (Cambridge: MIT Press).

Stopford, J.M. and Strange, S. (1991) *Rival States, Rival Firms* (Cambridge: Cambridge University Press).

Storper, M. and Scott, A.J., eds (1992) *Pathways to Industrialization and Regional Development* (London: Routledge).

Storper, M. and Walker, R. (1989) *The Capitalist Imperative* (Oxford: Blackwell).

Strange, S. (1989) 'Towards a Theory of Transnational Empire', in E-O. Czempiel and J.N. Rosenau, eds, *Global Changes and Theoretical Challenges* (Lexington: Lexington Books).

Strange, S. (1997) *Casino Capitalism* (Manchester: Manchester University Press).

Strange, S. (1998) 'The New World of Debt', *New Left Review*, 230.

Sutcliffe, B. and Glyn, A. (1999) 'Still Underwhelmed: Indicators of Globalization and Their Misinterpretation', *Review of Radical Political Economics*, 31(1).

Sweezy, P. (1992) ' "Monopoly Capital"after 25 Years', in Davis, ed., *Economic Surplus*, *op. cit.*

Sweezy, P. (1998) 'The *Communist Manifesto* Today', *Monthly Review*, 50(1).

Swyngedouw, E. (1997) 'Neither Global nor Local: "Glocalization" and the Politics of Scale', in K. Cox, ed., *Spaces of Globalization* (New York: Guilford).

Tachibanaki, T. (1998) [*Japanese Economic Inequality*] (Tokyo: Iwanami-shoten).

Therborn, G. (1992) 'The Life and Times of Socialism', *New Left Review*, 194.

Thompson, E. (1968) *The Making of the English Working Class* (Harmondsworth: Penguin).

Tickell, A. (1999) 'Unstable Futures: Controlling and Creating Risks in International Money', *Socialist Register 1999* (London: Merlin).

Ticktin, H. (1998) 'The Problem Is Market Socialism', in Ollman, *Market Socialism*, *op. cit.*

Todaro, M.P. (1994) *Economic Development* (London: Longman).

Trotsky, L. (1923) 'O Krivoi Kapitalisticheskovo Razvitiya' ['The Curve of Capitalist Development'], *Vestnik Sotsialisticheskoi Akademii*, 4. Cited in Day, 'The Crisis', op. cit.

Tylecote, A. (1991) *The Long Wave in the World Economy* (London: Routledge).

Underhill, G.D.R. (1998) *Industrial Crisis and the Open Economy* (Basingstoke: Macmillan).

United States Department of Commerce (1986) *The National Income and Product Accounts of the United States, Statistical Tables, 1929–82* (Washington: US Government Printing Office).

United States Department of Commerce (1998) *The National Income and Product Accounts of the United States, Statistical Tables, 1929–94* (Washington: US Government Printing Office).

United States Department of Commerce (1999) *The National Income and Product Accounts of the United States*, http://www.bea.doc.gov.

Uno, K. (1962) [*Methodology of Political Economy*] (Tokyo: The University of Tokyo Press).

Uno, K. (1971) [*Types of Economic Policies*] (Tokyo: Koubundo).

Uno, K. (1980) *Principles of Political Economy*, translated by T. Sekine (Brighton: Harvester Press).

van der Pijl, K. (1984) *The Making of an Atlantic Ruling Class* (London, Verso).

van der Pijl, K. (1996) *Vordenker der Weltpolitik*, second edition (Opladen: Leske & Budrich).

van der Pijl, K. (1998) *Transnational Classes and International Relations* (London: Routledge).

van Duijn, J.J. (1983) *The Long Wave in Economic Life* (London: Allen & Unwin).

van Zon, H. (1994) *Crisis in the Socialist International Economy: The Case of Hungary and the GDR*, PhD dissertation (Amsterdam: University of Amsterdam).

Vasko, T., ed. (1985) *The Long Wave Debate* (Berlin: Springer-Verlag).

Veblen, T. (1983) *The Engineers and the Price System* (New Brunswick: Transaction Books).

Veltz, P. (1996) *Mondialisation, villes et territoires: l'économie archipel* (Paris: Presses Universitaires de France).

Wade, R. (1990) *Governing the Market* (Princeton: Princeton University Press).

Wade, R. and Veneroso, F. (1998) 'The Asian Crisis: The High Debt Model Versus the Wall Street-Treasury-IMF Complex', *New Left Review*, 228.

Wallerstein, I. (1974) *The Modern World-System I* (New York: Academic Press).

Wallerstein, I. (1984) 'Long Waves as Capitalist Process', *Review*, 7(4).

Wallerstein, I. (1991) *Unthinking Social Science* (Cambridge: Polity).

Wallerstein, I. (1995) 'Response: Declining States, Declining Rights?' *International Labor and Working-Class History*, 47.

Warskett, G. (1991) 'The Regulation of Unstable Growth: L'École de Régulation and the Social Structure of Accumulation', *International Review of Applied Economics*, 5(3).

Webber, M.J. (1987) 'Quantitative Measurement of Some Marxist Categories', *Environment and Planning A*, 19.

Webber, M.J. (1989) 'Capital Flows and Rates of Profit', *Review of Radical Political Economics*, 21.

Webber, M.J. (1991) 'The Contemporary Transition', *Society and Space*, 9(2).

Webber, M.J. (1994) 'Enter the Dragon: Lessons for Australia from Northeast Asia', *Environment and Planning A*, 26.

Webber, M.J. (forthcoming) 'Theoretical Implications of the Asian Financial Crisis', *Geoforum*.

Webber, M.J. and Foot, S.P.H. (1988) 'Profitability and Accumulation', *Economic Geography*, 64.

Webber, M.J. and Rigby, D.L. (1996) *The Golden Age Illusion: Rethinking Postwar Capitalism* (New York: Guilford Press).

Webber, M.J., Sheppard, E. and Rigby, D.L. (1992) 'Forms of Technical Change', *Environment and Planning A*, 24.

Weber, M. (1961) *General Economic History* (New York: Collier).

Weber, M. (1978) *Economy and Society* (Berkeley: University of California Press).

Weeks, J. (1982) 'Equilibrium, Uneven Development and the Tendency of the Rate of Profit', *Capital and Class*, 16.

Weeks, J. (1985–86) 'Epochs of Capitalism and the Progressiveness of Capital's Expansion', *Science and Society*, 49(4).

Weeks, J. (1988) 'The Contradictions of Capitalist Competition', presented to the International Conference on Regulation Theory, Barcelona, June. (CONTACT JWIO@Soas.ac.uk)

Weeks, J. (1989) *A Critique of Neoclassical Macroeconomics* (London: Macmillan).

Weeks, J. (1998) 'The Essence and Appearance of Globalization: The Rise of Finance Capital', in F. Adams, S. Dev Gupta and K. Mengisteab, eds, *Globalization and the Dilemmas of the State in the South* (London: Macmillan).

Weeks, J. (1999a) 'Wages, Employment and Workers' Rights in Latin America, 1970–1998', *International Labor Review*, 138(2).

Weeks, J. (1999b) 'Latin America and the High Performing Asian Economies: Growth and Debt', *Journal of International Development*.

Weinstein, J. (1968) *The Corporate Ideal in the Liberal State, 1900–1918* (Boston: Beacon Press).

Westra, R. (1996) 'Periodizing Capitalism and the Political Economy of Post-War Japan', *Journal of Contemporary Asia*, 26(4).

Westra, R. (1999) 'A Japanese Contribution to the Critique of Rational Choice Marxism', *Social Theory and Practice*, 25(3).

White, L. (1978) 'The Evidence on Appropriate Factor Proportions for Manufacturing in Less Developed Countries: A Survey', *Economic Development and Cultural Change*, 27(1).

Williams, K., Cutler, T., Williams, J. and Haslam, C. (1987) 'The End of Mass Production?', *Economy and Society*, 16.

Williamson, J.G. (1968) 'The Long Swing: Comparison and Interactions between British and American Balance of Payments, 1820–1913', in A.R. Hall, ed., *The Export of Capital from Britain 1870–1914* (London: Methuen).

Willoughby, J. (1986) *Capitalist Imperialism, Crisis and the State* (London: Harwood Academic).

Wirth, M. (1977) 'Towards a Critique of the Theory of State Monopoly Capitalism', *Economy and Society*, 6(3).

Womack, J.P, Jones, D.T. and Roos, D. (1990) *The Machine that Changed the World* (New York: Rawson Associates).

Woo, J.E. (1991) *Race to the Swift* (New York: Columbia University Press).

Wood, A. (1994) *North-South Trade, Employment and Inequality: Changing Fortunes in a Skill-driven World* (Oxford: Clarendon).

Wood, E. (1997) 'Modernity, Postmodernity or Capitalism?', *Review of International Political Economy*, 4(3).

Wood, E. (1999) 'The Politics of Capitalism', *Monthly Review*, 51(4).

World Bank (1992) *World Development Report 1992* (New York: Oxford University Press).

World Bank (1993) *The East Asian Miracle* (Oxford: Oxford University Press).

World Bank (1994) *Adjustment in Africa* (Oxford: Oxford University Press).

World Bank (1995a) *Labor and Economic Reforms in Latin America and the Caribbean*, Reprinted from *The World Development Report 1995* (New York: Oxford University Press).

World Bank (1995b) *World Development Indicators* (Washington: World Bank).

World Bank (1999) *World Development Indicators 1999* (Washington: World Bank, CD-ROM).

Wright, E.O. (1979) *Class, Crisis and the State* (London: Verso).

Yamada, T. (1991) [*The Regulation Approach*] (Tokyo: Fujiwara-shoten).

Yeats, A.J. (1989) 'Developing Countries' Exports of Manufactures', *The Developing Economies*, XXVII(2).

Yeats, A.J. (1992) 'What Do Alternative Measures of Comparative Advantage Reveal about the Composition of Developing Countries' Exports?', *Indian Economic Review*, XXVII(2).

Young, A. (1991) 'Learning by Doing and the Dynamic Effects of International Trade', *Quarterly Journal of Economics*, 106.

Zoninsein, J. (1990) *Monopoly Capital Theory* (New York: Greenwood).

Zürn, M. (1998) *Regieren jenseits des Nationalstaates* (Frankfurt: Suhrkamp).

Zysman, J. (1994) 'How Institutions Create Historically Rooted Trajectories of Growth', *Industrial and Corporate Change*, 3(1).

Name Index

Aglietta, Michel, 124, 233–6
Albert, Michel, 235
Albritton, Robert, 124
Althusser, Louis, 232
Amin, Ash, 165
Arrighi, Giovanni, 129, 139

Barre, Raymond, 25
Bentham, Jeremy, 6
Berle, Adolf, 162
Blair, Tony, 97, 235
Bonapart, Napoleon, 5
Boyer, Robert, 124
Braudel, Fernand, 57, 59, 62, 64–5, 139
Brenner, Robert, 236
Bukarin, Nicholai Ivanovich, 136, 241–2
Bush, George, 34

Carnegie, Andrew, 8
Carter, James, 96
Castells, Mario, 10
Cleaver, H., 286
Clinton, William, 28, 63
Coeur, Jacques, 58
Cox, Robert, 15
Cullenberg, Stephen, 238

Davis, Mike, 235
Duncan, Colin A.M., 54

Engels, Friedrich, 98

Fabius, Laurent, 25
Ford, Henry, 18
Funke, Rainer, 12
Fukuyama, Francis, 124

Galbraith, John Kenneth, 46, 157
Glick, Michael, 236
Goerdeler, 7
Glyn, Andrew, 109
Gramsci, Antonio, 2
Greenspan, Alan, 34–5
Gronow, Jukka, 303

Hansen, 43
Harvey, David, 165
Hegel, G.W.F., 55
Hilferding, Rudolph, 111, 136
Hirsch, Joachim, 148
Hitler, Adolph, 7
Hobbes, Thomas, 4
Hobsbawm, Eric, 65
Hobson, John A., 136
Hubner, Kurt, 148
Hutton, Will, 27, 235

Itoh, Makoto, 139

Jessop, Bob, 176, 178
Johnson, L.B., 45

Kalecki, M., 21, 29, 31
Kautsky, Karl, 301
Keynes, J.M., 9, 18, 29, 35, 46, 108, 146–7
Kondratieff, 151, 247
Kuznets, S., 151

Lakatos, Imre, 239
Lenin, V.I., 111, 112, 136
Lipietz, Alain, 233
Locke, John, 4, 15

Maddison, A., 204
Mandel, Ernest, 162, 209–10, 301
Marx, K., xiii, 14, 23, 29, 58–9, 63–4,
    70–1, 98, 110, 138, 143–4, 179–80,
    209–10, 284, 301
Means, Gardiner, 162
Mensch, G., 66
Merton, Robert, 52
Mistral, J., 166
Miyazaki, 48

Norton, Bruce, 234

Overbeek, Hans, 5

Peck, J., 165

Subject Index

absolute surplus value, 221–2
accumulation, 8, 18, 57, 59–60, 63–4,
    77–82, 84, 86–90, 93, 95, 97, 103,
    104, 106, 128, 153, 165, 236, 292
  mode of, 39
  original, 2–3, 5–6, 12, 16
  regime, 18, 233, 236, 289
  strategy, 290
  see also, crises of overaccumulation,
    deepening accumulation, expanded
    reproduction, extensive regimes of
    accumulation, intensive regimes of
    accumulation, law of accumulation,
    primitive accumulation, social
    structure of accumulation, systemic
    cycles of accumulation
Africa, 28, 174
  sub-Saharan, 206, 271
agrarian, 6
agriculture, 44
  sustainable, 133
alienation, 3, 4, 139
American capitalism, 235
Amsterdam School, 166
anomaly, 73–5
anomie, 6
Arab fundamentalism, 226
Arbitration Treaty (1911), 8
Argentina, 8, 89
arms race, 10
Asia, 4, 11, 33, 34–5, 86, 107, 121, 123,
    138, 174, 269, 272
  Asian crisis, 35, 91, 102, 140, 284
  Asian Tigers, 22, 89, 206
Asia Pacific Economic Cooperation
    (APEC), 211
assembly line, 44
Atlantic Alliance, 83
Atlantic capitalism, 24, 292
Australia, 8, 250–52
Austria, 7
  War of Succession, 5
Austrian approach, 315
auto-centered development, 170

automation, 127
automotive complex, 9–11, 44, 128

balance of payments, 32, 83, 85, 100,
    134, 135
Balkans, 16
Bank of England, 134
Bank of International Settlement, 59
barbarism, 127
Barings Bank, 125
basic theory, 111
  see also, theory of a purely capitalist
    society
belle époque, 64, 66
big business, 104
  see also, transnational corporation
biosphere, 2, 11–12, 15
  see also, nature
bloc formation, 91, 107, 109
bonds, 101
boom, 34–35, 41, 76, 77, 81, 82–5, 87–90
  see also, growth, golden age
bourgeoisie, 2, 27, 30–1, 82, 168
Brazil, 19, 28, 31, 89, 107, 173, 198, 204,
    237–9
  brazilianization, 24, 28
Bretton Woods, 94, 98, 102, 115–16, 161,
    292
  see also, gold standard, International
    Monetary Fund, World Bank
Britain, 5–8, 10, 16, 17, 19, 23, 24, 28, 32,
    40, 59, 64, 65, 68, 78, 86, 97, 112,
    130, 134, 168, 224–5
  British Commonwealth, 6, 8
  British cycle, 59, 63, 67, 69, 70
Business Roundtable, 104
Business Week, 1

Canada, 8, 250–53
Capital (Marx), xiii, 63, 110, 111, 116,
    121, 230–31, 239–40, 286, 306–7
capital, 1, 3, 4, 77–8, 84, 89, 103–05, 111,
    290, 306–7
  circuits of, 3, 7–8, 14